THE GEORGE GUND FOUNDATION
IMPRINT IN AFRICAN AMERICAN STUDIES

The George Gund Foundation has endowed
this imprint to advance understanding of
the history, culture, and current issues
of African Americans.

The publisher gratefully acknowledges the generous support of the African American Studies Endowment Fund of the University of California Press Foundation, which was established by a major gift from the George Gund Foundation.

AMERICAN CROSSROADS

Edited by Earl Lewis, George Lipsitz, George Sánchez, Dana Takagi, Laura Briggs, and Nikhil Pal Singh

Jack Johnson, Rebel Sojourner

Jack Johnson, Rebel Sojourner

Boxing in the Shadow of the Global Color Line

Theresa Runstedtler

UNIVERSITY OF CALIFORNIA PRESS
Berkeley · Los Angeles · London

University of California Press, one of the most distinguished
university presses in the United States, enriches lives around
the world by advancing scholarship in the humanities, social
sciences, and natural sciences. Its activities are supported by
the UC Press Foundation and by philanthropic contributions
from individuals and institutions. For more information,
visit www.ucpress.edu.

University of California Press
Berkeley and Los Angeles, California

University of California Press, Ltd.
London, England

Library of Congress Cataloging-in-Publication Data

Runstedtler, Theresa.
    Jack Johnson, rebel sojourner : boxing in the shadow
of the global color line / Theresa Runstedtler.
        p.   cm. — (American crossroads ; 33)
    Includes bibliographical references and index.
    ISBN 978-0-520-27160-9 (cloth, alk. paper)
    1. Johnson, Jack, 1878–1946.   2. Boxers (Sports)—
United States—Biography.   3. African American
boxers— Biography.   4. Boxing—United States—
History.   5. Racism in sports.   6. United States—
Race relations—History.   I. Title.
    GV1132.J7R86   2012
    796.83092—dc23   2011027435
    [B]

Manufactured in the United States of America

20   19   18   17   16   15   14   13   12
10 9 8 7 6 5 4 3 2 1

In keeping with its commitment to support
environmentally responsible and sustainable printing
practices, UC Press has printed this book on Cascades
Enviro 100, a 100% post consumer waste, recycled,
de-inked fiber. FSC recycled certified and processed
chlorine free. It is acid free, Ecologo certified, and
manufactured by BioGas energy.

*Dedicated to Lolo Pacifico
and Lola Dalmacia Garcia*

*Stories of your courage, tenacity, generosity,
and resourcefulness in the face of adversity
continue to inspire me.*

Contents

Illustrations

Acknowledgments

This project has truly been a journey, from idea, to prospectus, to dissertation, to book. Along the way I have compiled a very long list of people and organizations to thank for their contributions to my work and my life.

My own journey to academia followed a route that was far from traditional. Before returning to school to study for a PhD, I spent several years working as a professional dancer, model, and actress in Toronto. Although I loved the energy and camaraderie of working with other performers (especially all my friends in the Raptors Dance Pak), I decided to go back to school for radio and television production at Ryerson University in the hopes of establishing a more lucrative and "legitimate" career on the other side of the camera. Realizing that I lacked the passion for media production, I dropped out of Ryerson and spent a year working in the public relations department of what was then CTV Sportsnet (now Rogers Sportsnet). In many respects this book is a logical outgrowth of these experiences. Working in the world of professional sport and entertainment has been an important source of insight when it comes to exploring representations of race and gender in popular culture. Part of my goal in reexamining Jack Johnson's story is to take seriously the political conversations stemming from this world. This book honors the many vibrant people who were central to this part of my life, including Greg and Chris Johnson, who introduced me to the sport of boxing.

When I finally arrived at Yale University in 2001, I launched into my studies with purpose and gusto. I have been blessed with the continued support of my graduate mentors, for whom I have the utmost admiration and respect. My dissertation director, Matthew Frye Jacobson, believed in this project even before I did, and his enthusiasm for each draft helped to sustain me through the difficult task of writing. Even when I visited his office, lost in a sea of ideas or drowning in the paperwork of the job market, he helped me chart a course for completion and success. Glenda Gilmore, who always inspired me with her encyclopedic knowledge of African American history, has graced this project with her incredible eye for detail, her love of good writing, and her chronological rigor. Seth Fein, one of the most brilliant historians I have come across, has been an invaluable resource for both unconventional ideas and practical advice. Finally, working with me in the prospectus phase of this project, Paul Gilroy was a fount of theoretical ideas and a wealth of contextual information on European race relations.

African American studies and History at Yale were great departmental homes. Alongside my dissertation committee, I had the pleasure of working with inspiring professors like Jennifer Baszile, David Blight, Hazel Carby, Jonathan Holloway, and Michael Mahoney. The staff members in both departments saved me countless times. Colleagues Jay Driskell, Sarah Haley, Jana Lipman, Shana Redmond, Anita Seth, Melissa Stuckey, and the rest of the GESO Organizing Committee sustained me through some very tough times. They hold me to a very high standard as a scholar and a person; I strive to be as strong in my convictions as they are.

I could not have completed such a far-reaching, transnational, and multilingual project without the financial support of a number of institutions. Funds from the Beinecke Library, the Yale Center for the Study of Globalization, the Gilder Lehrman Institute, the Organization of American Historians, and the Yale Center for International and Area Studies made my archival research possible, even as the value of the U.S. dollar plummeted. Other long-term awards kept me afloat over the years, including the Canadian Social Science and Humanities Research Council Doctoral Fellowship and Yale's Leylan Fellowship.

As an assistant professor at the University at Buffalo, a new set of resources opened up to me. The UB Humanities Institute, under the direction of Tim Dean, granted me a faculty fellowship, which along with my junior leave made it possible to quickly transform my dissertation into a book without having to compromise my vision. UB also provided start-up funds that allowed me to continue my work at the Schomburg Center for Research in Black Culture, to buy much-needed secondary sources, to hire professional researcher Jeannine Baker for work in the State Library of New South Wales, and to hire UB Caribbean studies graduate student Ernesto Mercado to help translate some of my Spanish sources. (A special thanks to Jeannine and Ernesto for all their hard work behind the scenes.) Assistance from the Julian Park Publication Fund enabled me to purchase the reproduction rights for the images in this book.

Since I spent much of my time researching abroad, I want to thank all those who helped make London and Paris my homes away from home. I am grateful to all the helpful staff at the Bodleian Library's John Johnson Collection in Oxford, the British Library's Newspaper Collection in Colindale, the National Archives in Kew, and also to Josiane Gandois at the Bibliothèque nationale de France for helping me get permission to see *La Boxe et les boxeurs*. Outside the library, Jeanefer Jean-Charles, Mark Hartley, and the entire Jean-Charles family—especially my English "mum," Mary, who taught me what it was like to be a St. Lucian immigrant in the 1950s—made my times in London some of the best of my life. They opened their hearts and homes to me, and even included me in their family activities. In Paris, Kader and Siham Bourhim let me stumble over my French words while continuing to invite me over for fabulous Moroccan mint tea. I will always remember our many conversations about race, cultural differences, politics, and the meaning of life (No6ra!). Naomi Hewitt-Couturier and her fashionable "amis internationals" let me tag along to all the hottest places in Paris, while Sara White Wilson inspired me with her artistic vision and wonderfully dry sense of humor.

This labor of love also required visits to various archives in the United States. The supportive staff at the Schomburg Center, the Library of Congress, and the National Archives in College Park helped me to navigate their holdings. Thanks to Larry Reynolds, my roommate and confidante in Adams Morgan, for offering me advice and support during one of the most tumultuous summers of my life.

During the writing stage, many people listened to and read parts of my evolving manuscript. My participation in panels at the annual meetings of the American Studies Association, American Historical Association, the Collegium of African American Research, the

Organization of American Historians, and the Popular Culture/ American Culture Association forced me to write faster and think more clearly. I also spoke at the following venues: the Race and Africana Studies Conference at the University of Connecticut; the Telling Stories Graduate Symposium at the University of Toronto; the Edward Bouchet Seminar Series, organized by Yale's Office for Diversity and Equal Opportunity; the Gill Lecture Series at Tufts University; and the UB Humanities Institute Scholars at Muse series at the Albright-Knox Art Gallery.

My graduate school colleagues were some of my most dedicated and exacting readers. My writing groups at Yale provided conceptual frameworks, constructive criticism, and life advice. Special thanks to Adam Arenson, Amanda Ciafone, Gretchen Heefner, Brandi Hughes, Lisa Pinley Covert, Camilla Schofield, Jenifer Van Vleck, and Helen Veit. I am especially grateful to Jana Lipman for being both a close friend and the closest reader of my dissertation. I cannot say enough how much her fellowship and intellectual exchange have shaped this project.

Writers and scholars from across the academy and beyond were also generous with their time and expertise. Adrian Burgos Jr. first encouraged me to write a project that involved boxing. Through her work on the 1968 Olympics, Amy Bass showed me that it was possible. Christopher Rivers gave me important leads in the French press. Patrick McDevitt offered advice about British sources. John Maynard introduced me to the Coloured Progressive Association of New South Wales and shared their photo with me. Matthew Guterl and Vivian Halloran encouraged my analysis of popular culture and black transnationalism. Satadru Sen helped me find Indian articles on Johnson, while Paul Kramer pointed me toward relevant Philippine newspapers. Andrew Offenburger not only offered keen advice about the history of race in South Africa, but he also volunteered to do microfilm searches in the bowels of Sterling Library. Johnson's most recent biographer, Geoffrey Ward, shared helpful leads over the course of this project.

My UB colleagues in American studies, Global Gender studies, African and African American studies, and History supported my work, even in the midst of the chaos and retrenchment caused by the economic crisis and ensuing budget cuts. Carole Emberton, Theresa McCarthy, and Cynthia Wu have sustained me intellectually and emotionally during moments of existential crisis and job-related stress. Alexis De Veaux has been a source of wisdom and inspiration. Theresa

McCarthy and the members of the Haudenosaunee–Native American Studies Research Group have taught me everything that I know about Indigenous studies and have inspired me to learn more. Students in my undergraduate and graduate seminars at UB have forced me to push beyond my own provincialisms and to better articulate my sometimes scattered and inchoate thoughts. They have all put their mark on this book, and on my life.

UB's Baldy Center for Law and Social Policy has been another important intellectual home. Through its funding of the Buffalo Seminar on Racial Justice, the Baldy Center has supported my dream of fostering a transnational community of scholars interested in questions of race, empire, diaspora, and indigeneity. It sponsored our symposia, "Building Connections" (spring 2008) and "Thinking beyond the Nation-State" (fall 2009), which brought together academics and community members from both sides of the U.S.-Canada border. The Baldy Center also funded a workshop for my book manuscript. I am grateful to Carl Nightingale and Rebecca French for their help in organizing and convening this workshop. Two outside experts, Kevin Gaines and Tracy Denean Sharpley-Whiting, offered insightful critiques. Other UB faculty from across several disciplines also challenged me to clarify the intellectual and political stakes of my work, including Ellen Berrey, Susan Cahn, Keith Griffler, David Herzberg, Peter Hudson, Carine Mardorossian, Patrick McDevitt, Ramón Soto-Crespo, Kari Winter, and Jason Young.

Parts of chapters 4 and 5 appear in the *Radical History Review,* the special issue "Reconceptualizations of the African Diaspora," 103 (2009): 59–81, and are reprinted here with the permission of Duke University Press. An earlier version of chapter 3 appears in the *Journal of World History* 21, no. 4 (2010): 657–89, and is reprinted here with the permission of the University of Hawai'i Press. Thank you to the editorial teams and anonymous readers of both journals for providing cogent critiques that shaped my book revisions. I am also grateful to the anonymous readers for the University of California Press; their suggestions helped me to better frame the book's arguments. My editor Niels Hooper has been a great proponent of my vision, even if it took me a little longer to achieve it than we initially expected.

Finally, I have to give a "shout out" to all the people in my life who are closest to me and have accompanied me on this journey. A million thanks to my parents John and Elisea Runstedtler, who have helped me out in innumerable ways and have always told me that they are proud of me. I am grateful to Allan, Sabine, Naomi, and Nathan Runstedtler for teaching me about the preciousness of life and family. Thanks to my Aunt Christine Runstedtler for her support, to my cousin Joy Garcia in Manila for her encouragement, and to Aunt Eva, Uncle Boy, Karina, and Jun Rojas for opening their home to me. My friends have been my second family. Thanks to Madonna Gimotea and Mary Sheridan for continuing to be such important people in my life. Maryjane Viejo has been the best friend ever. She has always kept me laughing and pumped me up even when I have doubted myself. Thanks also to the Viejo family for their hospitality over the years. Jill Sessa made living in Buffalo more fun than I ever imagined it could be. Her positive attitude is infectious and her fearless determination inspiring.

Joseph Johnson, my rock, my special someone, has been there to support me even when I felt the weight of the world on my shoulders. I could not have done this without him. Last but certainly not least, I thank Billie, who has become the pint-sized joy of my life, putting a smile on my face each and every day.

Preface

Just six months after my return from a research trip in Paris, France experienced its worst stint of civil unrest since the uprising of May 1968. On 27 October 2005, French police had chased three African teenagers from the Parisian suburb of Clichy-sous-Bois into a power substation, where two succumbed to electrocution. The deaths of Zyed Benna and Bouna Traoré produced an eleven-day shockwave of violence and car burning in disenfranchised *banlieues* (suburbs) all across France, from Lille to Rouen to Nice to Strasbourg. Reportedly, the young men had run away when they saw the officers, fearing that they would be subjected to the police interrogation and harassment customary in their largely immigrant and working-class neighborhood.[1] By 8 November President Jacques Chirac had declared a state of emergency, invoking curfews to help restore order. With copycat violence breaking out in Brussels and Berlin, some European officials even worried that the racial unrest would spread to other countries on the continent.

When the smoke cleared, France was forced to reckon with the origins of this violent rage. While the right-wing minister of the interior (now president) Nicolas Sarkozy denounced the rioters as "scum," Prime Minister Dominique de Villepin was more measured in his assessment of the problem. Villepin blamed some of the unrest on "criminal networks," but he also acknowledged that racial and religious prejudice, along with poverty and unemployment, had pushed many of the young rioters to lash out. "We must struggle against discrimination," Villepin admitted. "Everyone's behavior must change. . . . We must have a welcoming republic where everyone must be respected."[2]

As I read the various reactions to the riots, captivated by the debates about racism in the French Republic, I came across an interesting letter to the editor in USA Today. A reader from Tampa, Florida, took offense at journalist Souhelia Al-Jadda's suggestion that the French riots were "acts of civil disobedience," rooted in racial injustice, and therefore connected to the 1960s drive for civil rights in the United States.[3] The angry reader called this political characterization of the French riots and their supposed linkage to the U.S. context "not only irresponsible, but . . . also an insult to the memories of Rosa Parks and Dr. Martin Luther King Jr."[4] With his steadfast refusal to see any relationship between France's racial violence and the African American freedom struggle, the reader effectively negated the United States' own history of race rioting, along with its continued problems of racialized poverty and segregation.

The French were hardly innocent in this bout of discursive jabbing. They have consistently refused to acknowledge publicly the underlying connections between the legacy of U.S. slavery and segregation and their own history of imperialism and racism. In the wake of the riots, a political scientist at the American University of Paris reflected on this glaring blind spot. "After [Hurricane] Katrina, many French took an undisguised glee in poking the eyes of the Americans," Professor Steven Ekovich confessed. "They said this couldn't happen in France."[5]

Even though David Crary of the Associated Press maintained that the French riots and the U.S. government's slow response to Katrina's devastation of black New Orleans had forced these two "sparring nations" (his words, not mine) to move beyond this sport of finger-pointing, the fundamental connections between racial politics on both sides of the Atlantic have, for the most part, remained submerged, away from public scrutiny.[6] Most mainstream interpretations of these destructive events began with the assumption that racial discrimination is an inherently national problem—one that can be solved simply by exorcising the psychological demons of race prejudice from a few irrational white citizens. They rarely grappled with the larger global historical and structural forces linking the cultures of race in France and the United States. Defining the problem this way would force both nations to acknowledge their shared culpability in the same political economic legacies of slavery and imperialism. It would have deeper implications about the racial status quo than both countries, eager to declare the triumphant dawn of a color-blind and classless neoliberal era of peaceful global integration, are currently willing to address.

Such "sparring" contests between Western nations over their relative levels of racial tolerance are not new, and in particular black Americans have long served as important ciphers in these debates. Throughout Jack Johnson's infamous world championship reign (1908–15), France welcomed African American sportsmen and performers, all the while claiming the moral high ground over uncivilized Jim Crow America. In 1908 Johnson knocked out the Canadian fighter Tommy Burns to become the first-ever black world heavyweight champion. Two years later, when he took on the United States' "great white hope" Jim Jeffries, French sportsmen claimed to be above the racial dimensions of the match. They scoffed at white Americans who, blinded by a bad case of negrophobia, insisted that Jeffries would win against the much younger and more talented black fighter. Some Parisian sportswriters even blamed white American prejudice for transforming the interracial prizefight into a vulgar spectacle that played on people's baser instincts for the sake of profits. Johnson and his black American fans also joined in this discursive battle, praising France for its color blindness while critiquing white American racism on the world stage.

A century later, similar "sparring" matches surfaced with the rise of the United States' "great black hope," President Barack Obama.[7] Just months before his historic victory, Obama's visit to Berlin, Paris, and London in July 2008 became a celebratory story of European equality and democracy. Although most reports about Obama's fame in Europe argued that it was an outgrowth of George W. Bush's failings in foreign policy, race formed the subtext of the discussion. A kind of "Obama mania" had taken hold as largely white crowds cheered for the black American presidential candidate. A poll conducted by London's *Daily Telegraph* suggested that if Western Europeans could participate in the November election Obama would surely win, since 70 percent of Italians, 67 percent of Germans, 65 percent of the French, and 49 percent of Britons claimed they would vote for him.[8] The implicit message was that white Europeans were racially enlightened, and perhaps even more so than white Americans.

On 12 November 2008, CNN's *Situation Room* discussed Europe's reaction to the news of Obama's presidential win. Citing the "jubilant headlines" from across the Atlantic in celebration of Obama's election, the anchor Wolf Blitzer asked, "Is Obama's popularity there evidence that racism has essentially been wiped out of Europe?"[9] A report by CNN correspondent Carol Costello went on to show that "Europe's racist fringe" had reared its ugly head in the wake of Obama's victory, much to the chagrin of the majority of white Europeans. After the Italian prime minister Silvio Berlusconi jokingly described Obama as "young, handsome, and even tanned," Carla Bruni, the Italian-born wife of French president Sarkozy, called his comment offensive and declared, "I am pleased to have become French." Costello unearthed more virulent European criticism of the U.S. president-elect. A Polish politician and member of the conservative Law and Justice Party named Artur Górski decried Obama's win as "the end of the civilization of white men." Jürgen Gansel, a German legislator and neo-Nazi, issued a press release condemning Obama's popularity in Germany in which he stated that "Obama fever . . . resembles an African tropical disease." Interestingly enough, Costello's report never discussed Europe's historical or current treatment of its own nonwhite constituencies. Yet Europe's metropolitan centers are arguably in the midst of their own set of racial conflicts, as more and more people of color from the former colonies enter their borders demanding equality and respect. Although more strident than polite conversation would permit, the opinions of Górski and Gansel are hardly an aberration.

Back in the United States, commentators from both ends of the political spectrum were eager to declare that Obama's exceptional achievement proved that no other country in the world provided its racial minorities with as many opportunities, that the nation had officially entered a postracial era. As the election results came in on 4 November, CNN's Anderson Cooper asked a panel of experts what Obama's victory would mean for U.S. race relations. Bill Bennett, a conservative pundit, former U.S. secretary of education under President Ronald Reagan, and former director of the Office of National Drug Control Policy under President George H. W. Bush, launched into his interpretation: "I'll tell you one thing it means. . . . You don't take excuses anymore from anyone who says the deck is stacked, I can't do anything, there's so much in-built this and that. There are always problems in a big society, but we have just—if this turns out to be the case [with] President Obama—we have just achieved an incredible milestone for which the world needs to have more respect for the United States than it sometimes does."[10]

In other words, there was no reason to continue talking about any structural inequalities facing young black Americans, for the United States had proven to the world that its racial barriers could be scaled with hard work and determination. Taking a slightly different tack, the liberal journalist Nicholas Kristof of the *New York Times* was optimistic that "Barack Obama's political success could change global perceptions of the United States, redefining the American 'brand' to be less about Guantanamo and more about equality."[11] It could provide "a path to restore America's global influence," since white Americans were showing that they could "see beyond a person's epidermis." Whether in the United States or in Europe, this rush to claim racial progress and harmony based on the embrace of a prominent black figure effectively effaced any discussion of the broader historical, structural, and cultural forces connecting their continued problems of racial inequality.

Taking a closer look at the story of Jack Johnson and the world he traversed can help us begin to excavate these largely unspoken linkages. The surprising scope of Johnson's high-profile career throughout Europe, Australasia, and the Americas obliges us to think beyond the often-stagnant domestic squabbles over reformist solutions to racial disparities. The controversies surrounding his far-reaching travels highlight the intrinsic relationship between the rise of a global color line and the expansion of Western imperialism and capitalism. Even now, at a moment when many politicians have declared the dawn of a "color-blind" and "multicultural" era, racial inequality remains a defining feature of the contemporary world. Today's most powerful engines of global economic integration—multinational corporations, transnational financial institutions, and trade alliances—push an array of agendas that involve both discrimination and displacement on a grand scale. The transnational trade in racial ideologies and practices has also helped to spawn inequities in a variety of realms, including job and housing markets, welfare and educational organizations, legal and criminal justice systems, immigration policies, the state management of indigenous peoples, and environmental regulations.

Yet geopolitical and economic narratives of the race question have remained largely absent from popular and political discussions in the global North (North America, Europe, Australia, and New Zealand), particularly in the post–civil rights, postcolonial, post–cold war era. For the most part, race enters the public domain only during discussions of obvious interpersonal acts of racial hatred. "Racism" has been reduced to an aberrant psychological affliction that affects only a small percentage of the world's white population. According to popular logic, decolonized peoples and nations in the global South have been more or less responsible for their own failures, and persons of color in the global North who fail to adopt societal norms have simply chosen to be pathological and unproductive. Given these diagnoses, we often look to the War on Drugs, stricter law enforcement, the expansion of prisons, immigration restrictions, patriarchal family values, structural adjustment and bootstrap economics, counterterrorism, population control, cultural sensitivity training, and ultimately the passage of time as solutions to the enduring race problem.

The official response to the most recent uprisings in Britain sparked by the police shooting death of Mark Duggan, a twenty-nine-year-old black man from Tottenham, typifies this trend. Prime Minister David Cameron called for "tough love" in dealing with the rioters. "For some of the children who've ended up in this terrible situation there was probably a failure in their background, in their families," he said. "There probably was a shortage of not just respect and boundaries but also love. But you do need, when they cross the line and break the law, to be very tough." Cameron even considered hiring William Bratton, a famous American anti-gang czar who served as police chief in New York City, Boston, and Los Angeles, to help Britain reinstate law and order.[12]

While our leaders work together to prop up institutions of white supremacy, we waste our energy "sparring" over which nation is doing the best job of "managing" its racial tensions. It is no longer enough to point the finger elsewhere while thumping our own chests with national self-satisfaction, for the challenges we face require us to acknowledge the global routes and consequences of racial ideas, images, policies, and practices. The various controversies that followed Jack Johnson at the turn of the twentieth century can begin to shed some light on the racial disputes that plague us at the turn of the twenty-first. After all, Johnson's career spanned a period of profound change, as new cultural, political, social, and technological developments complicated prevailing racial paradigms and practices, not just in the United States but across the world. In tracing Johnson's journeys we can begin to uncover the real stakes of our own game of race.

Introduction

Jack Johnson, Rebel Sojourner

I thought Muhammad Ali touched the world community
like no other, but [Jack] Johnson did likewise.
—Leland Stein III, *Michigan Chronicle*, 26 June 2005

Jack Johnson was well aware of his place in the pantheon of global sporting heroes. In 1927, at the age of forty-nine, the retired African American prizefighter reflected on his "tumultuous career" as the first black heavyweight champion of the world. "I am astounded when I realize that there are few men in any period of the world's history, who have led a more varied or intense existence than I," he declared. "My life, almost from its very start, has been filled with tragedy and romance, failure and success, poverty and wealth, misery and happiness."[1] While Johnson claimed that these "conflicting conditions" had made him "somewhat unique of a character," he also believed that his diverse experiences in a variety of places suggested some larger lessons: "[The] story of the life I have led may . . . not only contain some interest if told for its own sake," he argued, "but may also shed light on the life of our times." While certainly not known for his humility, Johnson was by no means exaggerating his importance as a bellwether of racial and imperial conflicts in the early twentieth century.

In his day, Johnson was the most famous black man on the planet. Not only did he publicly challenge racial segregation within the United States, but he also enjoyed the same brazen and unapologetic lifestyle abroad, one of conspicuous consumption, masculine bravado, and interracial love. Like other successful African American heavyweights at the turn of the century who refused to be hemmed in by the strictures of U.S. racial politics, Johnson spent a great deal of his career

1

outside the United States, gaining admirers and goading critics of all different races, social classes, political persuasions, and nationalities. Even before he won the world championship in 1908, he had already fought in places as far off as Australia and England, and after his infamous conviction under the federal Mann Act against white slave trafficking in 1913, he fled the United States, lingering in exile throughout Europe and the Americas until he surrendered to U.S. authorities in 1920. In those places that he did not personally visit, his stories and images found their way into local newspapers, magazines, and movie houses, provoking spirited debates about the future of Western imperialism and the rise of a global color line. Often overlooked as a key part of his legacy, Johnson's impact in the wider world is the focus of this book.

Despite the vast geographic scope of his career, Johnson is still most remembered by historians and boxing fans alike for his many public battles against the laws and customs of Jim Crow America.[2] This tendency to frame the black American heavyweight's cultural and political significance within the borders of the United States has a long genealogy, rooted in racial conflicts within and beyond the boxing ring. After Johnson finally lost the world title to Jess Willard in 1915, white Americans were eager to bury any memory of his global pugilistic dominance and to ensure that such a sweeping travesty of white supremacy would never happen again. The world heavyweight championship remained racially segregated until the mid-1930s, when the young African American fighter Joe Louis rose to prominence. Hoping to break this boxing color bar and to secure a world title match for their protégé, Louis's managers went out of their way to distance him from Johnson's controversial legacy of irreverence and interracial relationships. This tactic paid off, for Louis wrested the world heavyweight championship from the white American favorite James J. Braddock in 1937.

These initial efforts to suppress the public memory of Johnson's contentious and cosmopolitan life dovetailed with the United States' racial and geopolitical stakes during World War II and the early cold war. There was simply no place for Johnson's ilk in the period's popular discussions of racial progress and respectability. Johnson and the global imagination of race and resistance that he had come to symbolize, especially for black Americans in the early 1900s, were increasingly submerged under the weight of crossover sporting heroes like Louis and the national priorities they came to represent, from desegregation and the expansion of civil rights to the construction of a positive image of U.S. democracy for people of color around the world.[3]

It was not until the rise of the Black Power movement in the late 1960s that Johnson came back into public view. Johnson's resurgence as a black icon owed much to the growing fame (and infamy) of another African American world heavyweight champion, Muhammad Ali. As Ali's resistance to the Vietnam War made him at once a pariah in the eyes of conservative white America and an anticolonial hero around the globe, he developed a close sense of connection with the man he called "Papa Jack." Although he disapproved of Johnson's preference for white women, he shared his predecessor's defiance in the face of white discrimination. "I grew to love the Jack Johnson image," Ali explained. "I wanted to be rough, tough, arrogant, the nigger white folks didn't like."[4] This Johnson "renaissance" also extended into the arts. *The Great White Hope,* Howard Sackler's play based on Johnson's life, was so well received by audiences in Washington, D.C., that it secured a spot on Broadway in 1968. The play's film adaptation, directed by Martin Ritt, opened to critical acclaim in 1970.[5] The following year Miles Davis released *A Tribute to Jack Johnson.* For the audacious jazz musician, Johnson embodied the period's spirit of open black defiance and black pride. "Johnson portrayed freedom," Davis's liner notes declared. "It rang just as loud as the bell proclaiming him champion. . . . His flamboyance was more than obvious."[6] This flurry of black cultural production was fleeting, and over the next thirty years Johnson's legacy languished in relative obscurity. His "bad nigger" image certainly did not mesh with the Reaganite myth of color-blind meritocracy, nor did it fit with the increasing calls for "law and order" in the turbulent 1990s.[7]

Now, in the first years of the twenty-first century, it has taken the attention of the celebrated white American documentary producer Ken Burns to bring Johnson back into the public consciousness of mainstream America. On 13 July 2004, on the eve of the Athens Olympics, Burns led a bipartisan and multiracial committee of politicians and celebrities in filing a petition with the U.S. Department of Justice for a posthumous presidential pardon for Johnson. Senators John McCain, Edward Kennedy, and Orrin Hatch, Representatives Charlie Rangel, Eddie Bernice Johnson, and Jesse Jackson Jr., boxers Sugar Ray Leonard, Bernard Hopkins, and John Ruiz, and entertainers Chuck D, Samuel L. Jackson, and Wynton Marsalis, among others, requested that the boxer's bogus Mann Act conviction officially be overturned. It seemed like a prime opportunity to raise public awareness in the United States about the indignities that Johnson endured at the hands of Jim Crow racism. "Our country will be represented in Athens by people of all races," Burns told reporters. "Today, American kids do not know who Jack Johnson was or what he accomplished, in part because his magnificent career was stolen from him by this wholly unjust legal decision."[8] With an air of nationalist triumphalism the Republican senator McCain added, "Pardoning Jack Johnson will serve as a historic testament of America's resolve to live up to its noble ideals of justice and equality."[9] A symbolic gesture, Johnson's presidential pardon promised to provide both an important teaching moment and a cathartic release from the country's racist past. Eight years and one president later, however, Johnson has yet to be officially vindicated.

It is rather ironic that Burns and his committee picked the eve of the Athens Olympics to place this pardon before the world. When his PBS documentary *Unforgivable Blackness: The Rise and Fall of Jack Johnson* premiered on Martin Luther King Jr. Day in 2005, it was, for the most part, interpreted as an *American* tale both at home and abroad.[10] In the final moments of the film, the black American writer Stanley Crouch described Johnson's life as "uniquely American," a quintessential bootstraps tale of black success. "America—for whatever its problems—still has a certain kind of elasticity and a certain latitude that allows the person to dream a big enough dream that can be achieved if the person is as big as the dream," Crouch maintained.[11] Across the Atlantic, a reviewer for Britain's *Manchester Guardian* put a more negative, yet still decidedly U.S.-oriented, slant on the racial moral of Johnson's story. Noting the recent proliferation of U.S. films celebrating white boxing heroes such as James J. Braddock (*Cinderella Man,* 2005) and the fictional Maggie Fitzgerald (*Million Dollar Baby,* 2004), he argued that "the rawest black boxing stories cut too closely to America's sense of itself to be likely hits." Critiquing white American hubris, he scoffed, "Count on Hollywood to concern itself with white boys—or girls—on the make, and not with black men taking on the whole white world, and knocking it flat on its arse."[12] In his eyes, *Unforgivable Blackness* offered a welcome correction to Hollywood's glaring omission, resurrecting Johnson's gritty story from "Ellisonian invisibility," a reference to Ralph Ellison's 1952 novel *Invisible Man.*

Yet, as the British critic's comments also suggest, the black American champion's career was profoundly global. He not only defied white America, but he also took on the "whole white world." While Johnson has posthumously reemerged as a symbol of the ultimate victory of U.S. freedom, individualism, and democracy, his global stature and its larger, more insurgent implications have for the most part remained buried. This domestication of Johnson's legacy points to the limitations of our own understandings of persistent racial inequality in this supposedly postcolonial, postracial era.

Johnson's numerous battles against white supremacy in far-flung spaces around the world provide the narrative thread for this global history of race, gender, and empire in the early twentieth century. Always traveling in search of an unprejudiced place to ply his boxing trade, Johnson was a "rebel sojourner."[13] His life defied convention and fixity, for he refused to "cast down his bucket" and stay in his ascribed racial place. Although his boxing skills and financial success turned out to be exceptional, his peripatetic existence was far from unique. Johnson was part of a hardscrabble world of black men who traveled extensively as professional fighters, minstrel performers, circus attractions, maritime workers, casual laborers, and sometimes all of the above. Although black women also participated in this migratory lifestyle, often as entertainers, it was still largely a male-dominated phenomenon.[14] Thanks to improvements in railway and transoceanic travel, Johnson and other black sojourners could not only chase opportunities throughout the United States but also try their luck across other countries and continents. Advances in communications technologies, from the democratization of newspapers and photography to the rise of the telegraph and moving pictures, also allowed for the unprecedented transmission of their likeness and life stories across the globe. However, as Johnson and his contemporaries discovered, no matter how far they journeyed or how widespread their fame became, they could never fully escape the shadow of the color line.

The relentless swirl of controversies that followed black pugilists like Johnson was emblematic of the deep-seated relationship between the rise of modern ideas of race and the expansion of global connections.[15] The color line they faced was not a relic of days gone by, nor was it just a simple matter of individual or national psychology. Although built on the racial regimes of an earlier era of slavery and empire, it was a quintessentially modern construction. While definitely shaped by local, national, and regional conditions, it was also a global structure routed in the transnational flows of capitalist imperialism, urban industrialism, and the expanding mass culture industries.

The eminent black American intellectual W.E.B. Du Bois certainly recognized this in 1900 when he addressed the first Pan-African Conference in London, England. "The problem of the twentieth century is the problem of the colour line," Du Bois declared; "the question as to how far differences of race . . . are going to be made, hereafter, the basis of denying to over half the world the right of sharing . . . the opportunities and privileges of modern civilisation."[16] As Du Bois later observed in "The Souls of White Folk," published in an August 1910 issue of the *Independent,* the rise of a "new religion of whiteness" had caused the proliferation of racial segregation in a variety of forms.[17] The world's many nations, ethnicities, and religions were increasingly becoming divided along a white-nonwhite binary. This binary was neither natural nor inevitable but actively constructed through the extension of imperial and commercial links in the early twentieth century. More than just an expression of white dominance, this zealous fixation on racial boundaries also indicated that conventional modes of racial control were in crisis—a crisis brought on by the active resistance of nonwhite peoples as they fought for greater access to the fruits of "modern civilisation" on their own terms. Perhaps influenced by the widespread white backlash against Johnson's defeat of Jim Jeffries just one month earlier, Du Bois likened this new religion of whiteness to the powerful waves of the ocean, for its destructive doctrine of exclusion appeared to be flooding the earth.

Its transformative strength came from its ability to speak to the hopes and fears of regular people. Although larger struggles over power, land, resources, and profit were definitely at the heart of this new racial religion, for its many adherents it also involved what Du Bois called the "discovery of personal whiteness."[18] The transnational circuits of commercial mass culture were instrumental to this sense of individual conversion since they carried the gospel of whiteness to folks from all walks of life.

Shifting ideals of manhood and the body, as well as the rise of mass production and consumerism, set the stage for this far-reaching religious revival. Both a physical activity and a commercial amusement involving man-on-man competition, boxing lay at the intersection of these modern developments. Although proper patriarchal organization remained an important marker of whiteness and civilization, and therefore the right to political self-determination, by the turn of the twentieth century Victorian notions of manliness grounded in the ideals of productivity, frugality, and self-denial were beginning to fall by the wayside. A new sense of masculinity emerged, expressed through recreational pursuits, the conspicuous consumption of mass-marketed commodities, and the public display of bodily strength.[19]

At the same time, Western nations became increasingly concerned with maintaining the physical health of their populations. With the rise of what the philosopher Michel Foucault termed "biopolitics," the policing of fitness versus degeneracy formed the basis of new racial regimes in the metropolitan centers and across their empires.[20] This desire to create strong imperial nations in the normative image of a white, bourgeois, heterosexual man inspired a variety of disciplinary mechanisms, from physical education to sexual purity campaigns to involuntary sterilization. Yet biopolitics was not just an apparatus of state power, for it spawned a host of transnational culture industries dedicated to the improvement, preservation, and celebration of white, and especially male, bodies.

This anxious drama often played out most prominently in the cultural realm. With the accelerating shift to mass production centered in cities, spaces of mass consumption (sporting arenas, vaudeville theaters, movie houses) became integral sites for public debates over questions of racial difference and imperial control.[21] Not surprisingly, in this same period professional boxing had begun to shift from a local, often criminalized activity practiced in seamy saloons by bare-knuckled proletarians to a transnational sporting industry complete with gloved competitors, official rules, and governing bodies. Progressive reformers and state officials also began to see amateur boxing as a powerful instrument of normalization—a means to remake white men from across class and ethnic lines into stronger and more productive patriarchs, workers, citizens, and soldiers.[22]

Because of their audacity and success in and out of the boxing ring, Johnson and other black pugilists became some of the most notorious heretics of this new religion of whiteness. Even though they lived on the fringes of respectable society, their geographic mobility, their public visibility, and most of all their physical conquest of white men put them at the very center of a developing black counterculture. Alongside the more conventional political work of black Atlantic activists and intellectuals like Du Bois, they played an integral role in the emergence of a popular black global imagination and a more confident race consciousness that touched the lives of ordinary people of color within and beyond the United States.[23]

Their dual status as both second-class citizens and sporting celebrities gave them a unique perspective on the global color line, along with a mobile platform from which to protest it. They often had more "real world" experience than their middle-class counterparts in negotiating the local conditions of racial oppression in various spaces outside the United States. They were at once reviled and adored as they traveled to destinations throughout the Atlantic world and across the Pacific Ocean. While overseas they publicly challenged the hypocrisy of white supremacy, gaining the admiration of people of color in different places. Stories of their successes and troubles abroad also inspired black Americans back home to expand their geographic imaginations and to envision their racial struggles as part of a global problem.

For Johnson and other rebel sojourners, their widespread fame ultimately was a double-edged sword. As they entered the transnational circuits of professional boxing, they became even further enmeshed in a complex racial economy that extended far beyond the purview of Jim Crow America. They soon became some of the most glaring symbols of the mounting confrontation over the terms of race and empire in the modern world.

BLACK BOXERS AS MODERNITY'S DISCONTENTS

Johnson was not the first black pugilist to experience such an expansive life and career. Throughout the nineteenth century black boxers were always on the move, their migratory lives often overlapping with those of sailors, itinerant laborers, and traveling performers. The legendary bare-knuckle boxer Thomas Molineaux, the first black man to claim the title of "American champion," was one such wandering figure. Likely born in Virginia sometime around 1784, the former slave was earning his living as a prizefighter in New York City's bustling Catherine Market by 1804, and by 1810 he had already journeyed across the Atlantic for a title fight against the reigning English champion, Tom Cribb.[24]

In the decades after Molineaux's celebrated career, scores of other black boxers continued to survive by their wits in the wider world. Recognized more for their skin color than their national affiliation, they were the quintessential black cosmopolitans. Born in Tangiers, Morocco, in 1813 to an African seaman and a local peasant woman, James Wharton, better known as "Jemmy the Black," started out as a cabin boy on a ship that voyaged between Cairo and London. During a violent altercation with the ship's cook, Jemmy's fighting ability caught the attention of an English passenger who encouraged the black youth to become a prizefighter. Although Jemmy initially found work at a British boxing booth taking on all comers, by the 1830s he had emerged as one of the period's most famous black pugilists. The next generation of black prizefighters gave rise to strong-minded men like John Perry, dubbed "The Black Sailor." The son of a white mother and a black British father in Nova Scotia, Canada, Perry fought in England and Australia throughout the 1840s and 1850s. In 1849 he even captured the heavyweight title in Australia, where his opulent clothing and confident demeanor unnerved many of the local white journalists.[25]

By the 1860s African American men had begun to emerge as the leading force in the transatlantic fight scene. A native of Washington, D.C., the black sailor Bob Smith developed into a successful bare-knuckle fighter popularly known as "The Liverpool Darkey." Much like his predecessor Jemmy the Black, Smith first tested his boxing skills aboard a ship bound for England. After enduring many attacks at the hands of his white mates, Smith fought back, beating them all. Sensing a chance for easy profits, the ship's captain offered to back the black American as a professional fighter in Liverpool.[26]

In the years just before Johnson's rise to fame, another black heavyweight named Peter Jackson garnered international recognition. Born on 3 July 1861 in Frederiksted, St. Croix, of the Danish Virgin Islands, Jackson, also known as "The Black Prince," had moved to Sydney, Australia, as a teenager. He started sparring as a deckhand and quickly emerged as a bona fide contender in the early 1880s. After winning the Australian heavyweight title in 1886, Jackson had difficulty coaxing white Australians into the ring with him. Intent on continuing his boxing career, he traveled to the United States and later to Britain, where he became a prominent prizefighter and performer. Despite his widespread success and genteel manner, Jackson was never able to vie for the world title since the reigning white American champion, John L. Sullivan, refused to fight him.[27] For early black sportsmen, from Molineaux to Jackson, their confrontations with the color line were never neatly contained within national borders.

They formed an integral part of a much broader history of black working-class travel and resistance, a kind of "vagabond internationalism."[28] Despite their low social position, people of African descent had long struggled to make their mark on the moral and political economy of the world. From the revolutionary period to the age of emancipation, maritime work had offered enslaved and free blacks a route to greater mobility and autonomy. Black seamen experienced a level of racial flu-

FIGURE 1. In the late nineteenth century Peter Jackson gained international recognition as he moved from country to country in search of white opponents who would fight him. He won the heavyweight championship of Australia (1886) and of England and Australia (1892), but he never got the chance to fight John L. Sullivan for the world heavyweight championship. National Library of Australia.

idity as yet unimaginable on land. They also helped to spread subversive information and ideas throughout the African diaspora. They were not simply a rebellious vanguard, for they built on an already robust network of underground connections across plantation, colonial, national, and even regional boundaries.[29]

This black global vision was borne out of the shared experiences of the enslaved, the dispossessed, the displaced, and the disfranchised—those who had virtually no claims to citizenship rights, no cause for loyalty to the nation-state, and very little stake in the capitalist system.[30] By the late nineteenth century the growing ranks of roving laborers such as black sailors, athletes, and performers proved difficult for white authorities to control. They often had very little to lose. They were no longer yoked to the plantation. Kept out of the economic sphere, most were not tied down by property ownership or lucrative businesses. Many were already separated from their families. Black seafarers continued to be key figures in the black transnational literature of the early twentieth century. Most famously, the meandering maritime narratives of the Jamaican-American leftist Claude McKay underscored the importance of black working-class travel in the development of radical global imaginaries, and the anticolonial and anticapitalist activism they inspired.[31]

The hard-drinking, fist-fighting black mariners featured in works like McKay's novel *Banjo: A Story without a Plot* (1929) were more than just metaphorical. Their fictional experiences on the margins of Western modernity resembled many of the real-life challenges facing Johnson and other rebel sojourners.[32] Even McKay himself noted that black boxers usually came out of "a milieu of the very poor proletariat" and were hailed as heroes in all the "Negro billiard halls, barbershops, and nightclubs of American cities."[33] Drifting in the undercurrents of late imperialism and industrial capitalism, they were part of a disposable and highly mobile workforce that moved in and out of the underground economy. Much like McKay's wandering seamen in *Banjo,* they were "nationality doubtful . . . with no place to go."[34]

Long before the Harlem Renaissance intellectual Alain Locke declared that "Uncle Tom and Sambo have passed on," Johnson and other black pugilists were already articulating their own masculine image of a proud, independent, and assertive New Negro.[35] However, unlike Locke's vision, their vision of the New Negro emerged from the subaltern, homosocial spaces of the diaspora, where anarchistic, evershifting communities of black men defied the gendered and sexual conventions of bourgeois domesticity. Theirs was a subversive camaraderie that cut against the normative grain of the white imperial order.[36] They refused to play by society's economic and social rules.

For them, boxing was not just a better way to make money; it was a route to freedom and independence. Although still managed by white promoters, black men often used the boxing industry as a means to escape from the discipline and degradation of menial low-wage work. The competitive and performative elements of boxing also provided them with opportunities to express themselves in bold new ways. Given the sport's widespread popularity, Johnson and other African American boxers were able to experience life beyond the borders of the United States. Transnational in their travels and resistant to the racial and imperial status quo, black boxers became some of Western modernity's best-known discontents. Yet they have more or less been written out of standard histories of the black renaissance and treated as little more than an amusing sideshow in histories of black transnationalism.

Born on 31 March 1878 in Galveston, Texas, John Arthur "Jack" Johnson became the most famous discontent of his time. The third child and first son of former slaves Henry and Tina (also known as "Tiny"), Johnson arrived in the wake of the U.S. Civil War and Reconstruction as new racial regimes emerged to reassert white control over the recently freed African slaves.[37] In the first decades of his life, the color line became increasingly rigid in the United States, reinforced by the 1896 *Plessy v. Ferguson* doctrine of "separate but equal." The late nineteenth century was also marked by widespread change and upheaval. Johnson came of age at a moment of unprecedented demographic and economic expansion, as societies around the globe not only shifted from rural to urban and from agricultural to industrial but also became increasingly interlinked through more rapid modes of transportation and communication. Despite the period's retrogressive racial politics, these sweeping shifts helped to instill an optimistic sense of possibility among many African Americans.

In search of greater fortune, Johnson's own parents had made the trek out of the plantation economy of the Deep South to the maritime hub of Galveston.[38] Even though they continued to struggle against racial discrimination and financial hardship, their decision to move to the Gulf Coast had undoubtedly opened up new prospects for their children. Young Jack's early experiences in the port city helped to shape both his cosmopolitan outlook and his utter contempt for the color line, two characteristics that pushed him along the path to a high-profile career in boxing.

Galveston's importance as a southern center of maritime trade made it much more demographically varied than other Texan towns further inland. Diverse groups of people passed through the busy seaport, including European immigrants and black sailors from across the Atlantic world.[39] These foreign visitors often mingled with the locals, developing a sense of camaraderie as they shared exciting tales of their journeys. Johnson likely gained his first glimpse of life abroad through such chance encounters.

Galveston was also comparatively lax in its policing of racial divisions. Its waterfront and rail yard were especially vibrant centers of interracial activity for the city's working-class youth. Johnson was a prominent member of the 11th Street and Avenue K gang, a motley group of white and black boys that roamed the docks. He even became best friends with the gang's leader, a white youngster named Leo Posner. "So you see, as I grew up, white boys were my friends and my pals," Johnson later reminisced. "I ate with them, played with them and slept at their homes. Their mothers gave me cookies, and I ate at their tables."[40] His boyhood experiences had raised his expectations for racial equality.

As Johnson grew up, life became far more complicated. Like many of his black classmates, Johnson abandoned school as an adolescent, taking a job as a stevedore. Despite the steady paycheck, he hated the monotonous, backbreaking work and left to try his luck at a series of odd jobs, riding the rails between Galveston and other south Texas cities. Johnson was a porter at a gambling parlor, a baker's assistant, and even a horse trainer.[41] Believing that mobility afforded him greater control over his life, he continued to travel as a stowaway, eventually reaching the international hubs of New York City and Chicago.

Far from provincial in his outlook, young Jack relished the opportunity to journey in search of new adventures and experiences. In his 1927 autobiography Johnson claimed that he had left home at the age of twelve in search of Steve Brodie, an Irish immigrant who became famous in 1886 after claiming to have survived a leap from the newly built Brooklyn Bridge.[42] While Johnson's tale of his quest for Brodie was likely more fiction than fact, the sheer scope of this childhood narrative reveals much about the beginnings of his expansive geographic imagination. "From the Texas town to New York was a long way, especially for a youngster without funds," Johnson recalled. Nevertheless, he was resolved to meet Brodie, the hero that he and his friends had read so much about in the newspaper.

As the story went, the determined yet naïve Johnson set out in pursuit of Brodie. "I spent more than a week trying to find a train out of the railroad yards," he recalled. "There were strings of box cars at my disposal and many times, seeing a train of cars moving in the direction which I believed would take me to New York, I hid myself in one of them and settled down for my long journey."[43] Unfortunately, he discovered that he was just circling the rail yards. Still, young Jack refused to be discouraged.

Rather than give up on his dream, he quietly stowed away on a steamship bound for New York City. His presence did not remain a secret for long. The ship's captain soon discovered Johnson and put him to work shoveling coal and peeling potatoes.[44] Although bruised from the many beatings he endured at the hands of ship's cook, young Jack arrived in New York brimming with optimism. As he explored the city he asked around for Brodie's whereabouts. The Irish daredevil apparently ran a local saloon, so Johnson made his way to the Bowery District. Although he never actually met Brodie, as Johnson later recalled, "I found a new entrance into life, and spent many happy, if not prosperous days in New York during which time I met many historic Bowery personages, [and] became more or less absorbed by Bowery life."[45]

Johnson considered himself to be in the midst of a new "career as a worldly young man."[46] Instead of returning home he journeyed from New York to Boston in search of another one of his idols, the Afro-Caribbean prizefighter Joe Walcott, also known as "The Barbados Demon." While Jim Crow segregation had pushed its way into the sporting realm ever since the 1880s, black athletes like Walcott had persevered, touring all across the United States to practice their fighting trade. When Johnson arrived in Boston he took a job in the stables of the city's society folk and later tracked down his hero. Enamored with the Barbadian welterweight, young Jack sometimes carried Walcott's gear to and from the boxing gym. Regardless of the exact dates and details of Johnson's northeast jaunt, he was clearly captivated by the adventuresome lives of Brodie and Walcott. Indeed, Johnson tried to emulate them. Throughout his teenage years he continued with his "roaming instincts and hectic experiences," splitting his time between Galveston and other U.S. cities.[47]

Much to the chagrin of his parents, Johnson had not chosen a conventional route to racial uplift. "My father would have had me take more interest in the church, and sought determinedly to have me extend my schooling," Johnson claimed.[48] Instead of working toward a respectable trade, young Jack gravitated to the seedy life of Galveston's dockyards, where he developed a reputation as a skillful fighter. Even when he took on an apprenticeship in carriage painting in Dallas at the age of fifteen, his experiences still pushed him further down the road to becoming a professional boxer. Walter Lewis, the white owner of the carriage shop where Johnson worked, trained him in the art of pugilism and encouraged him to pursue a career in prizefighting.

Johnson began to "think of the boxing ring as a profession."[49] A rising star, he quickly outgrew the local fight scene. As he recollected, "The purses offered me were truly minimal—10, 15 or 20 dollars at most." He could hardly make enough money to cover his expenses, and he soon found himself in debt, "so I decided to travel the world," Johnson later wrote, "to try to box from one coast to the other, and to attach myself to the training camp of a famous boxer."[50]

Such ambitions were not for the faint of heart. The young prizefighter's experiences tramping to Chicago, Kansas City, and other U.S. destinations had hardened him. "Fellow travelers . . . initiated me into the secrets of obtaining, here and there, scraps of food sufficient to keep me alive," Johnson claimed.[51] Hunger was just one of the many challenges he faced. "Hard-boiled train crews did not seem enthusiastic over having me as a passenger, and on countless occasions I was chased from boxcars, gondolas and blinds," Johnson recounted. "Brakemen impressed me with their earnestness by brandishing clubs with which they threatened to break numerous bones."

Struggling to survive during one of his forays north, he had participated in a battle royal in Springfield, Illinois. White promoters often trolled the rail yards in search of itinerant black youths to participate in these bloody free-for-all fights. Usually three or more blindfolded African American boys were pitted against each other in the ring. A Springfield man had approached Johnson about trying his luck in such a fight. Still without a manager to underwrite his expenses and arrange his matches, the half-starved Johnson agreed to participate in a battle royal in exchange for food, housing, and a $1.50 purse.[52]

Despite these difficulties, by his early twenties Johnson had distinguished himself as one of the premier African American boxers both in and out of the ring. As his winnings multiplied, he threw himself into the ostentatious, dandified lifestyle typical of the period's professional athletes. Much like he had during his boyhood days at the docks, Johnson continued to reject prevailing notions of respectability, choosing instead to run in the same circles as the motley collection of pimps, prostitutes, gamblers, and entertainers that frequented the saloons and flophouses of urban vice districts. In this way he retained a special appeal for poor and working-class African Americans, even as the black middle class remained somewhat ambivalent about his sporting success and audacious demeanor.

Not only did he hail from humble origins, but he also embodied a bold vision of black masculinity that spoke to the hopes and dreams of the dark proletariat.[53] Johnson openly publicized his enjoyment of luxurious clothing and jewels, sumptuous eating and drinking, and, perhaps most of all, beautiful white women. As a *Los Angeles Times* reporter described the black heavyweight in 1903, "The clothes that garmented the strolling colossus spoke emphatically." He sported trousers with "orderly creases," gleaming patent leather boots, a high-collared, "modish" dress shirt, "a scarf of ermine silk," diamond jewelry, and even a regal walking stick.[54] He was known for performing elaborate grooming rituals, usually with the help of white servants, and for openly exhibiting his well-muscled physique in front of curious journalists. While Johnson's dandyism undoubtedly mocked mainstream society's rigid divisions between masculine and feminine—the same divisions often deployed to mark black people as deviant—he was also notorious for perpetrating domestic violence against women.[55]

Beyond his focus on bodily aesthetics and his lavish taste in up-to-the-minute fashion, Johnson maintained a particular fascination with the power of cars and the mobility they offered. As one sportswriter declared, "He has never been without an automobile since they became available."[56] Over the years Johnson acquired a sizable collection of autos, including many of the leading U.S. and European makes. Johnson also prided himself on his ability to drive fast, and he ran into trouble for speeding wherever he traveled. Since he enjoyed flaunting his wealth and also thought of himself as a thoroughly independent and modern man, it is hardly surprising that Johnson focused so much of his leisure time on automobiles.[57] Conservative African American leaders like Booker T. Washington became some of Johnson's fiercest critics. The young prizefighter had not only eschewed the more predictable path of a tradesman, but he scoffed at the black bourgeoisie's standards of restraint.

Faced with pervasive racial segregation in the U.S. boxing scene, Johnson eventually chose to go abroad in pursuit of new opponents. The more recognition he received as a top-flight competitor, the more

FIGURE 2. Jack Johnson sporting his signature style, 1908. National Archives of Australia.

difficult it became for him to convince prominent white American boxers to meet him in the ring. As early as 1903 Johnson had emerged as the most logical challenger for the reigning white American world heavyweight champion Jim Jeffries, yet Jeffries steadfastly refused to fight him. Frustrated but not defeated, Johnson fixed his sights beyond the borders of the United States.

As Johnson ventured out on his first journey abroad in December 1906, he joined the transnational tradition of black working-class movement and resistance. Although Johnson's roving lifestyle failed to garner him the kind of respectability that his father had hoped for, it made him famous and gave him the freedom to express himself. Over the next thirteen years he became one of the period's most worldly and outspoken black American men.

Johnson and other rebel sojourners emerged as important "organic intellectuals" of the diaspora.[58] They often saw themselves as such. Through the rising black press they provided their African American fans with insights about their experiences abroad, and through telegraph reports about their triumphs and travails they gained ardent followers throughout the colonial world. As they publicly pushed the limits of possibility wherever they traveled, they pried open an imaginative space for utopian dreams of black freedom. Moreover, as great reservoirs of practical knowledge on the workings of the global color line, they laid the groundwork for the diasporic leaders and thinkers of the interwar years, from Marcus Garvey to Claude McKay, who endeavored to envision a more militant brand of New Negro politics through the prism of transnationalism. These rough-and-tumble men, whose education, for the most part, came from the school of hard knocks, simply refused to remain in their prescribed "place."

BOXING, BIOPOLITICS, AND THE WHITE MAN'S BURDEN

Even though Johnson left the United States to escape Jim Crow segregation, his search for greater liberty and opportunity in foreign lands was hardly an uncomplicated tale of cosmopolitan harmony and good fortune. Traveling aboard steamships and trains, he necessarily moved along the same routes as Western imperial military and political power, commerce, and culture. He also journeyed overseas just as the new religion of whiteness seemed to be sweeping the earth. As Johnson continued to beat white men in the ring and flout racial etiquette outside the ring, he frequently found himself embroiled in public fights against this wider culture of white supremacy.

Johnson's rise to global fame (and infamy) was not just a simple case of serendipity, nor was it a mere matter of individual personality. The various controversies surrounding his pugilistic success fit within a much larger pattern of geopolitical and cultural shifts at the turn of the twentieth century. While the disparate places he traversed had their own local logics and practices of race, the increasingly transnational flows of people, capital, commodities, and ideas had helped to bring them under the banner of the "white man's burden." Coined by the British author Rudyard Kipling in a poem published in February 1899 at the start of the Philippine-American War, this phrase took on a life of its own.[59] Originally invoked by Kipling to urge white Americans to join their European counterparts in the work of empire, the white man's burden and its gendered philosophy came to provide a ready rationale for numerous forms of racial exploitation and expropriation. In essence, it meant that white men had the collective moral responsibility to civilize the world's supposedly savage peoples of color. Whether expressed as a *"mission civilisatrice"* (civilizing mission) in the case of the French or as "benevolent assimilation" in the case of the United States, a collective sense of white racial destiny marked this moment.[60]

Although the inner workings of these imperial projects undoubtedly differed, white men from across national borders were discovering a racial common ground on the terrain of the body. This emerging culture of the white man's burden was closely intertwined with the global shift to biopolitics. From a theoretical and practical point of view, the disciplining of individual bodies—white and nonwhite— formed the centerpiece of this Western civilizing mission. White men had to make sure that they were not only politically and culturally prepared but also physically fit to carry out their imperial duties. As social Darwinist ideas about the "survival of the fittest" entered the mainstream, the health and purity of their bodies came to represent the strength and vitality of their nations in the global arena. This imagined mission to civilize also granted white men the authority to control the bodies of nonwhites, not just in the realm of battle or labor, but even in the most intimate domains of life, from the domestic to the hygienic to the sexual. Through this exercise of colonial conquest and discipline, white men and their nations could ultimately ensure their own racial regeneration.[61] These gendered notions of the body and the body politic seemed to sanction the Western powers' violent and invasive interventions into the lives of people of color.

The United States was no exception. Even before Kipling beseeched the young nation to take up the white man's burden, it had already managed to consolidate its continental empire at the expense of Mexicans and Native Americans. The United States then turned its sights abroad. By 1893 it had already made headway into Hawaii, and by the late 1890s the Spanish-American and Philippine-American Wars brought Cuba, Puerto Rico, Guam, and the Philippines under U.S. influence. U.S. culture and capital continued to extend their hegemonic reach throughout Mexico and the rest of the Americas.[62]

At the same time Britain was working to extend its influence abroad. Faced with the growing threat of nationalist unrest, Britain tightened its hold on India. British forces also began their campaign to consolidate the imperial nation's power and territory in South Africa. The bloody

Kaffir Wars culminated with the defeat of the Zulus in 1879. Britain then struggled to bring the Afrikaners' lands under the Union Jack during the First and Second Boer Wars (1880–81 and 1899–1902).[63]

With the establishment of the Third Republic in 1870, the French imperial government began touting its special duty to civilize the indigenous peoples of the world. During the last two decades of the nineteenth century France increased its holdings in Indochina and also established control over territories in North, West, and Central Africa, covering the areas of modern-day Mauritania, Senegal, Guinea, Mali, Côte d'Ivoire, Benin, Niger, Chad, the Central African Republic, the Republic of Congo, and Djibouti.[64]

Despite their blustering rhetoric and enormous scope, these expansionist projects exposed a pervasive sense of anxiety about white men's continued ascendancy in the modern world. Faced with economic depression and the contraction of foreign markets as well as a host of domestic social ills, U.S. and European officials had begun to see imperial growth as a way out of their problems. By the 1890s a self-consciously "new" imperial moment had come into play for Western nations on both sides of the Atlantic, as they looked to the colonies for more consumer markets.[65] For U.S. president Grover Cleveland, the control of markets "in every part of the habitable globe" became a national project.[66] This would improve the U.S. economy and help to resolve the ongoing conflict between labor and capital.

British and French officials also looked to their colonies for national revival. English politicians believed that their economic survival depended on securing more foreign markets for their surplus products. According to prevailing logic, white colonial settlers would boost the domestic economy as they consumed British-manufactured wares and procured valuable resources for British factories. In the wake of the Franco-Prussian War (1870–71), politically and economically vulnerable France began an emboldened pursuit of imperial prestige and profits. The ailing industrial power was looking for a way out of its recent economic slumps (1882, 1890), and the colonies appeared ripe with opportunity.[67]

In the midst of this restless imperial moment, white settler nations began to deploy a host of immigration restrictions and other modes of racial segregation. The influx of free people of color into formerly white preserves had aroused concerns about the control of land and resources and also challenged racialized notions of citizenship and democracy. In the United States, the racial reconciliation of white Americans in the North and the South, along with the rise of de jure segregation, had effectively relegated African Americans to second-class citizenship. Similarly, Australia, Canada, and the Union of South Africa seemed bent on excluding people of color from the political and economic benefits of Western modernity. In 1901 the newly formed Commonwealth of Australia further marginalized the Aboriginal people while also passing racial immigration restrictions in an effort to "whiten" the continent. Under the slogan "White Canada Forever," Canadian officials passed a series of immigration laws to prevent the entry of people of Asian and African descent. By 1910 even the British and the Boers had found common racial ground in the newly formed Union of South Africa as they worked together to exclude Africans, coloreds, and Indians from full citizenship.[68] Because of their physical proximity to nonwhite peoples, many white settlers believed that they bore the brunt of the white man's burden. They became some of the most fervent converts to the new religion of whiteness.

This urgent sense of shared purpose in the preservation of the racial and imperial status quo was not just the result of overlapping political and economic crises. It was also a product of the accelerating flows of commercial mass culture. The rise of transnational sporting industries was particularly vital to this emerging global economy of race. Competitive sports seemed to offer the perfect complement to the defensive physical stance of the white man's burden. Collective fears about the rising power of nonwhites were often expressed through gendered metaphors of the body. As the Australian politician Charles Pearson argued in his foreboding book *National Life and Character* (1893), white men had to remain on guard or else they would be "elbowed and hustled, and perhaps even thrust aside" by their nonwhite subjects.[69] Popular discussions about the supposed degeneration of white bodies at the hands of urban industrialism betrayed much deeper concerns about the diminishing power of white nations and empires.

In the midst of these widespread fears, elaborate rituals of physical fitness and grand exhibitions of the white male body gained mass popularity. By the 1890s, "heavyweight champion of the world" had become an internationally recognized title. The first modern Olympiad took place in Athens, Greece, in 1896. Around this time several international sports organizations also came into existence, including the Davis Cup of tennis (1900), World Series Baseball (1902), and the Fédération Internationale de Football Association (FIFA) (1904).[70]

At once intimate and public, boxing seemed best to encapsulate the growing struggles over the racial and imperial order. Boxing involved unscripted hand-to-hand combat between individual men who embodied races and nations in the eyes of their fans. As they fought barechested in the ring, with no weapons and only the protection of leather gloves, professional pugilists offered spectators an occasion to witness firsthand the "survival of the fittest." Although intimate in practice, boxing emerged as one of the world's most popular live sporting events and it also generated a myriad of inexpensive and accessible publications, souvenirs, exhibitions, and films that reached diverse audiences across national borders. Physical and highly visual, boxing always threatened to expose the hypocrisy of the white man's burden.

The stakes were high, for the boxing ring was more than just a metaphorical site; it was a public forum in which racial divisions were drawn and debated. By Johnson's day, the ring had become a space of heightened white surveillance, much like other intimate sites involving potentially subversive and sexualized interracial contact. However, as prizefighting slowly emerged from the criminal underworld, where race mixing was not as strictly policed, it presented white officials with a particular set of problems. Profit motives and consumer demand foiled their attempts to maintain a rigid color line in the boxing ring, while modern technology prevented them from keeping the triumphs of black men such as Johnson out of the public domain. Ironically, the overwhelming desire of white men to prove their own physical supremacy in the ring turned interracial title matches into massive commercial spectacles that reverberated around the world. Without the specter of black challengers, the victories of white boxers simply could not hold the same explanatory power for the white man's burden. Boxing's burgeoning popularity was closely tied to its very embodiment of contemporary battles over the racial boundaries of Western modernity.

COMMERCIAL MASS CULTURE AND THE GLOBAL COLOR LINE

This keen desire to showcase white dominance was not limited to the boxing ring. The exigencies of Western empire, technological advances, the growth of urban industrialism, and the rise of consumer capitalism had inspired a diverse and profitable trade in racialized amusements that stretched across national borders. Instrumental in spreading the new religion of whiteness, these popular diversions and their vast array of related products helped to enlist the support of regular people in the white man's burden. As Johnson and other black sojourners ventured abroad, they entered a complex racial economy driven by the increasingly transnational currents of commercial mass culture.

By the turn of the twentieth century boxing was just one part of a much "broader universe of white supremacist entertainments."[71] On both sides of the Atlantic world's fairs and imperial exhibitions encouraged the collective celebration of white control. Britain presented the Colonial and Indian Exhibition (1886) and the Jubilee celebrations (1887, 1897); France hosted the Universal Expositions (1889, 1900); and the United States staged the Chicago World's Columbian Exposition (1893), the Buffalo Pan-American Exposition (1901), and St. Louis's Louisiana Purchase Exposition (1904). In addition to these official state-sponsored events, scores of commercial amusements, including zoos, ethnological expositions, blackface minstrel shows, circuses, freak shows, museums of curiosities, dime novels, and Wild West shows reinforced prevalent ideas of white supremacy.

Writing in 1901, the English economist John A. Hobson called this white imperialist sentiment "the psychology of jingoism" in a book with the same title. He blamed the burgeoning entertainment and recreation industries for inspiring "the glorification of brute force and an ignorant contempt for foreigners" among "large sections of the [white] middle and labouring classes."[72] He believed that commercial spectacles had become "a more potent educator than the church, the school, the political meeting, or even than the press" because of their ability to reach the semiliterate masses. Indeed, imperialism and what Hobson called "spectatorial passion" went hand in hand.[73] Many of these commercial amusements put nonwhite men and women on display for the pleasure and edification of white audiences while also enacting visual narratives of white conquest over primitive peoples of color at home and abroad. They helped to create a more expansive sense of whiteness that defied not only national borders but also ethnic and class lines.

Since this growing trade in white supremacist entertainments relied intrinsically on the circulation and exhibition of nonwhite bodies, it presented men such as Johnson with many opportunities to compete and perform overseas. Yet this opportunity and visibility came at a price and never guaranteed political or social equality. Instead, so pervasive was this trade that black sojourners had difficulty finding work outside the realm of entertainment. Even those who initially went abroad as sailors and laborers often found themselves forced into sporting arenas and playhouses out of financial necessity. Their racialized bodies proved to be valuable commodities as they performed largely for the amusement of white spectators and for the financial gain of white promoters. Whether they were boxing or performing in vaudeville acts, or a combination of both, the ability of African American athletes and entertainers to stage their "blackness" was integral to their survival in this marketplace of race. The mechanical reproduction of their images only expanded this marketplace.[74] Although swept up in this trade, Johnson and other rebel sojourners refused to be defined by it. They began to develop their own counterculture of blackness as they navigated through the undercurrents of interimperial exchange.

Nevertheless, the expansion of mass culture was pivotal to the construction of a global color line. Commercial amusements helped to reshape older conceptions of race for modern consumption. As they separated white from nonwhite bodies, they effectively breathed new life into biological theories of racial difference, even as cultural explanations began to emerge in academic circles. They also spawned a visual shorthand for ideas of racial hierarchy that proved to be both adaptable and enduring across space and time. This trade in racial images emerged as one of the first examples of globalization in the late imperial age.

As the United States became a more powerful player in world politics, it moved to the forefront of this trade. U.S. commercial culture—amusement parks, circuses, vaudeville shows, dime novels, moving pictures—had already been spreading U.S. racial mores abroad since the mid-nineteenth century. Just as these cultural products had eased the process of racial reconciliation between North and South after the Civil War, so too did they help to reinforce transnational bonds of whiteness.[75] Circulating within this mix of media, stock images of the Western frontier, southern plantation slavery, Jim Crow segregation, and the "American negro" became reference points against which other nations judged the state of their own racial and imperial relations. Although U.S. race culture became inextricably linked with local conceptions of race across the globe, this was not merely a case of "Americanization." Instead, commercial amusements provided a shared "cultural space" in which everyday people in a variety of places "indigenized" American racial ideas to speak to their local circumstances.[76]

In the decades before Johnson's championship reign, the transnational careers of two rival heavyweights, the Irish-American John L. Sullivan and the black Australian Peter Jackson, exemplified these cultural dynamics. Both prizefighters' reputations reached far beyond their homelands. Their international celebrity revealed at once the growing influence of U.S. ideas of race abroad and the increasing importance of commercial mass culture in shaping modern conceptions of race.

In November 1887 New York City's *Life* magazine boasted that America was "doing a vast deal" for its British cousins by sending them two of its national heroes, the frontiersman William F. Cody, popularly known as "Buffalo Bill," and the champion boxer Sullivan, dubbed "The Boston Strong Boy." [77] Complete with Indian skirmishes and stagecoach races, Buffalo Bill's Wild West Show had already proven a smashing success alongside the summertime events of Queen Victoria's Golden Jubilee. Shortly thereafter Sullivan had arrived in London just as Buffalo Bill was about to embark on a tour of the English provinces. The Boston Strong Boy was already a well-known commodity in Britain. His photos, life story, fight record, and training methods had long appeared in inexpensive penny papers, pamphlets, and boxing manuals on both sides of the Atlantic. [78]

Known for his sturdy physique and his steadfast refusal to fight any black challengers, especially Jackson, Sullivan was the ultimate icon of white American working-class men. Accompanied by a troupe of boxers and the African American Bohee Brothers minstrel performers, he followed Buffalo Bill's lead, exhibiting his pugilistic talents throughout England, Ireland, Scotland, and Wales. In Birmingham Sullivan's tour converged with Buffalo Bill's Wild West Show, and the industrial city reveled in its white American heroes. Nearly twenty thousand spectators, including "a large number of Buffalo Bill's followers," attended Sullivan's exhibitions at Bingley Hall. [79] Both these spectacles of white American manhood—one a romanticized vision of Western conquest and the other a celebration of urban working-class strength—resonated with Britain's own racial and imperial mythology. Contemporary U.S. commentators recognized the sheer power of these images. An illustrator for *Life* magazine called it "The Triumph of the West," depicting a British royal procession that featured Buffalo Bill on horseback followed by Sullivan posing atop an elaborate float for scores of admiring fans. [80]

Alongside these grand displays of white American manhood, U.S. tropes of blackness were also central to the growing trade in racialized amusements. Just as popular ideas and images of the so-called East provided Westerners with a means to construct whiteness in opposition to an exotic "other"—what Edward Said called "Orientalism"—popular tropes of the "negro" had come to play a similar geopolitical role.

The negro was a hybrid construction, an admixture of black images from across the diaspora. Because of the cultural power of the United States, the archetypical "stage darky" of blackface minstrelsy emerged as one of the predominant images of blackness. The stage darky permeated not only the United States but also wherever African American performers and their burnt cork imitations traveled. Elements of the stage darky pervaded representations of black South African miners, colonial subjects in India, and even Australian Aboriginals. In this way, a local narrative of race situated in the specific historical realities of U.S. plantation slavery and Jim Crow segregation developed into a global story of white supremacy.[81]

This trade in stock images of black America was not without real-life consequences. Given white Britishers' limited contact with people of African descent, their racial education often came from commercial amusements emanating from the United States. Writing in 1885, Major A.B. Ellis of the First West India Regiment argued that the circulating images of blackface minstrelsy made it next to impossible for black soldiers to get any respect in England. As Ellis observed, "The popular idea in Great Britain of the negro is that he is a person who commonly wears a dilapidated tall hat, cotton garments of brilliant hue, carries a banjo or concertina, and indulges in extraordinary cachinnations at the slightest pretext."[82] As the frustrated officer maintained, this vision of blackness was just "as far from the truth" as the stereotypes propagated "by the vivid fancy of Mrs. Beecher Stowe." So popular was *Uncle Tom's Cabin,* as both a book and a play, that it continued to influence English perceptions of black people from all parts of the diaspora for many years to come.[83]

When Jackson traveled to England in 1892 to fight the white Australian Frank Slavin, he experienced the same kind of conflation. Many Londoners viewed him as a "curiosity," since they had only encountered black people through the "burnt cork darkies of minstrelsy."[84] Even though Jackson was technically a British subject and certainly saw himself as such, they still perceived him largely through the prism of U.S. racial narratives.

As much as Jackson and his generation of black pugilists remained trapped in this web of minstrel imagery, they also proved indispensable to the development of a cosmopolitan black counterculture. They were part of an expansive network of black cultural traffic, one that included the likes of Henry "Box" Brown, the famed abolitionist performer, and the celebrated vaudeville duo of Bert Williams and George

Walker.[85] The performative elements of boxing, both in and out of the ring, held a special appeal for the black masses. Through their pugilistic heroes, everyday people gained a sense of control over the black body and its gendered representation at a moment when prevailing ideals of citizenship and the nation remained interwoven with images of white manhood. After Jackson defeated Slavin to capture both the English and Australian heavyweight titles, an enthusiastic African American reporter declared that Britain was "One Spot where the Negro is a Man." As the reporter bragged, Jackson's "exemplary bearing in the ring" had garnered him "troops of friends of all ranks and grades in the social scale." In civilized England the black man could apparently "'live, move and have his being' on terms of absolute equality with the white man."[86] Although the foreign exploits of men like Jackson certainly provided African Americans with a means to critique the Jim Crow color line, they also exposed the limitations of commercial mass culture as a forum for collective resistance.

Whereas visual imagery and performance helped to translate counterhegemonic ideas of race across national borders, they were also susceptible to their own distortions and elisions. As black American sportsmen became some of the most infamous stand-ins for an imagined community of nonwhite peoples across the globe, their hypervisibility had real implications for the construction of black and anticolonial nationalisms and transnationalisms in subsequent decades. Their well-publicized version of black success was not only male-dominated but also overwhelmingly focused on the cultivation of the body, displays of physical strength and sexuality, conspicuous consumption, antisocial behavior, and outward performance. In turn, the growing prominence of African American images of blackness complicated later attempts to build transnational racial solidarity. The very ubiquity of black American sojourners and their exhibitions tended to obscure the complexities of race in different spaces while also pushing the concerns of their peers from across the diaspora and the colonial world to the margins of public debate.

Following in the cosmopolitan footsteps of men like Jackson, Johnson strutted onto the world stage in the early years of the twentieth century. Australia was his first overseas destination. Chapter 1 explores the controversy surrounding Johnson's relationship with a white Australian woman in 1907 in tandem with the public outcry over his 1908 defeat of the reigning world heavyweight champion Tommy Burns in Sydney. Placing these two incidents within the context of contemporary fears of impending race war in the Pacific region exposes the deep-seated relationship between modern ideas of race and the body. U.S. president Theodore Roosevelt's own fascination with boxing and the "strenuous life" echoed popular British and Australian concerns about their fitness for the white man's burden. With mounting anxieties over white degeneration, colonial spaces and interracial conflict became the imagined backdrop for the regeneration of Anglo-Saxon manhood.

Expanding on these themes of white degeneration and nonwhite subversion, chapter 2 examines the concerted efforts across the United States and the British Empire to ban the moving picture featuring Johnson's defeat of the white American champion Jeffries in 1910. News of this heavily anticipated interracial fight and its film recording traveled far beyond the confines of the actual event in Reno, Nevada. The many reports and visual representations of Johnson's victory inspired anticolonial discussions and celebrations around the globe, from South Africa to India to Fiji. They also provoked interimperial conversations about the maintenance of white supremacy in the modern world, especially given the increasingly transnational reach of commercial mass culture.

The next three chapters shift the spotlight to Johnson's European travels throughout the 1910s, exploring the tensions between his exhilarating freedom of movement and the realities of the global color line. The transnational tumult that followed the announcement of Johnson's world championship match against the British titleholder Bombardier Billy Wells in London, England, provides the centerpiece for chapter 3. As white men on both sides of the Atlantic joined together in their search for a "white hope" to unseat Johnson, the boxing ring became a space of intense discussion about the urgent need to police the racial divisions between citizens and subjects.

Unfairly convicted in 1913 under the Mann Act, which prohibited white slave trafficking, Johnson chose to seek refuge abroad rather than go to jail. Chapter 4 examines Johnson's European exile as part of a wider culture of black working-class resistance in the years before World War I. In Europe black sojourners found a ready market for their matches and exhibitions along with many opportunities to publicly critique the injustices of Jim Crow America. Yet, although European sportsmen often embraced African American boxers to demonstrate their own civilization and racial enlightenment, their sense of allegiance only stretched so far. As chapter 5 demonstrates, this was certainly true of black American boxers' experiences in France. Although they became instant celebrities in Paris, there was a darker side to their success. Exoticized for their physical prowess, hypermasculine sexuality, and flashy style, they remained commodities in the profitable trade of racialized spectacles.

As the Great War spread across Europe, Johnson was once again on the move. As chapter 6 shows, his subsequent journeys across the Caribbean and Latin America, particularly in Cuba and Mexico, coincided with the United States' growing influence in the region. Traveling along the same routes as U.S. power, Johnson found himself confronted by the profound irony of being black and American at a moment when the United States was beginning to take on a more prominent geopolitical role. Although Johnson eventually surrendered to U.S. authorities in 1920, bringing his long sojourn to an end, his rebellious feats in and beyond the ring had already unsettled the racial order in much of the late imperial world. Chapter 7 explores Johnson's insurgent legacy in the aftermath of his career. The storm of controversy surrounding the Senegalese boxer Battling Siki (dubbed the "French Jack Johnson") exemplified the escalating conflict between Western imperialism and black/anticolonial radicalism during the interwar years. Although he was no longer in the limelight, Johnson had helped to unleash a rising tide of color across the globe.

Embodying Empire

Jack Johnson and the White Pacific

This battle may in the future be looked back upon as the
first great battle of an inevitable race war . . . there is more
in this fight to be considered than the mere title of pugilistic
champion of the world.

—*Australian Star* on Burns versus Johnson, 5 December 1908

On 26 December 1906 Jack Johnson left San Francisco for his first
journey overseas, traveling to Australia aboard the steamship *Sonoma*.
At twenty-nine years of age, the African American heavyweight was by
no means a rookie; he was already well known in professional prizefight circles and had traveled throughout the United States. He was
also very well versed in the racist ways of Jim Crow America. What
Johnson knew less was the kind of reception that awaited him beyond
U.S. borders. As his manager, Alec McLean, assured him, Australia
could not be any worse than America.[1] Not in need of much convinc-
ing, the ambitious Johnson agreed to try his luck abroad.

Johnson's initial experiences matched his optimism. Although he
battled seasickness throughout the trip, he was sad to leave the "charming friends" he had met aboard the *Sonoma*. Johnson later recalled,
"For the first time in my life, I was pleased to find myself in a group in
which we did not take into account people's color."[2] When he arrived
in Sydney on 24 January 1907, the city's white sportsmen embraced
him with open arms, and local newspapers declared that he would not
be forced to confront a color line in Australia.

Despite this warm welcome, Australian fans had more in common
with their white American counterparts than they cared to admit.
As they viewed Johnson through the distorted lens of blackface min-

strelsy, he appeared more an exotic curiosity than a man. "He has a genial face," the *Sydney Truth* described, "somewhat babyish looking and of the type of the little coons who may be seen devouring watermelons in a well-known American picture."[3] Since the mid-nineteenth century, minstrelsy had been a staple in Australian theaters, providing white settlers with a glimpse of U.S. racial politics. Australians had eagerly embraced this U.S. import, adapting both its imagery and its language to their local scene. So-called "nigger" bands played on Australian steamers, and street minstrels paraded outside neighborhood pubs dressed in loud suits complete with oversized collars and coattails.[4] Not surprisingly, when the dandified heavyweight arrived, white Australians immediately cast him as a minstrel. Wrapped up in the sentimental tropes of blackface comedy, Johnson, for the time being, seemed harmless.

Over the next two years the black heavyweight transformed from an amusing spectacle to a serious threat in the eyes of many white Australians. They discovered that he was the farthest thing from a submissive stage darky. Much like in the United States, Johnson's conquest of white men in the ring and white women in the bedroom did not go over well Down Under. These were both serious violations of racial protocol at a time when preserving the strength and purity of white bodies was central to white supremacist thought. Thus, the public uproar over his relationship with a white Australian woman in 1907 and the subsequent backlash against his 1908 world championship victory over Tommy Burns in Sydney were essentially two sides of the same coin.

Though geographically distant and demographically different, the two nations shared the same underlying logics of race and the body. First forged in the performances of blackface minstrels, these transnational links proliferated with the expansion of mass sporting culture at the turn of the twentieth century. By the time Johnson reached Sydney, the athletic body had become an important medium through which white men expressed their mutual interest in the maintenance of global white domination. The image of an ideal citizen was a muscular white male. This focus on the physical provided an easy justification for the exclusion of people of color from mainstream politics and society. Their dark skin and exotic bodies became the tangible proof of their unworthiness for full citizenship rights and self-determination. It marked them as contaminating threats to the health of the white body politic.

The rise of rationalized physical training and organized sport also helped to naturalize social Darwinist theories about the survival of the fittest. "Man is and always will be, a fighting animal," declared the famed white American and former world heavyweight champion Jim Jeffries.[5] Countless articles in U.S., British, and French sporting magazines reflected the widespread idea that *how* a group of people (a race, ethnicity, or nation, for example) fought provided a clear demonstration of its relative cultural and political status.[6] Like many of his contemporaries, Jeffries believed that "the better fighter a nation was, the more quickly did it become civilised, because it tackled and downed the things which bound it to savagery more speedily." Conquering nations "were those that had learned the advantages of scientific fighting."[7] Boxing was especially suited to the needs of white men and white nations, for it promised to improve their productivity, self-discipline, courage, and self-reliance in the face of growing challenges to their authority.

White men, however, could never fully contain the fluid meanings of sport and physical culture. Wherever they traveled, Johnson and other black boxers publicly disrupted not only the mainstream ideals of the white male body and the white body politic but also the racial fictions of the degenerate stage darky. Thanks in part to the growing popularity of prizefighting, their powerful black bodies became the visual portents of racial Armageddon, at once feared and desired by white sporting audiences and celebrated by people of color around the world.

THE WHITE BODY POLITIC

Theodore Roosevelt maintained a longstanding fascination with boxing throughout his life in public office, first as the governor of New York (1899–1900) and later as the president of the United States (1901–9). The sport played a big role in Roosevelt's political self-fashioning as a rugged proponent of the "strenuous life." He often credited boxing with his early success as a colonel in the Spanish-American War. "A good deal of whatever it was that carried me through the San Juan business," Roosevelt once wrote, "I owed to the lessons I had learned as regards [to] temper and courage in the days when I used to box."[8] The heroic myths about his charge up Cuba's San Juan Hill with the Rough Riders had helped transform him from an effeminate "Jane-Dandy" to an icon of white American manhood.[9] Roosevelt actively cultivated this image, surrounding himself with professional pugilists like John L. Sullivan, Oscar "Battling" Nelson, and Robert Fitzsimmons. He even hired "Professor" Mike Donovan, a former bare-knuckle fighter and the head instructor at the New York Athletic Club, as his family's official boxing trainer. A regular fixture at both the governor's mansion and the White House, Donovan often sparred with Roosevelt. "I have noted his career in politics, [and] seen him go for the mark there with the same pertinacity that he shows when boxing," Donovan later recalled. "Resistance, discomfiture, [and] hard knocks in one domain as in the other serve only to make him keener."[10]

Roosevelt's pairing of physical fitness and political affairs was more than just an idiosyncratic trait. It was indicative of the rising importance of the body as a modern social construction at the turn of the twentieth century. The Muscular Christianity movement had first appeared in 1850s England, and by the early 1900s it had spread throughout the United States.[11] Its proponents argued that Christians needed to cultivate not only their spiritual and mental strength but also their physical health. To glorify the body was to glorify God, and white Anglo-Saxon Christian men had a special responsibility to develop their physiques for the battles of modern life. Over time this body culture became increasingly secularized.

The acceleration of industrialization, improvements in printing, photography, and cinematography, and the rise of consumerism contributed to this cultural reconfiguration of the body. The emergence of music halls, saloons, sporting papers, the penny press, and movie houses fostered a bachelor culture of mass spectatorship and readership in the growing cities of Europe, the United States, and their empires.[12] Physical strength and vigor became favorite topics of discussion in these homosocial spaces. Athletes and bodybuilders also became sought-after entertainers and heroes among the masses. Alongside traveling pugilists, physical culturists like Eugen Sandow of East Prussia and Bernarr MacFadden of the United States developed touring shows and established publishing empires. As these sports celebrities mingled with heads of state in the United States and Europe, the line between physical and political fitness blurred.[13]

The Hobbesian idea of a "body politic" had become much more literal in the minds of Roosevelt and his contemporaries.[14] According to popular belief, a nation's political and cultural dominance was directly linked to the physical condition of its citizens. In a speech before the Hamilton Club of Chicago in 1899 Roosevelt declared that "a healthy state can exist only when the men and women who make it up lead clean, vigorous, healthy lives."[15]

This focus on physical training also exposed a shared sense of anxiety about the decline of white men's control in the world. During the height of Roosevelt's popularity many believed that the shifting circumstances of modernity—industrialization, urbanization, immigration, women's social and political agitation, and imperialism—were wreaking havoc on the health of white nations. Since the 1870s fears of race suicide had been a part of public discussions in most Western countries, and by the early twentieth century some alarmists warned that the white race would die out.[16] The spread of tuberculosis among the white working class and the growing decadence of the white elite seemed ample proof of this impending racial downfall.[17] The flood of white ethnic immigrants and nonwhites into the cities (both metropolitan and colonial) also sparked new worries about racial competition and miscegenation, while white defeats in the first Italo-Ethiopian War (1895–96) and the Russo-Japanese War (1904–5) demonstrated the vulnerability of European powers. From New York to New South Wales, many imagined that whiteness was literally under assault.

Not even the United States' recent economic success could insulate it from the dangers of degeneration. Doomsayers like Bernarr MacFadden believed "old-time Americans" not only were dying out but were also being replaced by the substandard progeny of immigrants.[18] Europe seemed to provide a cautionary tale. A white American physical culturist argued, "The threatened extinction of the French as a race and France as a nation, should warn us on this side of the water of the dread possibilities which are to be found in a prosperity and a civilization which stifle the natural and encourage the abnormal in man." In 1907 the number of deaths exceeded the number of births in France.[19] Britain also appeared to be in decline. The lackluster performances of British soldiers and sportsmen on the international stage epitomized this national crisis. Britain's massive casualties during the Boer Wars had brought things to a head, inspiring numerous public projects for racial improvement.[20]

Regenerating the white body politic became tightly entwined with the social engineering of progressivism, the pseudoscience of eugenics, the discipline of anthropology, and the expansion of the state. Many physical culturists believed that crime, disease, and degeneration were related phenomena, particularly among the poor and working class.[21] The inclusion of sport and outdoor activity in formal education and in the programs of organizations such as the Boy Scouts and the Young Men's Christian Association was supposed to minimize this triple threat. With the help of rationalized record keeping and growing bureaucracies, governments began to play a bigger role in the classification and disciplining of their citizens' bodies. With measures like Britain's Contagious Diseases Acts, certain physical "abnormalities" became criminalized. The United States also pioneered laws requiring the sterilization of so-called degenerates.[22]

The rise of racial segregation at home and in the colonies accompanied these transnational efforts at white regeneration. New imaging technologies and the development of physical anthropology inspired the racial categorization of humans along a sliding scale of civilization. The intensification of Jim Crow segregation in the U.S. South, the codification of racial segregation in South Africa, and the rise of restrictive immigration legislation in Australia were just some of the ways in which these distinctions were put into practice.

Boxing seemed to offer some solace in these troubled times. Roosevelt and many of his sporting contemporaries believed that pugilism was the perfect antidote to the escalating problems of national degeneration and white race suicide. In his popular manual *How to Box to Win, How to Build Muscle,* the white American featherweight champion "Terrible" Terry McGovern claimed that boxing was one of the best ways for "any schoolboy or newsboy or office boy" to acquire a sound body and the skills of self-defense. The sport was inexpensive and easily practiced in the comfort of one's own home. McGovern also maintained that knowing how to protect oneself was "not only a convenience, but a duty." After all, General George Dewey and the U.S. Navy could never have conquered Manila "with a rotten, leaky fleet," let alone a bunch of effete and flabby recruits.[23] Boxing melded well with the modern demands of white supremacy both at home and abroad.

JOHNSON AND WHITE AUSTRALIA

The haunting specter of Johnson's strong and virile black body came to connect these white anxieties across the Pacific. Commenting on the black heavyweight's recent departure for the antipodes in December 1906, one white American journalist exclaimed, "He will go across and see how they look upon dark meat over in one of King Edward's lands."[24] Although undoubtedly filled with sarcasm, the writer's metaphorical use of the phrase "dark meat" rightly emphasized the physical dimensions of the color line that Johnson would soon be forced to face.

The most telling event of the African American boxer's first foray abroad was not a ring fight but a court fight stemming from his relationship with a white Australian woman named Alma Adelaide Lillian Toy. Lola Toy, as her friends and family called her, was a twenty-one-year-old traveling pianist whose mother owned the Grand Pacific Hotel, a popular pub in the Sydney suburb of Watsons Bay. The fact that Johnson and Toy's alleged intimacy provoked a public uproar in Australia is not surprising. Given the widespread belief that a nation was only ever as powerful as its citizens' individual bodies, the mounting efforts to maintain white men's physical fitness and white women's sexual purity were fundamentally intertwined. By the early twentieth century the bedroom, much like the boxing ring, was becoming a space of heightened white surveillance in a number of metropolitan and colonial locales.

When Johnson arrived in Sydney his commanding presence inspired white Australians to reflect on their own ongoing debate about the racial contours of citizenship, for he carried with him the freight of the United States' "negro problem." In 1901 the Australian Parliament had passed the Immigration Restriction Act. This legislation formed the centerpiece of what was popularly known as the White Australia Policy, or the collective political will to exclude nonwhite people, particularly Asians, from immigrating to the continent.[25] While fears of a "yellow invasion" from nearby Asian countries definitely drove the formulation of this policy, Australian politicians also looked to the United States' democratic experiment as a lesson in race and nation building. As the Free Trade Party opposition leader George Reid declared, "We have all seen the problem caused by coloured people in the United States. We do not want that to happen here. The Opposition wants the new Australia to be a land for the finest products of the Anglo Saxon race. This [immigration restriction] Bill will make that happen."[26] With this legislation they hoped to "whiten" the continent by deporting and preventing the entry of nonwhites and by encouraging white settlement.

Some Australian officials also envisioned interracial marriages between European men and indigenous women as "conduits of whiteness."[27] They believed that this particular process of miscegenation would allow for the genetic absorption of Aboriginal people into the nation. Grounded in the principle of white men's sexual privilege as well as the desire to seize Aboriginal lands and eradicate Aboriginal peoples' special entitlements, this view did not extend to sexual or marital relations between black men and white women. As Johnson and Toy discovered, much like their white American counterparts, many white Australians were passionate about preserving the purity of their women.

The two met in February 1907, when Toy went to Johnson's stage performance at Queen's Hall to inquire about her mother's missing gold pin. Someone in the heavyweight's entourage had apparently walked off with it during a drunken night at the Grand Pacific. Pressed for time, Johnson invited Toy to drop by his training headquarters at the Sir Joseph Banks Hotel in Botany so that they could resolve the matter. Toy first went to Johnson's hotel accompanied by her stepfather. However, it took a second trip out to Botany with her mother to retrieve the pin. During their visit Johnson invited the two women to watch him train. At just over six feet tall and two hundred pounds, Johnson's taut physique left both Toy and her mother mesmerized as they watched him, stripped to the waist, sparring in the ring. Despite the social taboo against the intermingling of black men and white women, Toy took a liking to Johnson, calling him "a great pugilist and a well-made man." Even Toy's mother had to admit that he was "a beautiful man." When Johnson offered to escort the two ladies home, Toy's mother allowed him to ride along in their sulky.[28]

Enamored with Johnson, Toy visited his hotel numerous times. She reportedly accompanied him on carriage rides, watched him spar, and waved mosquitoes away from him as the two nestled together on the hotel veranda. He gave her the pet name "Baby" and she called him "Jack." When the Tivolians, a group of Aussie chorus girls from the Tivoli Music Hall, visited Johnson's training camp, Toy stood next to the pugilist in a group photo. Johnson had his arm around her shoulders while she held his walking stick. Rumors began circulating about Johnson's escapades with Toy and the Tivolians.[29]

The two continued to meet. Toy apparently visited Johnson's hotel room at all hours of the day and night—so much so that her stepfather accused her of disgracing the family and kicked her out of the house, locking the door behind her. She finally had to call on a local constable to convince her stepfather to let her return home.[30]

Johnson's encounters with Toy had taken place during the lead-up to his match against the white Australian fighter Bill Lang in Melbourne. When Johnson stepped into the ring on 4 March, the white Australian spectators greeted him with a mixture of curiosity, derision, and downright awe. As one sportswriter claimed, Johnson looked like the "'Old Mammy' out of 'Uncle Tom's Cabin' in his noisy dressing gown and wraps."[31] The consummate dandy, Johnson reputedly arrived in a shiny robe decorated with flowers and frills. Despite the writer's obvious contempt for the black heavyweight's flamboyant and somewhat effeminate fashion sense, he could not disguise his admiration for Johnson's physique: "He is the finest black I have ever seen, and is just about as near physical perfection as mortal man can expect to get." With his superior strength and skill, Johnson dominated the match, and it soon became apparent to all in attendance that "White Australia was fighting a hopeless battle."

Even though Johnson knocked out Lang in the ninth round, this particular conquest of "White Australia" did not stir up much controversy. After the match Johnson toured throughout Victoria, exhibiting fight films and demonstrating shadowboxing in the small towns of Ballarat, Bendigo, and Geelong. He also garnered the praise of the Coloured Progressive Association (CPA) of New South Wales, an organization comprised of about forty to fifty African American, Afro-Caribbean, and Aboriginal men who crossed paths as sailors and stevedores on Sydney's docks. Johnson was an obvious choice of hero for the CPA, for he was part of the same hardscrabble maritime world as its members, having spent his formative years on Galveston's waterfront. Despite this warm reception, Johnson was frustrated with his inability to coax the white Australian champion "Boshter" Bill Squires into the ring for a big-money match, and he resolved to return to the United States.[32]

The CPA decided to host a farewell party in honor of the African American pugilist, announcing it "throughout the length and breadth of the land." Although this activist organization had been in existence for about four years, it was their celebration of Johnson that brought them into mainstream view. Held at Sydney's Leigh House, the CPA's farewell program featured performances by several prominent artists from the Tivoli and the National Amphitheatre, along with Johnson's own ball-punching routine.[33]

The white Australian press looked upon the whole affair with disdain, describing it as a kind of minstrel show. A reporter for the *Sydney Truth* called the party a veritable "coon corroboree"—corroboree being the European term for a ceremonial gathering of Aboriginal people.[34] "The gorgeous mirrors of the dance room reflected the gyrations of the coloured cult of the city," the reporter observed. "At the ballroom entrance several natty young coons attired in faultless raiment, passed in the guests. Just inside the door there was a typical Uncle Tom in evening dress." Women both "white and coloured" were also in attendance, including Toy and the Tivolians. At one point a group of "coloured damsels" danced a "captivating cakewalk" to the sounds of a "rattling good nigger song." When the guest of honor finally arrived in a stylish light tweed suit, the "big and little coons" greeted him with "admiring ejaculations of 'Mistah' Johnson." In one of the denigrating cartoons that accompanied the report, a blackface caricature of Johnson strolled by while a crowd of "coons" looked on in awe.

With the Tivolian Cassie Walmer on his "ebon wing," Johnson later ducked upstairs for a more exclusive party. The reporter for the *Truth* peeked in on the festivities, catching a glimpse of the "upper-crust coons" in attendance. Regardless of their class pretensions, Johnson's guests were apparently "going great game" and "chicken was disappearing at a fast bat." As the reporter recounted, "The sight of Mistah Johnsing picking his gold tooth with the wish-bone of a baked turkey was too reminiscent of a Cannibal Island King and stewed missionary." In the minds of many Australians the dissolute stage darky had come to epitomize all nonwhites, no matter their ethnicity or social status. As the reporter's reference to cannibalism implied, their colored excess was not just a matter of individual decline but also posed a threat to the white body politic.

These attempts to downplay the significance of this "coon corroboree" betrayed the reporter's uneasiness with the presence of this motley crowd of revelers in White Australia. Johnson's farewell party embodied white Australians' worst nightmares, from the interracial mixing of nonwhite men and white women to the open expression of a colored consciousness that transcended national borders. During the event the president of the CPA, "a former steamtug skipper" named Captain W. Grant, had expressed some of the group's political objectives. Although described as an "elderly colored gentleman" who appeared to have "struggled into a dress suit," Captain Grant "let it be distinctly understood that the Black Progressives didn't like the Commonwealth restrictive [immigration] legislation." As the correspondent for the *Truth* scoffed, "They want an open black door, which coons can enter at their own sweet will."[35] For years white Australian officials had tried their best to keep sailors of African and East Indian descent from entering the nation, forcing them to go through customs at every port, subjecting them to strip searches, and even preventing them from leaving their ships to come ashore.[36] As the CPA honored Johnson it supported the defeat of White Australia both in the boxing ring and at the border.

A surviving photo of the party further contradicts the white report-

FIGURE 3. Jack Johnson with the Coloured Progressive Association at their farewell party for him in Sydney, 14 March 1907. Johnson is in the center back wearing a beige suit. Aboriginal activist Fred Maynard is third on the right of the men sitting in the second to back row. Courtesy of Professor John Maynard.

er's dismissive account of both the CPA and its celebration of Johnson. In actuality the event appears to have been a rather refined affair, with most of the men dressed in dark suits with white shirts and seated around tables. While the *Truth*'s reporter claimed that the "coloured gentlemen and ladies were almost entirely of the American type," Aboriginals were definitely in attendance, including Fred Maynard, who later cofounded the Australian Aboriginal Progressive Association in the 1920s. Johnson's farewell celebration encapsulated the CPA's integral role in exposing the locals to the political ferment of the African diaspora, thereby paving the way for the influence of Marcus Garvey and other black internationalists on subsequent Aboriginal activism.[37] Johnson's iconic status had served to unite these men of color in a common cause, pushing their grievances into public view.

Along with his subversive political contacts, the rumors of Johnson's interracial romantic connections were making him increasingly suspect in the eyes of White Australia. Just before his scheduled voyage home a violent confrontation and ensuing court battle with his former manager

McLean forced him to remain in Sydney longer than expected. McLean claimed that the heavyweight still owed him money, but Johnson refused to pay. As he awaited trial Johnson told the *Sunday Sun,* "I expect to get married shortly, and I'm liable to make this my home. . . . I like the people here and I'm going to stop; and I'll go into business after I'm here a while."[38] "I hope," Johnson concluded, "that the people of Australia will have the same opinion of me now as they had before this trouble." Even though his problems with McLean did little to damage his reputation, his choice of fiancée did raise the ire of white Australians.

Contrary to what Johnson claimed in his interview with the *Sun,* when he lost his case to McLean he set sail for California aboard the steamship *Sonoma* in late April 1907. Shortly after his return Johnson's wedding plans made their way into several white American newspapers. A journalist in Oakland, California, asked the champion to confirm or deny the rumors circulating about his engagement to Toy. "Yes, it is true that I am to marry Miss Toy and I expect to marry her in November," Johnson reportedly affirmed. "She will come from Sydney, Australia, and I expect that our wedding will take place in this country."[39]

Though almost a year had passed since this story appeared in U.S. newspapers, when the Sydney *Referee* reprinted Johnson's words in March 1908 it caused an instant controversy. Although white Australians had tolerated Johnson's defeat of Lang and merely mocked his connections to the CPA, they now railed at the idea that he was romantically involved with one of their women. Johnson may have been safely tucked away in the United States, but Toy received abuse from all sides. Strangers screamed at her in the street and in the boardinghouses where she stayed while on tour as a pianist. Anonymous letters and postcards with Johnson's photograph arrived by mail, chock-full of condemnations for her rumored racial and sexual transgressions. In desperation Toy sent her attorney to the *Referee* to demand a printed retraction. She denied ever cavorting with Johnson, let alone agreeing to marry him. The *Referee* published a halfhearted disclaimer. "If the paragraph has caused Miss Troy [sic] any pain or annoyance we regret it," they wrote.[40] Despite this printed apology White Australia's abuse of Toy continued.

Determined to clear her name, Toy fought back in the courts. She sued the publisher of the *Referee* for libel, asking for £2,000 in damages. The publisher's attorney, G.H. Reid, called for the case to be dropped. He argued that it was not inherently "libelous to say that a white woman was willing to marry a black man" since no such color line had officially been drawn in Australia's courts.[41] As Reid emphasized, "The noblest woman in the world could marry a colored man without the slightest imputation being made against her morality, charity or modesty." Yet this was certainly not the case in practical terms. Regardless of Australia's laws, customary ideas about the natural laws governing race and the body made Toy a guilty party in the court of public opinion. Much like the discussions surrounding the CPA's farewell party for Johnson, the ensuing court case exposed the popular fears of interracial mixing and racial subversion in Australia's port cities. Toy, a single white working woman, had freely participated in Sydney's social life, opening herself up to illicit encounters with nonwhite men.

Reid cross-examined Toy in front of Chief Justice Sir Frederick Darley and a jury of four men. Strategically clad in white, the young pianist repeated under oath that she had never been in any kind of relationship with Johnson. Reid tried to break Toy on the stand using as evidence the group photo that showed Johnson's arm around her, but she refused to recant her story. Claiming to be "the unconscious victim of a harmless conjunction of events," Toy said she was unaware of Johnson's arm around her shoulders and that the photographer had given her the walking stick to hold. As she left the witness stand Toy fainted from the stress of Reid's scathing cross-examination and had to be escorted away.[42]

The defense then put Johnson's white trainers, Steven Hyland and David Stuart, on the stand. They provided some of the most damning testimony of Toy's racial and sexual wrongdoing, depicting her as a disreputable woman. Hyland had supposedly threatened to resign if Johnson continued to allow Toy to visit his hotel room. "I saw her there three or four times," Hyland told the court. "Her mother was only there once. At other times, when the mother was not there, the two were in the room by themselves."[43] He even alleged that one night Johnson and Toy had been in the room alone with the lights turned low. In cross-examining Hyland, Toy's lawyer, J.C. Gannon, asked, "Do you suggest anything improper between Johnson and Miss Toy?" While Hyland maintained he was not aware that anything "improper" had happened between them, he remembered hearing Toy say, "Here are all my rings. Come into town and marry me to-morrow morning!" Stuart added insult to injury when he claimed to have seen Johnson and Toy dancing together at a party. He also stated that he saw them flirting one evening at the Commercial Hotel, where Toy had been drinking "a brandy and soda" at the bar. The two had left together in a cab.

Toy's side called upon two witnesses, one a single woman named Ellen Gertrude Brown. Brown did her best to defend her friend's respectability, declaring that they had stayed together on the nights that Toy had visited the Sir Joseph Banks Hotel. She also maintained that she had never seen Toy dance with Johnson, nor, for that matter, had she witnessed "any familiarity at all" between the two. Still, Reid managed to reduce the young woman to a sobbing mess during his blistering cross-examination.

In a last-ditch effort to demonstrate Toy's "innocence," Gannon asked his client if she would be willing to submit herself to a chastity test and Toy said yes. Both the defense and the judge agreed that this measure was extreme given the parameters of the case, yet Gannon realized there was much at stake in proving Toy's sexual—and, by extension, racial—purity. In his closing remarks Gannon pleaded on Toy's behalf. He argued that if the public continued to believe that Toy had been intimate with Johnson she "would be stamped as an abandoned strumpet."[44]

His entreaty must have struck a chord, for the four-man jury reached a guilty verdict after two hours of deliberation, awarding Toy £500 plus court costs. Five years before Johnson's Mann Act conviction for white slave trafficking in the United States, his penchant for white women had already come under attack in Sydney. The Australian court had refused to endorse the idea that a white woman could desire a romantic or sexual relationship with a black man. This policing of the bedroom was part and parcel of the period's larger concerns about the preservation of white nations and the maintenance of white imperial control. It was also just the beginning of Johnson's numerous fights over the global color line, both in and out of the boxing ring.

WHITE POWER IN THE PACIFIC

A few months after Toy's lawsuit was settled a regular contributor to *Health & Strength* named Yorick Gradeley published a fictional piece about an interracial boxing match for the "championship of the Pacific" between John Jackson of Cuba and Tom Perkin of England.[45] This imaginary match, featured in the twelfth episode of Gradeley's serial story "The Battle to the Strong," closely resembled the potential meeting of Johnson and Burns in Sydney—a prizefight in the midst of negotiations and much discussed in the international press. Billed as "A Powerful and Exciting Physical Regeneration Story," Gradeley's "Battle to the Strong" was a manly tale of life in the British colonies.[46] Surviving natural disasters and savage battles, Perkin was a white protagonist tailor-made for the troubles of the day. He had fought in the Boer War and later founded a settlement in the far west of Canada. After learning that Jackson had decided to put his boxing title on the line, Perkin challenged the black champion to a match.[47]

Gradeley's fictional fight followed a familiar narrative of the period, as it pit a burly and brutish black man against a much smaller yet skilled white man. Jackson was a "mountain of mahogany." At six foot three and 210 pounds, his body seemed "to positively vibrate with strength."[48] Though slight in stature, Perkin was the ultimate frontiersman and imperial soldier. "The natural whiteness of his skin had been tinted a picturesque bronze by the caresses of sun and wind," Gradeley wrote, "and there were scars that were not disfigurements, but rather stripes of honour conferred upon him by the god of War."

Although the powerful yet dim-witted Jackson dominated the first few rounds of the fight, the quick and scientific Perkin made a mighty comeback to win by knockout. "Massa Perkin you am dasht clebber!" the fallen Jackson exclaimed as he looked up at his white vanquisher.[49] Through this utterance Gradeley managed to turn the "mountain of mahogany" into a stereotypical darky. Even if black men were physically strong, they were nevertheless mentally unfit for citizenship and self-government. In the months that followed, the publicity surrounding the impending match between Burns and Johnson echoed many of the same themes.

Though not as dashing or daring as his alter ego Perkin, Burns emerged as a popular embodiment of white manhood in the late imperial age. Born Noah Brusso on 17 June 1881 in a rural Ontario town, Burns personified Anglo-Saxon cooperation. Though technically French Canadian, Burns was still a citizen of a British dominion. Moreover, he spent so much of his fighting career in the United States that many mistook him for a Yankee.

Burns received his first knocks in the rough-and-tumble world of Canadian hockey and lacrosse. Known for his short fuse and his tendency to fight, he honed his boxing skills for self-defense on the ice and the field. Typical of most other pugilists at the time, Burns grew up working class, holding a number of different jobs, from house painter to factory laborer to tavern doorman. The young scrapper later found work aboard a Great Lakes steamship. In 1900, after a fight with the ship's steward, Burns lost his job and decided to stay in Detroit, Michigan, where he began his prizefighting career.[50]

At five foot seven and 175 pounds, Burns was relatively small for a heavyweight, yet he routinely beat men much larger than him. In 1905 when the reigning world heavyweight champion Jeffries retired undefeated, he handed his crown to Marvin Hart. A year later Burns beat Hart to claim the world title. Feeling the need to step out of Jeffries's shadow and legitimize himself as a bona fide champion, Burns declared, "I will defend my title as heavyweight champion of the world against all comers, none barred. By this I mean white, black, Mexican, Indian, or any other nationality without regard to color, size, or nativity."[51] Regardless of his bold claim, Burns ignored Johnson's many challenges, refusing to fight the rising African American star for anything less than £6,000 or $30,000, a prohibitively expensive purse for the time.

Undeterred, Johnson followed Burns first to Europe and then to Australia, trying to entice him into the ring. In August 1908, hordes of fans cheered for the white world champion as he moved through the streets of Perth. In Adelaide a large crowd greeted him outside the cathedral of St. Francis Xavier. The people of Melbourne even organized an official welcome for him at a local hotel, complete with speeches and free champagne. The prominent sportsman John Wren gave the keynote address, inviting Burns to "make himself at home" on the continent, promising him the "good-will" of the Australian people, "win or lose."[52]

Both Burns and boxing embodied Australia's way forward in challenging times. A correspondent for the conservative Lone Hand called his body "an exquisite fighting engine," akin to that of Hercules.[53] With his "clean-cut profile" and "gentlemanly manner," Burns also possessed the air of a statesman.[54] Some even claimed that he bore a striking resemblance to Napoleon Bonaparte. As Burns continued his travels across the continent by rail, fans greeted him at every depot. By the time he reached Sydney's Central Station eight thousand onlookers had gathered in anticipation of his arrival. Just outside the Crystal Hotel on George Street, a local alderman and two members of the legislative assembly, Edward William O'Sullivan and Colonel Granville De Laune Ryrie, greeted Burns with celebratory speeches. The physically fit O'Sullivan proclaimed that rugged activities like boxing had made England a great nation.[55] A veteran of the Boer War and a former amateur boxer, Ryrie also trumpeted the sport as "an important element in the bringing up of Australians." Given the ominous threat of a "yellow invasion," Ryrie argued, they needed "a sturdy young Australia to protect their hearths and homes."[56] Much like the Asians who seemed to be inundating the continent, Johnson would soon follow, forcing Burns to prove his mettle.

In the meantime another North American fighting wonder, the United States' Great White Fleet, arrived on the heels of the white world heavyweight champion. Ordered by President Roosevelt, the fleet's circumnavigation of the globe from December 1907 to February 1909 was designed to demonstrate the United States' rising military power. The correspondence of the Burns-Johnson match with the Pacific leg of the fleet's voyage was more than just a mere coincidence. These two spectacles of white male strength were linked both literally and figuratively. Given the deep-seated connections between boxing, militarism, and the white man's burden, they became an early exercise in cross-promotion.

The proposed interracial match must have seemed like it would provide the perfect climax to the U.S. fleet's Pacific tour, for boxing had long followed the transoceanic flows of U.S. imperialism. By the turn of the twentieth century pugilism and other forms of physical training had become popular pastimes aboard U.S. naval ships. Sailors honed their bodies with dumbbells and boxing bouts on vessels like the *USS Brooklyn* and the *USS Oregon,* both of which participated in the Battle of Santiago de Cuba during the Spanish-American War.[57]

When Admiral Dewey entered Manila Bay aboard the *USS Olympia* in 1898, boxing went along for the ride. Many of Dewey's personnel were ardent followers of John L. Sullivan, and throughout the ensuing Philippine-American War and U.S. occupation, scores of U.S. soldiers carried boxing gloves with them. Faced with alarming rates of desertion, suicide, venereal disease, and substance abuse among their troops, U.S. military officials began to see the utility of the sport as a means to prevent servicemen from degenerating and "going native" in the tropics. After all, boxers in training were supposed to avoid tobacco, alcohol, and sexual activity to help fortify their bodies for battle. By 1902 Major Elijah Halford had requested $200,000 of philanthropic funds to build a YMCA training facility in Manila.[58] Yet this imperial project of physical training was not without its own set of contradictions. African American soldiers stationed in the Philippines won a disproportionate number of the U.S. Army's athletic competitions. Boxing also brought together black Americans and Filipino rebels, encouraging camaraderie and collusion. Despite these ironies, pugilism and the practice of imperial control clearly went hand in hand.

The gleaming metal bodies of the Great White Fleet became traveling symbols of the U.S. nation's strength as a policeman of global white supremacy. Led by Rear Admiral Charles Stillman Sperry's flagship *Connecticut*, the U.S. fleet of sixteen battleships left San Francisco on the afternoon of 7 July 1908.[59] The fleet had already journeyed around South America, and as it set out for the Pacific region, each of its "white and buff ships glistened in new paint."[60] Thousands of onlookers had gathered in the hills to watch as America's very own armada departed for a long list of destinations, including Hawaii, New Zealand, Australia, China, Japan, and the Philippines.

The men onboard were just as important as the ships as representatives of the nation. In a special telegram to the fleet's crew President Roosevelt declared, "You have in a peculiar sense the honor of the United States in your keeping, and therefore no body of men in the world enjoys at this moment a greater privilege or carries a heavier responsibility."[61] *Physical Culture* published a feature article on the fleet's Pacific tour that included a detailed discussion of the crew's health.[62] Apparently the young sailors' exposure to "fresh air," "plenty of exercise," and "manly virtues" was ideal for the development of physical fitness and mental fortitude. The very practice of empire was making them stronger. In this moment of imagined white degeneration, the fleet was not only a demonstration of U.S. imperial might, but it was also a floating representation of the white American body politic.

British colonial officials were also keenly aware of the cultural and strategic importance of the Great White Fleet's voyage. To them, the fleet symbolized a developing body of white Anglo-Saxon collaboration, and they planned to do everything possible to make their U.S. allies feel the warmth of white brotherhood in the Pacific. New Zealand was the first British territory to roll out the red carpet on 9 August. Around fifty thousand Kiwis were on hand to witness the fleet's arrival in Auckland. Countless British and U.S. flags covered the city in a sea of red, white, and blue. New Zealand's prime minister Joseph Ward spared no expense on the public addresses, parades, military reviews, Maori pageants, banquets, tours, and sporting exhibitions held in honor of the U.S. servicemen.[63] "The day will come when a great fight will be necessary for the supremacy of the white races in the Pacific," Ward declared, "and when this time comes, Great Britain can have the assistance of the American fleet, and the two nations will be found fighting shoulder to shoulder to preserve to future generations the rights and privileges due to all classes."[64]

Several months before the fleet's arrival in the antipodes Australia's postmaster general had already commissioned a set of postcards featuring the British and American flags entwined. A squadron of British-Australian warships was also scheduled to greet the U.S. fleet in the port of Suva, Fiji. "It will be a picturesque gathering, when the Stars and Stripes and the union jack meet in the tropical seas and thundering guns awake the echoes in the recent haunts of the cannibal," one *Washington Post* reporter exclaimed. "There will be pomp in the great procession that moves onward to Australia, there to revive and strengthen the ties of friendship between far-separated white races."[65]

Despite this outpouring of support, some Aussies worried that the Great White Fleet would not be so white. Rumors circulated that the U.S. warships would be manned almost entirely by African Americans, who would inevitably chafe against the White Australia Policy. Given that many of the sailors who passed through the country's port cities were men of color, these fears were understandable. As the *Melbourne Age* tried to reassure its readers, "It is not at all probable . . . that a very large proportion of the crews will be found to be coloured. There will be some on the battleships, but they will not be nearly as numerous as rumour is suggesting just now."[66]

The impressive sight of the Great White Fleet and its British-Australian naval escort cruising into Sydney's harbor on 20 August helped to dispel any remaining reservations. The imposing vessels ranged from battleships to torpedoers, with a reported sixteen thousand men manning 850 guns.[67] An estimated forty thousand people, including Burns and his wife Jewel, converged on Watsons Bay to greet the U.S. sailors. As a report in the *Chicago Daily Tribune* boasted, "Fleetitis is raging all over the antipodes just now."[68] *Punch* magazine's special fleet edition broke all of its previous sales records.[69] There was also a record demand for U.S. flags and hand-carved replicas of American eagles. Many of these decorations graced the specially designated "America Avenue," which extended down Sydney's main street to the gates of the Federal Government House, symbolically traversing Australia's first white settlement.[70]

When the *Sydney Morning Herald* held a parade in honor of the U.S. Navy men, half the city's population attended, forming the largest crowd ever assembled on the continent. The Great White Fleet's men marched alongside ten thousand Australian troops. The festivities continued with a friendly game of baseball between the two nations, while Australian school children entertained their U.S. visitors with grand pageants.[71] A white American correspondent declared, "Balls, parties, luncheons, and smoke nights are sandwiched between gala fetes, water carnivals, military and naval reviews, and processions in a fashion calculated to turn the heads of the most callous cynics."[72]

These spectacles and social gatherings highlighted the transnational cultural and political bonds between the two white settler countries. Metaphors of familial relation permeated the public discourse. Melbourne's *Punch* published a cartoon depicting an Australian man asking a white American sailor, "Are we not brothers?" as the two stood side by side in front of a poster with the caption "One People, One Destiny, One Speech."[73] The popular stereotype of the obnoxious American who "spoke through his nose, made frequent use of a cuspidor, consumed vast quantities of cocktails, smoked green cigars, swore horribly, and was always in such a violent hurry" seemed to melt away as white Australians mingled with the visiting U.S. seamen. "They have the same ideals, the same habits of thought, the same ways of living as we have," one Australian editorialist observed.[74] He had even come to view the white American sailors as men of his "own blood" and his "own race."

For white Americans back in the United States, the numerous reports and photos from the fleet's Pacific voyage inspired both a growing interest in and affinity for their Australian counterparts. "There is much in the history of the island continent that resembles our own," one white American journalist observed.[75] As relatively young nations comprised of diverse populations, the two countries confronted many of "the same problems" and shared similar state structures. The Great White Fleet's travels to the antipodes even invigorated public demand for melodramatic plays featuring "Oriental and Pacific adventures" on the stages of New York City's Great White Way.[76] Amid all the pomp and circumstance, these distant strangers had come to feel a sense of common purpose.

The U.S. fleet's Australian stopover helped to cement the two nations as "partners in the business of dictating the white man's policy in the Pacific."[77] Some Australian commentators hoped that this partnership would soon replace the unstable and ill-advised Anglo-Japanese Alliance orchestrated by Britain, thereby uniting white men in control of the region.[78] On both sides of the Pacific alarmist articles about the so-called Asiatic menace coincided with the fleet's voyage. Not only did many white Australians and Americans worry that Japan was developing imperialistic designs, but they also feared that China would "awaken" and begin actively to resist the intervention of Western powers.[79] Australians felt especially vulnerable, for they did not possess their own army or navy to secure their isolated white outpost.

This regional fight for white dominance was also tied to a much broader sense of global white destiny. "If there is one clear principle amidst the welter of wrongs and reprisals and deceits called 'international politics,' it is the supremacy of the white man must be maintained," a writer for Australia's *Lone Hand* declared. "'My country, right or wrong,' may be questioned as a maxim of conduct, but most will confirm without a moment's doubt, 'The White Race Right or Wrong.'"[80] Keeping the world's dwindling resources for the exclusive use of white men was one of the major concerns driving this Anglo-Saxon cooperation. As President Roosevelt warned, nonwhite peoples everywhere in the world would certainly put up a fight, especially since they had learned about "the making of guns and other elements of progress" thanks to the Western civilizing missions.[81]

Still, the immediate crisis for Australia was a national one. The continued influx of Chinese laborers to the continent seemed to threaten the goal of a White Australia.[82] Local journalists turned to gendered metaphors of the body to describe this ongoing interracial struggle. An editorial cartoon in Sydney's *Bulletin* depicted a massive rock in the shape of an Asian man's head towering perilously over a white Australian maiden.[83] Moreover, there were anxious calls to reinvigorate Australia as a white body politic. As one reporter cautioned, if Australians "wanted to have the muscles of a body that could stand and defend the country in her hour of need they could not hope to secure it in sufficient numbers by the ordinary growth of population within their boundaries."[84] In order to remain "a clean-blooded limb of Greater Britain," Australia needed to restrict nonwhite immigration and also to encourage white immigration, preferably of Anglo-Saxon men.[85] In this moment of racial instability, white Australians welcomed the arrival of Burns and the Great White Fleet. They also cooled toward Johnson, for his penchant for white women and public grandstanding no longer seemed innocuous or entertaining. With the possibility of a Burns-Johnson prizefight on the horizon, white men from across the Pacific closed ranks.

BURNS VERSUS JOHNSON

Months after the U.S. fleet had moved on to its next destination, the Australian impresario Hugh Donald "Huge Deal" McIntosh found another way to reap the rewards of his nation's rush of Anglo-Saxon feeling. He finagled a deal to lease a large tract of land in Rushcutters Bay for just £4 a week. This vacant lot would become the site of a symbolic race war between Burns and Johnson. McIntosh had managed to drum up enough money to lure the white champion into the ring for a twenty-round title match. At the same time Johnson had obtained an official exemption from the White Australia Policy, which allowed him to enter the country for the fight.[86] Win or lose, Burns would receive £6,000, while Johnson would earn just £1,000 in cash.[87] McIntosh scheduled the match for the day after Christmas, a statutory British holiday otherwise known as Boxing Day.

McIntosh understood the rough sporting culture of white working-class men, and he had developed a knack for getting them to spend their hard-earned money. Born in Sydney in 1876, McIntosh was the son of a Scottish veteran of the Indian Mutiny who died when he was just four years old. As a young boy he supported himself through an eclectic mix of jobs. He was a miner, a surgeon's assistant, a dairy worker, and even a chorus boy. By the 1890s he had switched to entrepreneurial pursuits. He started off as a caterer, selling pies at parks and sporting events. He then segued into sports promotion, first managing a physical culture club and several prizefighters and later organizing international cycling events.[88] Most recently McIntosh had transformed the Great White Fleet's visit into a profitable venture. He speculated that boxing matches involving the white world champion Burns and the local fighters Bill Squires and Bill Lang would prove a lucrative complement to the fleet's Australian stopover. He believed these fights would attract both U.S. seamen and local boxing fans. Although few of the Yankee sailors actually turned out for the Burns-Squires fight on 24 August, McIntosh's gamble still paid off, since fifteen thousand eager Australians filled the stadium seats.[89]

Much like the fleet's visit, the upcoming Burns-Johnson prizefight presented the Australian public with another chance to ease their fears of interracial conflict in the region. In many respects, the color line appeared to be disintegrating right in front of their eyes. Chinese laborers continued to flood the continent.[90] In the week before the fight a mutiny of Lascars (East Indian sailors) onboard a British ship generated enough consternation to warrant a political cartoon on the front page of the *Bulletin*. Titled "More Perils of the Sea," it depicted white women armed with rifles, shovels, and spears boarding a ship staffed by Indian men while their families bid them a tearful goodbye from the docks.[91] One Australian editorialist blamed the "Anglo-jap alliance" for the Lascars' newfound belligerence.[92] Because of the treaty Lascars could now see "Japs playing cards in the smoking-room with British soldiers, flirting on deck with British maidens, [and] waited on and valeted by British servants." The writer complained, "He [the Lascar] reckons that if a Jap nigger is as good as a white man, a Lascar nigger ought to be the same." Whether Japanese or Indian, these "niggers" no longer seemed to know their place. Even Johnson himself had the audacity to be traipsing around Sydney with his white American girlfriend Hattie McClay.

White Australians had also noticed the Aborigines' growing admiration for Johnson. Titled "A Man and a Brother," one political cartoon showed a group of Aboriginal men watching the African American heavyweight speed by in a sports car. "That pfeller puts on heap plurry side, my wurrd," one of the men exclaimed. "What tribe that pfeller belonga?"[93] Johnson had apparently been treating the local Aboriginals to rousing demonstrations of his driving skills as he raced around the Sydney suburbs of La Perouse and Botany in his roadster. The African American heavyweight also expressed his admiration of Aboriginal culture, playing on white Australian fears of overcivilization and interracial conflict. "When I visit your museum and see the numerous specimens of prehistoric man's art, your boomerangs of many varieties, your stone axes from various States and the many examples of Palaeolithic and Neolithic man's skill—I simply envy you," Johnson told a group of Australian journalists. "Your central Australian natives must have been men of genius," he added, "to have turned out such artistic and ideal weapons."[94] For Johnson, Australia's greatness came from its "primitive" Aboriginal culture rather than the so-called "civilization" of its recent white immigrants.

Many white Australians came to see the Burns-Johnson fight through the lens of social Darwinism as a fierce evolutionary competition between racial representatives in which only the fittest would survive. One journalist called the match "a racial study," claiming that most Australian fans hoped "to see the triumph of the white race enacted under their eyes."[95] From a publicity standpoint, it certainly helped that the two boxers engaged in several public confrontations. "There is bad blood between the men. They positively hate each other,"

A MAN AND A BROTHER.

Johnson has been giving the inhabitants of La Perouse
and Botany a treat by scorching vigorously about those
parts in his car.

JACKY JACKY (of La Perouse): "That pfeller
  puts on heap plurry side, my wurrd! What
  tribe that pfeller belonga?"

FIGURE 4. White Australians poked fun at the Aborigines' growing admiration for
Jack Johnson. "A Man and a Brother," *Bulletin*, 24 December 1908.

one sportswriter declared. "Burns does not draw, as it is termed, the color line, but all the same the sight of a black man displeases him."[96]

Australian newspapers published physical and mental comparisons of the two fighters that conformed to the period's popular science of race. Burns was the thinking man, the "scientific" fighter, and an astute businessman, while Johnson was the physical man, the simpleminded savage and "over-grown boy."[97] The *Bulletin* even featured a contemptuous cartoon of the black heavyweight gazing at a gibbon skeleton in a museum. Johnson's caricature exclaimed, "My golly dem undersized niggers must have had a beautiful reach."[98] Since Johnson was supposedly bred from a "lower" species, most white fans believed he had a weak stomach as well as a "yellow streak" or lack of courage. They advised Burns to pummel Johnson with body shots in order to tire him out rather than going straight for his head with the hope of knocking him out.[99] According to popular belief, black men possessed thicker skulls and a higher pain threshold than their white counterparts. "A nigger has such a thick hide that no white man could make any impression on him, unless he went at him with a sledge hammer," one Australian woman explained in a letter to the *Tasmanian Mail*.[100] Consequently, if Burns won, his victory would demonstrate White Australia's readiness and resolve to defend its body politic from the incursion of nonwhites.

Yet there were no guarantees. On the eve of the great fight a visibly nervous Burns tried to assure reporters, "I am fit to fight the battle of my life, if it be necessary."[101] Much more confident in his prospects, Johnson had spent Christmas day on a hunting trip. "I'm going into the ring firmly intent upon winning," the black heavyweight announced, "and if I don't succeed, well, none will be more surprised than myself, and that's all there is to it."

Thanks to both the promotional wizardry of "Huge Deal" McIntosh and the racial angst of the white Australian public, the Burns-Johnson fight quickly became a huge event. The open-air stadium at Rushcutters Bay was enormous, with a seating capacity of sixteen thousand, not including its standing room. The number of tickets sold surpassed all expectations, far outpacing the box office of the recent Burns-Squires fight. For crowd control McIntosh planned to have two hundred policemen on patrol along with a staff of 222 gatekeepers, ushers, and ticket takers.[102]

To snag the best seats some fans spent Christmas night camped out in a park beside the stadium. Early the next morning special trams packed with fight-goers began to arrive in Rushcutters Bay. When the stadium doors opened at 6 AM, thousands of people rushed in, filling the seats in the cheaper sections, and by 10 AM the venue had reached its maximum capacity of twenty thousand spectators. Next to famous sportsmen and entertainers, numerous Australian politicians from the federal, state, and local level sat ringside. The famed white American writer Jack London and his wife Charmian were also in attendance, making it the first time a woman had ever been knowingly admitted to an important fight in Australia (other women reportedly snuck into the fight dressed as men). Both a longtime boxing enthusiast and amateur ethnologist, London had abandoned his South Pacific voyage aboard the *Snark* to cover the match for the *New York Herald*.[103] Another twenty thousand fans crowded outside the stadium, while several thousand more clustered on a hillside overlooking the ring. People even "swarmed up telegraph poles" hoping to catch a glimpse of the match.[104] Thanks to the railways and tramways, approximately forty to fifty thousand people from all across Australia had converged on Rushcutter's Bay, generating a fight gate of £26,000, or roughly $130,000.[105]

Meshing with the racial concerns of boxing fans in a variety of places, the Burns-Johnson match became an international phenomenon.[106] The telegraph cables remained busy the entire day, conveying updates of the fight to anxious fans in the United States and across the British Empire. Australia's deputy postmaster general later released the official figures on wire transfers: 22,061 messages were sent and 21,047 received. Including all other cables and messages in connection with the match, a total of 46,362 communications took place over the course of the day.[107]

By the time the two pugilists made their way into the stadium, "the tension was screwed up almost to breaking point."[108] The Australian fight crowd "was aggressively white in its sympathy," expecting to see the black challenger "beaten to his knees and counted out." Nevertheless, their anxiety was palpable, as dark storm clouds hovered on the horizon like "an omen of disaster."[109]

As Johnson entered the ring the Aussie spectators greeted him "with mingled cheers and hoots," calling him a "coon" and a "nigger."[110] Undaunted, the black heavyweight bowed, making the most of his moment in the spotlight. When Burns climbed through the ropes he "was nearly blown out of the Stadium by the crash of applause that thundered from 20,000 throats."[111] The stadium crowd "yelled itself hoarse" for five minutes straight, and just as they quieted down the thousands of fans outside the arena began cheering for Burns.[112] Yet as the white world champion stripped to his fighting togs, he looked far from majestic. Not only did he appear puny next to Johnson, "but he looked fat, and his muscles seemed flabby, and his face was of the strange yellow hue that bespeaks the sick man."[113]

Burns also wore large elastic bandages to protect his elbows. Citing an unfair advantage, Johnson demanded that Burns's armbands be removed before the start of the match. The white champion's Australian supporters began to chant, "Good boy, Tommy! Good boy, Tommy!" with a rhythm redolent of a "tremendous battle-song."[114] Above "the bass roar" of the crowd "came shrill voices adjuring Burns not to give way to the 'black cow,' and other animals."[115] Although McIntosh ruled the armbands admissible, Johnson remained in his corner, refusing to fight. Eventually Burns relented, and as he ripped off his bandages with righteous indignation, he received yet another noisy ovation from the Australian crowd.

Burns found himself hopelessly outclassed by Johnson. The black heavyweight was not only physically imposing but also highly skilled. As one correspondent recounted, "Burns looked like a small boy beside the beautifully-modelled giant."[116] Others argued that the match was akin to "a gorilla toying with a small meal," "a grown man cuffing a naughty child," or even "a gentle schoolmaster administering benevolent chastisement to a rude and fractious urchin."[117] Johnson remained "the personification of coolness and confidence," while Burns appeared "high-strung and nervous."[118] Burns's talent for infighting was simply no match for Johnson's combination of solid defense and blinding quickness.

The match displayed a frightening role reversal that challenged the racial protocol of the white man's burden. An Australian correspondent recalled, "With his native 'flashness,' Johnson grated all quarters of the amphitheatre just as a cannibal king might condescend to humor his most humble subjects."[119] Going against boxing's unwritten rule of silence in the ring, Johnson openly trash-talked his opponent. He also treated the crowd to his gold-toothed smile as he pummeled Burns.[120]

Johnson's audacious performance was especially troubling given that the match was being recorded on film for international distribution. Adept at the art of self-promotion, Johnson consciously constructed an image of black defiance that would not only rile white spectators but would also speak to the concerns of his far-off African American fans. To one journalist it appeared as if Johnson, in his contempt for Burns,

FIGURE 5. Australian artist Norman Lindsay painted Jack Johnson and Tommy Burns in action for the front page of the December 1908 issue of the *Lone Hand*. © H., C. & A. Glad.

thought only of the cinematograph—thought only of the black thousands of the Southern States. Mentally, he saw the coloured audiences crowding to see the pictures, and he gave them what they would love and applaud."[121] Johnson deliberately "postured and mouthed" for the cameras, as if to provide "a festival for the men of his own colour." He knew that his black American supporters would be closely following his feats in the ring. In the lead up to the match, many of them had bet heavily on him, including the likes of the famed vaudeville duo of Bert Williams and George Walker.[122]

As the fight began Johnson goaded Burns, "Come on Tahmy . . . you've got to get it."[123] In the first round it took him just fifteen seconds to knock the white champion to the canvas. Johnson continued his wisecracking as he blasted Burns with powerful shots to the body and head. "Ah, poor little Tahmy," he teased. "Don't you know how to fight, Tahmy? They said you were a champion." When Burns attempted to defend his swollen face, Johnson simply laughed, "That's right, Tahmy, feint away." Every so often Johnson even dropped his fists and stood up straight "in an attitude of indolent arrogance," daring Burns to take his best shot.

The subsequent rounds offered the increasingly dejected Australian crowd more of the same. During a particularly bad stretch of fighting in the third round, the spectators reprised their battle cry of "Good boy, Tommy; good boy, Tommy," as if their voices could convey their collective strength to the ailing white champion.[124] In the fourth round Burns called Johnson a "cur" and other choice names in a desperate attempt to get back into the fight. These epithets only served to inspire a more vicious attack from the black heavyweight. While Burns's condition deteriorated, his face bulging and eyes blackened, Johnson remained fresh, confident, and at ease.

In the final rounds of the match Johnson kept up his physical and verbal assault. At times it looked as if Johnson were actually holding up Burns so that he could prolong his opponent's punishment in front of the Australian crowd. "Jewel won't know you when she gets you back from this fight," Johnson taunted at the opening of the eighth round. In the ninth, he struck Burns repeatedly while shouting, "I'll teach you something. . . . Look at this, and this. . . . And this."[125] By the twelfth round it was obvious that the battered white fighter had absolutely no chance of winning, and many of the spectators began shouting for police intervention.

Fearing that Burns was on the verge of being knocked out, the police inspector entered the ring to stop the match in the fourteenth round, and McIntosh declared Johnson the winner by points. Johnson became the first-ever black heavyweight champion of the world. With an exuberant mix of joy and bravado, he jumped up and shadowboxed for the moving picture cameras. One Australian sportswriter likened Johnson's impromptu celebration to "a triumphant war dance—like the dance after the battle, before the cannibal feast began."[126] It was as if Johnson's "way-back ancestors" were "calling aloud their exultation through the muscles of their descendant." Johnson's body had become the public conduit for their longstanding grievances.

Every postfight report described the white spectators' quiet dejection. "Johnson waved his hands to the crowd that did not cheer him," one Australian journalist recounted. "A few straggling voices were raised but they were mere flecks of sound in an ocean of silence."[127] It took just twelve minutes for the stands to empty. Outside the stadium the "big crowd shook its head sadly, spat into the roadway, and silently dispersed. It hadn't a cheer in it."[128] Amid the hush one despondent fan muttered, "When a white man lowers himself to fight with a nigger it's time he got a licking."[129] An overwhelming sense of disappointment also permeated Melbourne, Wollongong, and Broken Hill, where throngs of the white fighter's supporters stopped traffic as they milled around outside newspaper headquarters and post offices in a state of shock.[130] Intended as a public spectacle of white supremacy, the Burns-Johnson match had gone horribly awry.

While the reaction of white Americans was predictably one of anger and disappointment, African American fans rejoiced at the news of Johnson's victory. As Lester Walton of the *New York Age* declared, "Every Negro, from the lad large enough to sell papers to the old man who is able to read the papers (if he can read) is happy to-day."[131] Some hoped that Johnson's display of skill and courage in the ring would help to redeem black people in the eyes of the world. "Every time Johnson knocked down Burns a bunch of prejudice fell," Walton exclaimed, "and at the same time the white man's respect for the Negro race went up a notch." Johnson's black supporters looked forward to his next fight against a white man. As Bert Williams told the *Indianapolis Freeman*, "If it is held outside the United States the colored people will migrate for a while to see it, but if it is held here it will bring together the largest single collection of colored sports ever assembled."[132] It was only natural for African Americans to assume a proud "peacock pose," since a black man from Galveston was now the "champion over land and sea."[133]

For Johnson's black fans, his triumph was more than just cathartic. They grabbed this chance to challenge established ideas about white men's physical, and therefore geopolitical, supremacy. As one African American editorialist maintained, Johnson's pugilistic success had forced the "unwilling civilized world" to acknowledge "the physical prowess of the black race."[134] If blacks and whites could compete on equal terms, it would undoubtedly threaten the racial and imperial status quo. The editorialist warned, "Let a wise world remember that the Negro race has an untouched store of physical perfection in Africa, as among the Zulus." Turning the disparaging discourses of black barbarism on their head, he argued that Johnson's victory proved that the "Negro's closeness to nature" was actually an asset rather than a drawback. The black man's "inherited strength and endurance, his ability to endure pain and punishment, his resource and ever presence of mind, [and] his confidence and courage" all combined to make him "the physical superior of the white man." J. Bernie Barbour, a well-known black composer and producer from Chicago, crafted an ode to the new champion titled "The Black Gladiator." Barbour placed Johnson within the classical tradition of ancient warriors, calling him a "Black Spartacus" and a "Black Alexander." For Barbour, Johnson was "A proof that all men are the same / In muscle sinew and in brain."[135] Contrary to popular belief, the black man possessed not only the physical ability but also the mental acuity and the strength of character to make him an important player in world politics.

Johnson's victory, coupled with his black fans' newfound confidence, undoubtedly rattled white boxing fans on both sides of the Pacific. One African American journalist predicted that if the black race managed to maintain its hold on the world championship for at least a year or two, "a few thousand prejudiced 'pugs' and sports" would end up "as inmates of insane asylums."[136] White Americans had already become increasingly sensitive to the apparent "uppishness" of their black counterparts in the wake of the fight. Walton provided a few tongue-in-cheek rules for his African American readers to follow: "Don't accidently [sic] jostle a Caucasian in the street car or on the street. Don't talk about prize fighting in public. Don't speak to your white brother other than in a quiet inoffensive manner." White Americans seemed to have little tolerance for any black assertions of "a spirit of manhood and independence."[137]

Back in Australia white sportsmen took out their frustrations on Johnson. Johnson complained to the *Sydney Morning Herald*, "Since I beat Burns . . . the people of New South Wales have suddenly taken a great dislike to me. . . . Burns is more popular here than I am, and all because he does what you Australians call the 'penitent smoodge.'"[138] Disgruntled white sports fans booed Johnson at postfight appearances and defaced his image in advertisements for the prizefight film. One reporter wrote, "Johnson's brown picture is invariably mud-bespattered or torn, and, wherever in reach, it is decked with such written legends as 'The Black Cow,' 'The big black skite,' and worse—far worse."[139] Some Australian vandals even used crayons to color in the black champion's so-called yellow streak.

Burns's pictures bore "no signs of disfigurement." Most white Australians remained loyal to their defeated hero, plastering his images with encouraging phrases like "Good old white man" and "You'll out him next time, Tommy."[140] As they sought to restore Burns's damaged reputation, the stock narrative of a courageous white man in the face of an overpowering black brute began to emerge. Burns encouraged this view of the match in the press. "I did my best," the white fighter reassured his fans. "I fought hard, but Johnson was too big, and his reach was too much for me. . . . I could do no more."[141] Australian reporters agreed. "However poor a showing Burns made as a boxer and hitter, he proved himself a man of extraordinary pluck and stamina," one sportswriter claimed. "His capacity for taking punishment is something altogether remarkable. His gameness is beyond all question."[142] Absolved of his pugilistic sins, Burns maintained his popularity, and his exhibitions continued to draw large crowds at theaters throughout Australia and New Zealand.[143]

The depth of Australia's racial partisanship surprised some. An editorialist for the *Australasian* declared, "In a population where the negro is not an ugly ever-present problem, as in the [United] States, it is impossible to concede that there was justification for the manifestation of this feeling."[144] Yet in making such a statement the writer conveniently overlooked his own nation's history of racial discrimination, from Aboriginal dispossession to immigration restrictions. Although one Melburnian accused her fellow citizens of being poor sports, she was careful to qualify her criticism. "I am not a sympathizer with coloured people," she reassured the readers of *Punch*. "I hate them, and I should die of disgust if I had to sit in the same compartment of a tram or train with one."[145] Despite any protestations to the contrary, white Australians were certainly no strangers to the concept of racial segregation.

The fallout of the Burns-Johnson fight made African Americans painfully aware of this fact, and it provoked discussions about the real stakes of the White Australia Policy. As a journalist for the *Indianapolis Freeman* observed, "While the [immigration restriction] act applies generally, it was brought about as a prohibition against the hordes of yellows and blacks that menace Australia on every side."[146] Even though relatively few African Americans traveled to the antipodes, this knowledge certainly helped to put their local problems of racial prejudice in a transnational perspective. "We," the journalist avowed, "may take courage of the thought that the 'colored' people of America are not so bad off as a race when compared with what is issued out to 'colored' people anywhere—everywhere." The white race's tendency to meddle with and steal from the darker races had created a global powder keg that threatened to explode. Western imperialism had effectively relegated people of color to the status of mere "nomads, fitting only as parasites on society—no real part of it." The writer warned, "Dispossessed peoples wandering over the face of the earth, evicted by brute force will smoulder—but not always." If whites continued to draw their own color line, he reasoned that blacks should be able to do the same in their own geographic domains. What was good for White Australia was good for Black Africa.

White Australians worried that the match foreshadowed a disturbing future of interracial mixing and conflict on both a local and a global scale. For some, Johnson's victory called to mind the terrifying image of "a grinning savage with his foot on the neck of White Australia."[147] They also feared that Burns's humiliating loss at the hands of the African American heavyweight would be "told, sung, and cinematographed everywhere where there is a black skin," thereby helping to promote widespread "unrest and sedition."

Johnson's victory could not have had more inauspicious timing. As a writer for *Health & Strength* noted, "We have at last a coloured champion at a white man's sport, following closely on the heels of a coloured race becoming recognized as one of the most formidable of the world's Powers."[148] The writer was undoubtedly referring to the rising fortunes of Japan in the Pacific region. Amid this geopolitical instability, the prizefight's significance could not be underestimated. "It was an ethnological study as well as a boxing contest," one postfight report declared, "and the white man's burden was too great for Burns to carry."[149] Much like Japan's military defeat of Russia just a few years earlier, Johnson's triumph over Burns had put white degeneration on full display, not only in Australia but all around the globe.

It certainly did not help that Johnson himself used his special access to the press to comment on the apparent decline of white world supremacy. As he told one Melburnian reporter, "While my people—the descendants of my ancestors in Africa—are increasing in numbers, the white man is decreasing all over the earth. Read the figures—those of your own country, of the United States, of England, of France, of all the white world."[150] Pointing to the burgeoning birth rates of "the colored peoples of India, Japan and China" and those of his "own race," he challenged, "Do you think it is to go on forever, this domination of the millions of people of color by a handful of white folks? I think it is not." He warned, "It may not come in my time or in yours, but the time will come when the black and yellow man will hold the earth, and the white man will be regarded just as the colored man is now." Johnson was more than happy to play on the widespread fears of white race suicide.

Given these political and demographic realities, some white Australians called for the maintenance of a strict color line separating whites from all nonwhites, whether they be the "brownish-yellow brothers/Up in China and Japan," the "Hindoo and Afghan," the "gentle Soudanese," or even the "smiling picaninny."[151] Assumed to be pagans, polygamists, and cannibals, these "colored brethren" were supposedly unfit to live alongside civilized whites. Taking up the banner of the white man's burden in the wake of Burns's downfall, the Australian poet Tom Beasley declared:

> It is only right and proper,
> It is only just and fair,
> That our brethren, black and copper,
> Who are scattered here and there,
> Should receive our old belltopper
> And the thrippence we can spare.

> But they're nicely isolated
> In their islands oversea, .
> And, as God has segregated
> Them with care from you and me,
> Let us keep them as they're rated
> By Eternity's decree.[152]

White men were morally obligated to assist their colored subjects; however, to mingle with them went against God's divine plan.

White Australian writers often couched this general fear of race mixing in sexual terms as a dangerous contamination of the white body politic. Henry Lawson, a nationalist author whose writings addressed themes of interracial conflict and the need to construct a White Australia, penned a passionate poem about the interracial fight's potentially negative effects. Lawson proclaimed, "For 'money' and 'sporting' madness—and here, in a land that was white!/You mated a black-man and white-man to stand up before you and fight." Lawson cautioned:

> You paid and you cheered and you hooted, and this is your need of
>   disgrace;
> It was not Burns that was beaten—for a nigger has smacked *your* face.
> Take heed—I am tired of writing—but O my people take heed.
> For the time may be near for the mating of the Black and the White
>   to *breed*.[153]

Lawson was not alone in his concerns. There was a sense that the Burns-Johnson prizefight had violated the boundaries of White Australia and that, with this violation, a race war inevitably would erupt. A clergyman from Bendigo prayed, "God grant that the defeat may not be the sullen and solemn prophecy that Australia is to be outclassed and finally vanquished by these dark-skinned people."[154] An ominous *Punch* cartoon depicted the African American champion's silhouette casting a shadow across the entire continent.[155]

Johnson's pugilistic victory seemed to presage a despotic future of colored control beyond the ring. His supposedly unsportsmanlike conduct became a horrifying example of what would happen if political power ever fell into the hands of nonwhite men. Johnson had "gasconaded in anticipation of the contest," "indulged in cheap, irritating airs during its progress," and then, afterward, "exulted exuberantly over his beaten foe." This behavior hardly represented "the bearing of a generous victor." Alongside the political failure of black self-determination in Haiti, Johnson's antics provided further proof that "the negro in the ascendant is not a very taking personality."[156]

White Australians poked fun at Johnson's unwarranted air of self-importance. *Punch's* boxing correspondent mockingly called him the "Champion of the Universe and All Dependencies."[157] Another caricature showed Johnson challenging the world to a host of contests, from riding to jumping to flirting to preaching.[158] Although some sportswriters excused Johnson's bravado, they still believed that his blustering behavior confirmed that black men were simply unfit for self-rule. "Johnson's conduct cannot be judged by white standards," argued one reporter. "He is great big, buck negro, very little removed by a thin veneer of civilisation from the fetish-worshipping savages of wildest Africa. He is not a white man in colour, thought, sentiment, or anything else."[159] Johnson's grandstanding had convinced many white Australians "how very necessary" it was "in a country like America to keep 'the black trash' under."[160] The well-known Australian adventurer and writer Randolph Bedford declared, "Blessings on the Immigration Restriction Act! I am forced to believe that much is to be said for Simon Legree."[161]

Yet Johnson clearly represented a new kind of negro, one much bolder than the brutal planter Legree's long-suffering slave Uncle Tom. Writing about a proposed production of *Uncle Tom's Cabin* that was to feature Johnson, one theater critic argued that the play would have to be "re-written to suit the principal's strength." "To expect Johnson to sit and humbly suffer while Simon Legree flogs him, would be preposterous," he contended. It would be "altogether too great a strain upon the public imagination." The critic also suggested that Johnson be allowed to "arise in his might and 'pass Legree out,'" for Johnson was neither hapless nor helpless like his predecessor Uncle Tom.[162]

Johnson's breach of the pugilistic color bar appeared to have unleashed a flood of colored ambitions in the Pacific. "Already the insolent black's victory causes skin troubles in Woolloomoolo," Bedford despaired.[163] An hour after the fight he had witnessed a Lascar publicly pontificating on the Marquess of Queensberry rules in front of two white men. Native Fijians had also become more rebellious with the arrival of press reports describing Johnson's victory. A white policeman in Suva recalled the inflammatory words of one native: "White man he no use; black man he knock him down every time."[164] Faced with such open defiance, the officer felt obliged to show the native that "not every coloured man is a Johnson."

In recounting his South Sea voyage in the aftermath of the fight, the Australian travel writer Jack McLaren acknowledged that maintaining an aura of white superiority sometimes "called for great ingenuity."[165] McLaren pointed to the collective efforts of white planters to keep the many reports and photos of the interracial match "away from native eyes" in the Solomon Islands. Despite this vigorous campaign of censorship, news of Johnson's triumph quickly spread throughout the native community, and, as McLaren recalled, "Our prestige began to rock!" To regain control of the situation, one of the planters called the native chiefs to an emergency meeting at which he tried to convince them that, all photographic evidence aside, Burns had actually made a courageous comeback to win the fight. The planter hoped that the chiefs would relay this story to their people, thereby reinforcing the idea that "no matter how big and strong a black man was he could not triumph over the strength and cunning of a white." Whether or not this scheme ultimately was successful, the white planters definitely understood that their political power rested on prevailing notions of white men's physical supremacy—especially since the natives greatly outnumbered them.

The Burns-Johnson match highlighted the need for continued white vigilance in the region. One boxing fan declared, "Let young Australia take heed, and when the black man (by black man I mean all coloured races) at last looks this way with a yearning to revenge the many insults, may we have many thousands of men of the Burns type to oppose their oncoming."[166] "It will be a 'degrading spectacle,'" he warned, "but must be faced, nevertheless."

In the meantime, boxing fans turned to the former champion Jim Jeffries to restore white dignity in the ring and beyond. "Does anyone imagine for a moment that Johnson's success is without its political influence, an influence which has only been checked . . . by the personality of Jem Jeffries?" one sportswriter asked. "It is not so much a matter of racial pride as one of racial existence which urges us so ardently to desire the ex-boilermaker's [Jeffries's] triumph."[167] Jeffries agreed, rallying his fellow physical culturists: "Unless we propose to become a nation of weaklings, it is about time that we woke up athletically speaking."[168]

White Censors, Dark Screens

The Jeffries-Johnson Fight Film Controversy

It seems absurd that a battle in faraway Nevada, disgusting
in its details and with the most sordid environment, could
have such wide-spread effects. But every student of native
life, every administrator of native affairs, and everyone
engaged in holding the balance between the white and black
races, will acknowledge that the prestige of the dominant
races has been lowered in the minds of the inferior races
by this brutal conflict at Reno.

—*Times of Natal* (South Africa), 6 July 1910

Reflecting on Jack Johnson's resounding defeat of Tommy Burns in
1908, the Australian promoter Hugh McIntosh declared that the
prizefight pictures had "influenced the various coloured races in each
country where they were shown." A self-professed "student of human
nature," McIntosh had noticed "the keen, eager interest displayed by
the coloured peoples of the earth in the personality, life, and career" of
the black champion. In South Africa the natives had gathered around
film advertisements graced with Johnson's photo. So enthusiastic was
their response that police throughout the Union had ordered promoters to "refrain from exhibiting posters, photos, or anything that might
excite the Kaffir mind."[1] Crowds of natives had flooded theaters to
watch the moving picture, cheering each time Johnson landed a blow.
Even more disturbingly, they congregated outside after the film, bois-
terously reanimating his victory. As McIntosh acknowledged, a couple
of celluloid reels had managed to transport this undesirable racial spectacle all the way from Rushcutters Bay to the street corners and movie
houses of South Africa.

The Burns-Johnson fight film had even stirred up people of color in Asia and the South Pacific. Stopping in Ceylon on his way from Australia to England, McIntosh had marveled as the "Hindoos and Cingalese . . . flocked to see the pictures in great numbers and displayed a remarkable knowledge of the smallest details pertaining to the contest."[2] Droves of Fijian natives had also seen the film, and many began to express a passion for professional boxing. By early 1909 Johnson was enough of a celebrity in Fiji to attract throngs of fans during a stopover on his way home from Australia. Even the "alien races" of Siam, Portugal, Burma, Japan, the Philippines, the West Indies, India, Egypt, and Mexico had reportedly shown great interest in the fight pictures. Regardless of their diverse cultures and complexions, these communities of color had each transformed Johnson's victory into a symbol of local resistance. Johnson had emerged as the world's first black movie star, and his fight films became the period's most widely disseminated representations of black male dominance.[3]

No wonder McIntosh worried about the possible consequences of "coloured superiority in the sport of boxing." His concerns were part of a much larger discussion about the impact of mass culture on racial and imperial politics across the globe. The increasingly transnational reach of commercial amusements such as sports was proving to be both the backbone and the bane of white supremacy's existence. While professional boxing was an important medium through which white men, especially white ethnic working-class men, envisioned their place in the political economy of empire, it also provided people of color with a public space for challenging the racial order.

Staged in Reno, Nevada, on 4 July 1910, Johnson's subsequent title match against the white American Jim Jeffries exemplified these competing dynamics. Alongside the question of the interracial fight's advisability as a live event, its reproduction and dissemination through the press, photography, and film became heated points of contention in places around the world. Transnational organizations like the United Society of Christian Endeavor in tandem with local white officials, newspaper editors, reformers, and clergymen led a concerted campaign to censor the Jeffries-Johnson fight film. Their collective efforts sparked interimperial conversations about the importance of preserving global white supremacy. The controversy surrounding the Jeffries-Johnson match and its moving picture also inspired open displays of racial pride and anti-colonialism in a variety of nonwhite communities. It not only encouraged people of color to view their own oppression as part of a worldwide race problem, but it empowered them to imagine a future of freedom and solidarity stretching beyond their local circumstances.

Through the boxing ring, journalists, politicians, progressives, and fans alike could see that the accelerating flows of mass commercial culture were connecting diverse peoples in new ways, thereby transforming the terrain of imperial power and resistance. The United States was at the forefront of this shift as one of the biggest purveyors of racial spectacles. Alongside blackface minstrelsy and other U.S. exports, the Jeffries-Johnson fight and its film pushed the American "negro problem" onto the world stage, making the United States the most talked-about space of racial conflict and African American men the most visible people of color around the globe.

Although most film scholars cite D. W. Griffith's *Birth of Nation* (1915) as the period's most prominent cinematic representation of U.S. race relations, by the early 1900s U.S.-produced interracial fight films had already achieved international distribution.[4] This genre emerged right alongside the intensification of racial segregation and Western imperialism, for it provided viewers with a dynamic image of Darwinian competition. Contained within the small space of a ring and organized into short rounds, boxing matches were well suited to the new medium's very real limits on camera movement and the length of celluloid reels.[5] Despite the fight films' often grainy images shot from a distance, the specter of light versus dark was undeniable and therefore applicable to a variety of racial contexts. The portability of film reels also made it easy for producers to market and distribute their prizefight pictures to an international audience. Since these films were silent, local exhibitors could add their own narratives, tailoring them to the language and cultural references of their viewers. As interracial fight films resonated with a combination of local and global debates over the color line, they garnered broad box office appeal.

Fight pictures (interracial or otherwise) were an essential part of the developing film industry. "The fortunes of the prize ring are apparently interwoven with those of the moving picture," declared one U.S. critic. "Without the moving picture your modern prize fight would be shorn of its financial glamour and possibilities; without the prize fight the moving picture would not appeal to as many people as it apparently does."[6] Much like the burgeoning boxing industry, the rise of commercial filmmaking accompanied the expansion of urban industrialism. The growth of cities and of working people's disposable income and leisure time had created a ready market for moving pictures.[7]

Although the advent of boxing films enabled the sport to draw a more diverse spectatorship across race, class, gender, and age lines, white immigrant and working-class men still comprised the majority of the genre's initial audience. Early fight films proved far more popular with the male spectators of burlesque shows than with the mixed-gender audiences of storefront movie theaters. However, once prize-fight pictures made their way into the nickelodeons' all-movie variety shows and the entertainment programs at amusement parks, fairs, and carnivals, their viewership began to expand. These films also had a long shelf life, often remaining in circulation for months.[8]

Though there were earlier productions, it was the Burns-Johnson match that solidified the interracial fight film as a touchstone for interimperial discussions about the maintenance of white supremacy. Cinematographers for the British division of the Gaumont Film Company had recorded the action from a platform that towered above the spectators at Rushcutters Bay. Just two days after the match the moving picture was ready for exhibition, and approximately seven thousand Australians attended screenings in the very same stadium where Burns had met his painful demise.[9] Over the next three months McIntosh traveled from Australia to Britain to the United States exhibiting the ninety-minute film all along the way.[10] In February 1909 the film debuted at England's National Sporting Club and then appeared in various music halls throughout London. The Parisian sporting magazine *La Vie au grand air* paid fifty thousand francs for the rights to show the film in France and its colonies.[11] McIntosh then sailed across the Atlantic to unveil the film in Chicago and New York City. Although African Americans were forced to watch the Burns-Johnson moving picture from the black sections of white-run venues or in separate "race theaters," they embraced the film as a public platform for racial pride, much like their counterparts in the colonies.[12]

Despite Burns's loss, screenings of the fight film also became exercises in racial solidarity for white American and British audiences, as they rallied for Jim Jeffries's return to the ring. Already retired for several years, the aging Jeffries was overweight, out of shape, and hesitant to challenge Johnson, yet these realities did little to dissuade his white fans. During a run of the fight film at the American Music Hall in New York City, Jeffries appeared on stage, and McIntosh roused the crowd by repeating Jack London's now famous call for a white hope to remove "the golden smile" from Johnson's face.[13] It was not long before Jeffries decided to enter the fray.

AN INTERNATIONAL MEDIA EVENT

Looking back on the Jeffries-Johnson prizefight, some European journalists charged that there was something particularly "American" about its promotion. They blamed white Americans' rabid racism, sensationalism, and commercialism for turning the fight into a virtual race war when it was merely a boxing match between two men. "The whole proceedings were organised on that colossal scale which appears natural to the citizens of the United States," declared one British correspondent.[14] The French sportswriter Georges Dupuy called the fight "a gigantic example of American spiel."[15] He argued that Jeffries's inflated pride coupled with Yankee race prejudice had produced countless exaggerations and extraordinary publicity in the U.S. press. "The savage hatred of the nigger in America, will never change, and I imagine that the lynchings and burnings of blacks will have better days than ever," Dupuy speculated. He argued that U.S. companies were largely to blame, for they had used the fight's racial dimensions to help advertise their products: "Six months before the combat, immense posters lined the streets of large cities, praising in the words of Jeffries the merits of certain soaps and laxative pills." White Americans' penchant for hype and profits, along with their rising preeminence in the global marketplace of commercial culture, had catapulted this race war across the world.

Yet these supposedly unique U.S. obsessions were far less exceptional than these foreign correspondents claimed. European sportsmen were also eager to cash in on the Jeffries-Johnson fight. The interracial match became a bona fide international media event as it resonated with the racial concerns of people in a variety of places.

In November 1909 Johnson and Jeffries signed a deal to fight each other for a purse of $101,000 and a share of two-thirds of the film rights.[16] Organized by the U.S. promoter Tex Rickard, the world championship match was set to take place on Independence Day in San Francisco, California. A group of white American reformers and clergymen came out in opposition to the proposed fight, arguing that it would prove to be both a barbaric spectacle and a national disgrace. Many African American sportswriters countered these criticisms, claiming that it was racism rather than morality that fueled the protest against the prizefight. Feeling the weight of public pressure, on 15 June 1910 Governor James Norris Gillett barred the Jeffries-Johnson match from the state of California. With just nineteen days until the bout, Rickard scrambled to save his event from cancellation by moving it to the frontier city of Reno, Nevada.[17]

Because of the contest's racial overtones, speculation abounded over how much revenue its moving picture would generate. *Harper's Weekly* estimated a box office of no less than $1,000,000, while *Moving Picture World* had a more conservative estimate of $160,000.[18] Most sportswriters agreed that the film's profitability ultimately would depend on which racial representative emerged triumphant. One British journalist argued that if Johnson won "the value of the pictures would be cut down largely," since they would likely face prohibition in the U.S. South and apathy in the North and West.[19] In light of this risk all three of the stakeholders sold their portions of the film rights before the fight: Johnson for $50,000, Jeffries for $66,000, and Rickard for $33,000.[20]

Despite all the commotion and contingencies, the fight attracted worldwide attention. In the week before the contest, hundreds of reporters from all over the United States descended on Reno along with a large contingent of foreign correspondents from Britain, Australia, and France. An African American reporter marveled, "Who could have ever thought that a Negro would have figured as a principal in an affair which drew on the newspapers of civilization . . . for representatives at the ringside?"[21] Telegraphers and cinematographers also reached the frontier city and began setting up their equipment. While the telegraphers would be on hand to send out round-by-round reports of the action, the J. & J. Company had won the license to produce a film of the fight for later display. J. & J. had assembled a group of camera operators from the Essanay Film Manufacturing Company, the Selig Polyscopic Company, and the Vitagraph Company to record the action. Endeavoring "to make the greatest sporting film ever," they stationed nine moving picture cameras near the ring.[22]

Adding to the bustle of preparations already afoot, tens of thousands of spectators began to arrive in Reno aboard special trains. They flooded the city, jamming the streets and overwhelming local restaurants and hotels.[23] On the morning of the fight, the crush of bodies only intensified as throngs of fans made their way to the venue in trolley cars, in automobiles, and on foot. By the afternoon, a boisterous crowd of more than sixteen thousand packed the open-air stadium. In addition to the "plain dips and stickup men . . . mine owners, stock brokers, touts, blacklegs, politicians, bank presidents and second-story men" from across the United States, "long-robed Chinamen, ultra-modishly attired Japanese, stolid Germans, vivacious Frenchmen,

[and] many Britons . . . rubbed shoulders in motley comradeship."[24] The match raked in a record gate of $270,775.[25]

Right from the opening bell, Johnson dominated the action, toying with Jeffries and showboating for the spectators. Although Jeffries managed to bloody Johnson's mouth in the fourth round, the African American champion still controlled the match. By rounds seven and eight it appeared as if Jeffries was simply too beat-up and tired to retaliate, and by round fourteen his eyes were swollen, his nose broken, and his body covered in blood. In the fifteenth and final round, Johnson knocked the beleaguered white challenger to the canvas several times. Fearing for the health and safety of his charge, Jeffries's manager, Sam Berger, jumped into the ring to stop the fight while Jeffries's trainer, Bob Armstrong, threw in the towel. As Rickard signaled Johnson's victory to the crowd, the black heavyweight became the undisputed champion of the world.[26] Much like Burns's supporters in Australia two years earlier, the disappointed spectators in Reno streamed out of the stadium in near silence.

A symbolic clash between white and black, the Jeffries-Johnson match marked the rise of a new kind of commercialized racial spectacle—one that earned immense profits as it moved rapidly across the globe in a variety of media. Although the fight was over, the news and images of the event began to take on a life of their own. Later that same day representatives from the Vitagraph Company rushed to New York City by train with the film reels of the historic fight. They arrived in record time on the morning of 8 July and immediately set to work editing the footage into a two-and-a-half-hour show.[27]

In the meantime, a communications network comprised of telegraphs and telephones carried the fight results to anxious boxing fans gathered at theaters, saloons, and newspaper offices in the United States and beyond. More news went out over the wires regarding the Jeffries-Johnson fight than the fall of Port Arthur during the Russo-Japanese War. The fight had broken all previous telegraph records, with more than eight hundred thousand words sent at an average cost of two cents per word.[28] One African American editorialist boasted, "Never before in the annals of history has telegraph wire sent to the four quarters of the globe two words which were received so anxiously as . . . 'Johnson Wins.'"[29]

Two thousand miles away in Johnson's home base of Chicago, the match results came over the wires and made their way onto bulletin boards throughout the city. At the popular Pekin Theater on the South

FIGURE 6. Jack Johnson in the ring with Jim Jeffries in Reno, 4 July 1910.
© Bettmann/Corbis. Courtesy of Corbis.

Side, owner Robert Mott read the postfight dispatch to an eager crowd of African American fans, unleashing a wave of celebration. "Men stood on their seats waving hats like mad," one black journalist recounted. "Women were equally as demonstrative; and through the windows, out of fire exits, and through the regulation exits, the big crowd surged to the streets only to be met by enthusiastic hosts coming from either direction on State street."[30] Thousands of Johnson's black fans streamed out of restaurants and saloons all along "The Stroll," forming an impromptu parade. Some waved Johnson banners while others pinned newspapers with Johnson's picture across their chests. White people passing through the enormous crowd "were made the butts of black folks' boisterous wit." Johnson's triumph over Jeffries had brought their submerged feelings of black pride to the surface for all to see.

The fight results made their way across the Atlantic and the Pacific. In Paris, many white American expatriates had converged on the offices of the French sporting daily *L'Auto* to await the telegraph reports. When the news of Jeffries's defeat arrived just after midnight, it spread throughout the city's white American colony causing "general consternation." Paris's African American community rejoiced. At about two in the morning a group of black American boxers and sportsmen entered the offices of *L'Auto* dancing with so much excitement that they scared the paper's editor.[31] The fight results also reached London, England, where thousands of people had gathered in the neighborhood of Leicester Square to discuss the match. By eleven o'clock that night the crowd of hundreds had grown into a throng of thousands. The "overwhelming majority" of these fans were ardent supporters of Jeffries. However, when the reports of Johnson's triumph arrived at midnight, all of a sudden "the coloured men seemed to become unusually numerous in the neighbourhood of Piccadilly, Leicester square, the Strand, and Fleet street."[32] Some scuffles ensued. A crowd of white men attacked a black music hall artist outside London's Alhambra Theater just because Johnson had won.[33] News of the fight even traveled to the North Coast region of New South Wales, Australia, where it roused debates among eager white and Aboriginal boxing fans.[34]

Thanks to this initial onslaught of information, the fight film became a hot commodity. A U.S. film critic declared, "The interest these pictures have aroused throughout the entire world and the advertising they are getting from people who think they should be stopped, should make them a gold mine for the exhibitor in sections where they can be shown."[35] The rights to exhibit the film in Canada alone fetched a price of $150,000. Australian and French promoters had initially bid $50,000 each to obtain the rights for their countries, and yet their offers were rejected as too low. The exclusive rights for Illinois sold for $60,000, Oscar Hammerstein offered $20,000 to exhibit the film in his venues, and one New York theater placed a bid of $12,000 to score the moving picture.[36] Even fake films of the match began springing up in a variety of locations, causing legal battles over patent rights.[37]

By early twentieth century standards, the Jeffries-Johnson moving picture was a marvelous production in its own right, providing a dramatic visual narrative of interracial competition. It took viewers inside both fighters' training camps as they prepared for the match, contrasting the stalwart white with the flashy black. A slow yet determined Jeffries punched the heavy bag, sparred, and skipped rope for the camera. He shook hands with the former white world champions John L. Sullivan and James J. Corbett in a show of racial solidarity. The cinematograph also captured Johnson's flamboyant personality. The black heavyweight fashioned himself as a prosperous man with panache and pride as he sparred, shot craps, fed chickens, drove a sulky, and even joked with his white entourage in front of the cameras.[38]

Although cinematographers filmed the prizefight from a distance, the color difference between the two boxers was stark, and Johnson's physical and tactical prowess were unmissable. "The pictures are very fine in quality and show the details of the fight with vividness," one critic maintained. "They show the great gorilla-like negro, with his cat-like pounce, striking in and retreating with dazzling speed . . . [and] they show the great frame of the boilermaker racked by grinding blows and his head shot back by the smashing force of the negro's attacks."[39] The footage from the fifteenth round featured the production's most intense moments. It left no doubt of Johnson's awe-inspiring triumph, as it showed the black champion pursuing Jeffries and pummeling him to the ground with a right uppercut and three left hooks. It also captured the potent left hook that left Jeffries sprawled across the bottom rope and the final moment when Berger jumped into the ring to end the fight. With its graphic images of black dominance and white defeat, the moving picture appeared to augur a frightening reversal of the racial and imperial hierarchies beyond the ring.

In the month after the match Johnson recorded a voice-over to accompany the film. Produced by the American Cinephone Company for distribution on phonograph, it had inspired one critic to "perceive the possibilities in the way of topic talking pictures."[40] Copies of this rudimentary "soundtrack" were marketed directly to African American fans, complete with a letter from Johnson guaranteeing the recording's authenticity.[41] Over the next year the voice-over remained in circulation, even reaching France in February 1911. To satisfy French viewers' curiosity about the black champion, the American Biograph Theater in Paris played the fight film together with the phonograph. "One can very clearly hear the champion explain the details of the 15th round of his great combat in Reno, while the translation of this speech is reproduced . . . on the screen in French," one Parisian reviewer described.[42] The Jeffries-Johnson fight film pointed to the real moneymaking potential of recorded racialized spectacles.

The film was part of a much broader universe of white supremacist productions that pervaded the early film industry. It circulated right alongside newsreels of events such as President Theodore Roosevelt's African safari and various fictional dramas of U.S. western expansion, including *Custer's Last Stand*.[43] The same individuals and companies that had recorded scenes from the Spanish-American War, including Edison and Bioscope, also took the lead in producing interracial prize-fight films. Thomas Edison had even used African American performers to play the conquered Filipinos in his filmed reenactments of battles from the Philippine-American War.[44] This interchangeability encouraged the conflation of African Americans and colonial subjects, and white spectators came to view these moving pictures as part of the same genre. As one bored little girl reportedly exclaimed at a screening of the Jeffries-Johnson film in the Forest Park suburb of Chicago, "This isn't near as nice as the cowboy and Indian pictures."[45] Regardless of the young girl's criticism, interracial fight films appealed to a transnational audience since they embodied contemporary racial conflicts with a heightened sense of immediacy.

The United States' moving picture community certainly realized the far-reaching significance of the Jeffries-Johnson match and its cinematographic exhibition. According to Reverend H. F. Jackson of *Moving Picture World*, just as the Spanish-American War had brought global attention to the United States, so too had the Jeffries-Johnson cinematograph made the medium of film a "world issue," especially with regard to "*its use*."[46] "It [film] is the world's eye," Jackson argued, "and the world is deciding what it shall behold and keep upon its everlasting retina." Since moving pictures were now a "universal factor to be reckoned with," they would have to be "governed accordingly." "The world at large acknowledges their value, respects their powers and recognizes their possibilities," Jackson observed. Given the growing backlash against the Jeffries-Johnson fight film, the reverend was not far off the mark.

THE CENSORSHIP MOVEMENT

Reverend Jackson was not the only one pondering the global consequences of the Jeffries-Johnson moving picture. In the weeks following the match a collection of coordinated movements to ban its exhibition arose in various locales throughout the United States, the British Empire, and Europe. Although some white reformers and officials joined the opposition because of their general distaste for boxing's barbarism, it was clear that the racial dimensions of the fight had sent them into crisis mode. *Moving Picture World* called the mounting protest "one of the strongest demonstrations ever started in the amusement world."[47] Troubling questions of race and representation were galvanizing concerned white citizens across ethnic, regional, and national divides.

Beginning in its home city of Boston, Massachusetts, just days after the Jeffries-Johnson match, the United Society of Christian Endeavor (USCE) organized a national campaign that quickly evolved into a transnational crusade against the exhibition of the moving picture. Heeding the complaints of Boston's USCE chapter, Mayor John F. Fitzgerald expressed his hope that the film would not be shown in the city and declared that Bostonians should take the lead in banishing prizefight pictures. Under the direction of its general secretary, William Shaw, the USCE then sent a telegram to all the state governors requesting their support: "Race riots and murder in many places following announcement of Johnson's victory in prizefight. These results will be multiplied many fold by moving picture exhibitions. Will you join other governors in recommending prohibition of these demoralizing shows? Save our young people. Wire answer."[48]

The USCE also urged former president Theodore Roosevelt to use his influence on behalf of its cause. In an article published in *Outlook* magazine, Roosevelt complained that prizefight films had "introduced a new method of money-getting and demoralization" to the sport of boxing.[49] "It would be an admirable thing," Roosevelt declared, "if some method could be devised to stop the exhibition of the moving pictures." Other progressive reformers and religious organizations began joining the movement. The Women's Christian Temperance Union built a coalition of civic groups to oppose the film publicly.[50] The International Association of Police Chiefs, the Juvenile Protective Association, the Young People's Christian Union, the Epworth League of Methodist Episcopal Churches, and settlement house workers such as Jane Addams also expressed their disapproval of the film.[51]

Even though few places in the United States had laws prohibiting prizefight pictures, police and government officials in nearly twenty states and thirty cities across the country made plans or issued orders to prevent the exhibition of the incendiary film. Actions against the Jeffries-Johnson moving picture arose in Washington, D.C., Alabama (Birmingham, Mobile), Arkansas (Little Rock), Georgia (Savannah, Atlanta), Kentucky (Louisville, Newport), Louisiana (New Orleans), Maryland (Baltimore), South Carolina (Charleston), Texas (Forth Worth), Virginia (Norfolk, Portsmouth, Richmond), California (Fresno), Illinois (Macomb), Michigan (Saginaw, Detroit), Missouri (St. Louis), New York (Rochester, Buffalo), Ohio (Cincinnati, Aurora, Cairo), Pennsylvania (Harrisburg), Rhode Island (Providence, Woonsocket), and Wisconsin (Milwaukee).[52] In the United States' empire, Manila's Municipal Board in the Philippines and the Cuban government took steps to ban the Jeffries-Johnson film, fearing the incitement of racial animosities.[53] In the face of this ever-expanding opposition, the Chicago syndicate that owned the film rights stood to lose a lot of money, and on 7 July they threatened to sue for permission to override the various prohibitions. Just two days later, however, they backed down from this stance, assuring the public that they would not fight the bans of any U.S. state or municipality.[54]

Hoping to extend the geographic dimensions of their crusade, Christian Endeavor leaders in the United States wired urgent messages to all the organization's branches around the world.[55] By 1910 the USCE had become an international force to be reckoned with, comprised of roughly four million members. This nondenominational Protestant society had more than seventy thousand chapters worldwide, mostly concentrated in the United States, Britain, Canada, and Australia. There were also chapters based in India, Madagascar, France, Mexico, Japan, the West Indies, Turkey, China, Africa, and Germany. The USCE's well-oiled publicity machine of letter-writing campaigns and press contacts, along with its own newspapers and international conventions, had helped the organization to sustain an influential voice in both the government and the public sphere.[56]

The USCE's movement against the Jeffries-Johnson fight pictures fit well within its dual vision of domestic regeneration and Christian imperialism. Its main constituents were white middle-class progressives with a decidedly global view of religious and moral reform. As part of the wider Social Gospel movement of the early 1900s, Christian Endeavorers also believed in the necessity of practical action. Worried that the exigencies of modern life were causing the decline of Western nations, the USCE worked to eradicate the disease and vice popularly associated with urbanization and industrialization, including consumption (tuberculosis), obesity, pornography, gambling, and drunkenness.[57] They believed not only in the importance of uplifting and disciplining the white working class at home but also in the necessity of civilizing colonial subjects abroad.

Christian Endeavorers railed against the commercialism and barbarism of prizefighting, a sport dominated by immigrant working-class men. Known for its materialistic, lascivious, hard-drinking, and race-mingling culture, professional boxing seemed to represent a dangerous trajectory for the modern world. The USCE worried that the interracial fight film would have an especially demoralizing effect on white children. In England, the Portsmouth and District C.E. Union chapter of the Society of Christian Endeavour passed a formal resolution against the moving picture on behalf of its 1,600 youth members. They claimed that any screening of the Jeffries-Johnson film "would be injurious to the moral welfare of . . . young people by fostering a taste for low and brutal amusement."[58] Despite their ostensible concern about the film's "brutality," what they really feared was the potential impact of its irrefutable demonstration of white weakness. Given the supposedly moribund state of Western civilization, this type of racial demoralization simply could not be tolerated.

The USCE's campaign seemed to have convinced some British authorities of the need to take action. Member of Parliament Sir Howell Davies announced that he would ask Home Secretary Winston Churchill to prohibit the moving picture in the interest of "public decency."[59] Although Churchill maintained that he had no direct power to bar it, he allowed local authorities to take action. The London City Council warned the proprietors of entertainment venues that they would have difficulty renewing their licenses if they exhibited the Jeffries-Johnson film, while the Glasgow Corporation of Scotland spoke disparagingly of the moving picture. In Ireland, both the Lord Mayor and the Roman Catholic Archbishop of Dublin came out in opposition to the "brutalizing" cinematograph.[60] Given the prevalence of concerns about white degeneration, it is not surprising that opposition to the fight film arose even in places where relatively few nonwhites resided.

As much as the USCE claimed responsibility for sparking a widespread white backlash against the Jeffries-Johnson film, it was not the only purveyor of doomsday news. With their traumatic accounts of Johnson's victory and its bloody aftermath, wire services and newspapers also helped fuel the public fire for a ban. Stories of race riots across the United States made their way into British metropolitan and colonial publications. The *Cape Times* shared a frightening cable report of black American unrest with its South African readers: "Troops have been called out. The prisons are overflowing. . . . Fifty people were injured in New York, where knives and revolvers were freely used."[61] The U.S. correspondent for Britain's *Boxing* magazine described a case in which four African American boys in Chicago packed a buggy full of guns and drove around terrorizing innocent white citizens. "Multiply this case by a few hundred," the correspondent cautioned, "and you can get some idea of what a state of high fizzle the Johnson victory has put the negro mind in."[62] Even though white Americans were actually the biggest perpetrators of racial violence in the wake of the fight, narratives of wanton black brutality dominated the pages of white newspapers.[63]

The cover of *Boxing* greeted readers with an ominous silhouette of the black champion's bust spanning the globe with the caption, "Jack Johnson in his Pride."[64] Throughout the British Empire political officials, newspaper editors, and police forces began calling for the prohibition of the Jeffries-Johnson film. On 8 July the *Times of Natal* in South Africa declared that a "world-wide movement" had coalesced around the issue. As proof, it pointed to the anti–fight film editorials in London's *Westminster Gazette*, Calcutta's *Englishman*, and Bloemfontein's *Friend* as well as the initiatives already underway in the United States.[65] The *San Francisco Examiner* captured the mood of this growing protest in a clever cartoon titled "And Not a Friendly Port in Sight." It showed an ocean wave of "opposition" pushing a projector labeled "Jeffries-Johnson moving pictures" away from three armed forts labeled "U.S.," "Europe," and "Africa."[66]

The calls for censorship were especially zealous in British colonies where nonwhites outnumbered whites. In Johannesburg, South Africa, the town clerk advised the agents and proprietors of local theaters against acquiring the rights to show the film since the town council planned to prohibit it, and the Germiston Municipality soon followed suit. By 9 July the minister of justice general, J. B. M. Hertzog, had ordered police forces throughout the Union to halt all exhibitions of the Jeffries-Johnson moving picture and to tear down any fight posters.[67] An editorialist for Calcutta's *Englishman* argued that the film would "do no good" in India since the natives would interpret it as "a race struggle."[68] He not only called on U.S. authorities to "secure and destroy" the interracial fight film, but he also hoped that "a spirit of sanity, or indirect official influence" would prevent the importation and exhibition of the film in India.

In Kingston, Jamaica, white colonials worried about the disruptive effects of Johnson's recorded victory on the majority-black island. Two years earlier Johnson's defeat of Burns had emboldened many black Jamaicans, creating difficulties for the island's white policemen.[69] Determined to prevent a repeat of this tense situation, several white colonials wrote to the *Daily Gleaner* protesting the newspaper's publicity of the Jeffries-Johnson match in "head-lines and pictures."[70] After the fight the prospect of its cinematographic exhibition generated even more condemnation in the *Gleaner*. "Can you think it will be good for the people of Kingston and Jamaica that moving pictures of the recent prize fight have been already noticed in the streets of Kingston?" a local clergyman asked. He argued that white Jamaicans should follow the lead of white Americans in calling for the prohibition of the moving picture.

Protesters in the white settler nations of Australia, New Zealand, and Canada also joined the movement. "The defeat of Jeffries is deeply felt in Australia, where racial prejudice is as strong, if not stronger than in America," one reporter observed. "The antipathy of the corn-stalk [native-born white Australian] to the Aboriginal is deep-rooted, and most white people hoped to see Tommy Burns's conqueror get the beating of his life."[71] Clergymen in Melbourne petitioned Prime Minister Andrew Fisher to bar the fight film's importation, while their counterparts in New Zealand waged a similar campaign.[72] Canadians took some of the swiftest actions against the moving picture. Perhaps reports that the postfight race rioting in the United States had spilled over the border into Windsor, Ontario, causing clashes between local whites and blacks, had pushed them to join the protest.[73] Out east, the United Baptist Association of New Brunswick passed a resolution asking the lieutenant governor to prohibit the film's exhibition in the province. In Montreal, Quebec, the owners of moving picture houses voluntarily refused to show the film. In Toronto, Ontario, the backlash against the Jeffries-Johnson cinematograph helped to usher in a new provincial law barring all prizefight pictures, with fines ranging from $50 to $300 or the alternative of three months in prison.[74]

Reports surfaced that the censorship movement had even reached Europe. Johnson's victory had apparently provoked "a campaign against negroes in Berlin."[75] In an effort to suppress any further "sensationalism," a committee of concerned citizens demanded that German authorities ban the exhibition of the fight pictures and bar the "braggart Ethiopian" from boxing anywhere in the country. They also hoped to "put a stop to the employment of negroes as sideshow freaks outside of would-be fashionable cafes and restaurants." Johnson was the target of broader frustrations over the recent influx of black entertainers who made the cakewalk, coon songs, and "nigger plays" all the rage in Berlin. In particular, the visiting black men's "disgraceful affairs" with "a certain class of white girls" had raised the ire of many Germans.[76] Seizing on the Jeffries-Johnson film controversy, this citizen group endeavored to rid the capital of the supposedly degenerate influences of black performers and their art forms. The fight film remained a subject of intense litigation between Berlin's concessionaires and police authorities for more than a year.

This concerted white backlash against the Jeffries-Johnson moving picture produced some unintended consequences. In their outspoken efforts to control its distribution, the fight film's white opponents had only made it more enticing for nonwhite audiences. White officials were understandably afraid that global distribution networks and market forces would trump local governance, allowing the film to permeate the colonies. People of color also recognized this possibility. "Do not worry," one African American reporter declared. "The Johnson-Jeffries fight pictures will be shown the world over. Public sentiment is one thing and the silver dollar is another."[77]

A VICTORY FOR THE DARKER RACES

The commodification of mass culture was changing the geopolitical landscape, into one defined more by the color line than by national or imperial borders. While mass culture's expanding reach and accelerating speed was uniting whites from across the globe in the preservation of the racial and imperial status quo, it was also uniting nonwhites in opposition to Western control. A drawing in Melbourne's *Punch* magazine depicted this emerging racial geography. Titled, "Knocked Out! Two Ways of Looking at It," it showed the defeated Jeffries lying face up in the ring while two anthropomorphized "worlds" looked on. The sad-faced "White World" gazed at his fallen hero, while his smiling black counterpart danced over Jeffries's body.[78]

Thanks to modern technology, news and images of Johnson's triumph streamed into nonwhite communities, where they took on a life of their own. A South African editorialist ironically observed, "The black and coloured races have been duly notified of the [Jeffries-Johnson] struggle by the agencies expressly invented by the civilized races for the dissemination of news, and the result will be a far greater injury to the white man's prestige than any defeat of the forces of a European Power by a barbarian horde."[79] He and many of his contemporaries believed that mass-marketed prizefights had the power to unsettle established racial scripts. Comparing the popularity of professional boxers with the legendary importance of medieval knights, he argued, "There is something more striking to the imagination in the ordeal by single combat than in the clash of arms of a multitude. . . . For this reason the knock-out blow given to Jeffries resounds throughout every region where the white man rules." Disseminated through an increasingly transnational network of communications, Johnson's victory was inspiring a wave of colored dissension.

The interracial match threatened to shake even the most secluded areas of the colonial world, for people of color had developed their own webs of exchange that extended far beyond both the reach of conventional news sources and the watchful eye of white officials. The same South African editorialist feared that reports of Johnson's victory would "be conveyed by that mysterious 'wireless' in vogue among the aboriginal peoples of the earth to the darkest recesses of the jungles and the dreariest heights of hill fastnesses." He predicted that in the United States, where the black was "a pariah," the fight would simply "embitter a race hatred . . . already terrible in its intensity," while in the Philippines, the match results would be "hailed with joy." He also agonized over the fight's potential effects in India and Egypt, where "semi-educated students" were "developing into seditious agitators." In southern Africa, exaggerated stories of Johnson's triumph would travel by word of mouth, "even in the most remote kraals of the interior." The "white man's prestige" was at stake, and with it, one of the bases of Western dominance.

This editorialist's fears of racial upheaval were not misplaced. Johnson's defeat of Jeffries had energized his black fans in the United States. "Oh, you Jack Johnson! O you undisputed champion!" the *Savannah Tribune* lauded the African American heavyweight. "Like Alexander [the Great] of old, Jack Johnson must weep because he has no more worlds to conquer."[80] The Talladega College professor William Pickens challenged white Americans who claimed that Johnson's victory would "do the Negro race harm."[81] "How, I ask, in the name of heaven can it harm a race to show itself excellent?" Pickens asked. "It was a good deal better for Johnson to win and a few Negroes be killed in body for it," he claimed, "than for Johnson to have lost and all Negroes to have been killed in spirit by the preachments of inferiority from the combined white press."

Far from doing harm, the match seemed to be awakening African Americans' racial and political consciousness. Reverend G. E. Bevens of the Mount Olive African Methodist Church in Philadelphia predicted that Johnson's win would "increase the spirit of independence in the Negro race" and "make the colored man politically more independent."[82] Johnson's victory had also stirred up more general discussions about nonwhite peoples' right to self-determination. One African American reporter pointed to the negrophobic postfight riots as proof that the white race was "unfit for self-control—self-government—even in so simple an affair as sport."[83] Another compared Johnson's victory over Jeffries in the boxing ring to that of the Japanese over the Russians in the Russo-Japanese War. "Johnson followed the Japs in demonstrating that the white man's burden was unnecessarily assumed," he declared. "Not only was Jeffries forced out of the ropes, but so also was race prejudice and domination."[84]

Although some African American newspapers called for the prohibition of the Jeffries-Johnson moving picture, most condemned the hypocrisy of the white movement against it. "What a folly!" one headline shouted in the *Washington Bee,* while the *Baltimore Afro-American* called the proposed bans "childish" and inappropriate, especially in a civilized country that prided itself on being the "land of the free and home of the brave."[85] Other black writers criticized white complaints about the fight pictures' supposed brutality. After all, no white reformers had ever decried the potentially riotous effects of the theatrical adaptation of Thomas Dixon's *Clansman,* nor had they taken any action against the barbaric crime of lynching. A clever cartoon in the *Chicago Defender* even showed Uncle Sam throwing a fight film promoter in jail while he allowed white lynchers to run free.[86] White Americans had evidently slipped into degeneracy. "They have made monkeys of themselves," one black reporter argued, "and have permitted themselves to become the laughing stock of the world."[87]

Yet white Americans were not alone in their hypocritical reaction to the Jeffries-Johnson moving picture. Leo Daniels, a black Canadian expatriate living in Glasgow, Scotland, bemoaned the "world-wide move" against the film.[88] In a passionate letter to the *Indianapolis Freeman* he explored the twisted reasoning behind this widespread white backlash. "Our victories must not be kept before the youth of a white man's country; it's too humiliating," he observed. "Had Jeffries won would this be so? No, they would have been used to cower these poor, simple, good-hearted natives to make them fear the power of the white man and make them feel their own insignificance before him." Those who protested the film were simply out to preserve the global color line. After residing in Britain for many years, "mixing and mingling with all classes of men and women," Daniels had come to one conclusion. "The black man must make his own way; no white man will do it for him, nor yet help him to do it," he maintained, "because the united white press, the united white Christion [sic] civilization (?), and the united white state rulers are at one side in all things where a Negro's interest is at stake." White solidarity was now the rule, not just in the case of the censorship movement, but in all aspects of life.

Despite this wall of white resistance, Daniels believed that Johnson's victory had the power to inspire and unify people of color, and, if properly harnessed, it could go a long way in reshaping the race's image on the world stage. As he explained, "Johnson has put the world to thinking; if there is a great muscular development and physical ability, there must also be great brain power somewhere." Now that Johnson had "established world-wide fame for himself and the down-trodden race" in the boxing ring, others could go out and "do likewise in their art, profession, science or trades." Given the sweeping efforts to suppress the Jeffries-Johnson film, black people needed to disseminate their own accounts of the fight's significance. "Publishers, give the world the history of this great battle in book form as it would have been shown on the screen," Daniels urged. "Give the biography of the champion, also that of others of your good men, and let the world read. Let it go down into history. Give the comments of the sporting world's presses of the injustice shown in that country to an inoffensive people and your champion." In an age of concerted white opposition, especially in the "yellow gutter papers" of the so-called civilized nations, Daniels argued that "colored journalists and the Afro-American press" were the "black man's hope." They could no longer remain focused within "the confines of the race-hating hordes of America." Instead, they could build on the momentum of Johnson's victory to sustain an alternative conversation about racial justice that stretched across international borders.

News of the fight had already spread to expatriate communities of black Americans, inspiring enthusiastic displays of racial solidarity. On the morning of the match the African American and Afro-Caribbean residents of Cuba's Isle of Pines (Isle of Youth) had flocked to saloons and other meeting places in the city of Santa Fe to await the results. Most were devoted Johnson fans. In the months before the fight they had even formed a club called the Jack Johnson Betting Pool, scraping together what little money they had in support of their black hero.[89] When the first confirmed reports of Johnson's triumph arrived at 1:45 PM, they organized a public celebration. The boisterous party had lasted all night long. "Some were dancing, jumping and doing every funny stunt that they could think of," a correspondent recounted. "Many toasts were said in honor of Jack Johnson, with many best wishes for our champion."[90]

No wonder Cuban officials moved quickly to ban the fight film. Not only did Johnson's triumph inspire the raucous celebrations of African American and Afro-Caribbean expatriates, but the film also threatened to aggravate their homegrown problem of rising Afro-Cuban consciousness. It did not help that black and mixed-race Cubans had begun to mobilize, in 1908 forming the Partido Independiente de Color (PIC), which demanded full equality for Afro-Cubans. Amid widespread rumors of a black conspiracy to gain control of Cuba, both the PIC and the Jeffries-Johnson fight film were outlawed in 1910.[91]

Regardless of the risks involved, Johnson's expanding fan base soon reached across the Pacific to the U.S. colony of the Philippines, where Filipinos embraced his racial triumph as their own, using it as a rallying cry for self-determination. Many were longtime fans of the black champion. Packed with laudatory tales of Johnson's exploits, African American newspapers like the *Chicago Defender* had long traveled to the archipelago via the black soldiers serving in the U.S. occupying forces. Thanks to the efforts of visiting U.S. pugilists and promoters, by 1910 boxing had also become a favorite Philippine pastime. It was especially popular among poor and working-class men in Manila, who used the sport to assert their masculinity at a moment when white Americans cast them as effeminate boys desperately in need of white tutelage. Catering to the growing demand for boxing reports, local newspapers provided front-page stories of the Jeffries-Johnson fight. The *Manila Times* even promised to post the fight results as soon as they arrived by telegraph from Reno.[92]

Hoping for their own chance to witness this historic match, Johnson's Filipino fans looked forward to the arrival of the moving picture. Fearing colonial unrest, Manila's Municipal Board banned its exhibition. The large numbers of *muchachos*, or male house servants, in the capital city, along with the recent rise of the Nacionalista Party for Philippine independence, likely influenced the council's decision.[93] One Filipino writer declared, "The punches thrown in Reno by the black boxer Johnson have reverberated in Manila, wounding the delicate eardrums of our Municipal Council." The reason for the ban was simple: "The victor is a black man. The vanquished is not."[94]

Thanks to the numerous postfight reports, Filipino fans were well aware of the violent white American backlash against Johnson's victory. Pedro Quinto of the *Renacimiento Filipino* argued that this backlash fit within a much longer history of white supremacy in the United States, dating back to the days of the founding fathers. "Even [George] Washington did not see in the black man anything other than a hunted slave in the African deserts and a trafficked object on the plantations of the new world," Quinto explained. "If in those days the black was a man in the United States, he was certainly not considered and treated as a man."[95] Evidently, "the equality of men was not written for the unfortunate black man." Instead, as Quinto emphasized, "The mere idea of a man of this [black] race raising his hand against a white man was considered a monstrosity, and it is the same even today." With the U.S. forces still occupying the Philippines, the nationalist Quinto was not only commenting on the unfair treatment of African Americans but was also critiquing the lowly status of Filipinos under the regime of benevolent assimilation.

Whether or not the fight film ever made it to Manila, Quinto hoped that Johnson's resounding defeat of Jeffries would help to overturn the "tyranny" of white supremacy, thereby promoting "civilization" and "social justice" throughout the world. In Quinto's estimation, the African American champion had provided "a service to Humanity" by "showing how far effort and 'training' can take individuals and peoples." The assumed inferiority of the darker races could no longer be taken for granted.

In the British colony of India the native press also followed the match, with an eye to its subversive significance as an interracial contest. Worried about the potential fallout, British officials monitored the numerous postfight reports in Indian newspapers, especially since Johnson's victory came on the heels of a politically charged physical revival among native youths. British ideas of Indian men's supposedly weak and womanish bodies had pushed many to join in this revival, whether in the gym, on the field, or through military service. They believed that British rule had softened them and that therefore they must cultivate their bodies in order to throw off the yoke of submission. A writer for the *Abhyudaya* warned that Indian men were in danger of losing their physical strength, "the most essential element in the formation of a nation."[96] Amid these biopolitical discussions, many Indian journalists claimed Johnson's triumph as a powerful symbol of their own fitness for self-determination.

They shaped their postfight reports into parables of pride and resistance. A correspondent for the *Arya Prakásh* provided eager readers with a graphic description of Jeffries's demise at the hands of Johnson: "The Negro got the better of his adversary and dealt one after another such heavy blows with his iron fist on the face of his white opponent that the latter's cheek bones were broken, blood gushed out copiously from his torn-up cheeks, one of his eyes got injured and finally he fell on the ground senseless and almost lifeless and was dragged out of the enclosure." A writer for the *Kesari* argued that any attempts to ban the fight film would ultimately prove misguided from both a practical and moral standpoint. "If the prohibitions are made to make the world continue in the belief that coloured people are of a lower order in everything than the Whites, they will be of no avail. Already the whole world knows the result of the fight," he declared. "The Whites should not delude themselves with the idea of such questionable prestige."[97]

The sweeping efforts to ban the Jeffries-Johnson moving picture had only further exposed the global scope of white supremacy. "Even Englishmen cannot overcome their prejudices against black skin and are apt to think that the Black man is inferior to the White man in point of civilisation," a reporter for the *Gujaráti Punch* argued. The censorship movement had laid bare the fundamental tensions between Christian pronouncements of "universal brotherhood" and the realities of imperialism and race prejudice. As another native writer sardonically suggested, rather than focusing on saving the heathens abroad, foreign missionary boards should "divert a great portion of their energies homeward to cure the maladies of racial animosity, colour mania, Negrophobia, &c."[98]

What disturbed Indian commentators most was the rabid postfight violence against African Americans. "One cannot but read with pain the account of the recent riots all over the United States—the attacks on poor Negroes in the country by white men," one writer expressed. The native press openly chastised white Americans, maintaining that black Americans were "entirely free from blame in the matter."[99] "What did the riots mean?" an editorialist for the *Indian Spectator* pondered. "They meant that the [white] Americans not only claimed superiority to the Negroes in every respect, even in physical strength, but they could not brook the idea of an individual Negro developing larger and tougher muscles than an American known for his strength." This petty jealousy over a matter of physical strength simply exposed the white man's "depth of barbarism."[100]

The violent repression of African Americans also spoke to the Indian subjects' own sense of frustration under British rule, for they still experienced daily rituals of humiliation and brutality. Several native writers noted that despite the continuing efforts of African Americans to uplift themselves, racial terror remained endemic in the United States. "Although slavery has been abolished in America Negroes are practically still treated as no better than slaves, as is evident from 'lynching' which is in vogue there," one editorialist declared. "The white people labour under the conviction that Negroes have been created to serve them, the sole aim of their existence is to work as slaves to the Whites,

and whatever be their other qualifications their colour alone is sufficient disability to deprive them of any better treatment."[101] Whether in
India or in the United States, no attempt to educate or advance oneself
seemed to offer people of color respite from assault and discrimination.

The Jeffries-Johnson prizefight and its bloody aftermath had
undoubtedly "brought to the fore the worthlessness of the vaunted
Western civilization."[102] Indian commentators argued that white barbarity was exemplified not only in the gratuitous violence of the sport
of boxing but also in white men's unwillingness to accept defeat graciously. "There is nothing more inhuman than spitefully to commit
outrages upon the black population from a false sense of injury. If this
be civilization, away with it to the devil! And let the East rot in its
uncivilized condition," a writer for the *Gujaráti* declared.[103] With or
without the film, the news of Johnson's victory was beginning to crack
through the armor of white supremacy the world over.

JEFFRIES-JOHNSON AND THE UNION OF SOUTH AFRICA

The expansion of commercial sporting culture was clearly helping to
link local and global issues of race in the minds of regular people,
both white and nonwhite. In the Union of South Africa a confluence of
local, national, and transnational factors had intensified racial feelings
in recent years, which made the Jeffries-Johnson fight seem like a matter of life and death for many white settlers. "To the average man in
the street, it was not the question so much of a boxing contest—it was
the colour element," a white South African later recounted.[104] In the
days before the match Britons and Boers alike had gathered together
to discuss the "upholding of the pride and prestige of the white race
against the black, and the probable effect upon negroes the world over
if the black man were victorious." Through the fight and the ensuing
controversy over its moving picture, they came to connect their own
racial difficulties with the broader project of perpetrating white world
supremacy.

Popularly known for having a "natural antipathy for negroes,"
Jeffries achieved a special celebrity among white South African sportsmen.[105] Although most had never seen, let alone talked, to Jeffries in
person, they embraced the white American boxer with an intimate
sense of racial brotherhood. As a correspondent for Johannesburg's
Sunday Times joked, South Africa seemed "to contain thousands of
Mr. Jeffries's oldest and dearest friends."[106] In pubs all across the Rand

he had encountered many men who "talked familiarly of 'Jeff.'" "Some of them had known him when he was a little white-headed boy, scores of them had taught him how to spar, [and] dozens of them had trained him," the writer wryly recounted. Still others claimed to have received "long cablegrams from him declaring he was in splendid condition and sure to win." They wove the many newspaper and magazine reports of the white American champion into the very fabric of their personal life stories, intertwining his racial trials with their own. When Jeffries lost, they were understandably devastated.

As white South Africans joined the transnational campaign to suppress the Jeffries-Johnson fight film, their motivations were wrapped up in local contests over political rule. A few months before the interracial match the British and the Boers had worked through their differences to establish the Union of South Africa as a "white man's country," effectively excluding native Africans, coloreds, and Indians from full citizenship rights.[107] White settlers, a small minority of the population, not only feared for their physical safety but also feared the potential ungovernability of their new nation. The British had made a major concession to the Afrikaners by refusing to mandate black suffrage. This calculated maneuver to unite South Africa's whites left natives without the vote in the former Afrikaner colonies and with limited voting rights in the Cape. A decade earlier the British high commissioner Lord Alfred Milner had already outlined the philosophy undergirding this maneuver, writing, "The *ultimate* end is a self-governing white Community, supported by *well-treated* and *justly-governed* black labour from Cape Town to Zambesi."[108] People of color were ancillary to the project of white nation building; they were there to work, but not to reap any of the Union's benefits.

Many white South Africans believed that it was their Darwinistic right to exercise this power, and they were not particularly concerned about the treatment of black laborers. For them, the establishment of the Union marked the end of a long "transition stage" from black to white control. An editorialist explained, "The struggle for mastery with the natives from the old Boer voortrekker days up to the last Natal rebellion [Bambatha Rebellion, 1906] has taught us one indelible lesson—that we have paid in blood for the dominance of the superior race . . . and that we are not to be cheated from what is due to us."[109] Johnson's irrefutable triumph over Jeffries undermined the validity of racial claims to political power by white settlers, who worried about the potential fallout of its cinematographic exhibition in theaters throughout the country.

On the same editorial pages that they discussed the negative consequences of Johnson's victory they acknowledged the insecurity of their
control, especially "in the midst of a teeming aboriginal population."
"In South African life, the native is always with us," declared the editor of the *Times of Natal*. "He is the dominant factor in our social
problem."[110] It was difficult to reconcile the native's supposedly stunted
evolution with the rapid march of Western modernity. "As an aboriginal there is much to admire in him," the editor explained; "as a savage,
with the rudiments of civilization badly planted in his brain, there is
much to regret in him." It was therefore the task of white officials "to
strike the balance between the two conditions." Inundated with numerous reports of postfight racial unrest in the United States, they feared
that the specter of Johnson's triumph would upset this delicate balance,
causing the natives to forget their subordinate position.

The rise of South Africa's mining industry and the nation's widen-
ing web of transatlantic connections had already disturbed this equi-
librium. The discovery of diamonds and gold in the late nineteenth
century had radically reshaped South African race relations. As the
opening of the mines created an insatiable demand for cheap labor,
native Africans found themselves relegated to the role of "hewers and
drawers" in a society increasingly divided by race rather than civilization. The growing consolidation of the industry under the ownership of
large foreign corporations had even forced formerly independent white
miners into wage work. Not only did they experience declining economic opportunities, but they found themselves in competition with
black laborers—the same laborers who had worked for them in the
early days of the mining boom.[111]

This industrial revolution also triggered the large-scale migration
of nonwhite men into urban spaces, creating new problems for colonial authorities. In mining areas such as the East Rand, bachelor communities of native laborers encroached on the edges of white towns,
sparking widespread fears of black men raping white women. Even
more disturbingly, old tribal enemies, now dislodged from their homelands, began to find a common ground in their shared experiences of
racial oppression. As they traveled back and forth between urban and
rural areas, this sense of racial solidarity began to permeate the native
community. It also began to extend beyond national borders as they
obtained unprecedented access to the outside world not only through
their encounters with black foreigners but also through their consumption of mass culture.

White settlers were most concerned about the natives' increasing encounters with African Americans. South Africa's industrial growth had attracted many black Americans to Cape Town, Durban, and other port cities, where they worked as stevedores, machinists, and tradesmen alongside a cosmopolitan mix of native Africans, Indians, and Afro-Caribbeans. Some black Americans even ventured further inland, laboring on the railroads, while others came as missionaries, helping to establish the African Methodist Episcopal Church (AME) across the country. White South Africans were particularly suspicious of the AME missionaries' role in the rise of "Ethiopianism," a religious tradition that embraced the need for greater black autonomy in both the sacred and the secular realms.[112]

They were no less wary of the subversive impact of visiting African American performers. Black American minstrel troupes like Orpheus McAdoo's Jubilee Singers had toured in South Africa since the late nineteenth century. Although these troupes certainly catered to the darky stereotypes of white audiences, they still managed to infuse their performances with a sense of sophistication and style, and through them, many native Africans across class lines came to see black Americans as exemplars of urbanity and modernity. Men like McAdoo encouraged this perception, often providing native fans with glowing accounts of black American achievements in education and business.[113] Inspired by one of the jubilee singers' performances in 1890, one native reviewer had asked, "When will the day come when the African people will be like the Americans? When will they stop being slaves and become nations with their own government?"[114] Although full of exaggerations about the extent of black American political independence, these performances influenced local black musical traditions and inspired African audiences to imagine a better life beyond the confines of their own circumstances. White South Africans came to blame nearly every example of native insubordination on the poisonous influence of visiting African Americans. Coupled with the urban migration of native men, this outside influence seemed to be inspiring a dangerous brand of black consciousness that transcended not only tribal but also national affiliation.

As part of this accelerating black cultural traffic from across the Atlantic, the postfight publicity and moving picture only threatened to exacerbate things. Even though nonwhites were prohibited from entering bioscope theaters in cities like Johannesburg, most white South African commentators still agonized over the special power of photos and film, both in terms of their visual impact and their ability to reach poor and working-class people of color. As one editorialist warned:

> Within a week or two the mail papers will be introduced, having full page illustrations of the fight and certainly posters will be issued with these journals depicting the defeated Jeffries prostrate and the victorious negro standing above him, ready to administer a final blow. These pictures will be exhibited in the shop windows and on boards in the public streets, and will have an even more demoralising effect upon the native mind than the mere news of the white man's defeat. Again, we shall be treated with numerous yards of bioscopic films giving every degrading phase of the contest, and as these pictures were obtained at a heavy cost they will be extensively advertised.[115]

Already tales of Johnson's triumph were not isolated to "the staid newspaper-reading citizens" but were making their way into the enthusiastic conversations of "cab-drivers, messengers, and every other class of the coloured population." The local natives in Bloemfontein reportedly cabled Johnson to congratulate the black heavyweight on his victory over the white American.[116] Likewise, signing himself "a Black Coolie," an Indian from Pietermaritzburg wrote a bold and contemptuous letter to the *Times of Natal*.[117] "The white races can do or say what they may, but the fact remains branded in the heavens 'that the Black man is wearing the laurels of the ring of the world,' and may he always be," the writer declared. "A white man cannot do as he pleases. Man proposes but God dispenses." Given the Indian's obvious lack of respect for whites as well as the strong likelihood that members of his community shared his sentiments, the barring of the Jeffries-Johnson fight film seemed justified.

White commentators were especially anxious about the large number of young native men living in urban areas, many of whom were houseboys (domestic servants) and mine workers with the disposable income to spend on fight reports and film tickets. Even before the Jeffries-Johnson controversy came to a head, the houseboys' growing impertinence had become a topic of public discussion. Their exposure to white civilization in the cities was apparently making these "young hot-bloods" all the more unmanageable.[118] One white writer joked, "It is unfortunately the case that as his [the houseboy's] intelligence expands his energy diminishes."[119] Given the houseboys' close proximity to white women and the longstanding belief in the hypersexuality of black men, their unruliness was no laughing matter. A letter to the editor warned, "We in these colonies, for the sake of good government and safety for our wives and children . . . should do our best to prevent the natives getting swelled head [sic] and attempting to imitate their dusky champion."[120] Many white settlers feared that the circulating images of Johnson would only make the natives bolder.

Although the specific conditions of industrialization and black migration differed between the United States and South Africa, black working-class men on both sides of the Atlantic were increasingly becoming connected through a shared culture of the urban dandy, an important facet of the rise of transnational New Negro politics. Rather than taking on the best of civilization, much like Johnson, the prototypical urban houseboy seemed to have contracted all of its vices. He was supposedly a spendthrift who wasted all of his money on gaudy suits with bright colors and loud patterns. Annoyingly smug, he considered himself "a member of fashionable native society," inviting "other house-boys to his room at night, where they [would] sit till the small hours smoking cigarettes and discussing house-boy affairs in stentorian tones."[121] Perhaps most importantly, he ended manual labor, often preferring to make easy money in the underground economy. White South Africans also painted a similar portrait of the archetypal black mine worker. His purported participation in the illicit diamond trade enabled him to afford elaborate outfits, cigars, and champagne. He often spoke loudly and swaggered along city sidewalks, refusing to be silent and invisible.[122] While the "nigger dandy" may have been a figure of derision in the eyes of white South Africans, native men actively adopted this flamboyant persona, in defiance of the racial order, as a means to express publicly their own class aspirations and masculine prerogatives.

These descriptions of African dandies bore a striking resemblance to Johnson's own New Negro lifestyle outside the ring, including his love of fashion, jewels, fast cars, and white women, his cultivated worldliness, and his general irreverence for white men. The African American heavyweight, along with the native houseboy and native mine worker, embodied all of white South Africa's worst fears of racial, gender, sexual, and class upheaval at the turn of the twentieth century. Thus, the Jeffries-Johnson prizefight provided native men with yet another unsanctioned and subversive connection with the wider black world. As gangs of native youths gathered in the streets to celebrate their black American hero's conquest, white South Africans looked to white America for direction.

The controversy surrounding the fight and its film encouraged white South Africa to see its racial destiny as closely linked with that

FIGURE 7. White South African officials worried that exhibitions of the Jeffries-Johnson fight film would only exacerbate the growing impertinence of native houseboys. "The Kaffir House Boy," *Sunday Times*, 10 July 1910.

of Jim Crow America. They openly expressed their support for white Americans' violent and repressive response to Johnson's victory. In contrast, many English metropolitan sportsmen used the match to claim a moral high ground over their colonial contemporaries. They lamented the imposition of race in the boxing ring, complaining that white Americans had violated the enlightened British ethics of fair play. Racial, ethnic, class, and religious divisions were not to intrude upon the neutral realm of sport, which in theory offered every man an equal chance at winning.

Yorick Gradeley of *Health & Strength* cautioned that it was "presumptuous" for English boxing fans "to dogmatise upon this racial problem." Located far from the realities of colonial life, they had come to regard the "negro" as their brother. Yet white settlers' arduous experiences in places like South Africa had proven that if the black man "fancied that he was mightier . . . he would strive to wrest the scepter from his master's grasp."[123] Gradeley emphasized, "He [the negro] is not your brother; he is no fit mate for your sister. He belongs to a different race; a race that, for its own sake as well as for yours, must be kept separate."[124] The metropolitan calls for a dispassionate spirit of fair play were simply inapplicable to the semicivilized, racially diverse, and highly contentious environments of both the United States and the British colonies.

Invoking the famous story of *Uncle Tom's Cabin*, Gradeley elaborated on these underlying connections between British colonialism and the American "negro problem." "Oh, it's all very well for you to remind me of the pretty, but maudlin sentimentality of 'Uncle Tom's Cabin,' little Eva, and all that. The negro of that day was a better man than the negro of to-day," Gradeley declared.[125] Under slavery the "negro" had been "pure"; now that he was free, he had become "intolerable." Gradeley insisted that he was not calling for a return to slavery but rather for the recognition that emancipation had not been "an unmitigated blessing." He maintained, "I tell you straight that we have no right to judge our Colonial and American kinsmen harshly . . . [just] because they do not love the black man quite as much as they do their own race."

Gradeley's candid assertions about the need for a color line both within and beyond the ring provoked a passionate debate in *Health & Strength*, which tended to pit metropolitan readers against white South Africans. This sporting debate built on the ongoing conflict between metropolitan liberals and white colonials over the political and social status of nonwhites in the British Empire. At the crux of the conflict was the question of whether citizenship rights should be dependent on civilization or skin color. English liberals frowned upon white settlers' often blatant displays of color prejudice, which they saw as rude and uncouth. They argued that demonstrating one's grasp of Western civilization was the key to obtaining full citizenship; therefore, nonwhites could aspire to it, even if their progress was slow. White South Africans, on the other hand, criticized English people in the metropole for their naïve and sentimental view of nonwhites. Determined to construct a white nation, they turned to the United States as a model for racial policy, from immigration restrictions to residential segregation.[126]

Some English sportsmen were critical of this apparent infiltration of U.S. racial values into the colonies. An outraged *Health & Strength* reader questioned, "Is Yorick Gradeley an Englishman? If so, then I am disgusted with him, because I think that every Englishman wanted the best man to win."[127] Critiquing white Americans' preoccupation with race, another Londoner advocated character over color as the true marker of manhood. "Some of us would as soon claim kinship with Booker Washington or Coleridge Taylor as with Charles Peace, though the latter's skin was undoubtedly whiter," he contended.[128] In this way they demonized their white American and colonial counterparts without acknowledging their own culpability in the imperial world order.

Coming to Gradeley's defense, white settlers argued for the strict enforcement of racial segregation. A Pietermaritzburg reader charged that Gradeley's critics would not be so quick to claim the black man as their brother if they actually lived in South Africa. He explained, "The black out here has a few centuries to live before he can compare even with the lowest white, let alone be acknowledged as brother."[129] He believed that "social equality" would be a "mistaken policy." A farmer from Wolvenkraal agreed, arguing that people in England were closing their eyes to the reality of interracial conflict in the colonies. "One thing is certain as far as South Africa is concerned, and that is that before long a serious war will result between the white and black races," he declared. "The authorities are all asleep, the natives are becoming more and more aggressive day by day, and I should not be surprised if one night they were to rise and massacre the whole population of South Africa, and that all through their being educated."[130] English sportsmen were only fooling themselves if they failed to see the merits of maintaining a strict color line.

Much to the relief of Gradeley and his supporters, the USCE and its transnational censorship movement managed, for the most part, to keep the Jeffries-Johnson film from appearing in either the British colonies or the southern United States. Still, however, they failed to shut it down completely. In the fall of 1910 the film started showing in a number of U.S. locales, in front of largely white male audiences. The small percentage of African Americans who attended screenings faced racial segregation and intimidation. The fight film appeared in theaters and outdoor venues in New York City, Boston, Brooklyn, Buffalo, Hoboken, Philadelphia, Pittsburgh, Detroit, Peoria, St. Louis, Kansas City, Denver, and a host of other U.S. towns and cities. Even in places where prohibitions were in effect, it played clandestinely for white audiences in hotel suites and summer homes and on Mississippi River barges. Across the border in Mexico it entertained packed crowds in local movie halls.[131]

The film was also a box office success in a number of European cities. Parisian journalists had encouraged France to remain "open" to the Jeffries-Johnson film, and when it finally arrived it was widely advertised in sporting magazines.[132] It ran for months not only at the American Biograph Theater in Paris but also at smaller venues in the provinces.[133]

The moving picture also enjoyed profitable runs at London's National Sporting Club and at theaters in Dublin and Brussels. Although the film had to be "revised" by police authorities before it could be shown, it played in Berlin and other cities across Germany.[134]

Caught up in a mix of local, national, and transnational debates over the color line, Johnson's triumph and its film recording had put white people on notice. Together these media events not only exposed the growing global influence of U.S. racial culture, but they also pushed the instability of Western imperialism to the forefront of public debate. White settlers urged their metropolitan counterparts to wake up to the frightening realities of the worldwide race problem in an age of increasingly rapid travel, trade, and communication. It seemed as if the fight had managed to shake some of the racial sentimentality out of England. As one African American correspondent complained, "The English [public], who usually take delight in anything it believes reflects adversely to the credit of America or Americans suddenly reverts to advice for suppression of the Negro."[135] These ideas could even be found in serious newspapers like the *Times*. "It is very easy for us in England, where we have no color problem, to talk with indignation and abhorrence of the lynchings and the outrages which occur so frequently in the Southern States of America," a *Times* editorialist acknowledged. However, they had "yet to see how the English would act if confronted with entirely similar conditions," and he feared that they "would be no more tolerant."[136] Johnson's arrival in London in the summer of 1911 would soon put them to the test.

3

Jack Johnson versus John Bull

The Rise of the British Boxing Colour Bar

Colored Men and Women Making Good in Europe—
No Color Line to Hamper Them and in Letters and Trade
They are Making Fame for Themselves and their Race
—*Chicago Defender,* 29 July 1911

This is a fight between black and white, and it will be
flashed in all its detail, printed and pictured, before men,
women and children, in places where races of different
colour live together. There is no problem more anxious,
for the present and for the future, than that of colour; none
about which there are more sinister features; none on which
instinct, passion, and prejudice are more inflammable;
none therefore, on which it is more imperative that nothing
should be done to inflame or excite.
—The Bishop of Winchester commenting on the Wells-Johnson
match, 1911

When Jack Johnson journeyed to London in June of 1911, the *Chicago
Defender* extolled the seemingly progressive racial mores of Britain.
"JACK TREATED LIKE MAN AND GENTLEMAN" its front-page headline
blazed.[1] The correspondent Sylvester Russell described everything from
Johnson's transatlantic crossing to his "grand arrival in the British capital" for the ready consumption of African Americans in search of hope
for a color-blind future. Russell repudiated the various white American
claims of Johnson's second-class quarters during his steamship voyage to London, arguing that the black heavyweight had stayed in the

engineer's cabin, a coveted location. He was also more than happy to recount Johnson's cold rebuff of a white southerner while onboard the steamer. When the southerner had warned the black champion not to get too familiar with the white folk in England, Johnson had told him to mind his own business.[2]

Russell's depiction of Johnson's first days in London provided a powerful refutation of the southerner's remarks. Upon Johnson's arrival a policeman had begged him to take a taxi, fearing that the throng of English enthusiasts that had gathered to greet him might become unmanageable. Obliging the officer, Johnson made his way to a cab, smiling and bowing to his right and left, as many in the crowd cheered raucously, struggling for a closer view. When the cab drove off Johnson waved his hat to the fans that followed him on foot. In recounting this wild demonstration of white British support for Johnson, Russell mused, "Perhaps the reason why Theodore Roosevelt condemned prize fighting in America is best described from the lionization of Mr. J. Arthur Johnson in England."[3] Johnson's popularity abroad seemed to portend a dangerous subversion of the racial status quo.

In September 1911, however, a heated controversy arose in the English press when word got out that Johnson was set to take on the British titleholder and former soldier in the British Indian Army, Bombardier Billy Wells. The match was scheduled for 2 October at Earl's Court in London, with a purse of £8,000.[4] Rather than casting the fight as an Anglo-American competition for world heavyweight supremacy, many English commentators imagined the proposed match as a colonial contest embodying the real-life race war threatening to engulf the British Empire.

Although incidences of armed anticolonial insurrection were relatively rare during this period, British imperial authorities still recognized the fragility of their control. Consolidating the nation's power and territory in southern Africa had proved difficult. During the Second Boer War (1899–1902) the British forces had sustained massive casualties as they struggled to bring Afrikaner lands under the Union Jack. Secular nationalist movements were also endangering British rule in India and Egypt, while African natives and Indian immigrants began to push for greater recognition in South Africa.[5] Making matters worse, Britain's nonwhite subjects greatly outnumbered its white colonial settlers and officials. An editorial in London's *Daily Chronicle* questioned, "It is from the capital of Britain, from the heart of the British Empire, which has so many colour problems and racial difficulties within its orbit, that films are to go forth depicting a fight between black and white—between a black champion and a white soldier?"[6]

Just as the London *Times* editorialist had predicted a year earlier, Englishmen now faced with racial troubles similar to those of the United States were proving to be "no more tolerant."[7] Some metropolitan elites feared that a highly publicized heavyweight title fight between the audacious African American and Britain's white champion would simply import U.S. racial violence into the colonies. Given that a cadre of British intellectuals and officials had long envisioned the United States' Reconstruction after the Civil War as an ominous example of the chaotic dangers of multiracial democracy, this reaction was not unexpected. Thanks to publications such as the British historian James Bryce's *American Commonwealth,* they were well aware of the "negative" consequences of giving black men political power.[8] With their own subjects calling for greater independence in the colonies, they had begun to see their fate as enmeshed with that of white America.

Johnson's impending fight against Wells only heightened this sense of shared racial destiny. Reverend Frederick Brotherton (F. B.) Meyer spoke out against the interracial match from his pulpit at Regent's Park Baptist Church: "God knows there is horror enough in the Southern States of America, trouble enough between ourselves, the settlers, in South Africa and the black population, difficulty enough and in plenty in India, and we do not want to make more bitter the antagonism between white and black."[9] Although Meyer had previously associated with prominent black people in London, even offering his support to the Trinidadian barrister and activist Henry Sylvester Williams for the Pan-African Conference in 1900, the possibility of a black pugilist shaming white British honor in the ring, in the very nerve center of the empire, was simply too dangerous a proposition.[10] Because of Johnson's proven popularity with the dark proletariat across the globe, he posed a different set of problems than more palatable members of the black bourgeoisie such as Williams. A writer for London's *Daily Telegraph* reminded readers that Johnson's defeat of Jeffries in 1910 had inspired brutal scenes across the United States that "were sickening in the antagonism between the two races."[11] He admonished his fellow Englishmen to wake up to their imperial responsibilities. "Even if you say that we have but few negroes in this country compared with them [white Americans]," he argued, "remember that you rule a mighty negro population." Reverend Meyer and others abandoned their already fragile sense of imperial brotherhood with British colonial subjects in favor of their growing racial kinship with white Americans.

Much as he had in Australia, when Johnson arrived in England he brought the United States' vexing "negro problem" with him. In many respects the black heavyweight posed the race question in the British metropolis with a breadth and intensity that formal political action simply could not, inspiring a surge of white opposition at the municipal, national, and imperial levels. After all, he threatened to blur the line separating white citizens from nonwhite subjects, not only through his physical prowess in the ring, but also through his public claims for recognition as a man outside the ring.

Johnson's difficulties in London exposed the intimate relationship between Jim Crow segregation and the racial fault lines of British imperialism. His black American fans initially had high hopes for their champion's overseas visit, especially since black boxers had a long and successful tradition of fighting in England. However, Britain's backlash against the Wells-Johnson match left many disillusioned, for it underscored the fact that their local experiences of racial oppression were just one facet of a broader effort to keep nonwhites outside the bounds of modern civilization. At the same time, the looming prizefight also made the specter of race war in the colonies all the more tangible for white sports fans in the British metropole, provoking empire-wide discussions about the merits of American-style racial segregation and the urgent need for white Anglo-Saxon solidarity around the world. Although it was the first time that an interracial match had received such criticism in England, the heated controversy helped inspire the rise of Britain's boxing colour bar. Even as Johnson and his black fans imagined and sought out better opportunities in Britain, they quickly discovered that Jim Crow and John Bull were not-so-distant relatives.

BLACK AMERICANS' ATLANTIC DREAMS

It was not easy for African Americans to interpret Europe's racial mores. From the moment Johnson arrived in London, the picture on the ground proved complex. Despite the glowing description of Johnson's British welcome published in the *Defender,* the black champion found it hard to move about freely in the capital city. Anticipating difficulty in securing accommodation appropriate for a man of his status, Johnson had sent his white valet to book a room for him at the Piccadilly Hotel.[12] The many conflicting reports of Johnson's overseas travels became an important aspect of the vibrant public debate over the racial progressiveness of Europe and its possibilities for African American exile and citizenship.

Black Americans had long envisioned Britain and Europe in general as spaces of civilization in contrast to the barbarism of Jim Crow America. Yet they often based this perception on a misunderstanding of the particular symbolic role that both U.S. racism and African Americans played in the complicated dance of European imperial politics. The United States served as a foil against which nations such as Britain and France could claim greater racial tolerance. Since the nineteenth century Britain had welcomed African American abolitionists like Frederick Douglass and Henry "Box" Brown, and it became a popular destination for black stage performers and professional athletes. Embracing Johnson and other African American rebel sojourners enabled white Britons to demonize white Americans while glossing over their own complicity in the racial and imperial status quo.

Nevertheless, many African Americans retained a special sense of optimism about the promise of freedom and equality abroad. Even as they faced racial violence and persecution at home, they found hope in Johnson's ability to cross borders and to explore opportunities in other nations. Their collective discussions of his overseas travels were part of their ongoing search for spaces of racial equality beyond the reach of Jim Crow. Contemporary debates about the benefits of migration out of the U.S. South addressed the potential for black settlement not only in the northern states but also in foreign places. "The number of dissatisfied and disgruntled colored people in this country is growing daily," one African American editorialist declared, "and the much heralded freedom from color prejudice of the old world has caused not a few strong and sensible colored men to ponder seriously the question as to whether they should not flee from the color-phobia of these shores."[13]

Still this same editorialist remained loyal to Booker T. Washington's call to "cast down your bucket where you are" and asserted that Europe was no better than the United States.[14] He cited Washington's observations on the desperate state of affairs for working people in Europe, published in 1911 as a series of installments in *Outlook* magazine. Titled "The Man Farthest Down," Washington's serial argued that the United States was still the best place for the future of black people.[15] For two months in the fall of 1910 Washington had traveled in search of the poorest of the poor in England, Bohemia (Czech Republic), Italy, Hungary, Poland, Russia, and Denmark. Instead of focusing on the impressive monuments in the capital cities, he investigated Europe's problems of unemployment, starvation, poor housing, primitive agricultural practices, and child labor.

Washington also claimed that during his trip many African Americans asked for his help to return to the United States since it was next to impossible for black people to find work in Europe. He recalled encountering an African American who had been stranded in London for fourteen months. "It seems to me that all Britain are against the Negro race," the beleaguered black man had told him. "Some say, 'Go back to your own country,' knowing if I had the means I would fly to-morrow."[16] Curiously sidestepping the continued problems of white American racial violence and segregation, Washington declared that because of the United States' free market democracy and class mobility, the average African American was much better off than his poor white counterparts across the Atlantic. Thus "the distance of Europe" seemed to be "almost her only enchantment."[17]

Whereas Washington maintained that the southern Negro was "just as proud to be an American citizen as he is to be a Negro," not all black Americans had the same kind of faith in the sincerity and inclusiveness of U.S. democracy.[18] One African American editorialist complained that Washington had used his European tour to spread false propaganda about the vast improvement in U.S. race relations. "He may succeed in deceiving the English people, but I don't think so," the writer argued. "He certainly will not if the colored people of the U.S. exhibit one-tenth as much courage, common sense, and ordinary perception as they have patience through all these long years of trial and suffering."[19]

Johnson's arrival in London offered African American journalists a chance to counter Washington's negative views of Europe. The *Defender* correspondent Russell seized on the possibility that the United States' color line was somehow exceptional among civilized Western nations. He took great delight in describing Johnson's dignified reception at the coronation of England's King George V on 22 June, since it suggested a kind of racial reversal that flew in the face of Jim Crow etiquette. "Jack is the London star, as a coronation visitor," Russell boasted. "Foreign royalties, Indian potentates and Colonial premiers and white folks from America are all completely overshadowed."[20] With a satirical touch he maintained, "The anxiety of a meeting between the two noble rulers rests alone with the King as everybody else is blissfully assured that Jack will be able to share in the enjoyment of the 'Man Higher Up,' as Booker T. Washington was to learn of the condition of the 'Man Farthest Down.'" Black Chicagoans reportedly feared that their great fighter would move to London for good, joining a group of "colored actors" that had already "settled down in amalgamation row never to return to America." Following the coronation festivities Johnson became a sellout sensation in London's music halls as he performed boxing routines and musical numbers in front of adoring crowds of British spectators. Moreover, other African American journalists touted the upcoming London meeting of the Universal Races Congress in July as an important step toward better relations between the different peoples of the world.[21] It seemed as if England was the place to be.

From the safety of London Johnson made an effort to publicly embarrass white America and set about courting the support of sympathetic British fans. An Irish correspondent interviewed him at Oxford Music Hall on U.S. Independence Day, exactly one year after his triumph over Jeffries. Johnson took this opportunity to protest the continued oppression of black people in the United States. "I never celebrate for America," declared Johnson, who also asked, "What has America done for me? Has it ever given me a square deal? Did it give me a shout when I won? Not on your life. Say son, I've given up thinking about America."[22] Johnson even maintained that if an international war ever broke out he would "never shoulder a musket for America," but would gladly fight for Britain. When the Irish reporter asked if he planned to return to the United States, Johnson replied, "Not until I am forced to, and then I'm coming back as quickly as I can. It is such a fine country—England." At a time when many African Americans viewed military service as an important marker of full citizenship, Johnson's assertions conveyed a particularly scathing critique of both the conventional wisdom of black uplift and the reality of U.S. democracy.

Yet Johnson's declaration of English citizenship through military endeavor was not without its own set of problems. The most recent British military invasion was a grab for imperial territory against the Boers of South Africa, and the English also maintained a standing army in India to ensure the efficient exploitation of their "crown jewel." Johnson's bold vision of himself as a wronged U.S. citizen who could simply shift his allegiance from the Stars and Stripes to the Union Jack seemed to have clouded his ability to see the deep-seated relationship between Jim Crow racism and the mechanisms of European imperialism. Throughout his time in Britain Johnson vacillated between optimism and despair, at times believing U.S. racial politics were exceptional and at other times recognizing they were simply one part of a global system of white supremacy.

Johnson's many public endorsements of British racial tolerance provoked white American discussions about the appropriate treatment of black people. Instead of interpreting Britain's embrace of Johnson as a challenge to U.S. racial mores, many white Americans viewed it with a sarcastic sense of humor. England's decision to include the black champion in the coronation ceremonies had apparently given Johnson an inflated sense of himself. *New York Evening World* cartoonist Robert Edgren poked fun at the black champion's pretentious "Anglo-mania," claiming that Johnson had wasted thousands of dollars on gaudy costumes for the coronation.[23] An editorialist for the *Washington Post* complained, "It would seem as though the vast array of dusky princes drawn from the wide suzerainty of the British Empire to witness the gorgeous pageantry of the coronation, should have been enough to satisfy the British pride without its capturing our own swarthy champion of champions."[24] Britain had let its own hubris get in the way of racial common sense.

There seemed to be an ocean of difference between U.S. and British racial customs. During his own tour of Europe in 1911, Jim Jeffries had also attended the coronation, and he had openly mocked England's apparent ignorance of appropriate racial conduct. Jeffries described his run-in with Johnson in a London pub named Romanos. As he recalled, "The Smoke came in with all his gold teeth shinin' and glimmerin' in the candle light." Greeted with affectionate cheers rather than sneers, Johnson seemed right at home in Romanos, and Jeffries concluded that "all niggers are white to them Englishmen."[25] Johnson had even tried to join Jeffries and the Virginia judge Walter Kelly at their table. "I was standing up at the time," the retired pugilist explained, "and as he looked my way, I had the pleasure of turning my American back to him." "The 'Smoke' knew what that meant," Jeffries bragged; "he did not linger one little moment."

Undeterred by Jeffries's snub, Johnson continued to use the transnational reach of the press to broadcast his grievances with white America. As the *Washington Post* reported, "He has spoken in no uncertain terms. The glories of America have faded before the wonders of England. . . . A careful study of England's political form of government, her social system, and her general resources and opportunities, has led to the conviction that a man of his caliber may go far in such a country."[26] Johnson's positive assessment of Britain directly contradicted the main conclusions of Washington's "Man Farthest Down." His vocal rejection of the United States inspired much criticism in the white American dailies. "We submit Mr. Johnson's defection as a proof of the blessings of reciprocity," the *Post* joked. "In letting him go so ungrudgingly we demonstrate to the full our sincerity in advocating the free and unhindered exchange of the best our country can produce. That we should get a duke or two in return may seem something, but it makes small amends for the loss of that golden smile."

Despite these attempts to discount the significance of Johnson's British welcome, black Americans continued to ponder the possibilities for greater inclusion and success abroad. Conflicting feelings of hope and disillusionment about Europe as a space for African Americans flowed throughout the black press. After participating in the Universal Races Congress, William Sanders Scarborough, the African American president of Wilberforce University, decided to vacation in Europe. "I have not seen in any instance any evidence of prejudice," he wrote from Germany. "The burning of the Negro in Pennsylvania is vigorously denounced here as is the malicious shooting of the Negro in South Africa."[27] Scarborough claimed that the only prejudice he and his wife had encountered came from the "cursed" white American tourists.

That same summer Mark A. Luescher, a promoter of black American entertainers, had spent five weeks in Europe arranging bookings for a musical comedy. "For years Americans have observed that the colored man in England and on the Continent was often received in good society," Luescher explained. "In the fashionable cafes and hotels one might see a black prize-fighter or vaudeville performer seated at the same table with white patrons."[28] To Luescher's great surprise, he had found new plays featuring black heroes in several European theaters. He maintained that the black man was now "receiving unusual attention" in Germany, where "the police had to be stationed near a certain theater to keep white girls away from the stage door." Yet he also tempered this heartening discovery with other disturbing trends. Luescher claimed that "the colored man" was no longer "being lionized in England as much as formerly."

A racist incident involving twenty African American grooms at the prestigious Royal Ascot horse race in June 1911 appeared to confirm Luescher's observation about the decline of English tolerance. When the U.S. racing team arrived several days early, the tournament officials had to scramble to secure temporary accommodations for the men.

While the white American riders had no difficulty finding places to stay, the fate of their black grooms was another story. Originally all of the grooms were to be housed at the Olympia Exhibition Building. However, when English officials discovered that they were black, a vociferous protest ensued and they were shunted to a nearby riding academy. As one African American editorialist declared, this hostile treatment signaled "the spread of race feeling against the Negro," and he emphasized that black people had become "the object of race hatred both far and near."[29] It no longer seemed to matter "what station in life a Negro may hold, how respectable and law abiding he may be or what fortune he may have amassed," since he was "never beyond the veil of racial discrimination." "In the south or in the north, in America or abroad it is ever the same," the writer maintained. "He is made to feel the ever present racial persecution which it seems is getting stronger and stronger with each succeeding day, and is beginning to assume world wide proportions." The European travels of black sportsmen provided some of the formative moments in which African Americans began to see the transnational reach of the color line. The growing tide of white Anglo-Saxonism was beginning to dampen their Atlantic dreams.

WHITE ANGLO-SAXON HOPES

Even with all of the celebration surrounding Johnson's arrival in London and his grand entrance at the coronation, English boxing fans had never given up on their own search for a white hope. Ever since the renowned U.S. novelist Jack London coined the expression "white hope" in the wake of Johnson's 1908 defeat of Tommy Burns, the public frenzy to dethrone the black heavyweight had taken on a life of its own. Johnson remained undefeated, making a public mockery of the white supremacist theories of social Darwinism and eugenics. "Are things what they seem? Is the Caucasian played out? Where is the white man who will take the conceit out of the big Negro Jack Johnson?" a correspondent for the New York's *Morning Telegram* lamented. "It seems as if this gross dark throwback stood invincible in the prize ring and defied the world to find a white man who can whip him."[30] Given the abysmal state of Johnson's white challengers, some African American sportswriters boasted that the quest for a white hope would soon be abandoned.[31] Yet their prophesies of white resignation never came true. Boxing promoters managed to transform London's original call for a white hope into a veritable industry with products and publicity that flowed across national borders.

By the summer of 1911 Bombardier Billy Wells had emerged as Britain's main contender for the heavyweight crown. Wells seemed to be the perfect man to conquer the black champion, for he embodied a mixture of Anglo-Saxon civilization and physical vitality. He was anything but a stereotypical professional boxer. Minus the crooked nose, facial scars, and missing teeth characteristic of his contemporaries, Wells was "perhaps the handsomest pugilist of the day."[32] Tall and slim, he resembled an English fiction hero with his skin "as white, as silky, and as glistening as ever."[33]

Regardless of these elegant descriptions, Wells's biography was very similar to that of other British pugs. Born and raised in a working-class neighborhood of London's East End, Wells learned to box in his spare time at local boys clubs and missions. At eighteen he joined the Royal Artillery and served in India. After Wells won the army's boxing championship, metropolitan promoters lured him back to England with the promise of pugilistic stardom. Wells himself believed it was his responsibility to come forward and fight Johnson. As he told *Boxing*, "I seemed to feel the strength creep in upon me; my veins tingled and my heart glowed with a wonderful pride at the thought that I, a British soldier—I, Bombardier Billy Wells—had been selected as the White Hope."[34] Some English sportsmen criticized the twenty-four-year-old novice for putting his, and therefore the race's, reputation on the line against the much stronger and more experienced African American fighter.[35] U.S. boxing writers characterized Wells as a second-rate fighter with little likelihood of winning against Johnson.

Nevertheless, the match promoter James White and British sports editors believed that Wells was a white hope candidate with whom English men and Anglo-Saxons in general could relate. With his military record and dashing looks, Wells would not only fill the stands at Empress Hall in the Earl's Court amusement park, but he would also make brisk business for postfight publications and the fight film. Who better than a former colonial serviceman to put the unruly black champion back in his proper place of subservience? This was a narrative that would surely resonate with the concerns of white men throughout the British Empire and the United States.

Writing in 1947, the British author Oswald Frederick Snelling looked back on the so-called white hope crisis of the 1910s through the lens of Nazism, pointing to an important link between the racial logics of

JACK JOHNSON, World's Champion.   Bombardier WELLS, Champion of Great Britain.

FIGURE 8. Framed as a contest between a former colonial serviceman and an unruly black braggart, the Wells-Johnson match resonated with the concerns of white men throughout the British Empire and the United States. Jack Johnson and Bombardier Billy Wells, *Boxing* supplement, 1911. From the author's collection.

imperialism and fascism. For Snelling, London's famous phrase embodied the competitive racisms of the 1930s and '40s: "Today he would be labelled Fascist, and it is almost certain that he would have fanatically followed the doctrines of Adolf Hitler had he lived in these days."[36] Although this comparison may seem particular to the post–World War II reflection on the atrocities of the Holocaust, a closer reading of the white hope crisis as an interimperial discourse on whiteness, manhood, and the body reveals the sharpness of Snelling's critique. The biological analogies of citizenship and the nation honed under Nazi rule had already begun to permeate the mass culture of late imperialism. By Johnson's day the physical fitness of the white male body had become an integral part of the prevailing myths of Western social and political superiority. The expansion of commercialized spectator sports such as boxing was helping to enlist white men—across ethnic and class lines and even across oceans—in the maintenance of Anglo-Saxon geopolitical power.

Boxing promoters capitalized on widespread white anxieties about physical degeneration and racial instability to advertise events and products and to maximize profits. Magazines like *Boxing* publicized white hope matches to sell copies, while sporting equipment companies like Spalding advertised their wares to fans at white hope elimination tournaments.[37] With circulations that stretched throughout Britain and its empire, Europe, and the United States, the London-based *Boxing* and its sister publication *Health & Strength* were particularly important in keeping white readers abreast of the imagined crisis. Boxing culture was helping to inspire a sense of Anglo-American rapprochement and interimperial cooperation that spread beyond the realm of government policy makers and officials.[38]

The search for a white hope had taken on new dimensions and a new sense of urgency in the wake of Johnson's triumph over Jeffries in 1910. Regardless of their nations' competition for preeminence in the global arena, in the ring white Americans and Britons began to recognize their mutual interests in the preservation of white supremacy. Echoing calls from across the Atlantic, *Health & Strength* columnist Yorick Gradeley declared, "The fact of the matter is, we're all anxious to find a champion; we don't care whether he's an Englishman or an American or what he is, so long as he's one of our race."[39]

The Australian impresario Hugh McIntosh saw his chance to market these racial fears in the heart of the British Empire. In August 1910 he announced his upcoming trip to London to arrange a full-fledged white hope campaign similar to the one ongoing in athletic clubs throughout the United States.[40] His original scheme involved erecting a pavilion in Earl's Court that would hold fight crowds of up to twelve thousand. He even banked on attracting white American fans to his London location, predicting that the puritanical blue crusades sweeping the United States would eventually outlaw professional prizefighting. With this gap in the U.S. market, McIntosh would develop London as the premier place for championship boxing and the center of the quest for a white hope.[41]

By the fall of 1910 McIntosh's grand vision seemed to be materializing as he staged "The Search for a White Champion," a series of qualifying tournaments for the British imperial heavyweight title.[42] Promoters in different parts of the world also began organizing their own local crusades. In January 1911 a troupe of U.S. boxers visiting Australasia reportedly inspired a white hope craze in the southern hemisphere.[43] From his home country of Canada, Tommy Burns tried his hand at promoting a white hope match in Calgary, Alberta, a prizefight that unfortunately ended in tragedy when the up-and-coming U.S. boxer Luther McCarty died from a blow to the head.[44] Although French fans remained far less passionate about the campaign than their Anglo-Saxon counterparts, even Parisian boxing managers began calling their heavyweights *"des espoirs blancs"* (white hopes).[45]

Despite the breadth and intensity of the hunt for a white hope, there was none to be found. Yet the historical significance of this phenomenon lies less in its pugilistic outcome than in its ability to inspire ordinary men to imagine themselves as agents in the white man's burden. White working-class men in the cities were the primary consumers of white hope fight tickets and paraphernalia. White hope matches were also imbricated in the larger world of working-class amusements, for they regularly shared the stage with blackface minstrels and physical culturists. It is hardly surprising, then, that after the Jeffries-Johnson fight some of the most violent racial attacks on African Americans occurred in white immigrant neighborhoods.[46]

Even the majority of the white hopes themselves were working-class men of immigrant backgrounds whose own claims to an Anglo-Saxon heritage were questionable. They included the likes of Carl Morris, an awkward six foot six engine driver of Irish and Native American extraction from Sapulpa, Oklahoma. Morris's popularity was fleeting as boxing fans abandoned him after his pitiful loss against another white hope named "Fireman" Jim Flynn. Born Andrew Chiariglione in Brooklyn, New York, Flynn moved to Pueblo, Colorado, where he developed his strength in the local fire brigade and later adopted an Irish boxing name.[47] The most prominent English hopes were the foot soldiers of empire, including Wells and Gunner Jim Moir, while in the southern hemisphere Australia touted Bill Lang, a man of French-Italian descent whose real name was William Langfranchi.[48] The diversity of this white hope contingent not only signaled but also helped to inspire an expanding sense of whiteness that defied ethnic, national, and class divisions.

Nevertheless, white hope elimination matches were not always successful ventures. Sports fans were not necessarily interested in paying to see white-on-white conflict, especially if the men involved were mediocre fighters. In 1911 several white hope tournaments in New York City, plagued with organizational difficulties and poor attendance, proved anticlimactic from both boxing and business standpoints. Scheduled fighters sometimes failed to show up. Even the matches that came to fruition were often lackadaisical or one-sided. Moreover, the very phrase "white hope" became so ubiquitous that it became meaningless, as managers used it indiscriminately to describe any second-rate heavyweights they represented.[49] Many boxing connoisseurs argued that the white hope crisis had placed undue focus on the heavyweight division, thereby ruining the quality of professional boxing.

Ultimately it was the promise of interracial competition and the vanquishing of the black champion that proved to be the driving force behind the profitability of the white hope phenomenon. In addition to his most famous fight with Jeffries, Johnson's matches against Stanley Ketchell (Stanislaw Kiecal) in 1909 and "Fireman" Jim Flynn in 1912, along with their moving pictures, were huge box office successes.[50] Johnson constantly played on the white public's anxious desire to test the relative strength of the races. In order to debunk the myth that black men had weak midsections, he once dared the famed British boxing writer Trevor Wignall to punch his stomach. As Wignall would later report, contrary to popular belief, striking Johnson's abdomen "was like hitting a piece of corrugated iron."[51] Despite Johnson's prowess, white boxing fans stuck to their hope that a white challenger would reinstate their racial supremacy in the ring.

McIntosh recognized this dynamic and geared his other promotions accordingly. To cash in on Johnson's infamy he planned to pay the African American champion a whopping sum of $90,000 for a barnstorming tour across the Pacific. McIntosh and Johnson eventually settled on the fall of 1911 as the proposed start of the tour, with tentative stops in India, the Straits Settlements (Malaysia), China, Japan, Australia, Fiji, Hawaii, and British Columbia, Canada.[52] McIntosh reportedly planned to make Johnson the backbone of his boxing trust. His grand idea was to contract Johnson and other major fighters, including both African Americans (Sam McVea and Sam Langford) and white hope challengers (Al Palzer and Dan "Porky" Flynn), to be part of his traveling show.[53] In this way McIntosh could corner a more promising segment of the market, taking advantage of the white hope craze while also capitalizing on Johnson's great popularity among people of color.

However, as profit motives clashed with imperial politics, interracial prizefights were not without potentially far-reaching consequences. In light of this, McIntosh devised a clever plan for calming British imperial officials' possible fears of native unrest. "Should the English authorities object to his boxing in India, Johnson is willing to become a lecturer and propagandist on the dominance of the white race," a report on the barnstorming tour explained. "He has already made plans for a series of lectures in which he will tell the colored races that white rule, particularly English, is beneficent. He proposes to detail his own treatment in England, which he says is the freest and most just country on earth."[54] Although Johnson never would have agreed to deliver a lecture on white supremacy, given his respect for Britain he may have consented to speak on behalf of British rule. If all went smoothly the black heavyweight's tour would benefit both McIntosh's pocketbook and Britain's reputation as a benevolent power.

In spite of its racist goals, the white hope crisis actually broadened the geographic horizons of African American boxers such as Johnson. Although McIntosh's Pacific tour never came to fruition, this transnational market for interracial spectacles provided black American pugilists with a ready source of income and opportunities abroad, even as Jim Crow segregation reached its height back home. Yet these opportunities were double-edged. Even though Johnson had become a vocal advocate of British racial tolerance, as the controversy over his match with Wells intensified he soon found that there was no real place for him in their white body politic. An African American sportswriter warned, "I am very much afraid that prejudice will come up a bit in England. Even that fairly fair country does not care to have a black-a-moor putting it over Englishmen. . . . I may be mistaken in this but we shall see what we shall see."[55]

RAPPROCHEMENT IN THE RING

To escape the growing commotion over his upcoming match with Wells in London, Johnson traveled to Paris for his training camp in late August 1911. White American and British observers were quick to criticize Johnson's obvious sense of entitlement in the French republic. In Paris Johnson apparently could live like a king, and he made every effort to make this public knowledge. William A. Nash, the president of the Corn Exchange Bank of New York, was in the midst of a European holiday when Johnson arrived in Paris. He went to see Johnson train at Magic City, a popular amusement park much like Coney Island. Nash recounted, "Johnson, who has been here only a few days, is attracting general attention, especially by his luxurious style of life. He arrived with a retinue of trainers and friends in four big automobiles and took a fine apartment at the Grand Hotel, where he entertains daily a host of admirers."[56] By late September Johnson and his white wife, Etta Duryea, had moved into a little chateau at the end of Boulevard Victor Hugo in the Parisian suburb of Neuilly. As one British correspondent described, "Here 'Jack' and Mrs. Johnson live, surrounded by companions, attendants, and servants, who compose the little 'court' of the negro boxing monarch, who, although quite a good-natured person seems to realise his importance and likes to be surrounded by white people."[57]

Regardless of Johnson's efforts to cultivate a regal persona, white American and British sports fans still cast him as a misguided minstrel who had forgotten his place. They assumed that the black heavyweight had chosen the City of Light because of its reputation for fetes, feasting, fashion, and freedom from discipline. London's *Boxing World and Athletic Chronicle* included a grinning caricature of Johnson smoking a cigar in Paris while dressed in a garish getup complete with a top hat, tails, and sparkling jewels.[58] Other British cartoons and articles described Johnson doing everything that went against the accepted ideals of physical culture and respectability, from gorging on chicken to avoiding training.[59] The white American dailies also turned their scrutiny on Johnson's Parisian hosts. They mocked the unusual French adoration of black boxers, suggesting that the overcivilized and effeminate Frenchmen were failing to uphold their end of the white man's burden.[60]

As Johnson continued with his training in Paris, the public backlash against his scheduled showdown at Earl's Court became even more expansive and impassioned. Reverend F. B. Meyer emerged as the representative "face" of the British crusade against the interracial fight. Born in London in 1847, Meyer was not just an outspoken pastor but also an adventurous globetrotter and a progressive reformer. Since the 1890s he had traveled throughout North America, East Asia, Europe, the Middle East, North and South Africa, and Australia.[61] As a reformer Meyer had first made his mark in the physical culture scene in April 1908, when he penned a manifesto for *Health & Strength* that called for a collective fight against white degeneration.[62] With his worldwide outlook and his concern for the well-being of white bodies, Meyer was the perfect man to spearhead the campaign.

On September 16 the *Times* printed a letter of protest signed by Reverend Meyer and Charles Brown of the National Free Church Council.[63] This letter ignited a firestorm of opposition to the prizefight that spread beyond the British Isles. Meyer and Brown called the Wells-Johnson match a brutal spectacle and urged all nonconformist clergy to dedicate Sunday's service to calling for its cancellation. In response to this public tirade, the promoter James White tried to reassure Meyer that the prizefight would be run in the most civilized manner, with three referees to enforce the Queensberry rules. White also promised that a board would review and edit the fight film before releasing it to the public. Even with these concessions Meyer refused to call off his campaign against the interracial bout.[64]

Instead he catapulted the protest into the realm of politics. Meyer asked the London City Council (LCC) to intervene in the situation. While the LCC did not have any direct authority to ban the match, it warned the owners of Earl's Court that they would jeopardize their license renewal if the interracial fight went on as planned. Speaking in defense of the match, the press manager at Earl's Court argued that the LCC's threat was simply unwarranted because Britain had a long history of tolerance for interracial bouts. Earlier in the year the African American Sam Langford had fought against Bill Lang at London's Olympia without any objections from the public.[65]

Undaunted, Meyer swiftly organized a petition signed by prominent clergymen that called upon Home Secretary Winston Churchill, who was then with King George at Balmoral Castle in Scotland, to stop the fight.[66] Feeling a sense of urgency, Meyer offered to travel north to deliver the petition personally. The home secretary, however, advised him to remain in London, assuring him that the matter was receiving the "closest attention."[67] Adding the support of the Anglican Church to Meyer's cause, the archbishop of Canterbury, Randall Cantuar, also advised Churchill that the match was "really a Home Office matter" since it would diminish Britain's reputation not only among its own citizens and subjects but also "in the eyes of other nations."[68] The crusade continued to gain momentum as the bishops of London, Oxford, Ripon, Rochester, Bristol, Manchester, Wakefield, Lichfield, Durham, and Truro; the headmasters of Rugby, Dulwich, Mill Hill, and Taunton schools; several members of Parliament; the Lord Mayors of London,

Manchester, Liverpool, Newcastle, Bristol, Nottingham, Portsmouth, and Hull; Lord Kinnaird (president of the Football Association); Lord Lonsdale (president of the National Sporting Club); Sir Robert Baden-Powell (founder of the Boy Scouts); and even the famous physical culturist Eugen Sandow all publicly denounced the match.[69]

The belief that race mixing in the boxing ring threatened to blur the line between white and nonwhite both locally and globally animated most of the resistance to the upcoming match. The fight's fiercest opponents argued that racial disturbances around the world had become increasingly interconnected as the rise of commercial media overrode the traditional buffers of geographic separation. "'Colour feeling' it is true, is still largely unknown in the British Isles, but it has already shown signs of unexpected growth," an English journalist maintained. "What is done at Earl's Court is not in any case to be done for Earl's Court alone. It will inevitably be spread by the Press and will have its effect on every community in which black and white live side by side."[70] The Wells-Johnson match became the focal point of a transnational debate about the boundaries of race, manhood, and citizenship in the modern era.

Even though Britain had a long tradition of hosting interracial prizefights, the stakes now seemed much higher. "The relations between white and black have undergone a vast change in the last century," a *Times* editorialist observed. "We have assumed throughout the Empire great and unparalleled responsibilities."[71] All across the newly formed Union of South Africa, newspaper editors and clergymen jumped on the bandwagon of metropolitan protest. The Wells-Johnson controversy inspired special concern in South Africa since its white minority population feared racial upheaval on a daily basis. The timing of the match also dovetailed with the ongoing racial reconciliation between Britons and Boers, as white settlers worked to exclude colored subjects from social, political, and economic rights. Cape Town's *South African News* called for the Union government to ban the importation of the fight film, while prominent leaders like the moderator of the Dutch Reformed Church pressed for the prohibition of *all* newspaper descriptions and illustrations of the fight.[72] Soon the *Mail* and the *Star* of Johannesburg, the *Bloemfontein Friend,* the *Cape Argus,* the *Cape Times,* and the *Pietermaritzburg Witness* joined the fray.[73] Following South Africa's lead, colonial officials in Uganda and Nigeria came out in support of the ban. A *Times* correspondent expressed, "There can be no doubt that in this part of British West Africa, and in such places as Sierra Leone and Cape Coast [Ghana], the news flashed over the wires that a physical struggle between a white man and a black man, attended by thousands of spectators, has been waged in the capital of the Empire, would have a thoroughly mischievous effect—especially if the black man won."[74] The British liberal concept of imperial citizenship marked by civilization, rather than color, seemed inapplicable, if not naïve, in this case.

This nervous recognition of the transnational reach and racial symbolism of the Wells-Johnson match also fostered a sense of Anglo-American solidarity. The white American dailies weighed in on the domestic implications of the foreign fight. "As a contest between a white man and a negro, the controversy has especial interest for America," a *New York Times* correspondent contended.[75] Many British commentators concurred, expressing their concern about the interracial prizefight's potential effects in the United States. As Reverend J. H. Shakespeare of the British Baptist Union predicted, "White and black will be pitted against each other in anger, revenge and murder, especially in lands like America in which the negro is the gravest of all problems."[76] Reverend Moffat Gautrey, the president of the Brotherhood Conference, worried that the match would actually damage Anglo-American relations. "What will the best of the American States say of Britain when they read the telegraphic accounts of the fight?" Gautrey asked. "How London can permit such a degradation amazes me."[77] White sentiments throughout the United States and the British Empire were beginning to align on the question of interracial competition in the boxing ring.

As the *Cape Times* stressed, interimperial cooperation was absolutely essential, for "localisation was no longer possible." Modern technology now had the power to disseminate "long accounts of such purely physical and often brutalising displays to every quarter of the globe."[78] Since both the threat and the use of physical force were still central to the maintenance of imperial order, they understood the degree to which such a fight would undercut white authority. The *Cape Times* warned that it would lead to the "grave danger of establishing in the native mind a vague theory of a physical force standard as between the two races." As a graphic transgression of the basic physical mores of imperial governance, the Wells-Johnson match jeopardized the colonies' delicate balance of power. "In the past the white man has been taught that it is degrading to maltreat a black; a coloured man that it is a heinous offence to attack a white," one British reporter declared. "The fact that the capital of the Empire sees no harm in such a contest as is now proposed must go far towards shattering this doctrine."[79]

Within this gendered discourse of power, white male physical and political control became inextricably linked with the sexual ownership of white women. For many of South Africa's social commentators, interracial mixing in the boxing ring would provide a dangerous pretext for interracial mixing in the bedroom. This was particularly disturbing since native African houseboys often lived and worked without male supervision in close proximity with the wives of white settlers.[80] The Wells-Johnson match seemed indicative of the ultimate breakdown of the color line—an affront to both the prerogatives of white men and the propriety of white women. This controversy had exploded in the midst of heated discussions over the so-called Black Peril. Widespread fears of native African men raping white women paralleled the U.S. hysteria about interracial sex, of which Johnson, with his many high-profile relationships with white women, was a prime target.[81] A South African editorialist claimed that the rape of white females by black men now seemed to "recur constantly." "The animus of the people will be kindled and the 'Lynch Law' applied," he warned. "I shall not be surprised to hear one of these days that an Association has been formed, with branches over the whole of South Africa, to see that such crimes be severely punished."[82] Fears of the Black Peril were inspiring in South Africa white vigilantism similar to that of the United States' Ku Klux Klan.

Given this social context, it was not a stretch to argue that if black men beat white men in the ring they would feel entitled to ravish white women in the bedroom. The decision to hold the Wells-Johnson contest in London had apparently "startled" white colonial settlers because of the "license freely granted to the black man, in all innocence, by white men and women."[83] Many white South Africans believed that British officials simply did not grasp the gravity of the Black Peril. The high commissioner of Rhodesia, Lord Herbert Gladstone, had recently commuted the death sentence of a native African servant accused of raping a white woman, inspiring protests across southern Africa.[84] As one editorialist declared, "We do not say the coloured man should be shunned as though he were a pestilence; we do say that his place is not amongst a family of comely, cheerful English girls."[85] He called for the barring of this "abhorrent" and "demoralising" exhibition, along with its film. "There should be no hesitation in this matter, no playing with fire in the midst of powder barrels," he cautioned. "We cannot afford to graft another branch on the 'Black Peril' tree."

Many of the antiprizefight activists claimed that the Wells-Johnson match was symptomatic of a broader trend of Western decline and a return to barbarism. They believed the interracial fight would have a detrimental effect on imperial management and also worried that it would allow the brutishness of the colonies—their violence, despotism, heathenism, and interracial mixing—to permeate the urban spaces of the metropole. In a fiery sermon at Regent's Park Chapel, Reverend Meyer drew a doomsday parallel between Britain's future and the fall of ancient Rome. He argued that the Romans were a "dissolute, money-loving race, from whom all the strength of their old nobility had gone."[86] The rich had monopolized Rome's resources, leaving the poor to live in crowded slums. Consequently, Roman rulers had to assuage popular discontent with the exhibition of gruesome gladiatorial contests that played to people's baser instincts. Meyer argued that interracial boxing matches functioned in much the same way for Britain's poor and working class. "The reason men like to see blacks fighting whites is because the black men fight so passionately," he maintained. "It introduces the element of animalism which you do not see in the case of two white boxers."[87] In Meyer's view, this kind of perverse miscegenation in the ring was a metaphor for Britain's descent into degradation.

Ironically, the English sportsmen who supported the Wells-Johnson match used many of the same arguments to bolster their case. The one thing that both sides seemed to agree on was the vulnerability of white control in the modern age and the need for collective vigilance. In an open letter to Meyer the editor of *Health & Strength* claimed that the banning of the interracial fight would provide the clearest sign of British decadence. He and many other physical culturists believed that economic prosperity and urban industrial life had caused in English society a breakdown that could be diagnosed through the declining bodies of its white citizens. Calling boxing a "social regenerator," the editor accused Meyer of "retarding the physical development of the race." "Abolish boxing," he wrote, "and you abolish the greatest of all man-making games."[88] Running away from this boxing challenge would dangerously debase white manhood in the eyes of people of color. As the editor of *Boxing* charged, Meyer and the other protesters were, in effect, tacitly admitting that white pugilists were scared to put the matter of racial supremacy to the test—an action that would have perilous consequences in South Africa, India, and beyond.[89]

Fearing the potential fallout of the Wells-Johnson fiasco, British commentators on both sides of the issue had begun to sound a lot like their white American counterparts. From his training camp in Paris Johnson realized that the door was closing on his match. Sick of being bad-mouthed in the British press, he told reporters, "It's just this, you don't want me to win, and that's the truth . . . but I am going to win."[90] Try as he might, Johnson could never really separate himself from the imperial context in which he fought.

JACK JOHNSON VERSUS JOHN BULL

These heated debates about the fate of the match exposed the tenuous position of African Americans in Europe. One black sportswriter exclaimed, "For the love of Mike, tell us, please what they are trying to do to our big black fighting champion over in England. Where he stood absolutely solid a month ago, today he has no standing at all."[91] Even when faced with stories of Johnson's difficulties, some black Americans refused to give up on their faith in English civilization. They could not fathom that "color" had anything to do with the British backlash against the match. Instead they blamed the "sensational-craving daily papers" of the United States for spreading lies to make it appear as if "other countries" were "equally guilty" of racial prejudice.[92] Still others chose to lay the blame at Johnson's feet. One sportswriter mused, "Was it Jack Johnson's pompous ways in England and the flashiness the colored champion displayed with his white wife that caused such a reversal of feeling in the land of King George?" It seemed as if Johnson's inappropriate conduct had "suddenly changed" things, since England had always been "a paradise for colored boxers."[93] Yet none of these interpretations adequately explained the great lengths that British clergymen and government officials went to cancel the interracial match.

A few weeks before the Wells-Johnson fight the British Home Office considered using the black heavyweight's precarious status—he was neither a first-class citizen of the United States nor a British subject—to stop the match. Although Johnson had seriously contemplated becoming a British citizen, government officials were not about to welcome him into the fold. In a Home Office report prepared by the barrister Sir John Simon, he considered England's right to deny Johnson reentry. "An alien who is so prevented from entering this country . . . can take no legal proceedings against the Government," Simon argued, continuing, "An American citizen like Johnson who is prevented from landing can only have recourse to his own Government and ask them to exercise diplomatic pressure."[94] Given white America's collective disgust for Johnson coupled with the unlikelihood of the U.S. government coming to a black man's defense, Simon realized the heavyweight would be left with no options. While optimistically seeking alternatives to U.S. citizenship, Johnson found himself abandoned, with little political leverage, in Britain.

Despite Sir Simon's clever suggestion, Home Secretary Churchill chose not to bar Johnson's entry for the time being, and on 23 September the black heavyweight returned to England to set up his training camp in north London's Epping Forest. Much to the disgust of Meyer and other opponents of the Wells-Johnson fight, the public controversy had driven ticket sales through the roof. With just a little more than a week before the scheduled match, the ten-thousand-seat Empress Hall was completely sold out.[95] The Barker Motion Picture Company had purchased the rights to the prizefight film for $100,000, and the flood of requests for it had already far exceeded the company's expectations.[96]

Johnson was now singing a very different tune about English racial tolerance. He turned against the Britain that he had praised so highly just months before, juxtaposing its racist hypocrisy with his recent Parisian welcome. "I am going on with my training expecting the fight to come off. We have signed to box under National Sporting Club rules and if they stop this fight, England cannot claim again she is the nation that allows fair play," Johnson declared.[97] Countering reports that he was just money-hungry, he contended, "Well, I'm just doing my work, and can any man be blamed for getting the best price he can?" Playing on the imperial rivalries of the day, Johnson warned that if Britain banned the fight the promoter would simply move it to the "fair country" of France.

The day after Johnson's return to London the protest against the prizefight finally came to a head. With public pressure mounting, the Home Office deemed the match illegal, declaring it a breach of the peace and counter to the best interests of the nation and empire. On 25 September the Variety Theatres Control Association added insult to injury by applying for an injunction to prevent the match, claiming that Johnson was already contracted to perform for them on 2 October. A few days later the freeholders of Earl's Court (Metropolitan District Railway Company) filed their own injunction to prohibit the lessees of their property (Earl's Court Company) from hosting the contest.[98] With the Home Office's outlawing of the fight, the director of public prosecutions then summoned Johnson and Wells, their managers, and the promoter White to the Bow Street Police Court to defend their actions. The Wells-Johnson match had managed to provoke the biggest test case on boxing on English record.[99]

The Bow Street case against the Wells-Johnson fight became a sensation in the British press. By 2 PM on 28 September "there were fully a thousand people" waiting for the principals to arrive at the trial.[100] Rather than hiring a solicitor, Johnson chose to speak for himself in court. He engaged the Crown's witness, Police Superintendent Duncan McIntyre, in an intense cross-examination. He showcased not only his own mental acuity but also McIntyre's embarrassing ignorance of professional boxing. Johnson objected to McIntyre's reliance on a book of newspaper clippings to answer his questions. "The witness does not know what he is talking about," Johnson declared. "If he only goes by the book his evidence is very thin."[101] Johnson even managed to get McIntyre to admit that he had never actually seen a boxing match. "You have no idea what they are?" Johnson questioned. "No," McIntyre confessed. By the time Johnson reemerged from the courthouse, the crowd had grown even bigger. "Spectators surged round the door and broke through the police cordon," making it difficult for him to leave the scene.[102]

That same day the freeholders of Earl's Court obtained their injunction from England's High Court, thereby preventing their lessees from staging the fight. The judge had upheld the freeholders' claim that the proposed match would go against the terms of the lease, which stated that all exhibitions "shall be of a high class and be conducted with due regard to the maintenance of order and shall be in no way contrary to decency or morality, and shall not endanger or in any way injuriously affect any of the licences in force for the premises."[103] Recognizing the futility of the situation, White agreed not to promote the contest in the British Isles or in any of Britain's domains and the Home Office dropped its legal proceedings.[104]

Now it was time for French sports fans to gloat, as they chided the British for their rigid, puritanical values. According to *Boxing* magazine's Parisian correspondent, many Frenchmen claimed that the English hysteria over the Wells-Johnson match provided the perfect justification for their own nation's "drastic action in disestablishing Church and State."[105] The various reasons against the interracial match

in England seemed to have no merit in France. Parisian boxing publisher and promoter Leon Sée scoffed, "Battle of the races? Fear of
riots between whites and blacks? There are not even 100 niggers in all
of France. To see an Englishman beaten? To us it's all the same, so long
as the best man wins."[106] Jacques Mortane of *La Vie au grand air* also
pointed to Johnson's citizenship dilemma, contending that the black
American's cold reception in England had convinced him to abandon
any thoughts of becoming British. If Johnson ever decided to attain
French citizenship, Mortane argued he could do so with ease.[107] As
French fans criticized the blatant racism of their Anglo-Saxon counterparts, they somehow managed to overlook the violence and exploitation of their own colonial endeavors.

Blind spot aside, French commentators were by no means the only
ones to level such a critique. After the cancellation of the Wells-Johnson
match, the black champion and the black American press also decried
the duplicity of British race relations. For them, the Home Office
ban highlighted the link between the racial oppression of African
Americans and that of British colonial subjects. This public outcry
coincided with African American discussions of European imperialism
at the turn of the century. With the rise of an organized Pan-African
movement beginning in London in 1900, concerned black scholars,
religious leaders, and activists from across the diaspora entered into
a dialogue on the worldwide race problem. These debates continued
through the developing black presses in the United States, Europe, the
Caribbean, and Africa.

Boxing provided the perfect forum for this expanding conversation
on race and imperialism, reaching well beyond the purview of black
intellectual and political elites. Johnson himself took a jab at the incon-
sistency of British policy, noting that their rhetoric of racial tolerance
was certainly not backed up with any real recognition of the rights
of nonwhite peoples. "You are funny people, you English," Johnson
scolded the readers of *Health & Strength*. "I cannot make you out at
all." Johnson used a humorous anecdote to poke fun at the arbitrary
nature of British "equality," noting the uneven benefits of so-called
British civilization:

> There were two missionary wives out there in Africa talking about their
> servants, as women always do when they get together. They both had black
> servants. . . . One of them had just engaged a maid from her husband's
> church—a "convert," they called her. "Oh, my dear," cried her friend, "I
> would never have a Christian servant on any account!" There's a lot of logic

in that, isn't there? If that missionary wife preferred the heathen to the convert, what was her husband drawing his salary for? But that's you English all over. You call the black man your brother; you say he is equal with you; that we're all one family. I must say you've got a queer way of showing your brotherly feelings.[108]

For Johnson, all this talk about interracial conflict was pure "bunkum." "We get it in the States; we're used to it there, but we did expect something different from England," he chided. The black champion was understandably bitter. Just as he was seeking out alternatives to life in Jim Crow America, British clergymen and government officials were instilling racial segregation in John Bull's boxing ring.

For many African American fans the prohibition of the Wells-Johnson match had shone a spotlight on Britain's central role in the preservation of the racial and imperial status quo. In an article titled "The Truth Out at Last," a writer for the *Cleveland Gazette* declared, "The plain fact was . . . that the spectacle of a Negro whipping a white man would give too much encouragement to the blacks of the English provinces [colonies], in several of which that country was and is having more or less trouble to keep them subjugated."[109] For Britain, banning the fight had become a basic matter of "self-preservation" since its "black belt stretched around the globe."[110]

An editorialist for the *New York Age* critiqued what he perceived as the "radical change of British public opinion on the race question within the last half century," a change that seemed to have coincided with their expansion into West and South Africa.[111] He viewed British Africa as a particularly rabid case of imperial exploitation that differed from their intervention in India. Although he acknowledged that British abuses of the Indian people had made the fear of colonial subversion ever present and the need for military occupation obligatory, Britain had never attempted to settle India. It now appeared as if the British policy of white settlement in Africa (and especially South Africa) was creating conditions of racial repression and segregation similar to those of the United States. "The natives are treated, for the most part, as aliens and are tolerated, under drastic restrictions, in the colonies or forced back into the interior," he explained.

The cynical protest against the interracial fight was really about race, power, land, and profit rather than about Christianity, morality, uplift, and civilization. One African American sportswriter charged, "Some who were eager to stop the prize fight in London are equally eager for dividends from South African investments where a far more degrading contest is going on involving the exploitation and debasement of millions of their fellow beings."[112] The writer predicted that the banning of interracial fights would spread across the Old World since most European countries had "holdings in Africa or a sphere of influence."

It was no longer possible to separate imperial politics from the tenor of metropolitan race relations because maintaining empires required that people of color remain a separate caste outside the benefits of Western democracy. This type of information would have been eye-opening for the many African Americans who imagined Britain as a civilized oasis, and for those who actively sought out opportunities for life and liberty across the Atlantic. As the *Age* editorialist emphasized, alongside the growth of British interests and the development of repressive policies in Africa, "prejudice against the blacks" had become "a national policy in the British Islands."[113]

He also viewed white American and British racism through the same lens, claiming that their policies betrayed the kind of imperial arrogance that had caused the fall of ancient Rome. He critiqued the overconfidence of Englishmen who boasted that "the sun never sets upon the British Empire." Comparing the Wells-Johnson controversy with the white American outcry against the Jeffries-Johnson fight film in 1910, he likewise contended that the United States had much to learn from Rome's tragic example. "'Render unto Caesar the things that are Caesar's' does not set well on white stomachs when Caesar happens to be black in the face," he maintained. "It proves that the white race has a big yellow streak in its nature; and moral cowardice is always associated with structural mental weakness." Rome's demise provided a glimpse of the Anglo-Saxon's troubled future.

Johnson's overseas travels and travails had brought the global color line into view for African American fans back home. "Poor, innocent Jack Johnson and his Reno have brought forth this world discussion, and perhaps for the better," one journalist declared.[114] The black champion's difficulties abroad seemed to confirm that it was best to "wage a universal war for the Negro's uplift, regardless of his whereabouts, with the thought in mind that the part will not transcend the whole." A year after the Wells-Johnson controversy a racial incident in the coastal town of Yarmouth, England, highlighted this interconnectedness. A group of white thugs attacked an unsuspecting black Jamaican man in the street as they shouted, "You dirty dog, Jack Johnson."[115] The status of African Americans was clearly tied to that of other Africans throughout the diaspora. As long as people of color anywhere continued to be deprived of their rights, there would be no real answer to the race question.

FROM COLOR LINE TO COLOUR BAR

Writing in the 1920s, Trevor Wignall reminisced, "It was Johnson's ill-fortune to transform a thin colour line into a colour bar that has become as wide as a continent."[116] Although Wignall's contention bordered on hyperbole, the Wells-Johnson case became a useful precedent invoked by the Home Office to ban many high-profile interracial matches in Britain. It also set the stage for the British Boxing Board of Control's decision to bar nonwhite men from British title fights until 1947.[117] Much like Jim Crow's color line, John Bull now had his own colour bar.

Since the racial boundaries of the boxing ring had become such a powerful metaphor for the boundaries of manhood and citizenship, they had to be policed. "There seemed to lurk a fear that the Negro all over the land would feel his ability to meet the white man on an equal footing," an African American writer later recalled of the Wells-Johnson controversy, "but no amount of suppression of what transpires on such occasions can stifle that inherent knowledge of manhood which every Negro knows is within him."[118] In subsequent years the British boxing magnate Lord Lonsdale wrote letters of protest to the Home Office, effectively thwarting two interracial matches involving the black American heavyweight Sam Langford. In 1913 Langford was scheduled to fight the German-American Frank Klaus in London. Even though Lonsdale admitted that the two boxers were "particularly well-conducted and respectable," he advised that it was still impossible "to overcome the fact that the competition [was] a 'coloured' one."[119] A year later Lonsdale took it upon himself to contact the Home Office regarding an upcoming match between Langford and the white American Gunboat Smith. Lonsdale once again admitted that Langford was a "straightforward and honest" man; however, he still warned that the interracial fight was likely "not in the interests of the Nation."[120] The Home Office agreed and told Lonsdale that he "would be doing a public service in getting the scheme dropped."[121] Not even respectable black men could scale the British boxing colour bar.

Commonplace ideas of social and political modernity remained tangled in a popular biology of race and the body that transcended

FIGURE 9. White sportswriters explained away the political significance of black ring success by tying black men's physical prowess to their alleged lack of civilization. "Snowy Baker's Search for an Aboriginal Hope," *Boxing*, 21 March 1914.

national and imperial borders. A British editorialist argued that *all* interracial fights should be banned because of the inherent physical differences between blacks and whites. As "neolithic" men, black boxers possessed thicker skulls and a "lower nervous organization," giving them an unfair advantage over their more refined and civilized white opponents.[122] It had been "scientifically and medically recognised that the higher a man's intellect the more he is sensitive to pain."[123] Such ideas were not limited to Britain, since many of them appeared in white American discussions of black athletes. White boxing fans explained away the political significance of African American ring success by tying black men's physical prowess to their alleged lack of modernity and, by extension, their unsuitability for self-government.

This discussion had even reached the fringes of the "civilized world" in Australia. Hugh McIntosh's assistant Reginald "Snowy" Baker gave *Boxing* a wry account of his search for an "Aboriginal Hope" in 1914. He outlined what many believed was the appropriate role for non-white men in the ring, assuring readers that Aboriginal pugilists were absolutely no threat to the racial order. "The Aboriginals aren't like the African negroes," Baker observed. "They're an entirely different race. They're full of humour, good-natured all the time, but they love a fight."[124] Mirroring contemporary discussions in the British metropole, Baker claimed that "Australian Aboriginals have the thickest skulls in the world. The African negro's skull is an egg-shell in comparison." "It's almost impossible to hurt an aboriginal with a blow," he added. "When they're fighting or being clubbed they laugh all the time." Baker's Aboriginals were the ideal men of color. They were physically gifted but mentally inferior, and they could withstand harsh physical punishment without complaining. Yet Baker's depiction revealed much more about white fears about the place of nonwhite men in the modern world than about the "true" nature of Aboriginals. His remarks exposed a nostalgic longing to return to the days before black men like Johnson dared to stand up against white men, whether in the ring, in the press, or in everyday life.

British subjects and black Americans continued to challenge these white racial fictions. An editorialist for the *African Times and Orient Review,* a London-based anticolonial weekly, complained that English sportswriters had the "'White Man's Burden' complaint in a particularly virulent form."[125] Turning the assumption of white civilization on its head, he argued that it was the Anglo-Saxon's appetite for brutality that had made interracial matches such a huge phenomenon. Similarly, the black American fighter Frank Crozier declared that the British boxing colour bar was a grievous insult against "the British-born black sons of the great Empire," and certainly "enough to make the coloured race cry out for self-government."[126] Crozier had long offered his own alternative theory of black physicality, boasting to white reporters that he had acquired his muscular strength by "mental suggestion." The real danger of interracial matches was that they implied that whites and nonwhites belonged to the same evolutionary category, not only in boxing but also in politics and society. Unlike Baker's fictive Aboriginals, New Negroes like Johnson were ready to fight for a legitimate place in the world.

The Black Atlantic from Below

African American Boxers and the Search for Exile

How incongruous to think that I, a little Galveston colored
boy should ever become an acquaintance of kings and rulers
of the old world, or that I should number among my friends
some of the most notable persons of America and the world
in general! What a vast stretch of the imagination to picture
myself a fugitive from my own country, yet sought and
acclaimed by thousands in nearly every nation of the world.

—Jack Johnson, *In the Ring—And Out*

In 1912 Jack Johnson found himself a political prisoner of sorts, unfairly
prosecuted by the U.S. government. His athletic prowess, his dominance
over white fighters, his refusal to follow the etiquette of Jim Crow, and,
most of all, his penchant for the company of white women had finally
caught up with him. With his dubious conviction under the federal Mann
Act against white slave trafficking in 1913, Johnson fled the United
States, lingering in exile throughout Europe and the Americas for the
next seven years. "I know the bitterness of being accused and harassed by
prosecutors. I know the horror of being hunted and haunted," Johnson
later recalled. "I have dashed across continents and oceans as a fugitive,
and I have matched my wits with the police and secret agents seeking
to deprive me of one of the greatest blessings man can have—liberty."[1]
Building on his global popularity as a pugilist, he soon became the most
widely publicized African American émigré in the world.

Johnson certainly remembered his foreign sojourn as a kind of exile.
At various points in his 1927 autobiography he called himself a "fugitive," a "voluntary exile," and a "wanderer."[2] He insisted that being
separated from his mother, Tina "Tiny" Johnson, was the most pain-

ful aspect of his time abroad. "It was she of whom I thought when I wandered as an exile in foreign lands," he later lamented, "but she died before I could negotiate the return, and while I was in distant lands, helpless to reach her, one of her last wishes was that she might see me."[3] Over the years Johnson had come to see his "flight to Europe" as one of his "greatest errors." He maintained a profound sense of ambivalence about his experiences overseas. "I had a delightful time in my travels and learned much concerning the world, [but] I was, nevertheless, an unhappy and restless individual," he recalled. "Nothing came into my life in the way of adequate compensation for the stings and grief I suffered over my separation from my friends and relatives."[4]

Far from an "error," Johnson's exile was a key episode in the already long-established tradition of African Americans who imagined and searched for better prospects in foreign spaces. During his sojourn, Johnson emerged as the ultimate emblem of a thriving black Atlantic counterculture from below. In the early 1900s there was a surprising fluidity of movement for poor and working-class black American men throughout the Atlantic world. There were still no sophisticated mechanisms in place to prevent their informal visits, even for those of little education and means who journeyed abroad as sailors, casual laborers, entertainers, and athletes.

The foreign travels of black American working men were symptomatic of their disenfranchised status politically, economically, and socially within the United States. Finding their horizons limited by the crushing repression of Jim Crow in the South and the de facto segregation of the North, many opted to join in the accelerating movement of goods, services, and commercial culture that permeated national borders. Some found a place in the rowdy multiracial milieu of port cities, laboring as maritime workers, stevedores, and longshoremen. Others ventured further inland in search of jobs in the mining sector and other dangerous heavy industries. Scores of black men also took advantage of the rising global preeminence of U.S. culture, and in particular the increasing foreign demand for African American popular culture. Often rejecting backbreaking manual labor in favor of more profitable opportunities in the field of popular entertainment, they became ever more ubiquitous figures of fear and desire.

Professional sports (particularly boxing) became tightly entwined with notions of freedom, mobility, exile, and racial progress in the folklore of the black American community. Black prizefighters were the cosmopolitan protagonists of some of the first widely available writings on African American travel and exile, helping to inspire a popular black global imagination that was much more about exploration and discovery than doctrinaire politics. In covering these boxers and their foreign destinations, black journalists educated readers about the possibilities and the pitfalls of living abroad. African American sportsmen also used their unprecedented access to the foreign and domestic presses to broadcast their own agenda on racial inequality. In addition to their role in this emerging print culture of the diaspora, they played an integral part in shaping a diasporic culture of performance, one that presented images of racial advancement that spoke to the imagination of the black masses. Their daring exploits and expressions in and out of the ring not only went against the conventional bourgeois narratives of racial uplift, but they also challenged the whitewashed visions of modernity circulating in the popular culture of late imperialism.

BLACK BOXERS AS BLACK EXILES

In November 1912 Johnson was arrested and charged with bringing his former flame, a white American call girl named Belle Schreiber, across state lines for the purposes of prostitution. Drafted by Republican congressman James Robert Mann of Illinois, the White Slave Traffic Act (Mann Act), which barred the interstate and international transport of women for "prostitution or debauchery" and "other immoral purposes," had gone into effect on 1 June 1910. So vague was the Mann Act's wording, with phrases like "crimes against nature" and "unlawful sexual intercourse," that prosecutors even used it to police sexual encounters between consenting adults, especially those involving black men and white women.[5] Although Johnson's relationship with Schreiber had actually taken place *before* the passage of the Mann Act, this did not prevent his arrest. A month earlier Johnson's newest squeeze, an eighteen-year-old white prostitute named Lucille Cameron, had refused to cooperate in the first Mann Act case against him. The second time around, however, officials were resolved to make the trumped-up charges stick. Not one to shy away from confrontation, Johnson added fuel to the fire by marrying Cameron in December 1912, just three months after his previous wife, Etta Duryea, committed suicide.

Johnson's well-publicized legal troubles signaled that the strict maintenance of a color line, particularly a sexual one, had become a national priority in the United States. Fears abounded over black migration to the North and its concurrence with the rising number of young, single white women living in urban areas. The failed attempt by Democratic congressman Seaborn A. Roddenbery to add an antimiscegenation clause to the U.S. Constitution, the passage of bills to ban black-white marriage in ten northern states, the frequent police crackdowns on interracial vice districts, and the many cases against African American men who dared to consort with white women occurred alongside the public uproar over Johnson's sexual escapades.[6]

Although the black champion openly fraternized with white women from the sexual underworld—a popular pastime of many professional athletes of his time—there was simply no evidence to suggest that he had ever solicited or sold their services for money. Johnson's eventual conviction, which carried a 366-day prison sentence and a $1,000 fine, underscored not only the second-class citizenship of Johnson but that of all African Americans. One black editorialist complained, "The pugilist as a citizen has not been given a square deal. As a Negro, a member of a despised race, he has been meted out a terrible punishment for daring to exceed what is considered a Negro's circle of activities."[7] The black heavyweight's ring successes and romantic choices had merely "violated public sentiment, not the laws."[8] Nonetheless, U.S. officials seemed bent on using the lowest possible means to discredit him. As one African American journalist declared, Johnson's Mann Act conviction was clearly "meant as a lesson to the black folk, the world around."[9]

Faced with the prospect of jail, Johnson sought his mother's advice. Although he was initially hesitant to flee, Tiny Johnson had begged him to leave the United States, insisting that she would rather see her son die than go to prison.[10] Seeking exile abroad appeared to be a safe and viable option. "The spotlight is a fearful ordeal," one black journalist observed. "It ran Roosevelt to Africa, Carnegie to Skibo castle, [and] J. P. Morgan up and down the continents."[11] Because of Johnson's color and the nature of his profession, he had even more reason to run. "When some big black colossus knocks the point from the head of a huge Olympus, not only the spotlight becomes overworked," the journalist argued, "but the cruel searchlight in his private character is done with a prejudice and a frenzy that would make the angels weep." Feeling the searing "heat of white hate," Johnson decided to take the transatlantic plunge in June 1913. The Bureau of Investigation, established in 1910 to enforce the Mann Act, led the heavily sensationalized manhunt for Johnson.[12]

A few weeks after his disappearance from Chicago, Johnson gave a British reporter the "exclusive story" of his escape from the clutches of

U.S. officials. He claimed to have taken a train across the border into Canada with his nephew Gus Rhodes, disguised as a member of the Negro Giants baseball team.[13] Even though Johnson knew that violations of the Mann Act were not extraditable offenses in Canada, his carefully choreographed exit north of the border was not without serious risks. Earlier in the year a report in the *Indianapolis Freeman* claimed that the Canadian government had issued a general order to all of its immigration inspectors instructing them to prevent Johnson's entry into the country. Canadian officials had called into question not only Johnson's physical health but also his moral character, the very same reasons typically used to bar the admittance of African American settlers and migrants.[14] As *Freeman* sportswriter Billy Lewis bemoaned, "Canada has caught the cure, and one feels to say, 'Etu [sic] Brute.'" Safe havens for African American fugitives like Johnson seemed to be disappearing. "On the last day it is said that the wicked shall flee and be without a hiding place," Lewis declared. "Are we now in those days? Have we been wicked? More wicked than others? Aren't we rather hard pressed for a hiding place?"[15]

Although Canadian authorities were eager to curry favor with the United States by "fetching Johnson under 'the disorderly' and 'undesirable person' rule," Johnson still managed to evade their grasp.[16] He and Rhodes had a brief brush with the law in Hamilton, Ontario, when police arrested them and took them to court. Two local lawyers helped to secure their release by arguing that there was still no official decree from the United States demanding Johnson's return.[17] He and his nephew then continued on their journey to Montreal, Quebec. Since Johnson had already purchased a ticket from Chicago to Le Havre, France, via Montreal, he was technically a "tourist in transit" passing through Canadian territory, and therefore safe from deportation. The new Mrs. Johnson had also quietly traveled to Montreal to join her husband on their passage to Europe.[18] An enemy of the state, Johnson was on the lam.

The black heavyweight was not alone in his decision to flee the United States. Johnson went into exile alongside a growing contingent of black American boxers who took their prizefighting, sparring exhibitions, and vaudeville tours overseas. Although most of these African American pugilists were not fleeing the United States for any specific legal or political reasons, their departure was a clear rejection of white American racism, for they sailed across the ocean in pursuit of greater liberty, respect, and economic prosperity. In the United States they often found themselves shut out of lucrative boxing matches and theatrical engagements, whereas in Europe they discovered a rising demand for their diverse talents. Yet even as black sportsmen searched for a space of exile beyond the color line, it was their color that ultimately shaped their opportunities abroad.

As they traveled they confronted and provoked the question of race in a number of contexts. Their itinerant existence on the margins of mainstream society exemplified the incompatibility of black freedom and Western modernity. Denied access to more conventional and stable forms of employment, they often found themselves pushed into the transnational marketplace of racial spectacles. They were wanderers "in an expanded West but not completely of it." The "striking doubleness" resulting from this "unique position" as, at once, second-class citizens and sought-after objects of white curiosity proved to be a source of both success and suffering for men like Johnson.[19] Despite the demand for their talents abroad, they kept coming up against the racial boundaries of modernity.

Molded by their ambiguous status, they became cosmopolitan renaissance men. Frank Craig, "The Harlem Coffee Cooler," an African American prizefighter in turn-of-the-century Britain and France, was one of the few who permanently expatriated to Europe. When English patrons invited Craig to London in the 1890s, his spectacular feats both in and out of the ring inspired public discussions about race and physical ability. Although at first British sportsmen questioned "what degree of boxing excellence might be expected in a debutant whose mother was an American Indian and whose father was a Cuban negro," Craig proved his courage and skill against white fighters. In addition to his ring prowess, Craig reputedly spoke English, Spanish, and German, and he was also adept at swimming, cycling, roller skating, dancing, and playing the mouth organ. A consummate performer, he even became a smash hit in British music halls, helping to popularize the cakewalk.[20] With his fight purses and the money he earned from his stage performances, Craig bought several London taverns. He enjoyed flaunting his wealth and often drove around with his white wife in an open carriage, wearing expensive clothes and sparkling diamonds.[21]

For Craig and those who followed in his foreign footsteps, the line between sport and theater was blurred. Many of them made as much money, if not more, on the stage as in the ring. The next generation of African American prizefighters gave rise to what some European sportswriters called the Coloured Quartette, a group of four internationally renowned and seemingly unbeatable African American heavy-weights that included Johnson, Sam Langford, Sam McVea, and Joe Jeannette.[22] Alongside these major stars a corps of black journeymen also ventured overseas in the early 1900s, including the likes of Eugene Bullard, Aaron Lester Brown (the "Dixie Kid"), and Bob Scanlon. As they developed thriving careers as touring athletes and entertainers, they came to embody an alternative vision of racial progress.

Even before they left for Europe, the majority of these hardscrabble pugilists had already spent their boyhoods wandering across North America in search of opportunity. Born in Weymouth, Nova Scotia, in 1886, Sam Langford, "The Boston Tar Baby," rode the rails stowed away on break beams and in boxcars. "I was a tramp when only a boy," Langford once told a British reporter. "I guess it was the rough-and-tumble I had then that has made me so strong and hard now."[23] Langford's early adventures as a hobo definitely groomed him for the grueling international life of a professional boxer. Likewise, born in Columbus, Georgia, on 9 October 1895, Eugene Bullard had roamed across the state as a youngster, crossing paths with a variety of folks, including a band of European gypsies.[24] Bullard later claimed that his friendly encounter with the gypsies had convinced him that a "social order tolerant of racial difference was possible" and that the chance for a better life existed on the other side of the Atlantic.[25]

With little formal education or access to steady work, black men gravitated to prizefighting since it was one of the best-paying profes-sions open to them at the time. Langford eventually settled in Boston, where he started off as a janitor and then became a sparring partner at the Lenox Athletic Club.[26] One evening he was hanging around out-side a Boston boxing arena trying to get in to see the bouts when the promoter ventured out in search of more fighters. Langford jumped at the chance to make some cash. "I was mighty hungry, I tell you, and was willing to do anything for a meal," he recounted, "so I ups and tells him if he'll give me five cents . . . for something to eat, I'll box for him." Langford took the nickel, filled up on doughnuts, and proceeded to knock out his opponent. The easy money convinced him to pursue a career in boxing.[27]

Joe Jeannette, a New Jersey native born on 26 August 1879, also began prizefighting because of economic woes. He told a British sportswriter, "I started life breaking in young horses for a large coal company, but my mind was centred on being a veterinary surgeon." Unfortunately, the small salary he earned for breaking horses stood in the way of his studies. "So, being always fond of boxing," Jeannette recalled, "I determined to scrape up the necessary money in the ring."[28] Initially a means to finance his education, prizefighting became Jeannette's primary occupation.

Although Bob Scanlon started out as a maritime worker and itinerant laborer, the harsh realities of unemployment eventually pushed him into the boxing business. Born Benjamin Lewis in Mobile, Alabama, on 7 February 1886, Scanlon at the age of sixteen moved to Mexico, where he worked as a cowboy for a year. He then crossed the Atlantic, slogging away as a ship's cook. Discharged in 1903 in Renfrew, Scotland, Scanlon later traveled to London, where a porter ran off with his luggage, leaving him destitute. After surviving rough times in the metropolitan capital, he journeyed to Cardiff, Wales, where he found another position aboard a ship. When he returned to Cardiff a few years later, he was once again jobless and had no prospects. Scanlon left for Pontypridd, Wales, hoping to labor in the coal mines, but he was unable to secure employment. Instead he found work in a boxing booth at a local fair, where he took on all comers for a small fee. From there it was a short step to the much more profitable world of professional boxing.[29]

The high demand for black pugilists in Europe coupled with the oppressive state of U.S. race relations pushed Johnson and many of his contemporaries overseas. Incidents of racial violence outside the ring drove some abroad. A popular welterweight named Dixie Kid, born in Fulton, Missouri, on 23 December 1883, left the United States in 1911 after enduring an eight-month jail sentence for defending himself against a white man in Philadelphia.[30] The following year, when a white boy cut Bullard's favorite suit pants with a razor, the sixteen-year-old vowed that he would travel to Europe and become a boxer like his hero Jack Johnson. Bullard caught a train to Norfolk, Virginia, where he stowed away on the *Marta Russ* for its three-week voyage across the Atlantic. When the ship reached Aberdeen, Scotland, the captain gave Bullard £5 and sent him ashore. At first Bullard was shocked at the friendliness of the local whites, who addressed him endearingly as "darky" or "Jack Johnson." Although he was viewed as an exotic novelty in Aberdeen, Bullard found that his new neighbors did not have the same contempt for him as white American southerners. Over the next two years he held a variety of jobs, from longshoreman to fish wagon vendor to midway attraction, eventually making his living as a vaudeville performer and professional boxer in Britain and France.[31]

American racism inside the ring propelled even the most successful black prizefighters overseas. When white American boxers ignored their challenges, black pugilists often chose to leave the country in search of new competitors and larger purses. Langford's earnings increased dramatically when he traveled to fight in Britain, France, Australia, and Mexico. During his early days as a professional boxer in the United States he received a paltry $150 to $200 per bout. Even his largest U.S. purse was only around $3,000, for his fight against the white heavyweight Gunboat Smith. However, in 1909 Langford earned $10,000 for meeting Ian "Iron" Hague in London, and he secured his next biggest purse of $7,500 in Australia. Money was not Langford's only reward for his foreign venture. He also had the opportunity to compete for and win the heavyweight championships of Australia and Mexico.[32]

Langford's contemporary Sam McVea, a Texan born on 17 May 1883, spent so much of his career abroad in England, France, Belgium, Australia, and South and Central America that he gained the moniker "Colored Globe Trotter." McVea made his biggest mark fighting in Europe, particularly in France, where fans affectionately dubbed him L'Idole de Paris (The Parisian Idol). Tired of meeting the same black opponents multiple times in rings throughout the United States, Jeannette also decided to try his luck in Europe. In 1909 he accompanied his Irish-American manager Dan McKetrick to Paris, where he had a string of fights against McVea.[33] All of these men publicly embraced their newfound fame and fortune overseas, indulging in fashionable suits, fast cars, and white women.[34]

Profiting from the success of these traveling athletes, African American managers and promoters also began to make their way across the Atlantic. An Indianapolis native and famed blackface comedian, Billy McClain became the booking agent for several African American boxers and performers in Europe, including McVea. McClain had left the United States in 1904, and, like many of his African American clients, he found his niche in the realm of entertainment. Known for being a bit of a braggart, he often sent back glowing descriptions of his overseas travels, including his enjoyment of high-powered automobiles and European women.[35] Maintaining that he was the "first and only Negro promoter of any note in the world," McClain felt that "it devolved upon him to show his mettle." He served as a "Ballet Master" and managing director at prestigious venues in London, Paris, and Brussels. In 1910 he also established a boxing gym in Brussels where some of the best pugilists in Europe reputedly trained. The multitalented promoter gained a facility with several European languages, enabling him to better guide his clients' transnational careers.[36]

Thanks to his journeys, McClain had also acquired a much more comprehensive view of the race question. "I am satisfied that the people of all races are for themselves," the black impresario declared. "In order that the Negro should become a factor in the world and take his place among men he must free himself from the abominable subservience to others which permits him to be treated as he is today."[37] From champions to journeymen to managers, black sportsmen embraced a transnational existence that challenged the traditional scripts of racial uplift and U.S. citizenship. These rebel sojourners were, as Claude McKay later described himself, "bad nationalists."[38] While abroad, they developed a critical eye for white American racism along with the confidence and creativity to protest it. Their well-publicized experiences outside the United States gave their black American fans a picture of life in the world beyond the confines of Jim Crow America.

NARRATIVES OF EXILE

Johnson, his wife, and his nephew Rhodes traveled first-class aboard the steamship *Corinthian,* arriving peacefully in the French port of Le Havre in July 1913. As the black champion disembarked, he greeted a gathering of European reporters and proceeded to explain his side of the story. His account of this public address, titled "Mes malheurs" (My misfortunes), initially appeared in *La Boxe et les boxeurs,* and the *Chicago Defender* subsequently translated it for African American readers. "Since my return from France to America I must say that I have been the most persecuted man in the whole world," Johnson announced. "The Americans, decidedly unable to stomach my victory over Jeffries and the relatively important sums I have won . . . seem sworn to destroy or ruin me. There has not been a day when I was not the victim of some plot, of some ridiculous accusation, which invariably ended in a great loss of money for me."[39] Since leaving the United States, however, Johnson's luck seemed to be changing. He claimed that the officers and passengers on board the *Corinthian* had treated him with respect, sympathizing with his plight as a persecuted man. Johnson graciously concluded, "I have always been welcomed in France and I hope that the Parisians are reserving a good welcome for me again this time. I count on settling permanently in their city and never returning to the United States."

FIGURE 10. Rather than go to jail after his Mann Act conviction, Johnson went into exile abroad. Jack Johnson and his wife Lucille embarking on a vessel, 1913. © Roger Viollet/Getty Images.

Widely covered in the black press, Johnson's exile provided African Americans from all walks of life with an optimistic story of escape from the racial injustices they faced on a daily basis. As tales of his foreign travels circulated on street corners and in barbershops and saloons, they took on a life of their own in black communities across the United States. Johnson became a cultural conduit through which African Americans could ponder the role of race in the wider world. The black champion used the foreign press to highlight the hypocrisy and brutality of white America on the world stage. In this way, his flight fit within a much longer history of black exile and the development of international alliances in the face of white American discrimination.

Johnson and his fellow black sportsmen were an integral part of a developing discussion on the global state of the race question in the African American press. In addition to acting as his uncle's road manager, Rhodes became Johnson's full-time publicist, sending laudatory reports of the champion's overseas endeavors to the *Chicago Defender*. The *Defender* played up this transatlantic connection, claiming that it offered readers "the most authentic accounts of 'Jack Johnson's Doings Abroad.'"[40] This was a particular point of prestige for the *Defender*, since most African American newspapers during this period did not have the funds to hire foreign correspondents. Their international news tended to come from two sources: reprinted or rearticulated reports taken from the white American press and letters from subscribers who happened to be living or traveling abroad. The fact that Johnson's nephew was the source of these special reports did not seem to detract from the newspaper's excitement at having access to regular updates. Even the newspaper's founder and editor in chief, Robert S. Abbott, later ventured overseas for a personal visit with the black champion.[41]

This interest in Johnson's travels was just one part of the *Defender*'s broader vision of cultivating in its readers a more optimistic and cosmopolitan outlook. Next to reports of racist white southerners objecting to educated negroes and lynch-happy rednecks in the Midwest, the *Defender* often featured news of black successes in Europe. It prided itself on giving "more foreign news of the race than any paper in America."[42] Around the same time that Johnson arrived in Le Havre, the *Defender* also featured travel articles promoting Paris and the historic town of Ghent, Belgium, as ideal tourist destinations.[43] Johnson's journeys as well as other transatlantic reports of racial tolerance helped to raise Europe's profile among African Americans.

With its British circulation sold from Daw's Steamship Agency in London, the *Defender* also attempted to vindicate black America in the eyes of white people abroad. Since white American correspondents for the British press sought to "magnify the faults of the colored Americans," the newspaper became a kind of countervoice. The editorial team vowed to show the outside world that not only were African Americans progressing as a race, but also that black men were continuing to be murdered simply because they dared to defend their households. These transatlantic efforts appeared to be working. An African American reader studying in Europe wrote that he was pleasantly surprised to find a copy of the newspaper in Glasgow, Scotland.[44]

Johnson, charged with the responsibility of telling all his foreign friends about the *Defender,* was the newspaper's most popular spokesman in England. Copies of the *Defender* sold out every week in London, attracting widespread attention. The British reputedly admired the black weekly because of "its bravery and fearlessness on behalf of its colored Americans."[45] Its many ingratiating reports of English civilization certainly did not hurt its cause. Comparing its transatlantic mission to that of the legendary black abolitionist Frederick Douglass, who had traveled to London to garner support for the freedom of African

American slaves, the *Defender* declared that this time the "power of the press [came] to speak in their behalf."

Regardless of these grand pronouncements, Leo Daniels, a concerned black Canadian expatriate who corresponded with the *Indianapolis Freeman* throughout the 1910s, believed that the African American press simply was not doing enough. Writing from Glasgow, he echoed many of his earlier pronouncements in the wake of the Jeffries-Johnson fight. He argued that "British and American white prejudice" had come together in "united determination to slander" black people.[46] Daniels explained, "If a Negro commits a grave offense in America to-day it is flashed across here for publication in the European papers for school boys and girls and other millions to read that same day so that is the way the millions of white people who are no better than we black people are educated and embittered against us."[47] He claimed that the "masses of the British and foreign people" had come to believe that African Americans lived "in a state of semi-cannibalism." They were "represented to be heathens, rapists of white women, indolent, ignorant, worthless pests only fit to be feathered, tarred, shot or burnt at the stake." Daniels called for the establishment of "news agents in foreign countries to advocate the cause of the American Negro," and he requested copies of black American newspapers to distribute abroad.

Daniels also worried that certain kinds of African American visitors were gaining too much visibility in Europe. "The only Negro that is apparently known here," Daniels maintained, "is the Negro who can sing, dance, sell quack medicine at street corners, box, wrestle or fight."[48] The intervening years had clearly tempered his optimism about the symbolic power of black pugilistic success. Meanwhile, to those back in the United States, the task of disseminating the truth about African Americans' many accomplishments in professions other than performance or pugilism seemed incredibly daunting. Adding to Daniels' observations, the editor of the *Freeman* lamented, "It is impossible to maintain propagandas abroad or 'floating' exhibitions of our status at home." It was difficult to imagine how African Americans would garner greater respect abroad when Johnson and his fellow black sportsmen had become their most famous representatives.

However, both Daniels and the *Freeman*'s editor underestimated the role of men like Johnson in shaping a transnational conversation on the race question. Because of their special access to the foreign press and performance venues, black boxers had developed their own ways of broadcasting their racial pride and their grievances to European audiences. They were instrumental in cultivating a broad base of international support for the ongoing African American freedom struggle.

Johnson and his contemporaries had already been courting French favor in the years before his Mann Act conviction and arrival in Le Havre. Not only did they help foster the rise of Parisian "negrophilia," but they also became a popular medium through which French sportsmen critiqued U.S. racism and Anglo-Saxon imperialism more broadly. Recognizing this dynamic, Johnson and his contemporaries actively pursued French sympathy as they called upon the protection of French civilization. Throughout the 1910s Johnson became a cause célèbre in the French press and arguably the most outspoken African American exile in Paris. French sporting journals afforded him many opportunities to circulate his critiques of white America. French readers, already well versed in sensationalized accounts of southern lynch mobs since the early 1900s, came to view Johnson and his black boxing confreres as exiles from the oppressive negrophobia of U.S. society.[49]

In January 1911 the sporting weekly *La Vie au grand air* published its first installment of Johnson's life story, titled "Ma Vie et mes combats" (My life and battles), and the serial continued for the next five months. Johnson was famous enough in France for the publishers, Pierre Lafitte and Company, to introduce his autobiography as one of the magazine's most important acquisitions of the year. Greeting readers with a full-page photo of the black heavyweight's fist, a preview for the series boasted that the story would be told by none other than Johnson himself.[50]

Johnson's French memoir was a quintessential text of African American exile and protest, a kind of New Negro manifesto that predated World War I and the Harlem Renaissance. However, historians have yet to plumb this important document for its insights into black working-class understandings of the global color line. "Ma Vie et mes combats" was the only autobiographical treatment of Johnson published during his career, and there appears to have been no contemporary English translation. In 1914 Pierre Lafitte and Company released an edited version of the series as a book *(Mes Combats)* to capitalize on the publicity surrounding Johnson's scheduled match against the white American fighter Frank Moran in Paris.[51]

Certainly there was a demand for Johnson's memoirs among his African American fans. As sportswriter Billy Lewis of the *Indianapolis Freeman* declared, "I can conceive of no more fascinating 'piece' of literature. . . . Not only would there be a recital of interesting facts, but their inspiration arising out of a quarrel of men about the rights of men. Then with Chicago, New York, London, Paris, as the backgrounds in the main including incidentally, the total world of civilization."[52] Lewis also recognized that such a book might be deemed too subversive in the United States. "Perhaps the story of his life too well told, as Hugo might tell it, or Balzac, would not be well for the present age," Lewis reasoned, "for when the rights of men are the theme we forget nationality and think of the individual. We exchange places with the subjects readily, and ere we are aware we are all aflame at our vicarious suffering." Comparing the potential effect of Johnson's autobiography to that of an abolitionist tract, Lewis added, "Harriet Beecher Stowe was such a writer, who could arouse the very rocks to mutiny." While Johnson could recount his life for a foreign audience, such a story was apparently too incendiary to be printed back home.

Although not tied to any specific political project, Johnson's French memoirs show that his transnational career and working-class origins enabled him to develop a nuanced critique of Western modernity. He played against prevailing discourses of race, manhood, and the body in a variety of often contradicting ways, not only speaking back to popular tropes of black savagery but also defying the rigid discipline of bourgeois life. Prefiguring the wandering nautical narratives of McKay, Johnson depicted a life characterized by masculine pursuits and geographic mobility.[53] His narrative not only indicted white American racism but also pointed to the global contours of white supremacy. Johnson refashioned the negative legacy of black slavery into a story of triumph, questioning the gendered justifications for the white man's burden. Moreover, Johnson's life story spoke explicitly to the challenges of working-class African Americans, casting them as agents in the fight against the color line. Even though Johnson had attained the financial trappings of sporting success, he continued to identify with the urban culture of the black proletariat.

The first episode of "Ma Vie et mes combats" was unflinchingly polemical, providing a sharp critique of white American negrophobia and of conventional ideas about the superiority of white Western civilization. As Johnson began, "When a white man writes his memoirs, as I will try to do here, it is customary to start with the history of his family from its earliest times."[54] Johnson disputed the popular belief that black people had no history of which to be proud. "Our memories are passed down, above all, by the tradition of father to son," he explained. "Whites don't believe it, but we are also proud of our ancestors and during the long days and even longer nights, when we knew neither schools nor books, we still passed on our memories from past centuries." Addressing his readers as *"les hommes blancs"* (white men), Johnson argued that even though it made white men proud to connect themselves to the noble soldiers of the Crusades, his ancestors had actually built the grand architecture the Europeans had discovered during their missions in Palestine. "Who constructed the Pyramids 40 centuries ago?" Johnson challenged. "Which race built the Egyptian monuments before such things were known in Europe, where the inhabitants, wearing animal skins, lived a miserable existence in caves?" Embracing the wonders of ancient Egypt as a usable, African past, the black heavyweight questioned the historical foundations of white supremacy. He echoed the claims of contemporary black scholars who argued that the Nile Valley was the cradle of all civilization.[55]

Turning a past of servitude into a virtue, Johnson declared that the physical trials of his enslaved forefathers had helped to make him world champion. "Undoubtedly, it is from my long list of ancestors who were all hard workers, men of the open air, that I have my size, the strength of my arms and the quality of my muscles," Johnson asserted, "all my inherited traits that make me just as proud as others would be of a baron's coronet." He argued that his rough childhood had only made him stronger. He recalled, "There were some very hard times in our small home in Galveston, [Texas,] and as soon as I was big enough, my father took me to help him because his job as a porter kept him very busy. At that time, we did not know carpet-sweepers or the vacuum cleaner. There were only old-fashioned brooms, with which I swept. I swept the entire day." He declared, "I believe that it was this sweeping . . . that strengthened my back and shoulder muscles." While French sportsmen, as well as the likes of Theodore Roosevelt and other proponents of the "strenuous life," contemplated the need for vigorous exercise and a return to nature to regenerate the white race, Johnson claimed that black men's myriad struggles against white domination had already made them more powerful and robust.[56]

Johnson also used his childhood narrative to counter prevailing ideas about the basic immorality and indolence of the black working class. He claimed that because he came from a tight-knit family he therefore tried to improve his station in order to provide them with a more comfortable life. He spoke lovingly of his mother as a woman with "too good of a heart" and of his older sister, Lucy, whose job it was to keep him in line. "Life was not easy in our small house in Galveston and the days when we had empty stomachs were far more frequent than the feast days. Often my mother had concerns and I sought to comfort her," Johnson recalled.[57]

The black champion portrayed himself as an ambitious and resourceful young man looking for a chance to better himself despite the odds. "[At] nine years of age," Johnson recounted, "I thought about earning my living. Pushing a broom behind my father hardly suited me. I wanted to go out and work on my own account." It was in the boxing ring rather than the more respectable realms of education or business that he gained more control over his own economic destiny and self-representation. Yet even during his early days as a professional prizefighter he regularly fought on an empty stomach. "I was sustained by the idea that I had to earn money if I wanted to assist my poor mother, who still had a whole brood of children to feed," he claimed.[58]

In addition to relating this righteous narrative of sacrifice and self-reliance, Johnson looked back fondly on the less savory aspects of his boyhood. He described a youth punctuated by street fights, gambling, and confrontations with white policemen as he roamed about Galveston's dockyards with his black friends. He also recalled being drawn to the large ships in the port. As an adolescent he decided to travel from Galveston to Key West to Boston, first as a stowaway, and then, after being discovered, as a ship's cook. He gave up on formal education, preferring to experiment with a slew of different occupations, including stable boy, horse trainer, bicyclist, and house painter.[59] Even after he set his sights on becoming a championship boxer, homelessness and pennilessness continued to plague him. Johnson claimed that these rough and roving years had prepared him for the vagaries of professional prizefighting. "I cannot tell you how happy I am now that I had to protect myself against hardship and understand poverty as intimately as I did."[60]

Johnson's French memoirs also revealed that he consciously performed a brand of urban black working-class masculinity that challenged the racial and sexual politics of the period. He was well aware of his reputation for decadence in the white American press, and he claimed to have kept a scrapbook of clippings. Johnson quoted one of the more amusing descriptions for French readers:

When he is out for a walk, he has the air of a true dandy and all his brothers of color are proud of him. He generally wears a large flat white hat, checkered clothing, a gaudy waistcoat, a colored shirt, gray or green gaiters, very pointed, patent-leather shoes and an enormous diamond as a tie-pin. He never forgets his cane, as large as a sapling, and his knotty fingers are covered with glittering rings. He does not have much money, but all that he has he spends on outfits and good meals.[61]

Rather than deny such derisive reports of his ostentation, Johnson chose to embrace his public image as a black dandy. "This description, as humorous as it was, was not in sum very far from the truth," he maintained. Although this audacious strategy of self-presentation made most middle-class African Americans cringe, it provided black sportsmen with a means to publicly recuperate their sense of personal dignity while also protesting the dehumanizing effects of late imperialism and industrial capitalism. For Johnson, his studied dandyism was not just a matter of style. It was also a form of political rebellion, one that not only went against established racial and sexual norms but also mocked the bourgeois Victorian values of industry, thrift, and restraint.[62]

Johnson's Parisian fans would have understood this point. Extravagant clothes, sparkling jewels, sports cars, sumptuous meals, and interracial sexual attraction had become the hallmark of African American prizefighters, many of whom ran in the same circles as the motley collection of pimps, prostitutes, gamblers, and vaudevillians that frequented urban vice districts. In Paris Johnson and his contemporaries lived on the edges of respectability, becoming fixtures in the city's raucous underground nightlife alongside adoring members of the French avant-garde. Although commonly associated with the intellectuals and artists of the Harlem Renaissance, African American sportsmen had long experimented with this modern sense of masculinity expressed through leisure activities, conspicuous consumption, and the public display of the body.[63]

Johnson's hardscrabble life in the transnational routes of imperial commerce and culture had made him openly skeptical of the white man's burden. He maintained that the "color question" had caused the "saddest moments" of his fighting career.[64] In recalling the widespread controversy over his 1910 defeat of Jim Jeffries, Johnson questioned the gendered justifications of the color line, whether in or out of the boxing ring. To make his point he included a short verse for his French readers:

For there is neither east nor west,
Border nor breed nor birth,
When two strong men stand face to face,
Though they come from the ends of the earth.[65]

While these may have been the words of famed British poet Rudyard Kipling's "The Ballad of East and West," Johnson remembered learning them from one of his sparring partners.[66] With a deep sense of irony, he used the imperial writer's appeal to popular ideas of manhood to critique his undeserved plight. Johnson maintained that he had chosen to operate above the arbitrary color line, for he viewed his title match against Jeffries as a question of courage, strength, and skill rather than race.

Two years later, when Johnson returned to Paris as a fugitive from U.S. justice, he was able to tap into the existing French fascination with and sympathy for African Americans. His Mann Act conviction apparently had no effect on his well-established celebrity in the City of Light. Local newspapers followed Johnson and his white wife wherever they went, printing photos of them surrounded by crowds of admiring French fans.[67] One of Johnson's sparring partners reported, "He still drifts around in two automobiles and is able to keep a chauffeur in furs and ice cream."[68] Johnson later recalled, "I was offered several engagements in theaters and music halls. Managers besought me on every hand, each trying to outdo the other in offering me inducements. I decided upon a short engagement at the *Folies Bergère,* where as long as I remained, crowded houses greeted me at every performance."[69]

It appeared as if he might stay in Paris permanently, for, as one African American sportswriter declared, "Evidently Monsieur Johnson is getting a square deal according to what he conceives to be his manhood rights."[70] The international community seemed to be embracing not only Johnson's cause but also the plight of African Americans in general. A report in the *Chicago Defender* claimed that the French Board of Trade had honored the black champion and his white wife.[71] French officials had reputedly declared that Johnson and any other black Americans were welcome in Paris and would have at their disposal all the liberties offered by the French government.

According to the *Defender,* around five thousand black Americans, including twenty from Chicago, had already made the French capital their home. Moreover, military officials had apparently given Johnson's nephew Rhodes a cadetship at the "West Point of France."[72] At a time when black Americans faced the prospect of menial positions in a Jim Crow U.S. Army, this must have sounded like something out of a utopian novel. However, these reports were most likely exaggerated since the major Parisian dailies never carried any corresponding news of the French Board of Trade event for Johnson, nor did they report any public proclamations of French authorities' desire to welcome African Americans as citizens. Nevertheless, through these circulating stories of their favorite boxing heroes, Johnson's black fans came to view Paris as a refuge from racial oppression. Johnson's exploits both in and out of the ring also suggested a more accessible and immediate form of social mobility outside the regular channels of politics, education, and business. After all, Johnson was "just a plain Galveston levee roust-about who found out he could fight and then got rich."[73] This roust-about had managed not only to evade U.S. authorities but also to trans-mit his story of racial persecution across Europe.

PERFORMING RESISTANCE

Starved for updates on Johnson's experiences abroad, sportswriter Billy Lewis opined, "If he were a great literary man, a great writer, such as Allegheri Dante [sic] was, doubtless the world would get some fine read-ing just about this time. He would take his tormentors to—[hell] . . . cutting out both purgatory and paradise. . . . O, if he could write like he could fight. But he can't. He's just a plain, blunt man."[74] Although for Lewis prose was the best medium of protest, Johnson and his cohort of black pugilists had developed other means to express themselves pub-licly and to advance their causes as they traveled overseas. They became masters of performance, not only in the ring but also on the stages and streets of Europe. They lived unapologetically as they competed with white men for jobs, became the headlining acts in theaters, made bold declarations to the press, toured around with impeccable style, and openly fraternized with white women. In Britain this influx of African American working men inspired a backlash, of which Johnson, the fugitive, became the most notorious target.

In August 1913 the black champion traveled to London, England, with his wife and entourage for another leg of his European exile. Almost two years had passed since the cancellation of his match against Bombardier Billy Wells, and behind the scenes Lord Lonsdale and the Home Office were conspiring to uphold a color bar in the British box-ing ring. It appeared as if the stage were one of the few spaces still open to Johnson in England, and he was determined to fight for his contin-ued access to both its financial rewards and public platform.

Sporting a·"smartly cut gray frock coat, giving full display to his dia-monds," he held a press reception in his West End residence. Johnson was reportedly set to earn $5,000 a week from his twice nightly per-formances of sparring, dancing, singing, and playing his bass viol at the Euston and South London music halls. However, objections were already surfacing from the Variety Artists' Federation (VAF), a British trade union representing vaudeville performers. The VAF had begun to instruct its members to boycott the venues where Johnson was slated to appear.[75] Despite this disturbing development, Johnson spoke confidently to the journalists in attendance. "They will soon come around and will be the first to lend a pal a hand," he declared.[76] When asked if he would return to the United States, Johnson joked, "I've got a good many friends there but when I meet them, if there is such a place as heaven, I hope it will be heaven and not America."

Over the next few months Johnson's bittersweet experiences in London painted a rather ambiguous picture of European tolerance. His own difficulties with segments of the English public seemed to betray an emerging, and disconcerting, trend in British metropolitan race relations. Just as growing numbers of black performers, athletes, and workers began arriving to fill the nation's demand for cheap labor and entertainment, Britain's policing of racial boundaries appeared to be tightening. The increasing visibility of African American men was causing white Britons to rethink the risks of living in an interracial society.

By the early 1900s there were already signs that England's racial climate was changing. Jim Crow seemed to be blowing through the British Isles in a new and more powerful way, within the larger context of what an editorialist for the *African Times and Orient Review* dubbed, "The Americanisation of England."[77] "American enterprise has captured the principal trades of our country," he observed. "The American accent rings through theatreland, and the variety art of America dominates the halls." Yet the most tragic development of all was that "the worst elements of American race-hatred" were being "imported into English Government." Even the "good old English characteristic of fair play" was becoming "a thing of the past."

Racial segregation and color consciousness appeared to be infiltrating British life in a variety of ways. English lawyers in the South Eastern Circuit had decided to exclude nonwhite barristers from eating in their mess hall.[78] They also urged aspiring lawyers from the colonies to return home after taking the bar exam, since their continued presence in the British metropole would inevitably bring them racial discrimination from all angles. White Londoners began to worry about the seventy African students presently in the city, calling for greater white supervision so that they "should not, from ignorance or inexperience, be allowed to drift among unwholesome influences."[79] Even visiting African American professionals were finding it increasingly difficult to secure hotel accommodations in London. A reporter for the *New York Age* declared, "The poison of American race prejudice is working powerfully in places where its presence was not heretofore suspected."[80] The characterization of this rising racial intolerance as an invasion of white American principles rather than a consequence of British imperialism not only exposed the pervasiveness of England's national mythology of racial tolerance, but it also revealed contemporary anxieties about the expanding international influence of the United States and its supposedly "peculiar" racial politics.

Yet the increasingly rigid construction of Britain's color bar was more than just a simple process of "Americanisation." The frightening reality of black men from across the diaspora converging on the metropole was giving everyday Englishmen a taste of their own imperial medicine. *Freeman* sports columnist Lewis complained that the England of old—the one of abolitionist William Wilberforce, the one that had "honored and protected Frederick Douglass"—no longer seemed to exist.[81] As a college sophomore he had come across what proved to be a prophetic passage in a British illustrated weekly. Pointing to the rampant negrophobia in the United States, it reasoned, "If the situation were here as there, our laboring men being jostled out of employment by the Negroes we would have the same conditions." This passage had left Lewis reeling with a sense of shock and betrayal, for as a young man he had placed his faith in the progressiveness of English racial mores. However, Britain's changing demographics had made the so-called Negro a local problem. Not only did the British have to contend with their African possessions, but now growing numbers of black men were landing on their own shores.

As far back as 1908, a London correspondent, whose story appeared in several U.S. newspapers, complained that a "Negro invasion" was overtaking the British Isles. Reportedly, thousands of African Americans had arrived in England over the past few years, and thousands more were expected to come. The first arrivals were "artists and athletes who realizing that they suffered in England but few of the disabilities attached to their race in the United States" had encouraged their friends to join them abroad.[82] According to figures furnished by the U.S. embassy in London, there were five thousand black Americans in England, and four thousand of them had arrived in the last year. A black quarter sprung up in London's Soho district, spawning two restaurants that served "fried chicken, sweet corn and other delicacies dear to the negroe's *[sic]* heart." Although one African American journalist believed that British reports were simply exaggerating the number of black Americans living in the capital alongside East Indian and West African immigrants, he acknowledged that there were more than "enough dark people in London to cause the oldest inhabitants to sit up and take notice."[83] African Americans were just one of many black ethnic groups living in London. Laborers, performers, and sailors from Africa and the Caribbean had also converged on the metropolitan capital in search of work. Nonetheless, it was easiest to blame the African American "outsiders" for bringing the "negro problem" to Britain, since it elided English culpability in the global project of white supremacy.[84]

Black American boxers were essentially cashing in on the increasing wages and leisure time of Britain's white working class. Many acquired steady, and often lucrative, employment in two working-class amusements, professional boxing and minstrel shows. By the early 1900s the boxing business was robust enough for venues in London and the provincial towns to host prizefights several nights a week. African American blackface performers were also gaining widespread popularity in Britain. While white minstrels wearing burnt cork had dominated English stages in the nineteenth century, by the turn of the twentieth century African American artists had begun to supplant them. African American blackface entertainers performed in town halls, assembly rooms, variety theaters, hippodromes, and cinemas throughout the country, rivaling circuses as the most sought-after shows.[85] They also became popular attractions in the seaside resort towns that catered to weekend crowds of middle- and working-class Britons. With the growing demand for "authentic" coon songs and plantation melodies, white minstrels found themselves "driven off the sands by the American negroes."[86]

While African American performers clearly catered to the imperial tastes and racial myths of English audiences, their access to the stage gave them greater control over their own image. Theater critic Lester Walton of the *New York Age* saw the British rejection of white minstrels in favor of African American blackface artists as an example of racial progress. Around the same time that Johnson arrived in London, Charles Hart, a black comedian in the same vein as Bert Williams, became a huge hit in the city's vaudeville scene.[87] Walton argued, "The fact that Charlie Hart is making good in England in blackface shows that the English theatregoer knows the difference between burlesquing a race and ridiculing a race." Even though the stage and sporting arena remained the only two venues in which the British public seemed to welcome them, touring African Americans like Johnson endeavored to make the best of this tenuous situation.

Yet the same assertiveness and ambition that had helped black Americans to achieve some success in the United States was now sowing the seeds for a backlash in Britain. "The English are called phlegmatic, and we, especially those 'brilliant' ones landing there for our country, are their very opposites," Billy Lewis explained. "The English do not take to our forwardness, even that of the white Americans," he claimed, adding, "And we are a forward race, the most aggressive, and also progressive on the earth when not hindered." Lewis admitted that this special "spirit" had turned out to be "both damning and saving."[88]

As black sportsmen pushed their way into formerly white preserves, they subverted British social norms, from the workplace to the bedroom. In a letter to the *African Times and Orient Review,* Stephen Hamilton, a disgruntled forty-one-year-old coal miner from Monmouthshire, Wales, raised a number of concerns about the increasing number of black men in Britain. "I must tell you candidly that I am not in sympathy with the class of coloured people that are in our district," he confided. "All the negroes we see are either pugilists or showmen."[89] As Hamilton explained, "I fancy we get the scum; they come in to Cardiff or Newport, two docks where coal is shipped, then they hear of the money got in coal mines, [and] they leave their ships and wander about the valleys of Wales."

Hamilton's observations were not unique. Throughout the late nineteenth and early twentieth centuries most of the black men in Britain arrived as sailors. Laid off from ships or attracted to the potential for work in the burgeoning coal mining industry, black seamen initially became a presence in Cardiff in the 1870s. By the 1910s Cardiff was second to London in its proportion of foreign-born inhabitants, including Africans, Afro-Caribbeans, and African Americans. Always the first crewmembers to be cast off, black seamen found it hard enough to find employment on new ships, let alone on land, since white sailors and laborers frequently refused to work with them. Many of them became destitute as they wandered from port to port in search of employment.[90]

Not only were black men competing in the local labor market, but they now infringed upon the sexual territory of white men. "Why don't they bring black women or girls with them?" Hamilton asked, "but they demoralise white girls by marrying them." Although he acknowledged that it was "not fair to judge the coloured race by Jack Johnson or Sam Langford or other pugilists," he obviously viewed these shifting demographics through the lens of popular stereotypes about African American prizefighters' pomposity, hypersexuality, and, most of all, their fondness for white women.

Hamilton's longtime exposure to the circulating fiction and rumor of Jim Crow America only reinforced his belief in the inevitable problems associated with race mixing. One of his uncles had taught him that before the U.S. Civil War, "it was not safe for a man to go to work in the morning and leave his wife by herself, because of the blacks breaking in and assaulting her." In turn, *Uncle Tom's Cabin* provided the overarching framework for his encounters with black Americans. Hamilton had read the novel and seen its theatrical adaptation. Yet men like Johnson were the furthest thing from Uncle Tom, colliding with the coal miner's ideal of a docile darky. Amid this hodgepodge of segregationist sentiments, Hamilton had come to the conclusion that colonial subjects "should marry women of their own colour" and "should stay in their own country."[91]

A report in London's *Evening Standard* resonated with many of Hamilton's views on miscegenation. Written by the manager of a local detective agency, the article caught the attention of the African American press. The detective warned, "The wave of indignation now sweeping over the United States against the recent marriage of Jack Johnson to a white girl in Chicago is nothing compared to the storm which will burst in this country if Englishmen do not speedily awaken to the real peril of the black invasion which has been going on steadily for the last two years."[92] London had apparently become "a paradise for the black man," since he was "permitted to mix with white women on social equality."[93] Given the growing insolence and hostility of the "Negro character," violence was a necessary reaction. As the detective declared, "Lynching seems to be the only way to prevent the wholesale commission of crimes against womanhood by modern Negroes because fear is the sole restraining influence they know." New Negroes no longer seemed to know their "place."

These collective concerns about increasing interracial contact in the metropole, along with the growing assertiveness of black men, continued to emerge in discussions of black boxers' exploits in and out of the ring. British publications betrayed an underlying anxiety about the preeminence of African Americans in the heavyweight division. Titled "The Dark Side of the White Hope Problem," a cartoon in *Boxing* encapsulated these fears, depicting a crowd of African American pugilists as a sea of apelike sambo faces, so numerous that they filled the page with blackness.[94] Another English sportswriter penned a sarcastic piece about black prizefighters' apparently unwarranted sense of pride. He explained, "The sensitiveness of some [black] boxers is abnormal and requires a rigid observance of numerous unwritten rules and regulations in its treatment."[95] Pluto, a hotheaded black pugilist from Coolgardie, Australia, seemed to provide a perfect example of this racial phenomenon. He had reportedly banged a white journalist's head against a doorstep for calling him a "nigger" in print. In some respects Pluto sounded a lot like Johnson. The sportswriter scoffed, "Clothe the negro in a suit resplendent with all the known colours on and above the universe, put spats upon his boots and crown him with the latest thing in hats, and no man dare call him equal. Add pugilism as his solitary accomplishment, and his value per ounce will exceed the price of radium per ton." Clearly confidence, honor, and aggression were not suitable expressions for black men to display in public.

Britain's "Black Scare" and its broader implications did not go unnoticed in black America. Although previous African American press reports from London had tended to tell a different story of interracial contact—one in which miscegenation excited no comment and fair-haired English ladies were free to marry men of color—an editorialist for the *Indianapolis Freeman* maintained that Britain's supposedly "new" racial paranoia was not so new at all.[96] "The black man's fight is around the globe, a fact we have been trying to make plain for years," he declared. "The world seems to be contesting the black man's right to exist."[97] In his view, the "Black Scare" revealed much more about white hypocrisy than black inferiority. "If it is said that the original intent was for each race to occupy its own zone, it can also be said that the white folks were the ones who thought to change things," he argued. "America must go to Africa to bring in black folks. England is puddling about in Negro affairs in Africa." British imperialism was no better than white American racism. "Great Britain and the rest of them go out of their way to cultivate the acquaintance of the barbarians," he declared. "They introduce schools and religions among them, teaching them the brotherhood of man, leading them to suspect that they are a part of the human family, and as such have rights in common." Regardless of this rosy colonial rhetoric, people of color still remained outside the bounds of civilization.

Johnson arrived in London amid this simmering controversy, and

FIGURE 11. British cartoons such as this one betrayed an under-lying anxiety about the preeminence of black Americans in the heavyweight division. "The Dark Side of the White Hope Problem," *Boxing New Year's Annual 1914.*

his well-publicized presence soon brought the situation to a boil. He had hoped for a profitable, if not peaceful, sojourn in the British capital. A local syndicate had booked him for the highest weekly salary "of any vaudevillian abroad," white or black. Among African Americans there was a sense of shared vindication in Johnson's international fame. "It must be refreshing to be treated as your position demands and not according to your color," theater critic Lester Walton maintained, "even if you have to go abroad to experience the unusual sensation."[98]

Johnson went out of his way to garner attention in London, sometimes waiting on "prominent street corners" for onlookers to gather so that he could stroll with an audience.[99]

However, Johnson's plans to become England's biggest vaudeville attraction quickly fell apart. Given the increasing visibility of African American sportsmen and performers in Britain, it is hardly surprising that Johnson's access to England's stages became a point of public debate. Claiming that the black champion's exhibitions would represent a clear "degradation of the music halls," VAF members decided to take collective action, launching a full-scale boycott of the venues where Johnson was set to perform.[100] Although some justified their stance as a defense of artistic standards and others pointed to Johnson's legal troubles, in many respects the VAF's protest fused racial prejudice with labor protectionism. As an escaped African American felon, Johnson was also proving a political liability for Britain. If the black heavyweight's performances were to proceed without complaint, "it would be a public scandal, if not an affront to the United States."[101] Much as he did through his campaign against the Wells-Johnson fight in 1911, Reverend F.B. Meyer tried to turn this controversy into a national issue. "Surely our variety stage will not stoop so low as to engage him," Meyer declared. "All that makes for national decency appeals to the variety managers to save us from the threatened disgrace."[102]

In response to this uproar, Britain's boxing luminary the Marquess of Queensberry urged his fellow Englishmen to speak with their pocketbooks. Although he refused to come out in direct opposition to Johnson's exhibitions, the marquess chided Londoners for taking Johnson too seriously and advised them to boycott his engagements and let the bad box office numbers speak for themselves. The marquess maintained that both the public and the press needed to acknowledge their role in creating the international Johnson phenomenon in the first place. Their unquenchable desire to see Johnson vanquished, along with their fascination with the lascivious and extravagant details of his life, had elevated the black champion to superhuman status. The English needed to remember that Johnson was just a mere man, and a black man at that.[103]

As English performers fought to keep Johnson out of their theaters, the African American champion chose to strike back in the court of public opinion. Rather than accepting defeat at the hands of the VAF, Johnson decided to call the trade union's bluff by going in front of audiences at the Euston and South London music halls to determine if *they* agreed his shows should be cancelled. He doubted that the antipathy toward him reported in London newspapers was actually true. Much as he had done from the docks of Le Havre, Johnson used his public appearances as a chance to explain his side of the story. ."If there is no popular feeling against me, I shall insist on all my engagements being fulfilled," Johnson announced. "I may produce a little sketch to exhibit the Mann act, under which I was wrongfully accused."[104] He would not only secure his engagements in England but also unleash a transatlantic protest against his maltreatment in the United States.

The African American press chose to focus on the positive, fashioning the news of Johnson's appeal to the British public into a vindicating story of white populist support. A correspondent for the *Chicago Defender* declared, "The man in the street showed tonight in an emphatic manner that he does not share in the hostility to Jack Johnson, the American pugilist. He regards the Champion as the victim of persecution which is due to color prejudice."[105] Johnson's presence had purportedly provoked public condemnation of white American racism, as London's streets were alive with talk of the Mann Act, lynchings, and Jim Crow segregation.

In reality, Johnson's public relations efforts were only a partial success, as British fans received him with a mix of curiosity, admiration, and outright revulsion. In anticipation of Johnson's arrival at the Euston music hall, spectators packed the venue, while a large, boisterous crowd waited outside hoping to catch a glimpse of the black heavyweight. After hearing that Johnson's show had been postponed for the night, the two VAF members who had refused to perform, British comediennes Maidie Scott and Beth Tate, finally agreed to go on stage. Of the two, Scott was the first to appear. Her comedy sketch was rather short-lived, as "the so-called vindicators of fair play" centered in the cheap seats of the pit and gallery shouted her off the stage.[106] Later, when Tate made her entrance, the same raucous spectators catcalled and booed, compelling the comedienne to leave in disgrace.

Outside the theater, the black champion's arrival inspired screams of excitement. "Johnson was almost smothered by the mob that got on all parts of the car, and the police had great difficulty in clearing a pathway for the pugilist," the *Defender* correspondent described.[107] Johnson slipped into the music hall during the darkness of a bioscope exhibition. When the lights came up, he bowed for his cheering fans, as several English ladies tossed him bouquets. Johnson's attempt to address the crowd inspired a counterdemonstration by several young men in the audience, who effectively shouted him down.[108] Police even had to intervene to prevent a brawl between these men and Johnson's supporters. With all of this commotion, the black heavyweight was forced to leave the theater in the middle of his planned speech.

Determined to be heard, Johnson traveled to the South London music hall to continue his protest. "My only crime is that I beat Jeffries," he declared.[109] According to the *Defender*, Johnson then made a bold gesture. Noticing that he was standing underneath a U.S. flag, the black champion stopped speaking immediately and ordered that the Stars and Stripes be replaced with the French flag. The English audience went into "convulsions" of applause and several white American visitors left the theater in disgust. Not only did Johnson send a clear message about his unwillingness to be bound by the racial antipathy of the United States, but in choosing the Tricolor over the Union Jack, he also made a powerful visual protest against British prejudice. Although this account of his appeal to the South London audience was likely more fantasy than fact, it revealed just how much African Americans hoped that Johnson would find a color-blind haven. Despite his best efforts, he was forced to cancel his London engagements.

In reflecting on Johnson's many challenges in England, Billy Lewis called the entire situation "disappointing." Although Johnson had tried to escape persecution in the United States, he now found himself in another jam. "He was not a criminal in his own judgment, nor in the judgment of many others," Lewis wrote. "He had a right to be heard."[110] Although disheartened by Britain's racism, Lewis attributed some of it to the "anti-Negro virus" brought there by the mainstream U.S. dailies and white American visitors. "If we will profit by our American experiences and those beginning in England," he argued, "we will act so as to preserve France and the rest of Europe as havens of rest when the goad presses sorely at home."

Johnson's tour of the continent in the fall of 1913 revealed that it was already too late. The black champion encountered protests against his exhibitions and faced hostile audiences. Belgium had even banned him. Where they would still have him, Johnson was reduced to engaging in cheap stunts, strongman feats, and wrestling matches for trivial sums of money.[111] The mix of curiosity and derision that greeted Johnson was hardly surprising since his tour built on a complex history of black American performance in Europe. By the turn of the twentieth century, cakewalk troupes had popularized African American song and dance and so-called "nigger fashion" in cities like Paris, Berlin, and Amsterdam.[112]

Johnson refused to admit defeat. More strategic than true, the *Defender*'s reports of his continued success in Europe shaped a narrative of Johnson as a celebrated and sophisticated New Negro. In the dispatches supplied by his nephew Rhodes, Johnson's continental tour was akin to a royal procession, enjoyed by Europe's common folk and aristocracy alike. As Rhodes described Johnson's visit to Vienna, "He is being greeted everywhere and is having the best of success. Besides giving boxing exhibitions he and Mrs. Johnson do the tango and the audience goes wild."[113] Rhodes's glowing account of his uncle's warm reception in Budapest also highlighted the barbarity of white American racism. "At the Budapest University, which is six times larger than the Chicago University, a boxing tournament was put on for the benefit of 'Jack,'" Rhodes boasted. "There is no discrimination against the colored man. When one sees how like a man he is treated here, he wonders why he remains in America to be treated as serfs [sic]."[114] Even with its long history of feudalism and monarchy, Europe still had a thing or two to teach the supposedly democratic United States about racial tolerance.

Regardless of Rhodes's impressive reports, black Americans appeared to have been relegated to the field of popular entertainment for the amusement of white European audiences. Whether in London, Paris, or Berlin, it was difficult for them to find jobs that did not involve a racialized performance of some kind. With few other options, black working-class men often jumped at the opportunity to do this type of work. In the eyes of many of their middle-class counterparts, this was hardly an ideal situation. One correspondent told the *Chicago Defender*, "If there was a better cultured class [of black people] in England than there is they could demand better positions and respect from the English people.[115] While there were few African Americans living in Holland and Germany, those who did were "of the unfortunate type that [gave] the dominant race a bad impression of the whole."

Years later Johnson effectively erased his own confrontations with Europe's color line from his 1927 autobiography, *In the Ring—And Out*. His desire not only to remake his notorious image in the eyes of the U.S. public but also to present himself as a cultured, cosmopolitan citizen of the world seemed to prevent him from publicly reflecting on the darker aspects of his European exile. The contemporary reports of Johnson's European sojourn, however, reveal that he traveled within a much larger network of black Atlantic sportsmen and performers who, try as they might, could never fully escape the shadow of the global color line.

Trading Race

Black Bodies and French Regeneration

What with the ostracising of coloured pugs in America
and Australia, France remains the only hunting ground for
them. Interracial contests will not be tolerated in England,
so that we may, before the passing of many moons, see Paris
occupied by the blacks. Already, and with but a slight pull
on the imagination, one might easily fancy oneself in bad
old Benin.

—F. H. Lucas, "Black Paris," *Boxing*, 4 January 1913

In April 1914, a few months before Jack Johnson's match in Paris against
yet another white hope named Frank Moran, the *Chicago Defender*
received a rather unfavorable report on the state of race relations in
France. Writing from the Hotel des Deux Gares, Ernest Stevens, the
well-traveled black chauffeur of U.S. industrialist and philanthropist
Julius Rosenwald, confided, "I have not seen many Afro-Americans
and I would not advise anyone to come here looking to better their
financial condition, as there are very few avenues of employment open
to them."[1] As Stevens noted, "The only exception, perhaps are theatrical folks and prizefighters, and even the latter is not advisable, Paris
having been overrun with fistic aspirants of every shade and kind."

Uncharacteristically negative in his assessment of life in France,
Stevens advised *Defender* readers that they were better off staying
home. "There is only one Afro-American in Paris who can say that he
is happy and that is Jack Johnson," he argued. Stevens recounted his
visit to the black world champion's home in Asnières, a "fashionable
suburb" about ten miles outside the city. Johnson had looked "robust

and healthy," occupying a grand residence that included a large playground and poultry yard as well as a garage housing "several first-class cars." In order to maintain this home, however, the African American heavyweight was constantly on the move with boxing exhibitions and theatrical performances in various countries. Despite Johnson's ostensible success, he was slipping further and further into debt. Johnson himself had even advised his black fans to "remain in America," where they could "become good and influential citizens" and could "get one hundred cents worth for every dollar they spend."[2]

Regardless of these practical realities, France had long cultivated an international image of racial tolerance, particularly among African American athletes and performers. At the same time, as men like Johnson searched for safe spaces of exile, they deliberately played into these French sympathies. Thus, French spectators and black American boxers ironically found their interests aligned, and yet this complicated relationship relied on an uneasy and unequal truce. Although French sportsmen enjoyed gazing at African American pugilists on stage and in the ring, they ultimately viewed black men not only as different from white men but also as fundamentally removed from Western civilization. As much as both sides claimed to operate above the color line, they remained imbricated in the racial and imperial politics of the day.

In 1908 the French sportswriter Jacques Mortane mused, "One must believe that our treatment of the niggers [nègres] is more pleasant for them than it is in America."[3] His proof was the recent influx to Paris of black American fighters such as Sam McVea, Joe Jeannette, and Jack Johnson. As Mortane acknowledged, these men left behind the pervasive racial segregation in U.S. boxing, where black American pugilists often had to fight each other repeatedly for second-rate purses in front of sparse and unenthusiastic audiences.

Struggling to gain notoriety and wealth as well as to find challengers worthy of their skills, African American boxers were drawn to the City of Light. The French sporting establishment actively promoted Paris as the one place where black men could thrive in an unprejudiced boxing ring. According to a *Washington Post* report, "Tales true enough of McVey's easy money from knocking out French champions . . . [had] reached America and tempted several others to enter the game."[4] McVea's victories as both a fighter and a businessman had convinced many African Americans that "Paris was a paradise for negro pugilists." As the report noted, "McVey, a Paris resident, manages himself, being clear-headed and taking advice from a Paris law firm."[5] Denied a fair shot at success back home, in France McVea was the quintessential New Negro—tough, determined, and independent.

McVea and his contemporaries formed one of the first black American expatriate communities in France. "We have at present, 'three negro villages' in Paris," one French sportswriter observed in 1911. Typically, white managers set up training camps for their "stables" of black fighters: Battling Guiller arranged the matches of McVea and Kid Davis; M. Galvin managed Dixie Kid, Andrew Dixon, Bob Scanlon, and Frank Crozier; and Joe Woodman handled the likes of Sam Langford, Bob Armstrong, and Cyclone Warren.[6] African American pugilists could be seen all across the city. They trained at Luna Park, and they fought at the Folies Bergère, Les Halles, the Hippodrome, Fronton Bineau, the Nouveau Cirque, and the Wonderland. They spent their free time in Montmartre and even frequented the glitzy nightspots of Montparnasse, setting the stage for the *tumulte noir* (black craze) of jazz-age Paris.[7]

Thanks in part to the well-publicized Parisian exploits of black boxers, narratives of French racial exceptionalism became ingrained in the African American popular consciousness. In August 1914 an editorialist for the *New York News* claimed that many black Americans were praying that France would emerge triumphant in the World War. Countering white American reports that trivialized "the black man's love for the Tricolor" as a childish reaction to the French embrace of Jack Johnson, the editorialist maintained that "the reason for the black race's convictions" was "far more sensible and substantial." "The Frenchman alone, whether at home or abroad, whether approached by a single black man or surrounded by ten thousand Guineans, treats the black man like a man," he declared. "The whiteman's [sic] burden to the Englishman means money, to the German it means conquest, to the Frenchman it means the spread of civilization."[8] Even though the writer downplayed the importance of Johnson's popular stories of success in Paris as a reason for African Americans' affinity with France, black boxers were some of the first black celebrities to praise the European nation's supposed color blindness.

Unlike the Anglo-Saxon powers of the United States and Britain, France appeared unafraid of black fighting men, whether in the boxing ring or on the battlefield. The fact that the French military had been actively recruiting black troops in preparation for a possible war helped to reinforce their reputation for racial tolerance. For many black Americans, France's use of African soldiers seemed to be a significant step toward the ultimate realization of black political independence. "Africa will eventually be for the Africans," the same editorialist declared. "Until that time the African favors France because France favors the African." Yet underlying these utopian narratives of French racial exceptionalism was a fundamental mistranslation of the significance of blackness, particularly black manhood, for constructions of white French nationalism and the French imperial *mission civilisatrice* (civilizing mission).[9]

Questions of color were at the very heart of black American prizefighters' great popularity in France in the years before World War I. Their physical presence inspired French sports enthusiasts to publicly reflect on questions of race, gender, empire, and civilization, for they provided a comfortable abstraction of the colonial question. As French fans embraced these black sojourners, they endeavored to project an image of enlightened imperial benevolence, one that stood in direct contrast to the racial oppression of Jim Crow America.[10] African American pugilists capitalized on this French fascination with "blackness." From Paris they not only critiqued the backwardness of U.S. negrophobia but also articulated their own vision of what it meant to be a New Negro. Eager to join in this interimperial conversation on race, white American journalists mocked the "peculiar" French adoration of African American boxers. Apparently, Frenchmen's joie de vivre, coupled with their Latin effeminacy, had rendered them incapable of shouldering the white man's burden.[11] Although the personal circumstances of black boxers often improved when they arrived in Paris, they remained tangled in the web of a transnational culture of race.

Despite France's official rhetoric of color blindness, it was a major player in this burgeoning trade of racial ideas, images, and spectacles. The transnational space of the boxing ring confounded French sportsmen's attempts to distance themselves from their supposedly race-obsessed Anglo-Saxon counterparts. The ring was an important cultural "contact zone" in which Parisian spectators actively engaged in the global flow of ideas about race, manhood, empire, and the body, translating and adapting them for their local circumstances.[12] Thus, their embrace of black American pugilists must be placed within the context of French imperial culture, the widespread fears of white degeneration, prevailing narratives of French racial exceptionalism, and France's longstanding fascination with U.S. race relations.

Boxing itself was a foreign sport, and in the years before World War I it became increasingly popular in France. Previously Frenchmen had practiced the *savate,* a system of defense involving both kicking and punching. Around 1905, however, the French public began to abandon the *savate* in favor of the British and eventually the U.S. style of boxing. Words like *knockout* and *fighter* came into use as a variety of French periodicals began to cover and support the fledgling boxing industry.[13]

Théodore Vienne, Frantz Reichel, Paul Rousseau, and Victor Breyer, the founders of La Société de Propagation de la Boxe Anglaise (Society for the Propagation of English Boxing, or SPBA), worked to legitimize boxing in the eyes of the French public.[14] The SPBA strove to develop French champions capable of beating Anglo-Saxon opponents and to promote boxing as a vital means of physical exercise and self-defense. They hoped the sport would help to strengthen and invigorate the French nation by fighting alcoholism and debauchery among its young men. The organization often brought in foreigners to fight French boxers and to tutor French fans in the nuances of boxing technique.[15] The SPBA's main venue, the Wonderland Paris, became a hub of social activity, attracting not only the *Tout-Paris sportif,* or the upper-crust connoisseurs of sport, but also considerable crowds of working-class people.

As the SPBA eagerly solicited the visits of African American pugilists in the early 1900s, questions of race soon entered the cosmopolitan space of the French ring. Parisian fans argued that their celebration of black prizefighters illustrated their greater modernity and, by extension, their more sophisticated relationship with the colonial world, yet the fame of black American boxers also exposed French anxieties about their place in the global arena, as well as their own ideas about racial difference and the cultural boundaries of civilization. Using this confusing mix of interimperial rivalry and trade to their advantage, Johnson and his contemporaries soon cornered the Parisian market for blackness.

BLACK BOXERS AND THE FRENCH BODY POLITIC

Long before the famed African American performer Josephine Baker arrived in the French capital in 1925, spectacles of blackness, especially black manhood, had already become a hot commodity in the Parisian sporting scene.[16] Although both vilified and feared in their own nation, African American pugilists became huge celebrities in France: they challenged white men in the ring, endorsed a variety of products, published articles in sporting magazines, toured the French provinces, participated in the underground nightlife of the Parisian *bals* (dance halls), and even gained the admiration of the European avant-garde. The early French boxing scene revolved around the lives and fights of African American heavyweights, and they emerged as central figures in the racialized and gendered aesthetics of transatlantic modernism.[17] Their pugilistic feats became an important cultural site for spirited discussions about race, the body, and the body politic.

Alongside other modes of African American performance, from the *danse du gâteau* (cakewalk) to the syncopated rhythms of ragtime, black boxers embodied a vision of modernity both in and out of the ring that appealed to French spectators. In the years before World War I, Parisian fans adopted American-style boxing for many of the same reasons they later embraced jazz. Popularized by African American fighters in France, boxing and its attendant culture seemed to encapsulate the presumed freedom, physicality, and vivacity of black culture. With the American style, one could fight with little appearance of strain or effort. Its crouched stance was more fluid than that of the traditional English method, allowing the boxer to punch and dodge with ease. Georges Max's Pelican Club and Grognet's school promoted their *salles de boxe* (boxing gyms) as places where Frenchmen could receive expert instruction in the new American method, often from African American champions. Outside the ring, Parisian sportsmen also began to appropriate the flamboyant lifestyles of their favorite black pugilists. Johnson and McVea helped to popularize chewing gum, while their dandified fashions found a place in the shops of local tailors.[18] Black American prizefighters exemplified the fundamental paradox of transatlantic modernism, for their combination of African primitivism and raw New World energy became the basis for the cultural regeneration of white France.[19]

Black American boxers' great popularity with French fans ultimately stemmed from their embodiment of primal black physicality, seen as the polar opposite of the effete intellectuality of white civilization. Unlike their white American and British counterparts, French sports reveled in spectacles of black strength. McVea's early matches against white fighters exemplified this growing fetishism of the black male body. When McVea knocked out English fighter Jack Scales in January 1908, his physical stature and boxing skill mesmerized French spectators. As Jacques Mortane recounted in colorful detail, with McVea's "avalanche" of blows, Scales's head had "oscillated three or four times from front to back, as if the shock would remove it from his trunk."[20] For McVea, who found himself effectively shut out of main-

FIGURE 12. French sporting magazines frequently featured news and photos of the major black American heavyweights, including Sam McVea (pictured here), Joe Jeannette, Jack Johnson, and Sam Langford. *La Vie au grand air*, 30 May 1908. From the author's collection.

stream U.S. boxing when first-rate white American pugilists refused to fight him, French journalists' graphic description and public celebration of his interracial triumphs must have seemed extraordinary. For close to two years he was an invincible hero, beating white opponent after white opponent in front of large crowds of Parisian fans. In France black male physicality was a saleable commodity rather than a cause for alarm.

Although bouts featuring two black pugilists had little mainstream marketability in the United States, *les combats nègres* (nigger matches) formed the centerpiece of the French boxing industry. In 1909 a series of fights between McVea and Jeannette captured the attention of Paris, provoking passionate debates about race and modernity. Through these matches sports enthusiasts discussed the nature of black masculinity, physicality, savagery, and solidarity and also pondered the intimate relationship between the survival of the French Republic and its African colonies. They eagerly consumed many of the same essentialist images of blackness circulating in white American and British publications and performances, reconfiguring them to suit their local cultural and political needs. As the McVea-Jeannette fight series linked sport with popular science, politics, and aesthetics, the boxing ring became an important arena in which all of these racialized themes intertwined.

The two African American pugilists traveled to Paris at a moment when calls for white physical regeneration in the face of modern decadence gripped the French popular consciousness. With its native-born population in decline, many physical culturists believed that France was, in effect, a dying nation, not only unable to protect its own citizens at home but also incapable of bearing its share of the white man's burden abroad.[21] While French fears of white degeneration centered on their diminishing birthrate in the face of German demographic explosion and the threat of German invasion, the African colonies emerged as the ultimate resource for national revival. Writing in 1910, Colonel Charles Mangin argued that France possessed an untapped human reserve, the *force noire* (black army), which would help to sustain the geopolitical strength of the imperial nation.[22] "All the French will understand that France does not stop in the Mediterranean, nor in the Sahara," the colonel explained, "that it extends to Congo; that it constitutes an empire vaster than Europe."[23] Despite Mangin's rhetoric of inclusion, this "expansion" would not only require continued white French stewardship, but it would also keep the majority of black subjects safely contained within colonial borders.

Rather than an endorsement of black sovereignty, Mangin's faith in the *force noire* had more to do with prevailing beliefs about the revivifying effects of primitive African manhood. He maintained that Africans had "the qualities which the long fights of modern war required: rusticity, endurance, tenacity, a combative instinct, the absence of nervousness, and an incomparable power of shock."[24] However, colonial posters, military postcards, drawings, and photographs always portrayed the soldiers of the *force noire* as endearing, humorous, and even happy-go-lucky. African American boxers also became nonthreatening symbols of colonial Africa. The consumption of primitive blackness embodied by men like McVea and Jeannette offered a means to regenerate white French manhood, and by extension the French imperial nation, in the safety of the metropolitan capital.

The amazing feats of black prizefighters often did more to support the French *mission civilisatrice* than to undermine it. The public fascination with McVea and others was an extension of France's already well-established culture of imperial spectacle. Black American boxers embodied the full range of African stereotypes already in operation in the French capital. In the late nineteenth century, elaborate displays of colonial peoples at the Paris Expositions Universelles (1889 and 1900) accompanied the expansion of French imperialism in Africa. Parisian theater had also taken to sensationalizing the French conquest of Dahomey (Benin) through epic plays, staged reenactments of battles, and ethnographic scenes involving "authentic" natives. This combination of state-sponsored exhibits and popular entertainments offered a glimpse of the supposedly colorful, brutal, primitive, and physical African lifestyle, thereby reifying the racial hierarchy while also helping to rationalize the need for white French intervention.[25] Black American fighters found themselves folded into this commercial culture of blackness as they boxed and performed in many of the same venues as these colonial spectacles. The Parisian sports columnist Henri Dispan admitted, "Each time Mr. Samuel McVea and other gentlemen of color fight, I am well aware of the emotions that a trip to the heart of Africa must give."[26] In his descriptions of their matches, Dispan freely melded stereotypical images of black slaves on the plantations of *la Louisianne* (Louisiana) with those of cannibalistic natives in the African jungle. It certainly would not have been a stretch for French audiences to view men like McVea and Jeannette as essentially "African," especially since black American performers often masqueraded as Zulus, Ethiopians, and Dahomeyans in marketing themselves to European audiences.[27]

Alongside these depictions of black colonial barbarity, the image of the African *tirailleur* (soldier) emerged as the epitome of the French civilizing process: a physically robust yet domesticated savage who had not only been tamed but trained to happily serve in the defense of white French interests. With its coverage of the Dahomean War in 1892, the mainstream French press constructed the African *tirailleurs* as faithful heroes—deferential, determined, and, perhaps most importantly, cheerful and comical. The *tirailleurs* first made their appearance in Paris in 1899, marching proudly to the cheers of white French spectators in the Bastille Day parade. By World War I their smiling pictures

FIGURE 13. The caricatures of black American boxers that appeared in French newspapers closely resembled popular images of the African *tirailleurs* (soldiers). "Après le match—Sen-Sen chewing gum," *L'Auto*, 28 March 1909. Bibliothèque nationale de France.

graced French advertisements for the beverage Banania, accompanied by the catchphrase "Y'a Bon!" (Dis be good!).[28] The blackface caricatures of African American boxers often spoke the same *petit nègre* (pidgin French). A popular advertisement for Sen-Sen chewing gum, a licorice-flavored breath freshener, featured a grinning McVea next to a battered white fighter with the caption "Moi, toujou vainqueur, toujou souriant, jamais knock-out, car moi toujou mâcher" (Me always winner, always smiling, never knock out, because me always chewing).[29] Much like the *tirailleurs*, McVea and his contemporaries exemplified the same duality of controlled ferocity, except this time it was in the service of white French amusement.

The McVea-Jeannette series also coincided with the rise of *l'Art nègre*, as avant-garde artists like Henri Matisse and Pablo Picasso began to experiment with the aesthetics of primitivism. These artists employed African motifs to shock viewers and disrupt conventions, thereby critiquing what they saw as the stultifying conformity of white French civilization.[30] Several of them were even known to frequent the matches of African American boxers, using them as a source of creative inspiration. "Since 1910, I had been attracted to boxing matches," the cubist painter André Dunoyer de Segonzac later recounted. "The black heavyweight champions Sam MacVea, Sam Langford, and Joe Jeannette amazed French sporting youth." He recalled seeing Johnson in a wrestling match at the Nouveau Cirque, "beautiful like an Apollo from the Congo."[31] Segonzac and others came to identify with the black heavyweights, for their savage vitality in the ring stood in direct contrast to the supposed degeneracy of the period. Even as the French tried to dissociate themselves from the imperial politics of their Anglo-Saxon counterparts, they actively participated in the very same ideas of race and the body that bolstered the global project of the white man's burden.

The announcement of the first McVea-Jeannette match had reportedly "revolutionized the world of Parisian sportsmen." A month and a half before the scheduled fight on 20 February, fans had already begun to inquire about tickets. "It is the question of the day," one journalist observed, "and in all the boxing clubs and athletic milieus, we discuss this subject with passion."[32] Another sportswriter claimed, "It is not just Paris, but all the regions [départements] and even abroad that are interested in the *great event* of February 20." Ticket requests had come to *L'Auto* from "London, Brussels, Liège, Anvers, Genève, Roubaix, Lille, Troyes, Rouen, Reims, Orléans, and even Bordeaux."[33]

The publicity surrounding the McVea-Jeannette match had ethnographic and social Darwinistic undercurrents, exposing French views on the inherent physicality of black people and their evolutionary separation from white civilization. Parisian spectators seemed to revel in the African American competitors' imagined brutality as an antidote to their own effete and effeminate modernity. Referring to McVea and Jeannette as *"les deux terribles nègres"* (the two terrible niggers), French sportswriters promised the match would be more gruesome than any other fight in the capital.[34]

This French eroticism of the virile black male body not only drew scores of fans (both men and women) to the African American fighters' training camps, but it also inspired the publication of countless pictures and the brisk sale of souvenirs. In describing Jeannette's first public workout, one sportswriter exclaimed, "I will not surprise anyone by saying that his musculature is superb: his large shoulders and supple, elegant legs."[35] Alongside Jeannette's "extraordinary virtuosity," he also touted McVea's "extraordinary power and speed."[36] Many Parisian sporting magazines showcased photos of McVea and Jeannette in just their boxing trunks, baring their powerful chests. The dark-skinned McVea had a stocky, muscular build, while the biracial Jeannette had a much leaner, chiseled physique. French fans could even treat themselves to figurines and silhouettes of the two African American pugilists, specially crafted for the occasion by local artists.[37]

Blackface images, neolithic caricatures, and simian tropes abounded in the prefight publicity, betraying the exotic, paternalistic gaze of French spectators. Despite the fact that McVea and Jeannette differed greatly in color and appearance, one cartoon reduced them both to white eyes and lips against a black background, while others featured the same markers of savagery, including dragging knuckles, exaggerated lips, jutting jawbones, and overhanging foreheads. A popular French cartoonist depicted McVea as a menacing gorilla and poked fun at Jeannette's seeming inability to find human sparring partners strong enough to train with him.[38] Even though Jeannette reportedly declared that he was a "mulatto" rather than a "nigger," European artists still defined him by the racial tropes of the day.[39] Many of their caricatures suggested that both fighters possessed an unrivaled animalistic strength.

On the evening of 20 February, hundreds of sports fans waited anxiously outside the Cirque de Paris on avenue de la Motte-Picquet well before the start of the fight card. Although the modern venue had a capacity of more than four thousand spectators, several thousand fans still had to be turned away. Many prominent European sportsmen attended, as did icons of the theater, arts, and letters. Also on hand were political and scientific leaders, from dukes to marquises to doctors. This historic match was not just the domain of the rich and famous, for the promoters had set aside a section of seats for the city's less fortunate. They had also expanded the betting services to accommodate the large number of transactions coming from every sector of society. In the end, the box office alone garnered a record-breaking eighty-five thousand francs.[40]

La Patrie called it "the greatest match that we have ever seen in Paris." French journalists portrayed the fight as almost titillatingly pornographic in its brutality. "For more than an hour, a half-breed as handsome as Hercules [Jeannette] and the strongest of the Ethiopians [McVea] worked patiently and furiously to send one another to dreamland," writer Georges Dupuy poetically recounted. "It was the assault of a tiger against a bison." Jeannette, the "tiger," was "agile, supple, powerful, aggressive, and perfectly composed," while McVea, the "unbeatable black bison," possessed a rock-hard forehead and enormous neck. With his many feints and dodges, Jeannette made his slower opponent look awkward at times. McVea, however, also hit Jeannette with pounding blows, knocking him to the canvas. Throughout the fight McVea struggled to counter Jeannette's assiduous technique with crushing force, and after twenty rounds he emerged the winner by referee's decision. The celebration of McVea's victory spilled into the streets of the capital.[41]

With the match ending by decision rather than by knockout, many spectators felt cheated. In the weeks before the fight French fans had anticipated "a butchering capable of causing future prohibitions" of boxing in Paris.[42] From the streets to the pages of sporting magazines, there was a flurry of discussion over whether the McVea-Jeannette match had been faked. Exposing underlying fears of black solidarity and conspiracy, many fans argued that the two fighters had entered into a secret "entente." One correspondent complained that McVea and Jeannette had not only "lacked determination and hate," but also had failed to bring "enough passion" to the ring.[43] Countering such opinions, another fan wrote a blistering defense of the fight, maintaining that those who questioned the match's veracity were simply uncivilized people "whose keen desire was to see a boxing ring transformed into a bullfighting arena."[44] As this fan so astutely observed, driving this controversy were basic assumptions about the inherent savagery of black men and the viciousness of African combat, especially since these allegations almost never arose in response to matches involving white boxers.

This "circus match between two niggers" had served to highlight the vital importance of physical training, and particularly boxing, for the reinvigoration of the French imperial body politic.[45] It had provided white French sportsmen with an excellent example of two primitive adversaries, stripped of all weapons, fighting to their maximum ability. Although France now appeared to be in the midst of a sporting renaissance, over the past half century Frenchmen had allowed their scorn for physical activity to make them lose sight of the importance of their muscles. Given the growing threat of war with Germany, boxing seemed to offer young Frenchmen the opportunity not only to revitalize their bodies, but also to acquire the critical skills of concentration, precision, and persistence necessary for survival in the modern world.

Back by popular demand, the second McVea-Jeannette match took place on the night of 17 April 1909 at the Cirque de Paris. To ensure a definitive result and, hopefully, a more ardent battle, the fight promoters arranged a *"match au finish"* (fight to the finish) for a purse of thirty thousand francs.[46] Guaranteed to test the limits of black physicality, the fight could only end in knockout or submission rather than by referee's decision. Such matches had long been illegal in both the United

States and Britain, and even in France white boxers rarely fought under such harsh conditions. The second time around the African American pugilists delivered, treating the audience to an exciting match, which continued for forty-nine rounds until a battered McVea threw in the towel. The arduous fight had lasted so long that many of the spectators had already left for the night by the time McVea surrendered. As Georges Dupuy exclaimed, "The rematch . . . was not only the most beautiful we have ever seen in France, but perhaps the most terrible and most savage in the history of boxing throughout the world."[47]

For many spectators, white civilization had triumphed over black savagery. Ségonzac contended, "I admired Joe Jeannette, the 'yellow' black, a learned boxer, more scientific than his pure black brothers."[48] Another Parisian sportswriter juxtaposed Jeannette, the "Greek athlete," with McVea, "the eldest son of a grand barbarian king." "In a boxing ring, with rules and care, the art and the energy of Joe triumphed," he maintained. "In a forest, the instinct of Sam would have overcome."[49] With its ten-second knockdown rule, rests in between rounds, the use of gloves, and the help of trainers, the regulated match had apparently given the more civilized Jeannette a distinct advantage over his primitive opponent. French writer Tristan Bernard forwarded his own anthropological analysis, arguing that McVea's submission had exemplified the "lack of perseverance inherent in the [black] race." The dark-skinned fighter's inability to go in for the kill stemmed from "a certain timidity" and "habit of subservience" also characteristic of African people.[50] In other words, regardless of the black male's superior physique, he still needed the guidance of white civilization.

In the lead-up to the final McVea-Jeannette match on 11 December 1909, French journalists once again went to great lengths to reassure fans of the fight's legitimacy.[51] Throughout the match the "nearly white" Jeannette seemed to have taken on the mantle of civilization, reputedly taunting McVea in the ring by calling him "nigger Sam." As one sportswriter described, McVea glared at Jeannette, much like the angry son of an African king sneering at an ill-mannered white explorer.[52] When the referee declared the thirty-round fight a *"match nul"* (tie match), cries of protest rent the air since many in the crowd believed that Jeannette should have won by decision.[53]

Throughout the 1910s, *combats nègres* continued to be the mainstay of the Parisian boxing scene, as many French fans jumped at the chance to participate in their own form of colonial ethnography. Paradoxically, while these matches embodied a racialized and gendered critique of the decadence of European modernity, they also provided a metaphorical showcase for the ultimate victory of Western civilization. Although white men apparently could regenerate their bodies through physical activity, black men seemed to be irredeemably inferior in the realms of character, intellect, and culture. Even as men like McVea and Jeannette generated astounding praise and profits during their Parisian sojourn, they quickly discovered the very real limits of French racial tolerance.

JIM CROW IN PARIS

Despite all these contradictions, the Parisian sporting press continued to celebrate African American boxers' apparent love of the Tricolor. "All negroes have two countries: America, and then France," one correspondent declared. He had noticed that an "admirable number of blacks" had found their way to the City of Light.[54] "In about twenty years," he speculated, "we will have in Paris, a whole army corps of adorable, young *café au lait,* vibrant and robust souvenirs of the champions' visit." Although the prospect of interracial liaisons and biracial offspring did not seem to disturb this particular journalist, the growing presence of African American men was certainly not welcomed by all.

The precariousness of black American sportsmen's social position gave them a glimpse of both the best and the worst of French racial politics. Unlike members of the African American intelligentsia, these rough-and-tumble men often experienced the full brunt of European racism. Even though McVea had become a popular "professor" at Grognet's school of boxing, where he instructed French students in the "American method," his large black entourage quickly became a bone of contention with the school's director.[55] Grognet openly despised the "army of negroes" that followed McVea around, calling them both "cumbersome and unpleasant."[56] When the director finally banned "these innumerable 'coloured men'" from the gym, McVea decided to take his business elsewhere rather than yield to Grognet's discrimination. While Frenchmen enjoyed watching and taking lessons from famed African American fighters, most did not want their social spaces to be overrun with black men.

The continued influx of black pugilists was forcing French fans to confront the practical problems of living in a multiracial society. Leon Sée of *La Boxe et les boxeurs* maintained, "Governed by our good hearts, we French have a tendency to consider the Americans veritable tyrants towards the black race in their country. In our total ignorance of the question, we gladly say, 'A nigger is a man like any other. He has the right to the same consideration as a white.'"[57] However, Sée and others were already beginning to rethink the wisdom of their supposedly naïve position. "We have not yet suffered of these 'coloured men' like our neighbors in America," Sée argued. "Some of us, who, since the invasion of boxing in France, have had dealings with the niggers are obliged to recognize that the [white] Americans are not totally at fault." Others maintained that the growing popularity of African American prizefighters and performers was a sure sign of France's increasing barbarism rather than its rejuvenation. As Armand Grébauval, a Paris municipal counselor, complained, "It's the Bamboula [a type of West African drum popular among American slaves] that now replaces the bygone tenor, and makes the men run and the women swoon."[58] Black boxers were just one part of the disturbing deluge of black culture into the French capital—one that seemed to be shaking the very foundations of French civilization.

Back home, some African American sportswriters remained suspicious of France's embrace of black prizefighters. *Indianapolis Freeman* columnist Billy Lewis maintained that in Paris McVea was not loved "in the best sense." Instead, "he was in about the same relation to the French public as a bull terrier pup is to a white lady millionaire." As Lewis explained, "She admires his chubby nose and monkey face in a way, perhaps, because rare—rare in ugliness. She pets him and fondles him; she permits it the liberty of her room, but she does not forget what it is."[59] Lewis cleverly captured the French public's exotic and paternalistic view of men like McVea while also exposing the unequal sexual dynamic between white French women and black boxers. Although the French public seemed to enjoy the African American pugilists currently in their midst, their racial tolerance had yet to be tested. "Of course they do not have our thousands [of black people] to deal with, our millions, many of whom do not present any too commendable fronts," Lewis warned. "France has seen us at our best, to put it honestly."[60]

Even at their best, these visiting black American sportsmen only seemed to confirm African inferiority in the eyes of many French spectators. Johnson was known for dressing in elaborate outfits and hobnobbing with the likes of the cubist Sonia Delaunay and the futurist Gino Severini at the *Bal Bullier,* a popular dance hall among the Parisian avant-garde.[61] His late-night jaunts had helped to inspire the dandified image of the *roi nègre* (nigger king), which emerged as a popular symbol of the inability of Africans to hold positions of political power. In French advertisements the *roi nègre,* much like Johnson, typically wore a top hat and monocle and carried a scepter. Despite this caricature's pretensions, his grasp of civilization was apparently incomplete, for his oversized feet were usually shoeless and his clothing both garish and ill fitting.[62] French sportswriters often poked fun of Johnson's own delusions of grandeur by cloaking him in images of African savagery. To Dispan of *La Boxe et les boxeurs,* the black champion carried himself like "kaffir royalty." "He endlessly masticates a piece of chewing gum," Dispan described, "his rolling eyes so white and ferocious that he seems to be chewing the tough flesh of an insufficiently roasted missionary."[63] While African American boxers attempted to fashion themselves as modern men in the Parisian capital, they found themselves folded into French imperial culture.

Nevertheless, both the growing presence of black pugilists and the rising popularity of U.S.-style boxing were forcing Parisian fans to contemplate and confront the color line in new ways. French sportsmen became better acquainted with U.S. racial mores through their participation in the commercial culture of boxing. Boxing publications, matches, and other spectacles provided a public forum in which French fans could experience firsthand the "peculiar" venom of U.S. race prejudice. Many of these cultural products were laced with stereotypical images of Jim Crow segregation, and the United States became a convenient foil against which white France could define its own relationship with people of color.

Although Parisian sports enthusiasts seemed to reject the obvious violence and vehemence of white American negrophobia, questions of race remained integral to the marketing of boxing in France. Banking on the widespread French fascination for black American boxers and U.S. racial politics, Parisian promoters decided to import an American battle royal in March 1909. Brutal and racist affairs, battle royals had become a popular amusement in the United States, providing many African American boxers with their start in the business. Usually a group of four or five blindfolded black boys would enter the ring and engage in a free-for-all fight until there was only one boy left standing. White American spectators would often taunt the boys with racial slurs and throw coins at them while they fought.

Given the proven popularity of matches involving African Americans, French promoters hoped that the battle royal would catch on and become a regular fixture on Parisian fight cards.[64] On the night of 20 March 1909, five black boys of varying shades entered the ring at the Hippodrome, and after a short charade of a fight the darkest boy in the group emerged the winner. The battle royal, however, never became a particular favorite of Parisian fans. As a representative for the local Society of Cinema-Halls named Charles Despland declared, "Let us leave aside, if you will, the 'Battle Royal' of the niggers."[65] According to Despland, this savage U.S. practice simply did not meet France's higher standards for sporting competition. Although Parisians enjoyed the often-bloody matches of men like McVea and Jeannette, the American battle royal was apparently too boorish for their sophisticated tastes.

Images of white American barbarism were commonplace in the French boxing scene. Parisian sportswriters often depicted the United States, much like Africa, as a wild and exotic frontier desperately in need of European civilization.[66] In recounting his travels to America, Gus Muller of *La Boxe et les boxeurs* claimed that the "majority of American [boxing] clubs" were not only "free from any decoration" but also "rudimentary" in their construction.[67] White American boxing fans appeared to be no better. "The noise of car horns and accordions and the vile outbursts of spectators during the engagements" were enough to drive the Frenchman to distraction. Muller's experiences in the United States had only emphasized his belief in the superiority of "French taste."

Muller had been struck by the bloodthirsty nature of an interracial boxing match that he had attended on the outskirts of Denver, Colorado. He recalled the racist milieu in which a white middleweight named Tom Kingsley had fought against an African American challenger named Arthur Collins. "The advertisement of this combat aroused enormous interest throughout the entire area," Muller described. "Many important bets were placed, and special trams were rented to bring the large and impassioned crowd to the match's location."[68] In the weeks before the fight, spontaneous brawls had broken out between white and black boxing fans as they discussed its probable result. Early on the day of the match, a crowd of about a hundred cowboys, along with a few African Americans, had pressed up against the venue's locked doors. With tensions running high, a gunfight had nearly broken out between a white cowboy and a black fan.

This interracial violence had followed the throng of men into the boxing arena. During the second round Muller remembered hearing,

"Kill that black bastard, Tom! Kill him!" The white cowboys in the stands had immediately drawn their revolvers, shooting them in the air and twirling them on their fingers. By the eighth and final round, full pandemonium had erupted. "It was easy to see that there was going to be some kind of tragedy," Muller maintained. "Several blacks frightened by the threats had tried to leave; however, unable to find a passageway, about twenty of them had escaped through the windows."[69] A black man was shot dead, and a general melee engulfed the ring as the white cowboys pointed their weapons at the remaining black spectators.

Although likely embellished, Muller's description of Denver's boxing scene closely followed formulaic French narratives of U.S. racial violence and the brutality of the Western frontier, shaped through their consumption of newspaper reports, popular literature, and moving pictures. A novella of the time titled *Les Nègres contre les Peaux-Rouges* (The Niggers versus the Redskins) provided French readers with a sensationalized view of racial conflict in the United States.[70] As the story went, a young white American named Fred became lost in the woods while riding his horse. He eventually made his way out of the forest and rode to the farm of a family friend in search of help. However, when Fred arrived old man Sadler was nowhere to be found. Sadler's home had been taken over by a band of menacing black men. Recently escaped from a Florida plantation, the black fugitives had made their way across the countryside stealing, massacring, and burning farms. Although the black marauders took Fred hostage, the young man still managed to break free. In the end, a tribe of brave Delaware Indians saved the day by killing all of the escaped African American slaves.

Not surprisingly, many Parisian sportsmen characterized racism as something that existed outside the political and cultural boundaries of France. These stories of interracial hatred in the United States stood in direct contrast to popular French myths about the nation's noble civilizing mission in Africa and the loyal service of its African *tirailleurs*. Parisian journalists tended to accuse white Americans of bringing Jim Crow racism to France. They blamed U.S. tourists for forcing French hoteliers and restaurateurs to erect a color line against African American guests.[71] In turn, they often showcased examples of white American race prejudice in their accounts of interracial matches in Paris. One French journalist described a colorful scene from a fight between the white American middleweight Harry Lewis and the African American journeyman Bob Scanlon. As Lewis rested in his corner between rounds a white American fan had urged him to "give the darned nigger a good 'licking.'" Lewis reportedly quipped, "The smell of coons is bad enough, without my wanting to taste 'em."[72] For many Parisian sportsmen, the prospect of witnessing this interracial friction in the ring was what drew them to the fights.

Indeed, interracial matches were big business in Paris, attracting not only European spectators but also visiting Americans, both white and black. French promoters took pride in the fact that they continued to host interracial matches, even after the boxing ring had become increasingly segregated in both the United States and Britain. When McVea fought against the white American Jim Barry in June 1909, French sportsmen threw their support behind the African American, while the white American expatriate colony sided with Barry.[73] On the night of the fight the two boxers seemed to have an equal number of fans in attendance. When the referee disqualified Barry, skirmishes broke out in the stands and the municipal guard had to be called in to restore the peace.[74] The match provided French sportsmen with a means to differentiate their racial politics from those of their white American contemporaries.

French promoters even went so far as to sensationalize the interracial hatred between black and white American fighters in order to drum up more business at the box office. They invited Parisian fans to be voyeurs of white American negrophobia in action. In April 1910, when Scanlon took on the white American Charley Hitte, French journalists billed it as a contest of the races. Betting was especially swift for this fight precisely because of its obvious racial overtones as a contest between a *"policier new-yorkais"* (New York policeman) and an African American. One sportswriter declared, "One knows that between Americans of different colors, such meetings are always sincere and always bitter because of the kind of race hatred that exists in the United States between the whites on the one hand, the Blacks, the Redskins and even the Yellows, on the other."[75] There was also a personal vendetta at stake. Hitte sought revenge against Scanlon since the black pugilist had apparently kneed Hitte's white American trainer and fellow boxer Blink MacCloskey in the groin during a previous match. Although the referee eventually deemed the Hitte-Scanlon fight a tie, the African American had physically punished his white opponent. So supposedly intense was their shared hatred in the ring that the Parisian columnist Dispan exclaimed, "If after having knocked him out, Bob roasted Hitte . . . and then devoured him gluttonously, it would only half surprise us."[76] While French sportsmen could certainly sympathize with the racial plight of black American pugilists, they could not help but view men like Scanlon through the prevailing tropes of African savagery.

In February 1912 MacCloskey finally got his own chance for revenge against Scanlon in the ring. When Scanlon triumphed, however, many Parisian fans began to ask "what occult power was at work . . . to so favour blacks in their fistic struggles with the white races." One French correspondent speculated that MacCloskey's loss may have been "a sort of punishment for the [white] Americans for their hatred of the coloured man."[77] In many respects the cosmopolitan space of the Parisian boxing ring exemplified the complex cultural forces shaping racial formations in the late imperial age. While boxing and other commercial amusements involving black Americans were instrumental to France's culture of racial denial, they also implicated Parisian fans in the increasingly transnational trade of white supremacist entertainments and ideas.

LES ESPOIRS BLANCS

Even as French fans attempted to distance themselves from the vicious racism of their white American counterparts, they promoted *un espoir blanc* (a white hope) of their own. France's beloved young champion Georges Carpentier fought against Jeannette in the spring of 1914. This Parisian match captivated the French sporting public along with the nation's intellectual and artistic community, putting questions of race, manhood, and the state of the French body politic at the forefront of public discussions. Not only was the interracial fight a question of black versus white, but it promised to showcase France's physical regeneration on the world stage.

As Scanlon later described in his memoirs, during a boxing tour of the French provinces in 1908 he had discovered a "little blond boy" named Carpentier who was managed by François Descamps.[78] "I could see that he was the makings of a champion, so I got them [Carpentier and Descamps] to come to Paris," Scanlon recalled. Over the next few years Carpentier's career took off and Parisian fans dubbed him "The French Idol."[79] Combining youthful effervescence, movie-star good looks, and great ring dexterity, Carpentier offered a strong counterpoint to the pervasive stereotypes of French effeminacy, overcivilization, and effeteness. More than just a question of athletic competition,

Anglo-Saxon sportswriters often used these gendered tropes to criticize France's supposed lack of both martial spirit and imperial discipline.

Through the boxing ring, French fans confronted their anxieties over their nation's racial and geopolitical standing. According to one Parisian correspondent, before the advent of men like Carpentier, one would often hear Frenchmen saying, "Oh, zee French vill nevair beat ze 'Roasbeefs' [British] with zee box."[80] They thought that their "fiery temperament" and small stature precluded them from success in the ring. "Comparatively puny in those days," the writer argued, "Frenchmen's eyes opened wide at the spectacle of two Englishmen doing their hardest . . . to do each other grievous bodily harm." With the emergence of pugilists like Marcel Moreau, Marc Gaucher, and then Carpentier, Frenchmen began to compete on even ground with Englishmen and white Americans alike. Daniel Rivoire of *Le Journal* believed that the upcoming Jeannette-Carpentier match would provide perfect "proof of the restoration of [the French] race from the physical point of view."[81] Carpentier stood as "a synthesis of all the efforts made for twenty years to restore energy to a languishing people." As one of the few white boxers in the world who dared to take on Jeannette, he emerged as an important emblem of the larger project of white French regeneration.

French fans still used this prizefight to make public claims about their color blindness. They argued that unlike most Anglo-Saxons, they approached interracial matches from a dispassionate point of view. They contrasted their embrace of the Jeannette-Carpentier match with the violent white American reaction to Johnson's victories against Tommy Burns and Jim Jeffries. "Fortunately, in the match of Luna Park there is for us, in Paris, only the sporting question," one writer declared. "We do not mingle it with other concerns of color. We do not think that in the boxing ring the superiority of a race, or even of a nationality, is at stake. It should simply be wished that the best man triumph."[82] The writer claimed that if victory smiled on Jeannette, Frenchmen would gladly congratulate the African American pugilist. "We will not take up with the niggers nor with the mulattoes of Paris; we will not massacre them," he assured. In other words, white French civilization would ultimately prevail even if the black American boxer triumphed in the ring.

Despite these declarations of impartiality, many French commentators were swept up in the racial dimensions of the fight. Jacques Mortane called Carpentier "the white hope that the whole world wishes to see triumph," arguing that if the young Frenchman defeated Jeannette it would not only be "a great day for the noble art" but a moment of glory for France.[83] While French sportswriters claimed to be color-blind, their portrayals of Jeannette tended to emphasize the black American's exotic blood quantum. One journalist described Jeannette as a "mulatto [with] the blood of a ferocious Indian."[84] Another sportswriter hailed him as "A Coloured 'White Man.'" "To quote the 'Duke' in 'Othello,' he 'is far more fair than black'—both as regards to colour and character," the writer maintained. "Although of the Mulatto hue, Joe is a 'white man' through and through."[85] While Jeannette's racial admixture and his gentlemanly behavior enabled him to become an honorary white man in the eyes of Parisian fans, Carpentier was still the undisputed French white hope.

With French honor at stake, many predicted that the Jeannette-Carpentier match would beat all previous Parisian box office records. The extraordinary demand for tickets had convinced the organizers to open the box office two weeks before the fight. Moreover, fake tickets were reportedly in circulation.[86]

On 21 March the fight at Luna Park attracted a diverse crowd of roughly seven thousand men and women, including "representatives of nearly every race" and social class.[87] Jeannette and Carpentier each had their own army of enthusiasts. After the weigh-in the grand boulevards of Paris were reportedly "invaded by a black crowd" of Jeannette's supporters.[88] Many of the white working-class men from the mining district near Carpentier's hometown of Lens also made their way to the match. The fight was so popular that organizers had to turn away hundreds of stragglers from the doors of the arena. As one journalist described, "The much-abused sardine was never so tightly packed as the crowd in the gallery, which disappeared almost entirely from view in tobacco smoke."[89] Alongside the masses in the cheaper seats, "the very cream of the Paris monde and demi-monde was present in all its glittering vanity." Another correspondent recalled, "One highly coloured queen of diamonds, in the front row, carried no less than the price of a king's ransom in those precious carbons."[90] The Jeannette-Carpentier fight went on to earn an estimated 150,000 francs, the highest gate ever recorded in Paris.

Staged in grandiose style, the interracial match had an almost dreamlike quality. A correspondent for *La Boxe et les boxeurs* described, "The two men are in the boxing ring, amid an extraordinary decor, an impressionist décor, worthy to tempt the imagination of a modernist painter. Above the narrow enclosure reserved for the fight . . . an intense pinkish light falls, and this light gives the two athletes colors and forms at once very clear and very surreal."[91] Carpentier had "the air of a beautiful statue of old ivory," while Jeannette resembled "a copper Buddha." Although both boxers were "very beautiful" in their own right, Carpentier was the crowd favorite. "Certainly, Carpentier remains our national Georges, for whom each Frenchman feels in his heart some fraternal fiber," the writer declared. Yet, French desires notwithstanding, Jeannette won by referee's decision in the fifteenth round.

Jeannette's victory inspired a public backlash that further emphasized the racial stakes of the match. Many French fans believed that the referee had unjustly awarded the match to the African American. Cries of protest filled the venue and continued to fill the pages of Parisian sporting papers in the days that followed. Thousands of Carpentier's supporters had waited outside Luna Park until the wee hours of the morning just to cheer him on.[92] *La Boxe et les boxeurs* received a deluge of letters disputing the referee's verdict. As the magazine's editor, Leon Sée, summarized the situation, it was "an admirable match, [but] a bad decision."[93]

Other reports suggested that Jeannette did, in fact, deserve to win, and that a case of wounded French pride was largely responsible for the outcry. "The French public is overly chauvinistic," a Parisian sportswriter declared. "It does not want to admit that its idol was beaten." Another argued that Jeannette had won because of his indefatigable strategy of blasting Carpentier with body shots. Jeannette had apparently "left the ring without the proverbial scratch, while Carpentier was badly disfigured."[94]

Over the next month the Jeannette-Carpentier match continued to inspire popular conversations about race as its moving picture played in Parisian theaters.[95] French journalists claimed that even though the younger and smaller Carpentier had lost against the more experienced and much larger Jeannette, his valiant effort in the ring still demonstrated the regeneration of white French manhood. "Who will dare to say after this . . . that our race is decadent?" Mortane challenged.[96] Mortane even advocated military service to help train Carpentier for his continued rise in professional boxing.

With all of the hoopla surrounding the match, French officials had become increasingly interested in developing a national sporting agenda, including a department and a university dedicated to the promotion of physical fitness. They argued that sport was an essential part of "the physical development of the rising generation" and they hoped that it would "serve as an exhaust valve for the excessive steam of those wound up in the every day battles" of modern life.[97] In a world of accelerating change Frenchmen could no longer afford to ignore their bodies. Much like their Anglo-Saxon brothers, they too had to prove their racial and martial mettle for the white man's burden.

BLACK PROTEST IN THE PARISIAN RING

Johnson, the consummate showman, certainly knew how to manipulate the cultural climate of the white man's burden to his own ends. Playing into popular French support for oppressed African Americans, the black champion couched his June 1914 fight against Frank Moran in images of primitive masculinity as a revenge match against white American and British racism. French sportswriters grabbed hold of this story of savage retribution, predicting an intense and bloody affair. Thanks to Johnson's knack for self-promotion and to French promoters' desire to make Paris the definitive capital of boxing, this white hope fight quickly became an international event, shaped by the exigencies of interimperial rivalry and racial protest.

In the lead-up to the interracial match, the English-speaking world backed Johnson's white American challenger. They celebrated the six-foot-tall, twenty-seven-year-old, "sandy-haired Pittsburgher" as an archetypical white man.[98] With a mixture of both brains and brawn, Moran was not only a former Navy man but also a university graduate with a dentistry degree. Fresh from a theatrical tour across the United States, the white fighter exclaimed, "The reception tendered me in the different cities made me all the more anxious to regain what Jeffries lost at Reno. . . . America and England are with me to a man, and I will make good."[99]

Moran was certainly correct in his assumption of white Anglo-Saxon support. Relatively low admission prices made the fight accessible even for "ordinary Britishers," and many thought it would be their last opportunity to travel to Paris given the ominous signs of war. Likewise, white American expatriates flocked to Moran's training camp and were expected to attend the fight en masse in support of "their hope."[100] Back home, mainstream newspapers like the *San Francisco Examiner,* the *New York Globe,* and the *Philadelphia Times* touted Moran as both a national hero and an assured winner—"a modern Lohengrin" who would "avenge the white race."[101] Each day Moran received telegrams of support from the United States, and some reports even estimated that hundreds of white American sportsmen would make their way across the Atlantic to witness the match.

Parisian sportswriters sensationalized the depths of white American negrophobia while also publicizing their own nation's racial exceptionalism. One journalist claimed that ever since Johnson had wrested the world championship from Tommy Burns in 1908, "America had but one thought: to punish the nigger."[102] Another prefight report reminded French boxing fans that Johnson's victory over Jim Jeffries in 1910 had triggered antiblack "riots" and "massacres" across the United States.[103] While white Americans' "hatred of the negroes" had apparently blinded them to Moran's pugilistic shortfalls, French sportsmen boasted that their racial impartiality had allowed them to see that Johnson was the superior boxer.[104]

Hoping to cash in on this interimperial competition, promoters scheduled the fight for the day after the Grand Prix, the prestigious French turf race that attracted thousands of sporting enthusiasts to Paris each year. It would take place on 27 June 1914 at the Velodrome d'Hiver, a modern indoor arena with a capacity of around thirty thousand people. The Associated Press, representing seven hundred U.S. newspapers, paid five thousand francs for the right to install a ringside telegraph wire that would connect directly to transatlantic cables. Round-by-round fight news would reach all four corners of the earth with amazing speed.[105]

Johnson took full advantage of this occasion to broadcast his critique of Anglo-Saxon supremacy. He expressed his determination to exact vengeance on his white American tormentors. "Even though I respect Frank Moran, I must make him pay for all the insults of the Americans," Johnson asserted. "The Americans are already dancing around my scalp," he complained. "They believe I'm finished, used up." However, he assured French readers, "It is not yet time for the whites to have my scalp."[106]

Every afternoon Johnson held an open training session at Luna Park to show off his physique and technique. One Parisian correspondent wrote, "This time, it is a warlike Johnson, slender . . . shining like a handsome thoroughbred—a Johnson who for two months has worked his body, his lungs, his heart, and his breath with the furious will to avenge himself against a new adversary."[107] Fans were assured of a bloody fight that would not only showcase the African American champion's incredible strength but also unleash his savage animosity for white America.

Despite Johnson's various efforts to drum up support, the results were mixed. He and his pursuit of savage retribution had apparently developed a particular appeal with the street urchins of Paris. On the evening of 27 June a crowd of white French boys stood at the entrance of the Velodrome d'Hiver chanting, "Vive le Nigger."[108] Although Billy Lewis tried to rationalize their use of the term "nigger," arguing that it was an "expression of endearment" in Paris, the boys' choice of words belied their paternalistic and exotic view of the African American boxer.

Later that night when Johnson entered the ring, followed by his imposing troupe of black trainers, he received only a smattering of applause. In contrast, an almost crazed clamor permeated the stadium as Moran arrived. All of the white Americans in attendance stood and cheered as Moran and his white entourage stepped into the ring. While the Velodrome d'Hiver in reality was only half full, it was such a large venue that the match still garnered a record gate of 181,000 francs.[109]

The lighting for the making of the fight film gave everything in the immense space a rosy tinge, adding drama to the scene.[110] Spectators from all sectors of society, most noticeably French women, attended in formal evening dress. As a report in the *New York Times* described, "The singular spectacle was presented of several hundred women in handsome gowns applauding the two pugilists as they struggled up and down the ring, feinting and dodging and hammering each other."[111] A French correspondent named Colette Willy, popularly known as a sportswoman, performer, and avant-garde writer, even covered the match for *Le Matin*.[112]

In addition to containing French women, the fight crowd was "amazingly international," with numerous dark faces dotting the predominantly white audience. Several hundred white Americans were in the best seats. Also in attendance were various public figures, including the likes of Spencer Eddy (former U.S. minister to Argentina), the Duke of Westminster, Louis Barthou (former premier of France), the Baron James de Rothschild (of the Rothschild banking family), and several marquises and dukes. When Moran's blows connected the white American fans in the audience rose to their feet, cheering on their white hope, while race baiting Johnson.[113] Not to be outdone, Johnson taunted Moran in the ring. When the Moran punched Johnson's stomach, the black champion held his arms up and grinned, as if to say,

"He [Moran] can do that as long as he likes."[114] Throughout the fight black American expatriates rooted for Johnson alongside black men from Senegal, Dahomey, and the Caribbean. The Guadeloupeans Gratien Candace and Rene Boisneuf, two black members of the French Chamber of Deputies, watched the fight with intense interest. Even Prince Dhuleep Singh of India and Omar Sultan, the pasha of Egypt, were in attendance.[115]

For all of its hype, the Johnson-Moran match was uneventful. Lasting twenty rounds, it ended with referee Georges Carpentier's decision in favor of Johnson. Even Billy Lewis admitted that Johnson had won only on the basis of his superior technique. Despite the previous claims of French journalists, the aging black champion was actually in much poorer physical condition than the younger Moran.[116]

When news of the match result reached Chicago's South Side, Johnson's African American supporters celebrated his Parisian victory in the streets.[117] Johnson had publicly transgressed the white man's burden on two fronts—the physical and the sexual. His superior strength and skill had prevailed, and he had gained the admiration of white French women. An editorialist for the *New York Age* declared, "The English speaking people in all quarters of the globe, who have decided that black men shall not have a fair chance . . . because the success of black men in anything over white men sets a bad example to the African and Asiatic colored people . . . have had another dose of 'White Hope Knock-Out' rammed down their throats by John Arthur Johnson."[118] Countering white American reports of Johnson's "dissipated mode of living," another black writer maintained that the black American's triumph proved that he had "lived a physically clean life."[119] Not only was Johnson's physique "truly marvelous, his strength . . . that of a gorilla" but he also possessed "a cunning, fighting brain." Johnson's black fans delighted in the fact that he ripped, tore, and jarred his white opponents into submission, leaving them physically damaged.

The African American press also highlighted Johnson's special popularity with white French women—a story of sexual attraction that could never have played out in such an open forum in the United States. Tales of the black heavyweight's interracial appeal in France continued to circulate in the African American community months after the Johnson-Moran fight. Taking his cue from French reports of the match, Billy Lewis described the subversive scene in exquisite detail for African American readers. "Four magnificently beautiful women in extraordinarily candid evening gowns" had crowded Johnson's corner of the ring. "They held each other by the hand, and shivered in stimulated ecstasy," Lewis added with a flash of drama.[120] The women had beckoned for Johnson as they tiptoed closer, calling him a "beautiful creature" and a "magnificent brute." One had even "stroked Johnson's bare, brown hide," while the others "pressed closer with little squeals." As Lewis tantalized his readers, "Their bare, round arms stretched through the ropes. Their eyes glistened. Filmy cloaks fell from their rounded shoulders. Johnson lay at his ease, his eyes half closed as they patted his great bak [sic] with slender hands from which they had frantically stripped the gloves." Reveling in the cross-racial eroticism of this spectacle, Lewis depicted an incredibly subversive image of black masculine sexuality and white female desire.

Yet, Lewis recognized the limits of this scenario. Whether French women considered the black champion to be beautiful or brutish, they simply admired him as a "physical man." Although this certainly beat the "general detestation" that white America had for black people, it was by no means an equal relationship.[121] A cartoon in the *Indianapolis Freeman* captured the essence of this French gaze, depicting Johnson as a blackface beast surrounded by the eyes of French boxing fans.[122] Lewis contended, "He was a Negro even in Paris. London was yet worse. Other European cities would not even tolerate him."[123] Europeans were now throwing their support behind the white Frenchman Carpentier. This seemed to be part of a trend of increasing race prejudice on the continent. Another black journalist explained, "Since American prejudice has crept into Europe it is not uncommon for a man of color who happens to be on the otherside [sic], to be made to understand that he has a dark skin and his privileges are limited for fear of offending some of the American visitors and loosing [sic] their patronage."[124] Some parts of Europe had even "adopted the American rule" against interracial boxing matches.

Unfortunately for Johnson, his victory over Moran coincided with the outbreak of World War I. Although Johnson never received any of his promised $14,000 in winnings, his black fans still managed to find a positive lesson in his victory.[125] His physical and sexual transgressions of the color line had convinced many of them that the white man's burden could also be fought on other fronts. As a postfight editorial in Grand Bassa, Liberia's *African League* declared, "You may not be a pugilist but you may be in your calling what Jack Johnson is in his calling—at the top, Dr. Booker Washington is there as an educator . . . and other Negroes of the United States are getting there as financiers and in other callings."[126] Johnson's ring success compelled black people to "take courage and move forward, along all progressive lines." As war engulfed the European continent, Johnson and his fellow black sportsmen had already paved the way for the momentous arrival of African American soldiers in France.

In August 1914 a correspondent for the *Chicago Defender* announced that Johnson had "shown his allegiance to the French flag by offering his services to fight for that country."[127] Rumors that Johnson, now a French citizen, had been named the colonel of a French regiment spread throughout black America. French military officials apparently believed that "if he could master the world in the prize ring, he could do so on the field of battle." The *Defender* even claimed that the French government had arranged for Johnson to receive a monthly pension if he were ever injured in combat.

Given the persistence of racial segregation and antiblack violence within the U.S. Army, these imaginary tales of Johnson's military leadership in France must have sounded revolutionary to African American readers. Stories of courageous black men in battle were central to African American understandings of racial equality in the French context. Commenting on France's decision to use black troops to fight the Germans, one black American journalist maintained that it was "the first time" such a thing had occurred in Europe "since the Moors of Northern Africa were driven out of Spain," and that he expected "none of them to fight more bravely under the Tri-Color than JOHN ARTHUR JOHNSON, the Champion Prize-fighter of the World."[128] Bob Scanlon and Eugene Bullard were two expatriate African American boxers who proudly served in the French Foreign Legion during World War I, earning medals and accolades for their bravery under fire.[129] It seemed as if the symbolic victories that Johnson and other black pugilists had achieved in Europe's boxing rings were now being realized in the actual theater of war.

The racial stereotypes circulating in the cosmopolitan realm of the French boxing ring, however, ran counter to this official rhetoric. Scanlon's public image encapsulated the French public's rather ambivalent acceptance of African Americans. Although Scanlon became a recognized war hero, during his years as a boxer Parisian sportswriters often cast him as a comical savage. When he knocked out the white Frenchmen Henri Marchand in 1914, a diasporic mix of black imagery pervaded the various descriptions of the match. For Henri Dispan, the fight was akin to an African ritual of cannibalism. "You devourers of pale men's flesh, monstrous idols squatted at the edge of the forest of coconuts, is your thirst for blood not yet quenched?" he asked.[130] It seemed as if "all of Africa and its American colonies" had come to see the "sacrifice" of Marchand, including "Toucouleurs, Mandingoes, Foulahs, Pahouins and those of Louisiana and Texas." In honor of their hero's triumph, they had danced all night "to the sound of the banjo and the tom-tom." While Dispan and other Parisian sportsmen viewed Scanlon's black fans with a sense of bemused contempt, they could still see that black Americans and French Africans had discovered a dangerous racial common ground in the boxing ring. Even as the French continued to profess their ideals of color blindness, the "invasion" of black American boxers was undoubtedly driving them to revisit the racial logics and practices of their Anglo-Saxon counterparts.

Despite all the reports of Johnson's military ambitions, unlike Scanlon and Bullard, he never actually stuck around to fight for the French. By the summer of 1914 the war had essentially foiled his plans for a peaceful and profitable exile in Western Europe. He also faced escalating threats of extradition to the United States. Chased by special agents from the Department of Justice, Johnson rushed to the U.S. embassy in London, where he managed to finagle the necessary papers for travel to Russia.[131] Since the Russo-American extradition treaty did not include the Mann Act, Johnson believed he had found his way to safety.[132]

Although Johnson would escape extradition by heading east, there were no guarantees that he would escape the race question. Russia was not necessarily a destination of great promise for African Americans in 1914. True, black sailors, artists, entertainers, and professional athletes had visited Russia since the nineteenth century, and stories about the absence of prejudice in Russia also appeared periodically in the African American press.[133] However, for some African American journalists Russia's anti-Jewish pogroms revealed that nation's own dangerous manifestation of race thinking, and they likened this "ritual murder" to the barbaric violence of the Jim Crow South.[134]

With few other options, the heavyweight champion and his entourage journeyed to St. Petersburg for a series of exhibitions organized by the expatriate black American promoter George Thomas. Johnson became fast friends with Thomas, a plucky Georgia native who had left the United States years before in search of his fortune. Through a combination of wit and grit, the former valet had managed to build a profitable amusement empire in Russia that included an immense glass-roofed park known as the Aquarium. As Johnson later described it, the Aquarium "was a veritable city, a city within a city." Alongside its many entertainment venues it included "residences, hotels, cafés, restaurants and other facilities."[135]

Johnson's plans for a lucrative series of boxing exhibitions at the Aquarium never came to fruition. Before the black heavyweight ever had the chance to perform, Germany declared war on Russia. Pushed out of St. Petersburg, Johnson and his party once again found themselves on the run in August 1914.[136] They hurried from Germany to Belgium and then to France, where many U.S. and British citizens were frantic to escape the approaching battles. Despite the chaos Johnson never seemed to lose his cool. One white American claimed to have encountered the black champion in Paris, "his face . . . wreathed in smiles" as large "crowds surrounded him urging him to fight for France."[137]

For a brief moment Johnson and his entourage were relieved to have made it back across the English Channel. Britain, however, had also entered the war. Caught in the midst of the mounting conflict, visiting and expatriate African Americans such as Johnson desperately searched for a way out of London. "Oh, how I long for State street," one black Chicagoan reportedly cried out, tears streaming down his face.[138] Unfortunately for Johnson, whose legal troubles in the United States were still unresolved, he could not yet return home like the others.

Viva Johnson!

Fighting over Race in the Americas

Este boxeador fifí,
en México un héroe fue,
aunque Sanborn le hizo—¡fu . . .
Pero el general Fafá
le dijo:—Amigo, ten fe,
que si alguno te hace ¡mú!
yo a dodos les hago mé.

This boxing dandy
was a hero in Mexico,
although Sanborn wouldn't serve him.
But General so-and-so
told him: Have faith, friend;
if somebody turns you away,
I'll make him pee in his pants.
—"Johnson Fifí!" *El Universal,* 1919

As war-torn Europe closed its doors to African American civilians, Jack Johnson sought refuge in the Caribbean and Latin America. Although the United States remained off-limits, he was happy to be moving closer to home. No longer in the prime of his career, the thirty-six-year-old champion had been on the run for a year and a half, and his exile was beginning to take a physical and emotional toll.

Johnson left Britain in December 1914 optimistic about the opportunities that awaited him in the Americas. His recent popularity in

¡Johnson Fifi!

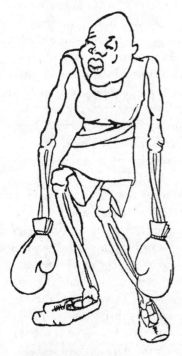

Este boxeador fifi,
en México un héroe fue,
aunque Samborn le hizo—¡fu....
Pero el general Fafá
le dijo: —Amigo, ten fe,
que si alguno te hace ¡mú!
yo a todos las hago mé.

FIGURE 14. Although Jack Johnson was by no means immune to color prejudice in Mexico, his audacious personality and flashy style made him an instant hero with local fans, especially the fashionably dressed young men known as the Fifi. "Johnson Fifi!" *El Universal,* 2 November 1919.

France had led him to believe that Latin peoples everywhere, regardless of skin color, were more racially tolerant than their Anglo-Saxon counterparts. Given the region's diverse demographics, he also hoped to find crowds of colored supporters. Over the next six years Johnson sailed to Argentina, Barbados, Cuba, and Mexico before surrendering to U.S. authorities in 1920. While Johnson and many of his black American contemporaries imagined and searched for a racial paradise in the Americas, they soon found that the color line had already etched itself into the cultural and political landscape.

This leg of Johnson's journey not only reveals the hemispheric impact of U.S. race culture, but it also provides an alternative perspective on black Americans' foreign encounters in the early twentieth century.

The controversies surrounding Johnson's world championship defeat in Cuba in 1915 and his Mexican sojourn from 1919 to 1920 epitomized the profound irony of being black and American at a time when the United States was expanding its influence in the region. World War I was not the only phenomenon that opened up new cultural and political spaces for the development of black transnationalism and internationalism in the 1910s. Turning away from Europe's metropolitan capitals, Johnson and other black Americans looked south for racial solidarities grounded in the shared realities of white American domination and cultural hegemony. They found some of their most powerful connections in the borderlands and colonial spaces on the fringes of the United States.

Despite its official stance of isolationism, the United States was beginning to see itself as a new kind of global leader, and its role in the spread of boxing seemed to be a perfect metaphor for its foreign policy agenda.[1] Rarely tied to any official state programs, this popular pastime of rank-and-file military men moved in very much the same way that U.S. influence aspired to—with a seeming ease and informality, and appearing to embody the character of U.S. democratic ideals while offering foreigners a means to express their own manhood, whiteness, and modernity. Boxing also came on the heels of U.S. capitalism and consumerism. White American promoters more or less controlled the boxing industry in places like Cuba and Mexico, catering to the interests of U.S. tourists and expatriates for the sake of profits. They often viewed the locals' enthusiastic embrace of pugilism as yet another example of the positive effects of U.S. stewardship. Through boxing, white Americans exerted a form of cultural power that helped them to advance the widespread adoption of U.S. mores and manners in their expanding spheres of influence.[2]

Yet boxing was truly a two-edged sword. Although it provided the framework for the ultimate public relations campaign for white American intervention, it also furnished a platform for popular expressions of political independence and transnational race consciousness. White elites in places like Cuba used the sport to showcase their nation's fitness for self-determination. Boxing also appealed to people of color living on the margins of both U.S. imperialism and elite nationalism. With his epic story of success in the face of discrimination, Johnson became a folk hero to men of color in the region, inspiring them to take up the sport on their own terms.

ALLIES IN THE AMERICAS

Johnson's return to the Americas intersected with larger debates about race and U.S. intervention in the region. By the 1910s the Caribbean and Latin America had become an important part of the global imaginary of white and black Americans alike. For white Americans the region was a space of profit and play. Most black Americans maintained an optimistic if ambivalent outlook on the area. Although it represented a refuge from Jim Crow racism, many feared that the United States' growing influence would undermine its racial fluidity. Still, Johnson and his contemporaries could not dismiss the fact that when visiting the region they often enjoyed greater privileges than the local people of color precisely because of their claims, however nominal, to U.S. citizenship.

Some even saw themselves as potential beneficiaries of U.S. intervention. A journalist for the *Chicago Defender* pointed to the Naval Academy's new emphasis on intensive Spanish-language training as proof of the rising importance of their southern neighbors. The United States had "waked up" to Latin America's possibilities, and many North Americans were now "endeavoring to capture their share of this rich plum." As U.S. high schools and colleges introduced more Spanish instruction, they were also "acknowledging the growing commercial and economic importance of Latin America." Rather than censuring this trend, the journalist argued that this southward expansion was particularly important for the black community since these lands would "offer equal opportunity to all men."[3]

Throughout the 1910s a smattering of reports in the black American press seemed to confirm their welcome, particularly in Johnson's first destination of Argentina. By 1913 Geneva Graham of Chicago had managed to establish a successful hair salon in Buenos Aires. "She is counted as one of the leaders of fashion, her wardrobe coming direct from Paris," one report claimed.[4] Having traveled through Brazil, Uruguay, and Argentina as the personal chauffeur of Julius Rosenwald, Ernest Stevens was convinced that black Americans could prosper in South America. In Buenos Aires he had witnessed men of color "filling every responsible position in government service." As long as they had money to spend, it was "no trouble to buy or enjoy anything."[5]

John R. Marshall, an African American colonel in the 8th Illinois Regiment, was reputedly named field marshal of Argentina's government troops in early 1914. "This government is always ready to accept the intelligence of the American Negroes, and offers to them the same opportunity that it does any of our citizens," a *Defender* report from Buenos Aires proclaimed.[6] The capital city had purportedly received more than eighteen thousand "well educated, well groomed and equipped colored men and women from the United States of America." Yet these were curious statements given that Argentina in the early 1900s was marked not only by large-scale white immigration from Europe (in a conscious effort to whiten the nation) but also by a corresponding decline in its black population. Although Afro-Argentines had a long history of military service, black soldiers rarely became high-ranking officers.[7] Regardless of these inconsistencies, many black Americans had come to view South America as a space of equality and possibility.

In mid-December 1914, Johnson's own arrival in Buenos Aires proved to be a festive occasion. He was the first U.S. boxing champion ever to set foot on South American soil. Pugilism in Argentina had heretofore been a largely elite and quasi-legal sport, practiced by British immigrants in private clubs. Johnson's visit, however, pushed it into the mainstream.[8] An honorary guard of soldiers and marines escorted him to places of interest throughout the capital. Local promoters also approached him to fill theatrical dates, and he performed in numerous exhibitions in Buenos Aires and its surrounding towns. As Johnson later recalled, "The South American city gave me such a rousing welcome and I was an object of much concern on the part of the people, all of whom treated me with the utmost kindness."[9] Shortly after Johnson's departure for Barbados in January 1915, a black American traveler named T. Grand Pre affirmed that Argentina was "the prettiest and most delightful place in the world to live." Although the "white [American] man took his prejudice there," he apparently "could not make it stick."[10] Despite increasing U.S. influence in the region, it looked as if Latin America would remain true to its spirit of racial egalitarianism.

At the same time, the bidding war commenced for permission to host the world heavyweight championship match between Johnson and the white hope Jess Willard. Many white Americans believed that Johnson would finally meet his match. Nicknamed the "Pottawatomie Giant" after his home county in Kansas, Willard was not only nine years Johnson's junior but also substantially larger, at a whopping six feet six inches and 230 pounds. Before trying his hand at boxing

Willard had held a variety of demanding jobs, from a horse breaker and trainer to a teamster who transported goods by wagon.[11] He was not just a boxer but a bona fide American cowboy who embodied the "strenuous life."

In January 1915 the syndicate promoting the Willard-Johnson match, led by Jack Curley, met in New York City to decide on a location. A contest between U.S. promoters, this bidding war illustrated that prizefighting was an important part of the ever-expanding reach of U.S. capital and consumer culture in the Americas. Representatives for U.S. sporting interests in Havana, Cuba, and the Mexican border cities of Tijuana and Juárez competed, and in the end it came down to a fight between Juárez and Havana.[12]

Curley and his syndicate eventually chose Juárez, setting a fight date of 6 March 1915. With its proximity to the United States, Juárez seemed like a perfect location for maximizing profits, especially since the match would coincide with the Southwestern Cattlemen's Convention. A frontier space that served as a playground of vice for U.S. tourists, Juárez had six railroads passing through it on the line to California. At least ten thousand spectators could be drawn from its U.S. sister city, El Paso, Texas, alone. Curley also expected upward of fifty thousand spectators to come from across the United States, and he believed that, with a few alterations, the Juárez racetrack could accommodate up to 100,000 people. The revolutionary Mexican general Francisco "Pancho" Villa had even sent Curley a letter with some words of encouragement: "I feel sure that the great American public that will attend the match will see for themselves that this city is lawful and normal, and that we are indeed a law-abiding community."[13] The Willard-Johnson fight offered the turbulent Mexican nation an opportunity to showcase its legitimacy and modernity in front of a white American crowd.

Not everyone was excited at the prospect of an interracial bout involving the brash black American champion in Juárez. Some white Americans believed that this was not the kind of example that the United States should be setting for its less civilized neighbors south of the border. A committee from the First Christian Church in El Paso wrote a letter of objection to Secretary of State William Jennings Bryan. Reverends Perry Rice, Wesley Webdell, and J. F. Williams pleaded with Secretary Bryan to prevent "this brutal and brutalizing event" and, if possible, to extradite Johnson so that he could finally serve jail time for his Mann Act conviction.[14] The clergymen confided, "We are so confident of your personal attitude and desire in matters of this kind that we feel it wholly unnecessary to make any further representation of the case to you." Bryan was already a well-known advocate of U.S. military intervention in the Mexican Revolution.

Included in the reverends' correspondence to Secretary Bryan was a translated version of their protest letter to General Villa. "Such an event would be very deeply deplored by all the good citizens of El Paso and of the United States," they cautioned Villa. Using the language of paternalism, they added, "We sincerely believe that only harm can come to your own people as a result of this contest." They warned Villa that his people would be "placed under influences" that would "only be detrimental to their development," for prizefights caused "civilization" to suffer wherever they took place. The clergymen urged Villa to work with them to "avert this impending disaster."[15]

Although the reverends' arguments centered on their desire to protect Mexico's supposedly impressionable citizens from barbarity and vice, it was obvious that the racial dimensions of the Willard-Johnson match had pushed them over the edge. Prizefights were already a well-established part of the sporting scene in Juárez, and yet this was the first time that they had ever bothered to register a complaint. Worried that Juárez's racial and moral laxity would seep across the border to infect El Paso, Reverend Price and his cronies felt more than entitled to petition U.S. federal officials to intervene in Mexican affairs.

The Department of State ultimately refused to do anything to stop the fight. Given the revolutionary upheaval in Mexico "and the lack of a central government . . . recognized by the United States," they were averse to making any requests for Johnson's extradition.[16] Furthermore, U.S. officials did not believe that it was their place to advise Mexican authorities to stop the fight, especially since it appeared to be a singular event rather than a recurrent problem that would continue to haunt El Paso. Not only would the white hope match go on, but Johnson would be able to continue his travels, raising the profile of boxing and gaining a colored following throughout the Americas.

The black champion, accompanied by his wife, Lucille, and his Australian sparring partner, Frank Hagney, did just that. The three left Buenos Aires aboard the *Highland Harris,* arriving in Barbados on 7 February 1915. "Quite unexpectedly, the privilege has been afforded Barbadians to see a celebrated fighter, although, strictly speaking, not in the same category as Kitchener, Joffre, or French," a *Defender* correspondent declared.[17] Through his many conversations with the residents of the majority-black island, he had discovered that Johnson was already a crowd favorite. Although the black heavyweight may not have been a military commander along the same lines as Herbert Kitchener, Joseph Joffre, or John French, many Barbadians had read of his successes in Paris. They had even heard rumors that Johnson "had become a Frenchman, and had been called on to put aside the gloves and shoulder a rifle."

Johnson came on the heels of black American entrepreneurs and tourists who had forged their own links in the region. The successful businesswoman Madame C.J. Walker had journeyed to the islands of Jamaica, Cuba, and Haiti to introduce her company's hair products, sometimes spending her winters abroad. Even lesser lights of the black community such as Calvin C. Lewis, the captain of the Tea Room at Chicago's American Hotel, had visited Cuba and Jamaica.[18]

African Americans had long admired the Caribbean as a space of black resistance and self-government. From 1889 to 1891 there was much optimism surrounding the appointment of Frederick Douglass as the U.S. minister to Haiti and the U.S. chargé d'affaires for the Dominican Republic. By the 1910s, however, the promise of greater black control in the region appeared to be diminishing.[19] One black American journalist claimed that the Caribbean was now "threatened with the danger of being Americanized."[20] He believed that Caribbean people were drawn to the "enterprising spirit of the United States," particularly when contrasted "with the inertness of Great Britain." The U.S. occupation of Puerto Rico, its administration of Cuba, and its building of the Panama Canal seemed to have "excited their admiration." The "numberless" white American visitors were also knitting closer commercial and social ties between the United States and the islands. Yet this closeness would come at a cost. The journalist predicted that this growing "intimacy" would soon culminate in the U.S. occupation of Haiti.[21]

Against this backdrop of race and international relations, Johnson became a huge celebrity with black Barbadians. A large crowd of fans accosted him at customs. Later that same day many gathered to greet him in front of the Standard Hotel, where they made High Street virtually impassable as they gave him "an ovation only equalled by those bestowed on royalty."[22] Local newspapermen descended upon Johnson, and J.E. Branker, the manager of the London Electric Theater, booked him for a boxing exhibition. When Johnson ventured into Bridgetown in search of a schooner to take him to Cuba, "the crowds that followed his automobile were so great that a guard of honor comprised of mounted policemen escorted him all about."[23]

On the night of Johnson's much-anticipated appearance at the London Electric Theater, there were more spectators than seats. The event started with a screening of the recent Johnson-Moran fight film, followed by the display of life-size portraits of the black champion. When Johnson finally appeared on stage in his fighting togs, the crowd greeted him with "tremendous applause." Johnson engaged in a little self-promotion, regaling the audience with stories about his foreign travels and past fights, assurances of his integrity as a boxer, and news about his upcoming match against the white American Willard. Next he invited challengers from the crowd. A Trinidadian man volunteered to put on the gloves against Johnson, but his courage was short-lived. At the first sign of Johnson's powerful blows he sprinted into the stage wings.[24] Johnson and his partner Hagney then closed the triumphant evening with a sparring exhibition.

Black American boxing fans took great pride in Johnson's commanding presence as their representative in Barbados. When Barnard Bonnafam of the schooner *Lillian Blaubelt* sued the black heavyweight for breach of contract, Johnson decided to defend himself in court. Bonnafam claimed that Johnson had agreed to pay $1,000 for passage to Cuba but later reneged on their agreement, choosing to travel aboard a different ship. Bonnafam, however, failed to produce any supporting documentation, and Johnson won the case. An "extraordinarily enthusiastic demonstration" greeted the black pugilist as he left the courtroom victorious.[25] Even the white-run *Barbados Globe and Colonial Advertiser* had to admit, "In appearance as well in speech Jack Johnson is brimful of refinement and polish, and, by the pictures of him produced in the American press, has been wickedly libelled." Despite his legal troubles, Johnson had "made many friends" on the island.[26]

As Barbados embraced Johnson the controversy over his upcoming match with Willard deepened. Although Reverend Rice and his fellow protesters initially failed to get the fight moved from Juárez, in February 1915 they finally got their wish. Mexico's political turmoil had forced the fight's U.S. promoters to search for an alternative location. According to Andres Garcia, a Mexican consul in El Paso, the newly installed president Venustiano Carranza vowed to oppose Johnson's entry into Mexico, since the prizefight would bring revenue to his rival, General Villa.[27] For Johnson to make it through any port controlled by Carranza's men—who, at that time, held the eastern seaboard and occupied Mexico City—he would have to present a recent U.S. passport. A fugitive since 1913, Johnson did not have the requisite papers, and he feared arrest at the hands of Carranza's men. When he arrived in Cuba aboard the steamship *Henry Krager* he decided to remain in Havana rather than continuing on his journey to Tampico, Mexico.[28] Undeterred by Johnson's sudden change of plans, Curley and his fight syndicate moved the match to Havana.

CUBA'S WHITE HOPES

By the 1910s the multiracial island of Cuba, much like Mexico's border cities, was a popular space of play for U.S. tourists—one that promised to furnish the desired box office figures for the white hope match. During the U.S. military occupations of 1898–1902 and 1906–9, boxing on the island had been more or less limited to U.S. servicemen. Thereafter the locals began to embrace the sport, and the Academia de Boxeo opened its doors in 1910. Yet interracial bouts and the victories of black boxers quickly inflamed the island's racial frictions, and the Cuban government banned the sport in 1912.[29]

Over the next few years Cuban officials lifted the ban as they recognized boxing's ability to bring in U.S. dollars. On 1 January 1915, the Cuban government granted the U.S. promoter Billy Gibson permission to conduct fight cards in the capital city.[30] As Gibson told the *New York Times,* "Cuba is destined to be the home of boxing, and everybody in Havana, including the President of Cuba and Mayor of Havana is enthusiastic over the plan to stage championship battles at Havana."[31] Gibson had big plans to build a sporting empire in Cuba. "When you consider that the park at Havana can be reached in fifty hours from New York," he argued, "it can readily be seen how encouraging the prospects are. It is a delightful trip in the Winter and the climate appears to be made to order." The Willard-Johnson match would certainly appeal to a race-conscious U.S. crowd, enhancing Havana's reputation as a fun place of transgression. Safely contained beyond the borders of the United States, the city's exotic appeal for white Americans stemmed, in large part, from its racially mixed and, therefore, racially charged atmosphere.[32]

U.S. tourists and dollars were not the only benefits that boxing would bring to Cuba. U.S. sportsmen and promoters saw it as a kind of progressive tool that would help Cuban men to develop a better appreciation for democracy, discipline, and civilization. Gibson's boxing enterprise had reportedly inspired Cuba's elite to cast off their "lethargic condition." As a *New York Times* correspondent criticized, over the years Cuban youth "had apparently acquired the Spanish mañana habit—tomorrow is good enough."[33] These young elites had forgotten their obligation to lead, and in particular their responsibility to "teach the Cubans the finer points of the game which is the major sport of all civilized nations." Thanks to Gibson's entrepreneurial "Yankee hustle," their growing participation in boxing supposedly signaled Cuba's emergence as a modern capitalist nation. Boxing gained popularity right alongside other physical education programs designed to fashion Cubans into bourgeois citizens, including those of the YMCA, which opened in Havana in 1905.[34]

The rising fame of black American fighters in Cuba during this period also attests to boxing's racialized appeal for Afro-Cubans. In February 1915 the editor of the English-language *Havana Daily Post*, George M. Bradt, had attempted to arrange a match between the black heavyweights Sam Langford and Sam McVea. Bradt and the two fighters' managers believed that the twenty-five-round match, to be held in a new fifteen-thousand-seat stadium located in Maine Park on the Malecón, "was the sort of thing that the Cubans wanted."[35] Even though this fight never occurred, a twenty-round match between McVea and Battling Jim Johnson did take place on 20 February in front of ten thousand fight enthusiasts.[36] The U.S. tradition of battle royals involving young black boys had also become part of the Cuban fight scene.[37] Although the promotion of black-on-black matches and battle royals suggests an element of white voyeurism at work, one cannot underestimate the impact of black American fighters on Afro-Cubans' race consciousness, especially at a moment when the Cuban government was trying to suppress black political mobilization.

As Johnson practiced a sport that was both a mode of colonial discipline and a forum for countercultural resistance, his presence provoked contentious debates about the racial trajectory of the new Cuban nation. Like other black Americans who traveled to Cuba, he found himself at the fraught intersection of the growing networks of U.S. hegemony and black transnationalism in the region. Johnson and his contemporaries looked to Cuba as a space of possibility and solidarity, yet the realities of U.S. imperialism still governed their actions.

Black American participation in the Spanish-American War in Cuba exemplified this ambivalent relationship. Many African American leaders such as Booker T. Washington urged the men in their communities to enlist. They believed that black soldiers' bravery on the battlefield would not only demonstrate their loyalty to the United States but also prove their worthiness for full citizenship. The four black regiments of the regular army—the 24th and 25th Infantry and the 9th and 10th Cavalry—became a source of collective pride. Black Americans also saw the Cubans as their racial relatives and believed that the Cuban fight for independence paralleled their own domestic struggle for equality.

Despite U.S. officials' public rhetoric in support of the Cuban revolutionaries, it became apparent that they had no real intention of granting the island its independence. Some black Americans criticized their nation's imperial stance. They feared that white American rule on the island would be even more brutal than that of the Spanish, especially since the United States did little to ensure the freedom and dignity of its own black citizens back home.[38] When the Spanish forces left Cuba in 1899 the United States remained, installing a military government. Although the inclusion of the Platt Amendment principles in the Cuban constitution of 1901 brought an end to the first U.S. occupation, in reality this step represented only nominal independence for the new nation. The amendment not only sanctioned continued U.S. involvement in Cuba's domestic and foreign affairs, but it also permitted the United States to maintain a naval base at Guantanamo Bay. U.S. interests continued to flow onto the island, and the threat of U.S. annexation remained.

Still, many African Americans saw postwar Cuba, with its nearby location, arid land, good climate, and multiracial population, as an ideal destination for black emigrants. Some argued that black Americans needed to assert their influence on the island before white American prejudice became an integral part of Cuban politics and culture. Black civil servants, educators, and missionaries from organizations such as the African Methodist Episcopal Church signed up to work on the island's reconstruction. The concurrent escalation of negrophobic violence in the United States only increased black American interest in Cuban emigration.[39]

Cuba's promise lured black American sportsmen, businesspeople, professionals, clergy, tourists, and performers. Independent black baseball teams had been barnstorming throughout the island since 1900, and by 1907 black American players had begun to join Cuban rosters.[40] In March 1912 Madame E. Azalia Hackley, a famous black American singer, writer, philanthropist, and activist, traveled to Cuba to raise money for her fellow black classical musicians. "America's queen of song" gave a spirited press interview in Havana, contrasting race relations in the U.S. South with those of the island. "Now what, with the unclean system of dealing with our [black] travelers, and the immoral designs which are forever in the minds of the southern white men regarding our women and the very lax way in which the health authorities regard the welfare of the race in the south," she noted, "one will not wonder at my being so enthusiastic over the extreme cleanliness and equality shown in Cuba to those of my race."[41]

Others focused on the island's economic opportunities. In the same month as Hackley's Cuban sojourn a group of Chicago's leading black men organized a banquet dedicated to exploring the benefits of investment on the island. Professor Charles Alexander urged the attendees, "Cuba is really the future hope of those ambitious colored men and women who really are seeking a home where there is no color line, and where the possibilities of making an independent living are greater than in any other country."[42] The evening's keynote speaker, William L. Barth, even hoped that "in a short while the island of Cuba would become one of the possessions of the United States," causing land values to skyrocket.

Unlike Barth, other black Americans remained suspicious of U.S. annexation, worried that white American racism would infiltrate the island. Popularly known as the Race War of 1912, the summertime uprising of many mixed-race and Afro-Cuban people in the eastern provinces confirmed that the island was in the midst of racial turmoil.[43] As one African American reporter saw it, Cuba's Race War was the "yield of the harvest from the seed of [white American] race prejudice." After fourteen years of U.S. intervention Cuba's interracial relations had worsened and the Cuban government was considering legislation to prohibit black and Asian immigration to the island, even as it subsidized European immigration to whiten the nation.[44]

Yet the so-called Race War of 1912 was not just a case of outside intervention gone wrong. Even before the United States invaded, the island already had in place a two-tier racial system that separated white from nonwhite by virtue of visible black ancestry. The military occupation had simply exacerbated existing racial inequities as U.S. officials put conservative white and light-skinned Cubans in positions of power. These elites often instituted policies that discriminated against Afro-Cubans. They also manipulated the new nation's founding myth of racial equality not only to justify the status quo but also to repress Afro-Cuban cultural expression and political mobilization. Pointing to the absence of legal segregation, the general tolerance of race mixing, and the upward mobility of prominent mulattoes, white Cuban elites blamed Afro-Cubans for their own socioeconomic problems.[45]

Frustrated with this state of affairs, Afro-Cubans began to organize, and in 1908 they founded the Partido Independiente de Color (PIC). However, with its platform of Afro-Cuban equality and working-class empowerment, the PIC was outlawed in 1910. By 1912 party leaders had come to believe that only armed protest would bring the PIC official recognition in Cuba. They simply wanted the right to organize for Afro-Cubans' full integration into the political, economic, and social life of the island.[46]

Taking a page from their white American counterparts, the Cuban elite couched the PIC's protest in narratives of black savagery versus white civilization, branding it a "race war" directed against the island's white population. The uprising had rekindled longstanding fears of an Afro-Caribbean conspiracy to make Cuba a black republic like Haiti. The mainstream Cuban press also revived the ominous specter of the black male rapist, rousing white men in the defense of the sanctity of their women and their families, and by extension the Cuban body politic. An editorialist for El Día even argued that Cuba should consider adopting the United States' racial practices of lynching, segregation, and disfranchisement to better control its own black population. The white repression of the protest was both swift and deadly. Not only were there mass arrests, but the racialized hysteria led to the indiscriminate massacre of thousands of Afro-Cubans.[47]

Even in the wake of this violence, many black Americans still held out hope for the fledgling nation. "If the present [Cuban] president can hold out and put the administration on a sound financial basis and carry out his policies, there is no reason in the world why they should not paddle their own canoe," an editorialist for the Chicago Defender declared in 1914. Yet this would require steering against a strong current of white American culture. With the "advent of the 'Yankee,'" Cuba, especially the Cuban elite, was "absorbing more of his bad than his good traits." The island needed to "shun annexation" to maintain its integrity as an inclusive multiracial nation.[48]

The Willard-Johnson match provided a perfect test case for determining which way Cuba's leaders would navigate. Johnson arrived in Havana on 21 February 1915, and by late March both he and Willard had set up their training camps in the city.[49] The rush of publicity surrounding the match was giving boxing a newfound popularity among the locals. As Johnson attested, "The growing number of individuals who attend my training sessions, as well as the applause they dedicate to me each time I perform a fast and elegant movement . . . gives me the authority to believe it."[50] Although initially marketed to U.S. visitors, boxing was quickly becoming a Cuban favorite.

The white hope fight was set to take place at the Oriente Park race-track at Marianao, an open-air stadium that could hold roughly twenty thousand spectators. Its U.S. promoters expected Cubans to buy up the cheaper seats, while the private boxes and ringside tickets would be sold principally to U.S. sportsmen.[51] An advertisement in the *Havana Daily Post* urged U.S. expatriates and Cuban elites alike, "This is Havana's chance to become the Sporting Mecca of the World. Do your share!"[52] A lot was riding on the fight both from the standpoint of Cuba's inter-national reputation as a modern nation and its future as a profitable center of big-money boxing.

White hope matches had already served to publicize and enrich fron-tier cities in the United States, including Reno, Nevada (Johnson versus Jeffries, 1910), and Las Vegas, New Mexico (Johnson versus "Fireman" Jim Flynn, 1912). Local officials had banked on the fact that hosting a white hope fight would confer a status of civilization and whiteness on their rough and multiracial communities.[53] They also hoped the fight publicity would bring in businesses and investors to boost their local economies.

Cuban officials and U.S. promoters saw the same potential for prof-itable cross-promotion in Havana. As a new nation, Cuba was endeav-oring to fashion itself as a civilized body comprised of civilized citizens. This involved using the latest techniques of social science (anthropol-ogy, criminology, and eugenics) to improve a population supposedly degenerated by its slave and colonial past.[54] Social Darwinism and pos-itivism undergirded Cuban fans' (particularly the elite's) understand-ings of race in general and the interracial fight in particular. Attuned to this context, U.S. promoters emphasized both boxing's and the match's regenerative possibilities for the nation. A white hope fight would not only put Cuba on the map of the civilized world, but it would also pro-vide free advertising for the island as a fun and adventurous space for U.S. tourists.

Yet this plan was not without complications. The potential for racial unrest simmered beneath the surface as Cubans of different stripes chose sides. Cuban officials threw their support behind the white hope fight, giving it the air of a state event. President General Mario García Menocal received "elaborately engraved" tickets for a special ringside box to share with his friends and cabinet officers. Next to Menocal's box was another set aside for the U.S. minister to Cuba, William Gonzales. The governor of Havana province, the mayor of Havana, and the commanding general of the army also scored their own private boxes.[55] On the day of the big fight the Cuban congress took a holiday, and twenty of Havana's leading stores closed in the morning so that the owners and employees could attend. "The entire sport world favors Willard to bring home the bacon and title to the white race," the *Havana Daily Post* declared, while *La Lucha* noted "that [Cuban] public opinion in general sympathizes with and supports Willard."[56]

Afro-Cubans embraced Johnson as their race hero. "Hundreds of negroes, the best sports on the island, are anxious to attend the fight, but cannot afford the admission charge," the *New York Times* reported. "In many cases they are scraping every penny together in their eagerness to see the Samson Johnson facing the white Goliath."[57] The epic match held a particular appeal for Cuba's working-class as "streetcar drivers . . . coachmen, and even the guys in the streets" were seen "stretching their arms and doing all kinds of pirouettes as if they were 'training' for a boxing 'match.'"[58] As the white American sportswriter Damon Runyon observed, "On every corner brown-skinned small boys are seen squaring off at one another by way of illustrating the American amusement."[59]

Even though Cuban authorities had authorized the Willard-Johnson match, they claimed they would ban all future fights between local whites and blacks. "They say they are not concerned with foreign race problems, but have their own to deal with," a reporter for the *New York Times* explained. "They are not taking any chances of untoward happenings on Monday, however, as Militia will be freely disposed about the race track where the arena has been constructed."[60]

The racial dimensions of the fight also put Havana on the radar of white and black Americans alike. In late March a sensational story circulated in the mainstream U.S. press about a Cuban manicurist named Monica Valdez who lost her job when she refused to wait on Johnson's wife, Lucille. After an exchange of "heated words," Valdez reputedly grabbed Lucille by the hair, dragging her and punching her in the face. The other women working in the salon called the police to break up the fight. Johnson demanded an apology, and although the salon owner apologized, Valdez refused to back down. According to the *Milwaukee Free Press,* "She flung a wet towel in the proprietor's face, told the champion what she thought of him, and left the place."[61] Johnson was incensed and threatened to sue, while Cuba's "white element" stood behind Valdez. Fearing that news of the catfight would incite "race trouble," the Cuban police forbade any publication of the incident in the local press.[62] The story still managed to catch the eye of a group of white citizens in Denison, Texas, who expressed their solidarity with the "little Cuban maicurist [sic] . . . who had the courage to give up her position rather than attend to Jack Johnsons [sic] wife." W. N. King, secretary of the Denison Chamber of Commerce, had even written to the U.S. minister Gonzales for help in sending a $10 donation to the embattled Valdez.[63]

The upcoming match seemed to be threatening both racial peace and U.S. power on the island. Captain Cushman Albert Rice, a white American ranch owner and soon to be the president of the National Sporting Club of Cuba, had traveled to New York City back in February, when he cautioned a group of men at the Army and Navy Club about the island's instability. "Now let me say for myself as well as every man of means on the island that a bout between Jack Johnson and Jess Willard will not be tolerated for a single moment," Cushman declared.[64] This was not just a local matter, but one that could potentially affect white American control of the island's resources. "Our interests are too valuable to allow the flames of race feeling to be fanned into a riot," Cushman advised. "If I find that they propose to pitch a battle ground for the pair I will rally all the powerful interests at my command to fight the proposition." He and other white American investors feared that an Afro-Cuban uprising would disrupt business as usual. "We don't want any civil war and that's what it would mean if a black started to muss up a white man," Cushman cautioned. The ranch owner knew from experience that the Afro-Cuban laborer was not afraid to exercise his rights: "You can tell him to get a move on in the fields; he'll either quit or stick a knife in you." Referring to the Race War of 1912, Cushman warned, "You know they went off into the woods to run a government of their own about three years ago and we had to go out and shoot them. We don't want that. We don't intend to do anything that would put the idea in their heads again."

Lester Walton of the *New York Age* countered Cushman's characterization of Cuban race relations. Like many other black Americans, he believed that white Americans had infected the island with their well-honed racism. "Not many years ago color prejudice was unknown in that country," he claimed, "but as is invariably the case, the invasion of Americans, with their contagious notions on the color question, has inflamed the whites against the blacks."[65] Walton asserted that as soon as the Afro-Cuban decided to "show a spirit of independence and demand his manhood rights," Cushman and his cronies would have another thing coming. Yet, in emphasizing the shared plight of Afro-Cubans and African Americans at the hands of white Americans, Walton effectively glossed over Cuba's own deep-seated racial problems.

Other black American correspondents provided triumphant reports of Johnson's popularity in Cuba. "In all, those who speak of him, speak of him as a polished gentleman," boasted a reporter for the *Chicago Defender*.[66] Although Willard apparently attracted little attention in Havana's streets, Johnson drew crowds as he and his wife, dressed to the nines, toured around in an automobile. Cuban journalists reportedly favored the black American heavyweight because of his friendliness and accessibility. During his training sessions Johnson put on a real show for his Cuban fans. He "sparred" with President Menocal's son and with the moving picture actress Miss Dixie.[67] Rumors circulated that Menocal had even placed a wager on Johnson. However, in a letter to Minister Gonzales the president countered these rumors and threatened to put an end to boxing in Cuba if reporters sent any more false and slanderous stories abroad. Betting on a black prizefighter was apparently considered conduct unbecoming a chief executive of a nation.[68]

On 5 April 1915 an audience of roughly thirty thousand spectators, including around one thousand women, squeezed into and surrounded the Oriente Park racetrack generating a box office of $110,000. Since streetcar lines could not accommodate the crush of fans, some Cubans walked the twelve miles from Havana.[69] As a band played ragtime in the background, "groups of soldiers and barefooted natives dotted the distant green landscape," and American "black derbies" mixed in with the Cubans' "bobbing straw hats."[70]

Even though promoters had billed the event as a tourist attraction for white Americans, around twenty-five thousand of the spectators were actually Cuban. A number of black Americans were also sprinkled throughout the stands. Still, most in the crowd were Willard supporters, and many had placed bets on the white hope.[71] As Herbert Swope of the *Chicago Daily Tribune* described the scene, "Never in the history of the ring . . . was there such a wild, hysterical, shrieking, enthusiastic crowd [as] the 20,000 men and women who begged Willard to wipe out the stigma that they . . . believed rested on the white race. . . . Nowhere was the feeling stronger than in Cuba, whose race hatred is near the surface, although the negro is ostensibly received on parity with the white."[72] Many fans in the venue waved white flags as symbols of their racial affiliation in the impending fight.

For the first seven rounds the black champion controlled the match, using his ring dexterity to make the giant Willard look awkward. As the crowd chanted, "Yellow, yellow, yellow," Johnson shouted back, "I wish I was . . . then everybody would think I was white."[73] From the eighth to the tenth round Willard managed to get some shots in and his fans began yelling, "Kill the black bear!"[74] By twentieth round the action had slowed and Johnson appeared to be tiring. Over the next six Willard started to take control of the fight, and in the twenty-sixth round he felled Johnson with a blow to the chin. Johnson lay on his back with his right arm shielding his eyes from the sun, causing many observers to speculate later that the fight was fixed. After twenty-six rounds of intense slugging in the heat, Willard came out on top, scoring a knockout against the infamous black American. It was the first time that Johnson had lost to a white man since becoming the world heavy-weight champion in 1908. The search for a white hope was finally over.

Cuban soldiers piled into the ring, drawing their sabers and revolvers to protect both fighters from the rush of fans.[75] "Something approaching a race riot followed," recounted Runyon. "Thousands paraded the race track, chanting, '*Viva El Blanco!*' . . . [while] blacks drew off in little groups." Swope even claimed that white American postfight celebrations were "mere apathy" compared to those of the Cubans.[76]

Many Cubans took great satisfaction in knowing that their capital city was the site of the notorious black American's downfall. Cars returning to Havana after the match flew white flags, spreading the word that the new world champion was white. Later, "cheering crowds" of Cuban fans followed Willard wherever he went, waving "flags and linen handkerchiefs tied to sticks," patting him on the back, and throwing flowers at him. As the sun set, the streets of the capital remained "ablaze" in Willard's honor, and the citizens of Havana even organized a victory dinner and reception.[77] Willard certainly did not disappoint, for he declared that he would never fight another black man.

Black Cubans were conspicuously absent from their regular haunts the night after the fight. Refusing to accept Johnson's defeat, a group of black children had greeted the new white champion by waving black flags. Although an Associated Press correspondent assumed that the

FIGURE 15. This postcard advertised Jess Willard's Wild West Show, which toured the United States after his triumph over Jack Johnson. "'The Count' that made Jess Willard Cowboy Champion of the World. Appearing with Miller Bros. & Arlington's 101 Ranch, Wild West," circa 1916. From the author's collection.

Afro-Cuban youngsters had mistakenly heard that Johnson had won, it is far more likely that they stood in defiant support of their black sporting hero.[78]

Back home, black Americans took the news hard. When several whites walked along South State Street waving the *Chicago American's* special fight edition with the headline "WILLARD CHAMPION," a group of black Americans attacked them, sending three to the hospital.[79] The sense of disappointment was palpable. Billy Lewis of the *Indianapolis Freeman* had to admit, "Jess Willard was a eugenic man—made to order."[80] In Chicago's Black Belt, "It was as if the community had had a promised holiday recalled," and Johnson's friends and family expressed their utter disbelief. In Harlem his fans remained loyal, arguing that the fight must have been a frame-up.[81]

Johnson's fall in Havana pushed black Americans to ponder the state of the worldwide race problem. Prominent activist and writer James Weldon Johnson connected the black heavyweight's struggle against the color line to the larger geopolitical struggle of nonwhite peoples. Born of parents with ties to the Bahamas, and having spent time as a U.S. diplomat in Venezuela and Nicaragua, Weldon Johnson was keenly

aware of the global scope of Western imperialism and white supremacy. "Johnson fought a great fight," the longtime admirer of the black
champion observed, "and it must be remembered that it was the fight
of one lone black man against the world."[82] Johnson's winning record
"has been something of a racial asset," Weldon Johnson claimed, since
"the white race, in spite of its vaunted civilization, pays more respect to
the argument of force than any other race in the world." Referring to
the Russo-Japanese War, he remarked, "As soon as Japan showed that
it could fight, it immediately gained the respect and admiration in an
individual way."[83]

Weldon Johnson recognized the link between notions of white supremacy and assumptions about white intellectual and physical prowess. "One of the delusions fostered by the Anglo-Saxon is that white
men are superior to those of 'lesser breed' not only intellectually, but
also in physical strength and stamina," he observed. White men believed
"physical stamina" was "a matter of mind," and since they supposedly
possessed a superior mind, they could survive "the grueling grind" that
would take "the heart out of other men." Weldon Johnson reflected,
"Before the Johnson-Jeffries fight, the papers were full of statements to
the effect that the white man had the history of Hastings and Agincourt
behind him, while the black man had nothing but the history of the jungle."[84] Johnson had helped to erase these false conceptions, giving people of color their own battle hero. As one editorialist put it, "His own
individual achievements in the ring had put new life and backbone in the
colored races from the China Wall to Niagara's Falls."[85]

Back in Cuba, local authorities saw the Willard-Johnson fight as
another step forward in their nation's development. According to one
official, the excitement of the fight had caused "Cuban boys and even
men to yearn for skill in the manly art of defending themselves with
their fists instead of with knives and pistols."[86] Others remained skeptical of the benefits of prizefighting, arguing that it did not befit a modern, independent nation. An editorialist for *Diario de la Marina* called
the match "mercenary and grotesque." Although he saw the necessity
of "body workouts" in these "cretinous and degenerated times," he was
not in favor of public fights.[87] Another compared boxing to the barbaric Spanish practice of bullfighting, noting that both were brought
in by the island's colonizers. He argued that his compatriots' embrace
of boxing was indicative of their colonial habit of "self-denigration,"
for they devalued their own traditions while blindly adopting the customs of those who despised them.[88] A few Cuban writers even likened

professional prizefighting to other U.S. colonial ventures on the island. The white American promoter Curley had initially gone out of his way to express his personal investment in Cuba and its people. When he later cheated Cuban workers out of money for services rendered, they realized that his investment was more profit-driven than sincere.[89] Disgusted by the Willard-Johnson affair, one editorialist urged the Cuban public to stop putting up "with those foreign frauds that make fun of your 'frock coats' and your charming tropical innocence."[90]

Despite these reservations, boxing, much like other U.S. imports, was gaining in popularity. In the years that followed the island developed its own boxing industry. On 12 May 1915 Cuba's Supreme Court legalized prizefighting on the island.[91] By 1919 there were two new boxing rings in Cuba—el Ring Cuba and el Black Cat Ring—run by the Cuban businessmen José María Villaverde and Angel Rodrigo Vivero. A professional boxing association, el Havana Boxing Committee, was also established in 1920, followed in 1921 by a government regulatory board called the Comisión Nacional de Boxeo y Lucha.[92]

Some sportsmen saw Cuba's trend toward athletics as part and parcel of its economic, political, and cultural progress. Writing in 1923, Fernando Gil, the official judge appointed by the Cuban Boxing Commission, contended, "Cuba is not only abreast with the times in her commercial development as the largest cane sugar producing country in the world; she is also the greatest producer of first class all round athletes south of the Rio Grande."[93] Every "fair sized city or town" in Cuba had its own athletic club complete with a ring or stadium with space for thousands of spectators, and Cuban newspapers had sports sections devoted to boxing. This burst of pugilistic activity had also revealed the true nature of Cuban manhood. "The Cuban has proven he possesses the indispensable requirements of an athlete in the strict sense of the word," Gil declared. "He is quick in action, determined, has a good eye, he is naturally strong, and courageous, assimilates punishment wonderfully, will accept advice readily and is always ready to try." With the help of boxing, Cubans were becoming brave and honorable "men"—modern masculine subjects capable of self-determination.

Although disaffected by both U.S. imperialism and white Cuban nationalism, Afro-Cubans became some of the most ardent fans and practitioners of pugilism. For them, boxing formed an important strand of countercultural connection with black America. In the decades following the Willard-Johnson match Afro-Cubans continued to idolize the audacious black American heavyweight for his public stands against white American racism. By the time the legendary Afro-Cuban featherweight Eligio Sardiñias-Montalbo (Kid Chocolate) picked up the gloves as a young boy in the Havana barrio of Cerro, boxing had already become an integral part of the local scene. Kid Chocolate and his friends learned the details of Johnson's career and emulated the black American's bold dandyism.[94] Ironically, they expressed their black pride and solidarity by appropriating the very sport that was supposed to signal Cuba's entry into the white world.

The official end of the seven-year search for a white hope had certainly not softened the hearts of U.S. officials. They were determined to make Johnson serve his time. When he applied for a passport in Havana, U.S. minister Gonzales consulted with State Department officials in Washington, D.C. Secretary of State Bryan denied Johnson a passport on the grounds that he was a fugitive from U.S. justice. When Curley and Willard departed for the United States, Johnson lamented, "It's hard to see you all go back to America, as much my country as it is yours, and I can't go there, and did nothing to warrant this persecution against me."[95] Still a wanted man back home and worried that Cuban officials might deport him, Johnson traveled to Spain with Lucille in a luxurious suite aboard the *Reina Maria Cristina*.[96]

Over the next four years (1915–19) Johnson became increasingly disillusioned about the real potential for black freedom and fortune in Europe, particularly among the Anglo-Saxons. Shortly after arriving in Spain Johnson left for London, where he gave exhibitions and later became a recruiter for the British military.[97] Even though Johnson remained a celebrity of sorts, his British sojourn was bittersweet. The former champion not only faced legal troubles and poor box office returns, but he also had to contend with slanderous reports of his "inappropriate" advances on English women. By January 1916 the Home Office had used the provisions of the Aliens Restriction Act to force Johnson out of the country.[98]

Cast out of Britain, Johnson returned to neutral Spain, where he and his wife settled in an exclusive area of Barcelona. In this Latin nation things seemed to take a turn for the better. Johnson took advantage of his exotic status as a black performer as well as Spain's relative racial fluidity to embark on a number of new business ventures. He opened a boxing academy and a café, tried his hand at bullfighting, became a patron of King Alfonso, purchased an interest in a Spanish socialist weekly, and continued to engage in the occasional prizefight.[99]

As he publicly critiqued the United States and made various pro-

German statements, Johnson remained a target of the U.S. government.[100] Military intelligence officers trailed him in Spain, providing
a record of his mounting frustration. John Lang, a military attaché
in Madrid, caroused with Johnson and his ragtag interracial posse of
embittered expatriates, gamblers, bohemians, radicals, and prostitutes.
Johnson drowned his resentment in liquor, his words often betraying
his disenchantment with the Allies' pronouncements of democracy. He
once asserted, "The Germans treat me as a man and my wife as a
lady."[101] Johnson's declaration revealed his overwhelming sense of disappointment more than any real affiliation with Germany. He had concluded that Britain and France were no better than the United States.
Their rhetoric of freedom appeared to be just that—empty rhetoric.

BLACK AMERICANS AND THE MEXICAN REPUBLIC

Although Spain proved to be a more or less hospitable place, ultimately
it was still too far from the United States for Johnson's liking. Yearning
for home and increasingly disaffected with Europe, the former champion shifted his sights to "Latin America, the garden of the world."[102]
He believed the region offered black Americans "all the golden privileges of a land that has never known racial prejudice." He claimed
that Mexico would not only grant black Americans citizenship but also
stand up for their rights. "If you want us, Mexico," Johnson challenged,
"we are ready to dwell among you and make you rich as we have made
the southern white man rich." In his eyes, the postwar period marked
a critical moment for his people. The "Negro" was "on the auction
block," and "the nation or community" with the highest bid would
receive his loyalty.

Johnson did not waste time in executing his plans. On 18 January
1919, Military Attaché Lang reported, "It is rumored that two rich
Mexicans at present in Madrid . . . have entered into agreement with
Jack Johnson to send him and his wife to Mexico where a fight will
be arranged between him and some American."[103] Shortly thereafter
Johnson left Spain, stopping in Havana on his way to Mexico City.

As Johnson encouraged Mexico to make its bid for the "Negro," he
was not only tapping into longstanding images of Mexico as a space of
exile for black Americans, but he was also playing on white American
fears about the potential for cooperation between black Americans
and Mexicans against the United States. After Reconstruction, Mexico
became the haven of choice for many African Americans in search of

a reprieve from racial violence and segregation. The 1890s brought the rise of Mexican colonization schemes often spearheaded by black Americans and supported by the Mexican government. These schemes involved recruiting black Americans from the South to grow coffee and cotton in the Mexican states of Veracruz and Tamaulipas. Like Cuba, Mexico was especially enticing because of its proximity to the United States in comparison to Liberia and other African destinations. Enterprising black Americans relocated with the hope of working for themselves on their own land.[104]

In 1902 the black American pugilist Bob Scanlon traveled to Mexico as a teenager in search of opportunity and adventure. He found work as a ranch hand in Veracruz. That same year the Chicago journalist G. W. Slaughter began his annual visits to Mexico. "It is a glorious land, free from race prejudice and all the little qualities that make up this country we live in," Slaughter wrote upon returning from his eighth trip south of the border in 1910.[105] "Black and white mingled together in even closer intimacy than the Jews do in the United States," he declared. "There is not a drug store in the capital city that will refuse a Negro a drink of ice cream soda, and in several cases whites and blacks have intermarried without causing even comment." He had also seen "prosperous, industrious Negroes"—including entrepreneurs, railroad engineers and property owners—"carrying on business of their own." As Slaughter concluded, "On the whole Mexico can be said to be the black man's country." It was a place where New Negroes could be "men" rather than "Sams, Georges, Shines, Coons and the like."[106]

Other accounts suggested that not all Mexicans would greet black Americans with open arms. Some worried that disease, vice, and vagabondism would accompany the black influx from across the border.[107] In reality, Mexican settlement was far from an unmitigated success. Often faced with hunger, disease, financial troubles, and inhumane treatment, many black migrants gave up and returned to the United States. Even for those who persevered, their position was shaky at best in a nation that not only marginalized its own black population but also worked to erase any African elements from its collective memory and consciousness.[108]

Throughout the 1910s the violence and instability of the Mexican Revolution brought additional complications. Although the dictatorial regime of President Porfirio Díaz had overseen a massive program of national development, building infrastructure such as railroads, highways, and telegraph lines, political and economic control had become increasingly concentrated in the hands of a select few. This select few also included white American financiers and corporations that not only invested heavily in Mexico's rail, oil, mining, and banking industries but also brought their racial prejudices with them. Mexicans from all classes joined in the revolt against this centralization of power and wealth. With the ouster of Díaz, many factions vied for control, causing political upheaval.[109]

Despite black Americans' historical affinity for Mexico, during the revolution the United States began to rely more heavily on black soldiers to police the border region. Although men like Sergeant John L. Hunt of the 9th Cavalry were a source of pride for fellow black Americans, he and his troops remained vulnerable to white American slander and violence. In the fall of 1912 Hunt wrote a letter to the *Statesman* in defense of his comrades. He lauded the "great courage and bravery" his men had shown as they guarded the border near Douglas, Texas, against a band of Mexican rebels. "For just that brief moment I felt proud to be a soldier," Hunt recalled, "but as we can be appreciated and respected only when we are on the battle field I sometimes regret that I ever donned the uniform of a soldier."[110] Given the region's harsh racial climate, U.S. officials worried about the potential impact of Mexican radicalism, from labor organizing to socialism to anarchism, on these armed and often disgruntled black soldiers.[111]

The stories of black American servicemen in Mexico contained many of the same declarations of New Negro manhood that permeated the tales of Johnson's successes abroad. It seemed as if black men had to leave the United States to gain respect and admiration for their bravery and skill, whether in the boxing ring or on the battlefield. Rumors about the Mexican rebel leader Pancho Villa's supposed black and Cherokee heritage exemplified this recurrent theme. Some black American veterans argued that Villa was actually Sergeant-Major George Goldsby, formerly of the black 10th Regiment of the United States Cavalry. As the apocryphal story went, Goldsby had deserted the 10th Regiment in 1879, fearing that he would be unfairly punished as a black man after being threatened with a court martial.[112] The mythical Goldsby was not alone, for other Spanish-American War veterans from the 9th and 10th Cavalry and the 24th and 25th Infantry had also defected to the Mexican Army. Goldsby's was a cautionary tale about the fragility of black American loyalty to the United States and its expansionist designs.[113]

When President Woodrow Wilson sent U.S. warships to attack and occupy Veracruz on 21 April 1914, it looked as if the United States might go to war with Mexico. Although black servicemen took part in the attack, their participation in a full-scale conflict with Mexico remained a subject of passionate debate back home. "Should they volunteer to fight for this country in view of the abridgement of their rights, and suffering . . . at the hands of the dominant race in America?" one black editorialist asked.[114] For some, the potentially positive impact of the black regiments' courageous exploits at the border overrode questions of racial discrimination at home.[115] Echoing Johnson's earlier pronouncements that he would never "shoulder a musket" for the United States, others could not justify fighting for a country that not only degraded them at every turn but also shunted them into the thankless job of border service while a real war was heating up in Europe. They argued that the United States had no right to interfere in Mexican affairs, and they questioned President Wilson's feeble claim that this was "a war of service" to bring peace to Mexico rather than a war of conquest.[116] Together, the Mexican rebels' defiance and black Americans' tenuous loyalty created a subversive combustion of colored interests. The underlying fear that had driven the furious pursuit for a white hope a few years earlier now appeared to be manifesting itself in the spheres of war and politics.

With the possibility of world war on the horizon, U.S. officials worried that Japan and Germany were allying with Mexico and courting the support of African Americans in a bid to attack them from the south. Rumors of such an alliance had already been circulating in the black community. In condemning the persistence of virulent white racism in South Carolina, a *Defender* report warned of a transnational and multiracial coalition against the United States. Its headline declared, "While Government and Southern States Were Making Ways and Means to 'Keep the Nigger Down' Japan Has Placed Fifty Shiploads of Guns and Munitions of War in Mexico and [President Victoriano] Huerta Now Defies the American Government to Show Her Hand—Japan with Mexico and the Philippines Allied with the Hawaiians Are Planning to Trounce Uncle Sam Soundly."[117]

By 1915 rumors of an imminent colored uprising on the U.S.-Mexico border had surfaced. The Plan de San Diego, so named for its suspected origins in a Texas town of the same name, offered a frightening example of what could happen if discontented men of color on both sides of the border united in opposition to their white American oppressors. According to the plan, Mexicans and Mexican-Americans would take over the Texas border region, declare their independence from the United States, and then invade the rest of Texas, New Mexico, Arizona, California, and Wyoming. The plan also included provisions for the annexation of six more states for the formation of an independent African American republic, along with the repatriation of stolen lands to the Apache Indians. Most disturbingly, it called for the extermination of all white American males above the age of sixteen. A transnational Liberating Army of Races and Peoples, comprised of Mexican-Americans, African Americans, Native Americans, and Japanese, would execute the plan, fighting under a red and white flag emblazoned with the words "Equality and Independence."[118] Even though the plan's provenance was unknown and its authenticity questionable, its vision of cross-border, multiracial resistance offered a harrowing prediction of what people of color could accomplish if they worked together.

Still, when the United States entered World War I in 1917, it remained dependent on black soldiers to secure the border. There was no guarantee that this gamble would continue to pay off. Alongside the Bolshevik Revolution and the flowering of black radicalism, public displays of black protest in the United States were reaching new heights. U.S. officials also worried that German agents were targeting both Mexicans and African Americans with racially charged anti-American propaganda. In 1918 a confidential government report described a black American soapbox orator in New York City who was advising black soldiers to kill their white officers. The report warned that this idea "once planted might well bear fruit on more than one foreign battlefield."[119]

Disaffected after years of persecution, Johnson also seemed to be shifting to a more concrete platform of colored solidarity, and he remained a target of U.S. military intelligence. An informant who claimed to have befriended Johnson reported, "I can positively assert that he has sent money and written articles to aid the Negroes in their struggle in the United States. He makes collections among the Negroes and their sympathizers." The informant even claimed that Johnson had "tried to go to the Antilles, especially Cuba, to foment a rebellion among the Negroes." These were exaggerations, although the black heavyweight had become much more deliberate in his critique of white supremacy, adding to white American fears about the various political instabilities in their own backyard. Though not a strict "Socialist," Johnson called himself a "DEFENDER OF HIS RACE."[120]

Amid all this uncertainty Johnson arrived in Mexico City by train on 26 March 1919. Similar to the black troops who tried to navigate the complicated maze of interracial and international relations in the border region, Johnson held an ambiguous position in Mexico. On the one hand, he became a conduit of U.S. commercial culture. Johnson's visit helped to expand the reach of U.S.-style boxing (and its cultural products) from the border towns to cities across the nation. Mexican newspapers began to report on matches in the United States, while U.S. boxers (black and white) streamed into Mexico for exhibitions and fights.[121] On the other hand, Johnson emerged as a symbol of anti-Americanism in the eyes of his Mexican supporters. As Mexicans endeavored to define their own way forward in the shadow of their more powerful neighbor to the north, Johnson's racial conflicts with white Americans provided a rallying point for independence and national pride.

Johnson's legendary fame as the former world heavyweight champion, his audacious personality, and his flashy style made him an instant hero with local sports fans, particularly the fashionably dressed and gender-bending young men known as the Fifi.[122] A crowd of more than two thousand people gave him a rousing ovation at the train station, complete with bullfight music and the "unanimous cry" of "Viva Johnson." Even little children greeted him with shouts of "Bravo Jack!"[123] A journalist for *El Universal* declared, "Jack Johnson is now the talk of the day." With his arrival, everyday conversations came to revolve around "exotic" words like "punch, upper cutt [sic], heavy weight class, *pesos de pluma* [featherweights], rounds etc. etc."[124]

Johnson's first match in Mexico City was against a white American former soldier who fought under the name Captain Bob Roper. Johnson's public training sessions drew many Mexican spectators, helping to initiate them in the pugilistic arts of shadowboxing and bag punching. Some even brought their English phrase books to Johnson's workouts in an effort to converse with him.[125] The Johnson-Roper fight took place at the Plaza de Toros on 22 June 1919. In some respects the match embodied Mexico's progress as it marked the shift away from the "backward" Spanish tradition of bullfighting to the more "civilized" U.S. sport of boxing. While the fight proved to be a flagrant physical mismatch, garnering cries of disappointment from the crowd, it also served to educate Mexicans in the basics of modern pugilism. Many of the advertisements and prefight articles in *El Universal* and *El Demócrata* had included the Marquess of Queensberry rules for the benefit of local spectators.[126]

In addition to adopting U.S. sporting culture, some Mexican fans unfortunately seemed to be appropriating white American racism as well. One black American journalist wrote, "Jack played with his opponent [Roper] and the copper colored Mexicans, who are just as predudiced [sic] against dark-skinned colored people as any other race, hooted and jeered the black American, who, as of old, came back strong and aroused their ire."[127] White American newspapers were more than happy to note that Mexicans were giving Johnson a hard time. The government of the Federal District requested that municipal authorities refuse to grant licenses for Johnson's boxing matches. Other reports maintained that Johnson was in trouble with Mexican officials because he failed to honor his contracts. They apparently planned to deport him for his defiance of police authority and disorderly conduct.[128]

The black American press mostly countered this disparaging news. "Anyone who thinks Jack Johnson . . . is down and out should take a trip to Mexico City, where the Negro fighter is living like a king in one of the palatial residences of the Mexican capital," a journalist for the *Louisville News* charged.[129] Johnson's home was reportedly something of a social center. He had managed to ingratiate himself with several generals and high-ranking Mexican authorities, becoming their official boxing instructor. He also had a gym in the house of General Alfred Breceda, a local power broker who owned one of best residences in the capital. The journalist maintained that Johnson "is still looked upon as a champion by the Mexicans, attracts attention on the streets, and has access to all places of business and amusements." Johnson even befriended President Carranza, who attended his ring exhibitions, and the two shared wide-ranging conversations. Carranza "was greatly interested in world politics and in the future relations between his country and the United States," Johnson later recalled. "He questioned me concerning my experiences in Europe and drew from me my views on international politics."[130]

Johnson's most famous run-ins were with white American expatriates. As he challenged their segregationist sensibilities he not only gained Mexican support but also garnered the praise of black Americans back home. His difficulties highlighted the intrinsic connection between both groups' experiences of racial discrimination at the hands of white Americans.

In April 1919 Johnson's troubles in a U.S.-owned restaurant named The House of Tiles provoked a public scandal.[131] The restaurant's proprietor, Walter Sanborn, a white American expatriate formerly of Los

Angeles, California, refused to serve the black boxer. One Mexican journalist drew a parallel between Sanborn's racist actions and the white American backlash in the wake of Johnson's victory over Jim Jeffries. The journalist maintained that Johnson had become accustomed to eating wherever he liked in Mexico and therefore felt entitled to fight back when Sanborn denied him service. Although Johnson initially left and went to another restaurant, he returned three hours later with three Mexican generals, two colonels, and several more men in tow.

When Johnson and his party sat at a table, Sanborn's staff waited on all of them except the black American. One of the generals confronted Sanborn, arguing that in Mexico, unlike in the United States, there was no difference between blacks and whites. Mexican laws protected everyone equally, Mexicans and foreigners alike. Still, the white American owner remained obstinate. "You are in Mexico, not in the United States!" one of the colonels exclaimed. "Here there are no color differences, here everyone is equal!" The other two generals then drew their pistols, instructing Sanborn that Mexico was "not a white man's country" and that he must serve everyone "regardless of color."[132]

A big and boisterous mob gathered outside the restaurant, shouting, "Viva Johnson, viva Mexico!" The police later arrived to keep the peace, and in front of the crowd Johnson declared, "I am a negro, Mr. Sanborn, my skin is black, but I have a whiter heart than you." The spectators followed his defiant statement with more shouts of "Viva Johnson!" One of the generals then threatened to close Sanborn's restaurant, while another threatened him with physical harm. Even a lawyer in the restaurant raised his cane to strike Sanborn. The American proprietor eventually bowed to Mexican pressure, shook Johnson's hand, and served him ice cream. One report claimed that Sanborn was forced to close his restaurant when Mexican officials revoked his license.[133]

For Johnson's black American fans, not only did such stories present a perfect opportunity to critique white American racism, but they also provided instructive moments about the potential for transnational racial solidarity. To help explain the difference between Mexico and Jim Crow America, a correspondent for the *Chicago Defender* described a confrontation between Johnson and a visiting white American named D. H. Moore of the New Orleans chamber of commerce. Moore and his delegation had entered a restaurant in Mexico City just four days after the incident at Sanborn's. Upon seeing Johnson, Moore declared that "no [nigger] could eat with white people in the South where he came from."[134] Johnson apparently overheard the comment and hit Moore with an uppercut. Despite Johnson's violent reaction, Mexican police reportedly refused to arrest him, for he "was in a country where the color of a man's skin" was "no bar to him receiving justice." As this incident seemed to prove, "in Mexico no man can insult another on account of his color or creed and get away with it."[135]

U.S. authorities worried that Johnson was using his platform in Mexico to stir up trouble for Washington on both sides of the border. A State Department official warned the U.S. embassy in Mexico, "It has been reported that Jack Johnson . . . has been spreading social equality propaganda among the Negroes in Mexico and has been endeavouring to incite colored element in this country."[136] He called upon the embassy to report back on all of Johnson's subversive activities and propaganda. Things back home had already turned violent during the Red Summer of race riots in 1919. Black radicals also increasingly questioned the validity of U.S. intervention in Mexico. A writer for the socialist *Messenger* wondered why black troops continued to risk their lives protecting the property of "American oil owners, copper mine investors and ranch owners" while the U.S. government did nothing to stop the lynching and burning of black people.[137] Black Americans who went against the Mexican people were simply enabling the spread of Jim Crow values. Rather than continuing to fight on behalf of U.S. capital, black Americans could seek out a better life in Mexico.

Johnson became the new figurehead of Mexican settlement. "He is the promoter of one of the largest land corporations in Mexico," a *Defender* report boasted. "Through this concern hundreds of men from the southern states are settling here."[138] During a meeting at the Mexican National Sporting Club, Johnson maintained, "Brazil may have its opportunities, but there are far better ones here in this city. I believe this to be the best place in the world for our people."[139] Advertisements for Johnson's Land Company appeared in the *Messenger* and other black newspapers:

COLORED PEOPLE

You, who are lynched, tortured, mobbed, persecuted and discriminated against in the boasted 'Land of Liberty,' the United States,

OWN A HOME IN MEXICO

Where one man is as good as another, and it is not your nationality that counts, but simply you.[140]

Who better than Johnson to pitch such a scheme? He was the most famous black American exile, pushed out of the United States because he dared to challenge the racial status quo. The advertisements declared, "Rich, fertile land only a few miles from Mexico City . . . is now on sale for $5.00 an acre and up." In addition to rich soil, a pleasant climate, and beautiful scenery, Mexico offered African Americans the promise of a prosperous modern life. They could enjoy "practically every advantage obtainable in improved suburban sections of the United States . . . excellent roads . . . telephone lines; electric lights; and numerous trolley lines." "Best of all," the ads claimed, "there is no 'race prejudice' in Mexico, and severe punishment is meted out to those who discriminate against a man because of his color or race."

Johnson's land venture, coupled with rising black protest in the Southwest and black migration to Mexico, was alarming enough to catch the attention of the Department of Justice and the Bureau of Investigation in 1919. They closely followed the military intelligence reports of Captain W. M. Hanson of the Texas Rangers. "Over the entire south . . . particularly Texas, Louisiana and Arkansas[,] there are spread secret societies of Negroes for the purpose of aggressive action against the whites," Hanson warned in one missive. Spurred on by Johnson's defiant stance, returning African American soldiers were "fostering this society" and procuring arms "in great numbers."[141] In another report Hanson stated, "Twenty [negroes] were counted at the theatre in Mexico City one night. They are publicly in favor of riots in the United States and are conferring with many Carrancista generals in Mexico City, with a view, supposedly, of assisting the Carrancistas in case of trouble with the United States."[142] He cautioned, "It is an open secret in Mexico City that Carranza is working with labor organizations through [Samuel] Gompers and others, and with the protestant churches . . . to further propaganda in the United States." Moreover, moving pictures featuring a well-dressed Johnson stating that he was a member of Mexico City's best clubs had been shown in San Antonio, fanning the flames of local black discontent.[143]

Although not involved in any subversive political plot, the poet Langston Hughes was part of this larger movement of black Americans south of the border. Right around the time that U.S. officials were tracking Johnson, the teenaged Hughes traveled to Mexico to visit his father. Langston recalled that his father had gone to Cuba and then to Mexico, "where a colored man could get ahead and make money quicker." Unable to gain admittance to the bar in the U.S. South, James

Hughes had become a lawyer in Mexico. South of the border James's brown skin was actually advantageous, since the locals preferred him over the gringos. His color not only saved him from having to flee during the revolution but also helped him to land the job of general manager at a U.S.-owned electric light company. He wanted his son to become an engineer in order to cash in on Mexico's mining industry. Langston, however, had other plans.[144]

Although some black Americans like James Hughes were most concerned with getting their own piece of the Mexican pie, others sought to build alliances with Mexican radicals. In August 1919 an informant spotted Johnson in the Mexican border town of Nuevo Laredo, accompanied by the Carrancista generals Juan Perez and Manuel Mijares, who were believed to be supporting the black heavyweight with funds.[145] Johnson still appeared to be fostering anti-American solidarity between blacks and Mexicans. A U.S. spy in Mexico's Socialist Party reported that Johnson had given a speech to a crowd in front of Nuevo Laredo's Vega Hotel in which he "said that when and if the gringos invaded Mexico, American blacks would stand alongside their Mexican brothers."[146] Charles H. Boynton, executive director of the National Association for the Protection of American Rights in Mexico, warned the Department of Justice, "Some time ago Johnson gave an exhibition in Nuevo-Laredo and about 20 negroes from different parts of the United States were there to meet him."[147] Boynton suspected that Carranza was using Johnson to spread propaganda to black communities in the United States. He also believed that several African American musicians were involved. To calm Boynton's fears, John Suter of the Department of Justice assured him that Johnson was "receiving appropriate attention" from Washington officials.[148]

Johnson's subversive influence even seemed poised to spread beyond Mexico and its citizens. In February 1920 a U.S. official in Panama wrote to the attorney general warning of Johnson's possible visit to the Isthmus of Panama, the site of the strategic canal.[149] That same month, when Johnson headed north to Tijuana, a group of Yaqui Indians hijacked his train in Sonora. However, they stopped after discovering the black heavyweight was on board. "I was surprised to find that they did know who I was," Johnson recollected. "Leaders of the band were profuse in their apologies for molesting the train," and the black American fugitive "mingled freely with the Yaquis" until they allowed the train to depart.[150] No wonder U.S. officials worried about Johnson's growing celebrity across Latin America.

Yet Johnson had no intention of staying abroad. When he arrived in Tijuana he opened the Main Event Café and began making plans to go home.[151] As he later revealed, "I was not satisfied with my lot in life. There was nothing, I felt, which would compensate me for continuing as an exile from my home and friends, so I thought constantly of returning but was at a loss as to how I should proceed."[152] Rumors that Johnson would remain in Mexico and become a citizen circulated in the African American press. However, without any legal status in the chaotic Mexican Republic, Johnson found himself in deep trouble after the assassination of his political patron Carranza in the spring of 1920.[153] On 5 June 1920 a Tijuana judge ordered Johnson to leave Mexico within thirty days, and on 20 July, seven years after fleeing the United States, the forty-two-year-old boxer crossed the border, surrendering himself to federal agents. Johnson's rebellious sojourn had finally come to an end.

7

The Empire Strikes Back

The "French Jack Johnson" and the Rising Tide of Color

When you summarize the great achievements and
accomplishments of the darker people of the world in
their upward climb you do not wonder that you hear
so much from the thinkers of the white world about
the rising tide of color.

—"The Darker Races of the World Coming Back to the Front,"
   Negro World, 21 October 1922

From the colonial viewpoint, a Carpentier-Siki match is
worth more than one hundred gubernatorial speeches to
prove to our subjects and protégés that we want to apply
to the letter the principle of equality between races.

—Ho Chi Minh, "About Siki," *Le Paria,* 1 December 1922

When Jack Johnson crossed the U.S.-Mexico border, spectators
swarmed as he posed with U.S. officers in front of the clicking motion
picture cameras. The African American heavyweight appeared to be
"in a joyous mood, laughing and talking with those about him."[1] "I'm
back home, and it sure feels mighty good," Johnson exclaimed. "It is
home sweet home for me and no one who has never been away can
know how good it feels to get back again, whatever is in the future."[2]
As Johnson recalled, his "viewpoint," while "never provincial," had
been "considerably broadened by the varied experiences and contacts"
he had made throughout his journey:

There are few countries in which I have not traveled. I have not only loitered along the beaten paths of old and new worlds, but I have gone into many strange and out-of-the-way corners of the globe and mingled with strange and little known people. . . . Having thus often found myself in the most exclusive circles of men the world over, I have on the other hand leaped to the other extreme and lived side by side with the aborigines and savages of the South Seas, of the Fiji Islands, and the Hinterland in Australia; the provincials of French and English possessions; the semi-savages—the Yaqui of Mexico; ruffians and adventurers of South America and the West Indies.[3]

Although not immune to the civilizationist ideas of his time, Johnson was a transformed man. His journeys had given him a greater appreciation for the oppressive circumstances facing people of color the world over. His journeys had also pushed questions of race and empire to the forefront of public discussions in a variety of locales. The defiant heavyweight had, in many respects, changed how his colored fans saw themselves, laying the groundwork for an increasingly militant and global movement against white domination. He had also forced the white world not only to confront its shared vulnerability but to question the moral and ideological underpinnings of its geopolitical supremacy.

Johnson surrendered his passport to U.S. authorities, making his homecoming complete. "Foreign lands are all right for the foreigner, and I have no complaint to make regarding the treatment I have received in the many different countries in which I have lived during my seven years' absence from home," Johnson declared, "but I am an American through and through, and no country, however generous, can take the place of my country."[4] After short stops in San Diego and Los Angeles, he took a northbound train under the watch of two federal agents. Crowds cheered for Johnson at every station.[5] Fearing that disturbances would arise as thousands of fans, many of them African American, gathered to greet the black heavyweight in Chicago, deputy marshals stopped the train before reaching the Windy City. They locked Johnson up in the Will County Jail, where he awaited his bail hearing. On 14 September 1920 federal judge George Carpenter decided to make an example out of the unruly and arrogant fighter. Carpenter not only denied Johnson's request for bail, but he also ordered the black heavyweight to serve out his 366-day sentence at the Leavenworth Federal Penitentiary.[6]

During his time in prison, Johnson continued to fight his sentence. He sought parole, applied to the president for clemency, and asked the attorney general for early release. In a letter to Attorney General

Harry Daugherty dated 25 March 1921, Johnson professed his innocence and argued that his trial had made "flagrant appeals to passion,
race hatred and moral infamies."[7] When Daugherty publicly pondered
the possibility of releasing Johnson a couple of weeks early letters of
protest flooded in calling for the defense of white American womanhood. One handwritten note dated 25 June 1921 and signed by "three
white ladies" challenged, "Would you insult the women by pardoning this man? Do you know his crimes against white women? Why
this clemency towards the despoiler of homes? Disgusting." Daugherty
responded by announcing that Johnson would have to serve out his
final weeks at Leavenworth.

Even after Johnson's pugilistic decline and imprisonment, the aspirations of nonwhite athletes and their fans could not be contained.
Johnson's defiant legacy had already taken hold. Dubbed the "French
Jack Johnson," the Senegalese-born prizefighter Battling Siki rose to
stardom in the early 1920s. Much like his flamboyant predecessor, Siki
publicly flouted the constraints of colonial etiquette. Siki also faced
concerted white efforts to strip him of his world light-heavyweight
championship title and to cast him as a savage unprepared for the discipline and complexity of modern life. For people of color, Siki's battles encapsulated the period's intensifying struggle over the racial and
imperial status quo, and the balance seemed to be tipping in their favor.
Alongside Siki, the Philippine flyweight Francisco Guilledo, nicknamed
Pancho Villa in honor of the Mexican revolutionary, and the Argentine
heavyweight Luis Firpo, who had a vast number of fans across Latin
America, further threatened white North American and European control of the ring.

Were white men up for the challenge? Frank O'Neill, a correspondent
for the New York–based *Ring* magazine, pondered the state of white
physical fitness after touring Asia with a group of U.S. baseball players in 1925. "We of the Caucasian race have a happy conceit that we are
the world's natural athletes," he asserted, "that we have created all the
records in every sport, and that the white athlete dominates the earth.
And it is no doubt true."[8] Yet O'Neill was not so certain of the white
man's continued dominance. "Off in the jungles of Africa are men who
can high jump seven feet, who leap twenty-five feet chasms, and who can
walk down a deer in the jungles," he warned. "Comanche Indians could
run for hours across deserts," and Asia teemed with "athletic material,
rich almost beyond dream." White America's "John W. Average Man"
was also becoming "an athletic slacker of the worst form" who pre-

ferred to take "his exercise by proxy." All the evidence suggested the decline of white men's power, at least in the physical realm.

A *Ring* reader from Chicago, Illinois, claimed that O'Neill was "unnecessarily apprehensive."[9] "As long as America is a Mecca to Europe's million, her manhood and womanhood will be continually strengthened and invigorated by the infusion of new blood," he proclaimed. "Instead of deteriorating, I expect to see the American athlete achieve still greater renown in the world of sport." Tied together by "blood," white people on both sides of the Atlantic would help each other to maintain the upper hand.

Such concerns about the strength of white bodies were not uncommon in the wake of World War I. The mass destruction and death had exposed the physical and political liabilities of white men, raising troubling questions about the preservation of white control. Eugenics reached new heights in this moment of geopolitical instability. In *The Rising Tide of Color Against White World-Supremacy* (1920), the Harvard-educated political theorist and eugenicist Lothrop Stoddard warned of the racial implications of what he called "the first White Civil War." Their internecine conflicts had distracted them from the mushrooming population of colored peoples who threatened to encroach on their power and space. Stoddard feared that the "frightful weakening of the white world during the war" had opened up "revolutionary, even cataclysmic possibilities." He warned that the darker races, "long restive under white political domination," were developing "a common solidarity of feeling against the dominant white man."[10] Japan's growing military force and the eruption of postwar race riots, from the Red Summer in the United States to the numerous clashes between whites and black soldiers in Britain, offered an apocalyptic vision of the future.

The African American radical Hubert Harrison believed the eugenic ironies of the recent conflict presented people of color with an unparalleled opportunity. Although the war had been waged to determine who would "dictate the destinies of the darker peoples and enjoy the usufruct of their labor and their lands," it was actually undermining white authority.[11] "Not only will the white race be depleted in numbers," Harrison explained, "but its quality, physical and mental, will be considerably lower for a time." The war had claimed the white race's strongest and bravest men, ensuring that successive generations would come from a weaker stock. As people of color felt the grip of white control loosen, they could "demand[,] and finally secure, the right of self-determination." U.S. President Woodrow Wilson's appeals for a new postwar order built on the principle of international equality seemed to sanction this call for self-determination, heightening expectations. When the Paris Peace Conference (1919) left white supremacy and Western imperialism intact, many people of color felt betrayed.[12] The powerful waves of the "new religion of whiteness" that W. E. B. Du Bois had first seen washing over the earth a decade earlier now faced an angry surge of heretics.

This "rising tide of color" was more than just a consequence of World War I; it also grew out of a longer tradition of black working-class travel and resistance. By the 1920s and '30s the transnational black counterculture inspired by Johnson and other rebel sojourners was manifesting itself in a more urgent and organized manner. In the United States African Americans took their cues from Johnson's brash persona, embracing the masculine ethos of the New Negro. As the scholar Alain Locke explained, "Uncle Tom and Sambo have passed on" and now the "[white] American mind must reckon with a fundamentally changed Negro."[13] This New Negro was not only militant in his pursuit of manhood rights but also proud of his race. In the cultural realm, artists and intellectuals of the Harlem Renaissance, much like the Francophone proponents of the Négritude movement and the Latin American advocates of El Negrismo, worked to reshape both the self-perception and public opinion of black peoples. This cultural reconfiguration accompanied an explosion of black radicalism and diasporic politics. Du Bois and a Senegalese member of the French Chamber of Deputies named Blaise Diagne convened a Pan-African Congress in Paris in 1919, bringing together fifty-seven delegates from across the United States, Europe, the Caribbean, and Africa. Marcus Garvey's Universal Negro Improvement Association (UNIA) endeavored to unify the world's scattered peoples of African descent in opposition to their white oppressors while also encouraging black economic and political self-sufficiency. Inspired in part by the Bolshevik Revolution (1917) and faced with continued problems of labor exploitation, other black activists looked to communism, socialism, trade unionism, and anarchism as modes of collective struggle. They closely followed the exploits of other nonwhites fighting for independence, from Indian and Turkish nationalists to advocates of "Asia for the Asians."[14] United in its critique of the racial, imperial, and capitalist world order, the empire was striking back.

Boxing remained a popular metaphor for these escalating fights over racial equality and political self-determination. In a speech to the Brooklyn division of the UNIA in 1922, Garvey declared that the post-war period was no time for cowering or complacency: "The age for turning the right cheek if you are hit on the left is past. This is a Jack Johnson age, when the fittest will survive." Black people had to step up because Africa now had the upper hand, with an opportunity to shift the balance of power: "The bankrupt nations of Europe, unable to rehabilitate themselves through their own countries, are looking to Africa as their hope. British East Africa must support Britain, French West Africa must support France with resources to rebuild. Italian Africa must also serve the same purpose."[15] Garvey lashed back at members of the black bourgeoisie who criticized his organization for being "too radical." They were simply out of touch with reality, for the world was rapidly "reorganizing." "Every race is seeking a place of its own," Garvey explained. "Japanese is [sic] looking for a greater Japan, India—a free India, greater India; Egyptian, a free and independent Egypt. The Irish, who had been clamoring for 750 years for a free and independent Ireland, have got an Irish Free State." Just as Johnson had fought for the right to live freely on his own terms, colonial peoples everywhere were claiming their independence.

The masculine aesthetics and international travels of African American boxers had opened up a space for the black radical imag-ination of the interwar years. When the Harlem Renaissance writer and leftist activist Claude McKay traveled to London in 1919, he was immediately confronted with Johnson's legacy. During McKay's first encounter with his literary hero George Bernard Shaw, the Irish Fabian writer declared, "It must be tragic for a sensitive Negro to be a poet. Why didn't you choose pugilism instead of poetry for a profes-sion? . . . You might have developed into a successful boxer with train-ing. Poets remain poor, unless they have an empire to glorify and pop-ularize like [Rudyard] Kipling."[16] While Shaw's assumptions about the inherent physicality of black men annoyed McKay, Johnson's success both in and out of the ring had challenged the masculine politics of the white man's burden. Boxing had also become one of the most popular pastimes of radical men's organizations. As McKay recalled, several African American boxers had joined the International Club, a multi-racial leftist group in London that counted Jews, Italians, Irish, East Indians, and West Indians among its diverse membership. Sparring exhibitions and prizefights were a regular part of the club's social cal-endar.[17] Boxing clearly resonated with their vision of proletarian revolt.

As this colored militancy took shape, boxing also became part of a biopolitical program of white regeneration and defense. With their weakness exposed by the war, the United States and other white nations tried to stem the tide of nonwhite immigrants through restrictive laws and stepped up efforts to bring white ethnic working-class men into the racial fold through programs of assimilation.[18] Boxing became an integral part of the global efforts to reinvigorate white manhood. Not only did it mesh with prevailing ideas of race improvement, but the sport had long modeled a more flexible, cosmopolitan sense of whiteness. Boxing's official use as a military training method for troops during World War I had also given the quasi-legal working-class sport a newfound legitimacy in mainstream culture.[19] As boxing entered a "Golden Age," black fighters found themselves effectively shut out of world heavyweight championship contention. Johnson's reign had passed, and white American pugilists like Jack Dempsey and Gene Tunney moved to the forefront as international stars.[20]

Despite these attempts to keep championship boxing white, increasing numbers of colored men took up the sport. By 1924 *Ring* magazine had received subscription requests from Brazil, Sumatra, Egypt, and Puerto Rico. Its reader feedback section also attested to boxing's popularity in India, the Philippines, China, and Panama.[21] While the expansion of boxing followed the global movements of imperial troops and civilians, people of color actively appropriated the sport to project their own vision of a new world order, one based on racial justice and colonial liberation. Johnson's pugilistic career may have been over, but his political and cultural legacy still cast its shadow across the globe.

SIKI BATTLES THE GLOBAL COLOR LINE

Battling Siki's comparisons with Johnson were well deserved. The Senegalese fighter lived large, with little concern for his proper racial place in society. He loved big-city excitement, fashionable suits, absinthe, wine, cigarettes, exotic pets, and, most of all, white women.[22] The black American boxer Bob Scanlon once happened upon a crowd of Parisians watching Siki "with two big Great Danes and a revolver firing it in the air and trying to make the dogs do tricks."[23] Even as white writers expressed their dismay, most offered a fairly benign interpretation of Siki's brazen behavior. To them, it showed he was unfit for civilization. As one of Siki's opponents, Harry Reeve, told *Boxing*, the Senegalese was "like a wild man let loose in Europe," a kind of "nigger minstrel" in both his dress and mannerisms.[24] Unaccustomed to modern life, Siki fell prey to its worst vices. He was in desperate need of white tutelage. "I myself am sorry for him as although he is almost a wild man, he is as harmless as a baby when under proper control," Reeve explained.[25] This description melded well with the grinning, childlike depictions of the Senegalese *tirailleurs* (soldiers) fresh from fighting on behalf of their French masters. Much like the *tirailleur,* Siki found himself cast as an anachronistic throwback at the very same time that the rising tide of color was calling for a more prominent place in the modern world.

Hardly a throwback, Battling Siki was well acquainted with the underside of late imperialism and industrial capitalism from a young age. His roaming life was remarkably similar to that of Johnson and other African American boxers. In 1898 Siki was born Amadou M'barick Fall in Saint-Louis, Senegal, then the administrative center of France's West African empire and a busy coaling station for ships destined for Europe or South America.[26] When his father, Assane Fall, a local fisherman, drowned on the job, his mother, Oulimata, was left to raise her young child alone. Amadou lived a hardscrabble existence, and, much like Johnson, he learned to defend himself on the rough-and-tumble docks and streets of Saint-Louis.

In 1908, the same year that Johnson became the world heavyweight champion, the ten-year-old Fall sailed to Europe under the supervision of a white European patron. Fall's benefactor brought him to the rowdy port city of Marseilles, but they parted ways, and the young Senegalese was left to fend for himself. To survive, Fall worked a variety of odd jobs—dishwasher, boxing booth performer, stevedore, doorman, locksmith, and messenger—and he spent the rest of his time in the boxing gyms of southern France. At fifteen he began his professional fight career, assuming the moniker of "Battling Siki." World War I intervened, however, and Siki was one of the 134,000 Africans who took up arms for France. He served on several European fronts as a private in the Eighth Colonial Regiment, proving his valor on the battlefield. In 1919 he left the military, bedecked with the prestigious Croix de guerre and the Médaille militaire, and he soon found his way back into the boxing ring.

A black veteran of the Great War and a successful black boxer in an era of primitivist modernism and mounting black militancy, Siki embodied the transnational debates over white supremacy and Western imperialism in the 1920s. He became a stand-in for the colonial world, albeit a rather extreme example of black male savagery. Although white journalists painted Siki as a "child of the jungle," his life story actually pointed to the blurring boundaries between Europe and Africa, white and nonwhite, and citizen and subject. "A lot of newspaper people have written that I have a jungle style of fighting—that I am a chimpanzee who has been taught to wear gloves," Siki complained. "That kind of thing hurts me. I was never anywhere but in a big city in my life. I have never even *seen* a jungle."²⁷ Even though Siki felt slighted by the white press, he was also keenly aware that primitivism paid. Like Josephine Baker and other contemporary black performers in Paris, the Senegalese prizefighter accentuated his exotic physicality and sexuality to the delight of white fans. While Baker played African princesses wearing little more than a banana skirt, Siki traveled around town with his pet lion cubs.²⁸

Yet Siki's pugilistic success tested the limits of French *négrophilie* (negrophilia). The better his record became, the more difficult it was to find white French opponents. Siki's African American fans took notice when Georges Carpentier, a decorated war hero and France's only world champion, initially declined to meet the black fighter in the ring. A reporter for the socialist *Messenger* asked, "Has the uncultured American, bigoted, uninformed, and unsportsmanlike—become the ideal of the former gentleman Carpentier, the national motto of whose country is '*Liberty, Equality and Fraternity?*' If so, France is rapidly becoming Americanized."²⁹ Carpentier seemed to be emulating his rival Jack Dempsey, the white American heavyweight who refused to fight any black boxers. Even more disappointing was the fact that many French sportsmen supported Carpentier's decision to avoid the African. In a familiar refrain, the reporter blamed this apparent transformation on the influx of white American soldiers and tourists in Paris. "Wherever they go, they carry their propaganda of race prejudice," he complained. "France's imperialism is bad enough without her taking on any more of our bad American customs." At the very least he hoped that France could remain the lesser of two evils.

This sporting discussion echoed earlier conversations in the African American press about the implications of Stoddard's *Rising Tide of Color*. A reviewer for the *Chicago Defender* agreed with at least part of Stoddard's analysis: "That there is an awakening [of colored peoples] cannot be denied. One sees it on every hand, in a more assertive press, in the pulpit and in the field of industry."³⁰ Ironically, the United States seemed most responsible for this increasingly militant countermove-

FIGURE 16. Although cast as a savage throwback from the jungles of Africa, Battling Siki was actually a cosmopolitan man and decorated veteran of World War I. Battling Siki, promotional photograph. From the author's collection.

ment. Not content to control its own affairs, white America endeavored to spread its racial gospel everywhere. "THE AMERICAN is nothing if not a missionary," the reviewed declared. "He has carried his color madness to all points of the world. . . . He has made his dislike of the Negro's color a theme for discussion in the bar rooms and hotels of England, and as a soldier upon the battlefields of France." Yet this global crusade appeared to be backfiring. White Americans' strident racism had not only "stirred" African Americans "with the deepest resentment" but touched "a responsive chord in all the colored peoples of the civilized and semi-civilized world." As the reviewer cautioned, "Among the republics of South America, in Mexico, China, and Japan, in every land where dark blood prevails, the tide is rising in might to protest against the overwhelming arrogance of assumed superiority." He predicted the emergence of organized, even violent, opposition to white supremacy in the decades to come.

As much as these editorials pointed the finger of blame at white America, they also exposed the connection between the United States' "negro problem" and other forms of racial inequality and imperial exploitation. True, by the 1920s the United States had begun a push for the moral leadership and financial mastery of the world. It had also become a preeminent player in the areas of racial theory and policy and in the production of racialized entertainments. However, this renewed focus on preserving white supremacy was more than just a simple case of "Americanization." It was indicative of the shifting geopolitics of race, as the white world grappled with nonwhite peoples' rising race consciousness and ethos of self-determination—what a columnist for the UNIA's *Negro World* called "the spirit of the age."[31]

As Siki climbed the pugilistic ladder, he exemplified the aggressive push for colored liberation. His struggle for fair treatment also showed the lengths to which white nations and empires would go to protect their prerogatives. On 24 September 1922 Siki finally got his chance to challenge Carpentier for the world light-heavyweight championship. With the twenty-round match set to take place at the Buffalo Velodrome in Paris, Siki was the first black boxer to fight for a world title in any weight division since Johnson's loss to Jess Willard in 1915. Promoters marketed this interracial contest, much like those of Johnson and other African American boxers, as a battle between white civilization and black savagery.

French reporters reproduced these established racial tropes. While Carpentier, "le Gentleman," boxed with "science" and "understated vigor," Siki, the "jungle beast," brawled with more instinct than skill.[32] Although Siki would most certainly win in a fight to the death, modern boxing was a civilized sport and therefore weighted in favor of Carpentier's studied finesse.[33] Apparently Siki did most of his "training" at Parisian nightclubs, where he danced to the sounds of "banjoes" reminiscent of the "tom-toms" of his native Senegal.[34]

Siki's manager, Charley Hellers, encouraged international fight fans to see his charge as primitive and subhuman. "A long time ago I used to think that if one could find an intelligent gorilla and teach him to box one would have the world's champion. Well, that's what I found in Siki," Hellers announced at a press dinner a few days before the fight.[35] British boxing commentator Trevor Wignall had attended Hellers's party, and he later described Siki as "a blend of animal and human being . . . more closely allied to a primitive cave-man." Wignall believed that Siki was not only mentally and physically but also temporally out of place in civilized society. "Born long after his time," the African boxer "should have lived when the world was very young."[36] Regardless of whether Siki won or lost in the ring, he was considered unfit for modern life.

At 6 AM on 24 September, throngs of fight fans were already waiting outside the doors of the Buffalo Velodrome. A veritable sea of humanity inundated Parisian buses, subways, and trolley cars, and by the start of the fight approximately thirty thousand people had squeezed their way into the venue.[37] When Carpentier entered the ring the crowd greeted him with a standing ovation. He was not only France's most famous boxer but an accomplished aviator who had won the Croix de guerre and the Médaille militaire for his bravery during the war. "He was our proudest possession," one sportswriter recounted, "smiling and debonair, a picture of manly beauty." French fans hoped that Carpentier's victory would help to rebuild "the spirit and vigour" of their ailing postwar nation.[38] They called him "the Ambassador of Muscle."[39] Carpentier also appealed to white American and British boxing enthusiasts, for he represented the revitalizing white world in the face of the rising tide of color.

Battling Siki had his own group of enthusiastic supporters from across the African and Asian diasporas. "Many Americans of color from all parts of France and from England, as well as a few from Germany, were in attendance," a correspondent for the *Chicago Defender* noted. "Among those countries having representatives of the darker races were British provinces of Africa, Turkey, India, French and Dutch possessions and Morocco."[40] They had high hopes for Siki, for he "was a picture of power, his muscles rippling under the ebony skin."[41] Scanlon witnessed the match from ringside. Although he was friends with both boxers and had worked in both of their training camps before the fight, he hoped the Senegalese would not disappoint his colored fans. As Scanlon recalled, "The first round Carpentier clipped Siki with a right. Siki went down . . . so I signaled to Siki to get up; being a colored man myself I didnt [sic] want to see him beaten in a way like that."[42]

Most postfight reports gave the first few rounds to Carpentier.[43] Then, after dropping Siki again in the second round, Carpentier got careless. "He began to play with Siki, pulling faces at him," Scanlon recounted, "so all of a sudden Siki caught Carpentier with a terrible left hook and poor Georges went to the boards . . . and at that moment Siki saw his chance."[44] He was relentless in his attack, and in the sixth

FIGURE 17. Battling Siki's triumph personified the white world's worst fears and colonial peoples' greatest hopes. Georges Carpentier on the canvas in his fight with Siki, 4 August 1922. © Bettmann/Corbis. Courtesy of Corbis.

round the shell-shocked white Frenchman fell, knocked senseless by the Senegalese slugger. As a black reporter for the *Savannah Tribune* described, "Georgeous *[sic]* Georges was lying on the canvas his bloody face caressing the floor while the Senegalese, smiling and unblemished, stood above him."[45] With his unexpected comeback to beat Carpentier, Battling Siki's performance in the ring personified the white world's worst fears and colonial peoples' greatest hopes.

The crowd quickly turned on its fallen French idol, jeering at him while cheering for Siki. When the referee gave the match to Carpentier, claiming that Siki had tripped the white fighter, they shouted with rage, storming the ring. So great was the protest in the Buffalo Velodrome that after an hour's consultation the fight judges reversed the referee's decision. Victor Breyer, the president of the French Boxing Federation, climbed into the ring to declare the new winner, awarding Siki with both the world light-heavyweight and European heavyweight titles.[46]

White French fans feted the Senegalese champion on the streets of Paris, while in the suburbs they carried him on their shoulders. Siki visited all the major newspaper offices, gave public speeches, waved from balconies, received countless flowers and garlands, and entertained a number of commercial opportunities.[47] A local contingent of black men from the French colonies organized a party for Siki and started a collection to purchase him a commemorative art object in honor of his historic victory.[48]

Some African Americans back in the United States expressed renewed hope in the persistence of French racial tolerance. "The most significant phase of the Siki-Carpentier bout was the pronounced spirit of sportsmanship and fairplay displayed by the French spectators," a writer for the *Messenger* claimed. While "an effort was made to cater to the American color line" by declaring Carpentier the winner, French fans had refused to succumb to racial prejudice. They also seemed less fearful of race mixing, a hopeful sign for the socialist writer. The fancy Parisian restaurants Siki frequented were "crowded with white women eager to touch his hand and pat his ebony cheek."[49] French fans did not seem to care that the dark-skinned Senegalese was married to a blue-eyed blonde from Holland.

Comparing the positive French reaction to white Americans' violent backlash after Johnson's defeat of Jim Jeffries in 1910, a writer for the *Chicago Whip* even went so far as to declare, "France cannot see the color of Siki's skin, nor the texture of his hair, the line and angles of his face nor the arch of his foot. Siki is a Frenchman and France loves her Frenchmen. . . . Vive La France."[50] Yet French fans fetishized Siki's blackness. Parisian women reportedly imitated his hairstyle, wore ochre-colored powder to darken their skin, and even sported tattoos of Siki's silhouette.[51] In the streets fans often mistook African American jazz musicians for Siki, surrounding them until they felt forced to flee for their safety.

The Senegalese was a fashionable object of curiosity rather than a social and political equal. French sportsmen could still point to Siki's ring victory as further proof of his, and by extension all Africans', essentially primitive nature. Siki tried to break out of this restrictive mold. In a letter to the readers of *L'Auto* he insisted, "I am not a cannibal." He also noted that he spoke and wrote in French just like them, and he considered himself to be a good son of France.[52] "I am not a Negro," Siki declared. "I am a Frenchman of color . . . a full-fledged Frenchman like Carpentier. I vote and pay taxes."[53] He had hoped that his victory would bring him full recognition as a Frenchman; instead, it had stirred up submerged fears about black power. Some French journalists questioned the advisability of interracial matches given their nation's imperial holdings in Africa. Another columnist warned against showing the Siki-Carpentier fight film in the colonies. Siki's defeat of

Carpentier had also sparked opposition to a proposal to allow black men to serve as officers in white French regiments.[54]

Battling Siki's triumph inspired more vehement disapproval in white British and American sporting circles. In London, *Boxing* called Carpentier's loss a "tragedy," while writers for the *Daily Graphic* and *Daily Express* hoped that the Siki-Carpentier fiasco would be the last interracial fight permitted in Europe.[55] White American journalists castigated Carpentier for allowing his moving picture career and pampered lifestyle to distract him from serious training.[56] Siki's victory had also shocked white American expatriates in France, leading to violent clashes with the "Parisian Negro colony," particularly in Montmartre, where celebrations of the Senegalese champion were ongoing. The white American troublemakers aimed most of their ire at black men who dared to cavort with French women.[57]

White Americans also reserved some of their ire for French sporting and political officials. In permitting such a match to take place in their metropolitan capital, they had committed a grave error in imperial management at the most inopportune time. A columnist for *Literary Digest* dubbed Siki "A Dark Cloud on the Horizon."[58] "The prestige of the white race, in danger now as never before in recent history . . . is threatened by the victory of 'Battling Siki,'" he warned. Turkish nationalists had recently scored a military victory against the British-backed Greeks to defend their independence, and there now appeared to be growing unrest among the Mohammedan populations of Asia and Africa. Siki's victory would have far-reaching effects, for it resonated with the political aspirations of the darker races. It would "be used by agitators in Egypt, in India, in Africa, and in numerous islands of the sea."

The match became a metaphor for the unraveling of white imperial control. The shortage of white manpower and money both during and after the Great War had forced European powers to rationalize and streamline their empires. The British experimented with indirect rule, appointing local peoples to police their own territories on behalf of English interests. Faced with difficulties mobilizing colonial forces and resources on behalf of the metropole, France also imbued local African institutions with greater authority.[59] "Politically, it was an indiscretion for France to incur the risk of such a victory," argued one writer for the Springfield *Republican*.[60] "Prestige rather than force," he maintained, "is the power by which the colonies are ruled." If the darker races lost their respect for white men, the already strapped European powers would have to govern by force, a strategy that would prove "costly, wasteful, and difficult, if not impossible."

This strategy of force was especially perilous given the role of black soldiers in the recent war. Hundreds of thousands of the African colonies' best men had risked their lives on Europe's battlefields, and now those who had survived "brought back the infection [of militarism] to their native land."[61] A French journalist questioned, "Flattered and courted by white women, written up and flattered by the press, jollied and flattered by our politicians, is it strange that they believed they had arrived?" In addition to their newfound confidence, they had carried their combat skills back to the colonies. Many black soldiers also remained in Europe. Some were recently demobilized, while others were redeployed to protect French interests. Referring to the use of African troops in his nation's occupation of the German Rhineland, the same Frenchman lamented, "We fancied that we could thus humiliate the [German] barbarians, forgetting that we were at the same time humiliating the entire white race." In relying on the *force noire* to fight its battles, France had made a deal with the devil to preserve its status as a world power. He worried that all of these choices, alongside Siki's victory, had "prepared the way for lynch law" in France's colonies.

Battling Siki faced the same wall of white opposition that Johnson had tried to break through in the previous decade. His troubles deepened in late October, when news surfaced of a possible fight against Britain's heavyweight champion. For one African American journalist, the match seemed like "a desperate effort to bolster up 'white prestige.'"[62] "The British are pushing forward their lone 'white hope,' Joe Beckett, on the chance that he may accidentally succeed where Carpentier so ignobly failed," the journalist joked. Carpentier had already beaten Beckett. However, "the British sporting world, backed by the sentiment of imperialistic circles," crossed its fingers and hoped for the best.

The memory of Johnson's victories still haunted some. Much as he had in the 1910s, Lord Lonsdale, the president of London's National Sporting Club, warned the British Home Office about the potential fallout of the interracial match. Lonsdale continued to believe that prizefights "between white and black men" had a "detrimental effect on their respective races."[63] In a heated letter to Lonsdale, Major J. Arnold Wilson, the Siki-Beckett promoter, countered that things had changed since the days of Johnson. "Surely if these [black] men were fitted to take a chance with us in the war, then they are fitted to take part in our sports," he charged. Banning the match would be an "open insult . . . to the black subjects of His Majesty, Indian and otherwise."[64]

With the Beckett fight on the horizon, Siki's involvement in a minor tussle set off a chain reaction of white efforts to undermine him. At the French middleweight championship between Maurice Prunier and Ercole Balzac on 8 November 1922, Siki worked in Balzac's corner. Balzac was in command of the match until Prunier fouled him with a low blow. When the referee counted Balzac out, declaring Prunier the winner, Siki and Balzac's other men jumped into the ring. In the ensuing scuffle Siki shoved Prunier's manager, Fernand Cuny.

Still embittered by the fall of Carpentier, French boxing officials saw their chance to stop the Senegalese fighter. The French Boxing Federation (FFB) met to determine Siki's fate after his supposedly savage attack of Cuny. Even those who defended Siki against censure painted him as a primitive. Cuny himself claimed that Siki had not meant to hurt him. "Of course, it [his behavior] is deplorable, but is he entirely responsible?" Cuny questioned. "He holds a title too heavy for him? He is a child who has been allowed to play with a gun."[65] Of course, Cuny overlooked the fact that Siki had used a gun quite capably for France during the war. In his own defense Siki declared, "When I was just the nigger Siki nobody bothered with my jokes, or [they] laughed at them; now that I'm champion, they get angry!"[66] The FFB tribunal slapped the Senegalese prizefighter with a nine-month suspension. It also took away Siki's boxing license and stripped him of his French light-heavyweight title. Making matters worse, exaggerated tales of Siki's allegedly criminal ways flooded the French press, as Parisian journalists accused him of selling drugs in Montmartre and fraternizing with an underage French girl. In the mainstream U.S. press, writers were attempting "to build up a wall of prejudice against this black Senegalese fighter simply because he ha[d] married a white wife."[67] In response to this hullabaloo an editorialist for the *New York Age* argued, "We do not believe that very many people, either white or colored, realize how deeply the factor of sex enters into what is called the race problem. Some day we are going to write a plain spoken article on the subject."[68]

Siki's ban expanded into other countries. Following the FFB's suspension, the British Home Office jumped at the opportunity to prohibit the Siki-Beckett fight on British soil, arguing that it would engender racial feeling and was therefore not in the best interests of the nation. The New York State Boxing Commission also followed suit, announcing that Siki would not be permitted to fight in the state until he was cleared of all charges. Italian boxing clubs subsequently closed their doors to Siki, and even the city of Rotterdam, located in his wife's home country, instituted a ban on all interracial fights.[69] A black American reporter complained, "Since the colored fighter became champion, there has been a systematic campaign of propaganda to discredit him before the public." It did not help that Siki openly enjoyed the company of white women and the excitement of Parisian nightclubs: "By his indiscretions in private life, Siki has become known as the 'Jack Johnson' of Europe."[70]

White settlers in the British colonies were happy the Home Office had taken a stand. Their own encounters with "the negro" had convinced them of the potentially negative effects of interracial contests. "A negro is *physically* different to a white man, and is able to bear blows on his body which would simply stun and seriously injure a white man," one settler wrote to the Home Office. "Anyone who, like myself, has lived in negro countries, knows this from personal experience."[71] He believed it was "*most unfair* and *unsportsmanlike* to pit a white man against a negro." "The only vulnerable part in a negro's body is his *shins*," he claimed. "A negro's *shins* are so tender that a white boy's kick will double him up, and put him out of action." Since the rules of boxing did not permit kicking, interracial matches left white men at a distinct disadvantage. In a letter to the *African World,* another English settler agreed that mixed matches were a bane to those who bore "the burden and the heat of the day 'neath Africa's sun." "The stirring of racial consciousness in millions of men barely higher than savages in the scale of evolution," he maintained, "must inevitably detract from the standing and safety of the European."[72] These letters about prize-fighting exposed not only the brutal and inescapably physical nature of the white man's burden but also its increasing vulnerability.

This white antagonism only enhanced Battling Siki's fame as a transnational symbol of nonwhite resistance. The Senegalese parliamentarian Blaise Diagne brought Siki's case in front of his white colleagues in the French Chamber of Deputies. During the budget appropriation for physical education Diagne moved that it be reduced by three hundred thousand francs, charging that national sporting societies like the FFB had purposely set out to derail Siki.[73] According to Diagne, the FFB was punishing the African fighter for celebrating his victory in the cafes of Paris, yet no one ever complained when white pugilists did the same. The FFB's suspension was also depriving Siki of his ability to earn a living. Diagne charged, "These men who are as French as you are, though they are of different color, have a right to the same justice as you," and he cautioned his fellow deputies about the danger of giving the impression that France had two unequal forms of justice—one for white Frenchmen and another for colored subjects.[74] Despite Diagne's impassioned appeal, his motion failed to pass by a margin of 408 to 136.

The Vietnamese anticolonialist and communist leader Ho Chi Minh made some of the same arguments in the radical journal *Le Paria*. As he considered the importance of the Siki-Carpentier match and the white backlash it inspired, Ho declared, "The boxing championship has changed hands, but national sporting glory has not suffered, because Siki, a child of Senegal, is in consequence a son of France, and hence a Frenchman."[75] Even though they operated on different cultural terrains, Ho saw Siki and René Maran, the Martiniquan author of the anticolonial novel *Batouala* and winner of the Prix Goncourt, as making similar contributions to the fight against white supremacy. "Following Maran's ironical pen," Ho argued, "Siki's gloves have stirred everything, including even the political sphere." "A Carpentier-Siki match is worth more than one hundred gubernatorial speeches to prove to our subjects and protégés that we want to apply to the letter the principle of equality between races," Ho claimed. He also criticized the British Home Office's banning of the Siki-Beckett match. "This does not surprise us," Ho scoffed. "As His British Excellency could digest neither [Mustafa] Kemal's croissant nor [Mahatma] Gandhi's chocolate, he wants to have Battling Siki swallow his purge even though the latter is a Frenchman."[76] Taking it a step further than Diagne, Ho argued that Siki's struggles were symbolic of the continued capitalist and imperialist exploitation of the world's "indigenous proletarians."[77]

Among black Americans, Siki's struggles also sparked public conversations about the transnational reach of the color line. Many saw the cancellation of the Siki-Beckett match as an obvious case of British race prejudice. They accused the Home Office of hiding behind the hypocritical subterfuge that mixed matches provoked racial disturbances. As one reporter pointed out, "Siki stirred up no racial feeling when he fought with shot and shell against the Boche [German soldiers] when England's back was to the wall."[78] For now, John Bull had leveled Siki with a low blow. "It will not be ever thus, however," the reporter warned, "for the horizon is bedimmed with black and yellow clouds."

Yet this was much bigger than just Britain or France. In a speech at Liberty Hall in November 1922, Garvey argued that Siki's tragic plight validated the UNIA's international platform. "We have always held to the opinion that there was absolutely no difference between the Englishman and the Frenchman and the American when it comes to the race," Garvey explained. Siki's treatment in France was similar to that of Johnson in the United States. White Americans "had to find some excuse to get rid of Johnson to restore the championship to the white man, because they could not allow a Negro to hold such an honor, as it would make the Negro realize that he is really a man." Now "France sought ways and means of getting rid of Siki." Garvey declared, "There is a set position for the Negro not only in America, but all over the white world, and any man who flatters himself to believe that his position is one of equality depending upon conditions as they are has a false opinion and a false idea of life."

Claude McKay came to a similar conclusion. He used Siki's quandary to critique the conservative nationalist agendas of the black bourgeoisie in the United States and France. "The black intelligentsia of America looks upon France as the foremost cultured nation of the world," McKay noted, "the single great country where all citizens enjoy equal rights before the law, without respect to race or skin color." Closing their eyes to the "vile exploitation of Africans by the French," they had come to believe that "one imperialist exploiter" could be "better than another."[79] Siki's troubles were like a slap in the face to the black bourgeoisie—especially to Diagne, whom McKay saw as a puppet of the French government. Although Diagne supported Siki in the Chamber of Deputies, he had recently abandoned the Pan-African movement because its increasingly radical and militant stance clashed with his assimilationist aspirations. McKay believed that the white backlash against Johnson, Siki, and other black boxers was ultimately about the need to maintain a compliant black workforce. "The Negro must not show himself capable of fighting and winning," he argued. "It is not entirely safe for capitalistic America, which makes twenty million Negroes bow down."[80]

Any changes to the status quo would come too late to save Battling Siki. By January 1923 the Home Office had decided to use the provisions under the Aliens Restriction Act to bar Siki from even setting foot on British soil. The International Boxing Union also stripped Siki of his remaining titles.[81] After his FFB suspension ended, Siki's career continued its downward slide. On St. Patrick's Day in 1923 he lost a controversial decision to the Irish-American Mike McTigue in Dublin, and later that year, when Siki traveled to the United States, his fight record was mediocre at best.

In December 1925 the Senegalese fighter was found shot to death in the New York City neighborhood of Hell's Kitchen. His untimely death, much like his life, personified the escalating fight between so-called civilization and savagery. Typical of other white press reports, the *Times* of London observed, "At heart he remained a savage, with all the weaknesses of a savage thrown into a doubtful atmosphere in the white man's world."[82] Although many black American sportswriters had expressed their support for Siki over the years, they, too, saw him through the lens of prevailing tropes of African primitivism. With a tinge of irony, a *Chicago Defender* journalist declared, "They [the white press] say he died of too much civilization. And perhaps they are right. Siki did die of civilization—the civilization as dished out to him by White America."[83] Much more critical of the Senegalese "Jungle Boy," another African American writer pronounced, "Siki challenged civilization, civilization accepted his challenge, they fought a good fight, and civilization won."[84] At least for now "civilization" had come out on top, but Battling Siki's contentious career, much like that of Johnson in the previous decade, pointed to a "rising tide of color" that threatened to topple the imperial order.

Even as white officials endeavored to eradicate the black global vision inspired by boxing's rebel sojourners, that vision had already permeated the ideas and strategies of activists throughout the diaspora. Much like Johnson and Siki, Garvey became the target of white authorities precisely because of his transnational appeal, particularly among working people of color. The same U.S. Bureau of Investigation that led the manhunt for Johnson after his conviction under the Mann Act in 1913 was now charged with the surveillance and persecution of Garvey, McKay, and black activists of various political stripes.[85] Similar to Johnson, Garvey and the UNIA also attracted the consternation of British colonial officials in Africa, and not without reason. Even though Garvey never managed to cement his political power or bring revolutionary change in his lifetime, both he and Johnson remained potent symbols of black pride and black autonomy that reverberated across the decolonizing continent in the decades to come. As the king of Swaziland later told Mrs. Amy Jacques Garvey, he knew the names of only two black men in the West: "Jack Johnson, the boxer who defeated the white man Jim Jeffries, and Marcus Garvey."[86]

Epilogue

Visible Men, Harmless Icons

In 1929 James Thurber of the *New Yorker* chose Jack Johnson as the subject of a "Talk of the Town" piece. Though Johnson still walked "proudly," Thurber noted that "his face no longer gleam[ed] in the ebony and gold splendor which admiring Londoners compared to a 'starry night' almost twenty years ago."[1] Now living in a modest dwelling on 148th Street, the former world champion still enjoyed recounting his international travels for anyone who would listen. "He loves to talk of his favorite city, Budapest," Thurber observed, "and of the time at the start of the war when the Germans did not molest several trunks containing all his wife's sables."[2]

In 1932, the year before the Nazis came to power, Johnson traveled back to Europe to perform in Paris and to visit Berlin, where he had received an offer to open a boxing school. During his time in the French capital Johnson made frequent appearances at the Parisian nightclub of fellow black American Ada "Bricktop" Smith, much to the delight of distinguished personalities like Josephine Baker, Maurice Chevalier, and Cole Porter. Although Johnson was no longer the European phenomenon he once had been, he remained a symbol of black achievement. As Bricktop recalled, "If anybody ever made me feel proud of who and what I am, it was Jack."[3]

By 1933, however, Johnson had become a kind of museum piece as he "boxed" with youngsters in Dave Barry's Garden of Champions at the Chicago World's Fair. On the outskirts of this "Century of Progress

FIGURE 18. The former champion never gave up his cosmopolitan flair. Jack Johnson in retirement, 21 May 1931. © Bettmann/Corbis. Courtesy of Corbis.

Exposition," the once illustrious and notorious Johnson appeared alongside the Midget Village, the exotic dancer Sally Rand, and the Aunt Jemima Cabin. In exchange for a dollar, each child could take a few swings at the former champion.[4]

The following year the black American heavyweight Joe Louis burst onto the professional boxing scene, demolishing opponents in the ring while maintaining a low profile outside the ring. No longer able to command large audiences or lucrative theater contracts at the age of fifty-six, Johnson saw an opportunity in Louis. After Louis's 1935 victory against the Italian boxer Primo Carnera, Johnson made his move, pitching his skills as a trainer to the young up-and-comer. Louis's management team, however, unceremoniously rejected his offer. Fearing that any association with the infamous black fighter could push their protégé out of world championship contention, Louis's handlers would not allow the young boxer to follow in Johnson's irreverent footsteps. As his trainer, Jack Blackburn, warned, the "White man hasn't forgotten that fool nigger with his white women, acting like he owned the world."[5] Determined to construct Louis as a respectable black icon, they kept his encounters with white women, his love of fast cars, and his frivolous spending out of the press.[6]

In 1937, the same year that Louis won the world title against the white American fighter James J. Braddock, Johnson found himself relegated to the basement of Hubert's Museum and Flea Circus on New York's 42nd Street. Johnson appeared next to a mishmash of sideshow acts, including a sword swallower, a trick dog, a half man–half woman, and even a performer who styled himself as "Congo the Wild Man." Dressed in a suit with a blue tie and French beret, the former champion answered visitors' questions in an affected British accent.[7] Although he had been reduced to a mere relic of his former worldly self, he still clung to the cosmopolitan air of his past. No matter his circumstances, Johnson refused to relinquish his dignity. In a cruel twist of fate, he died in a car wreck in 1946 at the age of sixty-eight, after angrily speeding away from a North Carolina diner that declined to serve him.

For decades after his tragic death, Johnson remained an obscure figure in American popular memory. Thanks to the efforts of documentary filmmaker Ken Burns and the multiracial, bipartisan Committee to Pardon Jack Johnson, scattered reports about his unfair conviction began appearing in the mainstream media in 2004. However, by the end of President George W. Bush's second term in office, the committee had yet to procure Johnson a posthumous pardon.

With the election of the nation's first black president, Barack Obama, in 2008—a century after Johnson became the first black world heavyweight champion—the committee saw an opening. It stepped up its campaign, and dual requests for a posthumous pardon passed the Senate and the House in the summer of 2009. Ironically, it was two white Republican boxing aficionados, Senator John McCain of Arizona and Representative Peter T. King of New York, who were the main drivers behind these requests to (according to the House resolution) "expunge a racially motivated abuse of the prosecutorial authority of the federal government from the annals of criminal justice in the United States." Although they claimed their efforts were not politically motivated, they believed that a pardon would be a "strong symbol of racial and political harmony" (one sorely needed by the Republican Party).[8] Yet less than a month after signing the House request to pardon Johnson, the white Republican representative Lynn Jenkins complicated matters when she declared that her party was searching for a "great white hope" to stop Obama and the Democrats' policy agenda during a town hall forum in Kansas. Predictably, Jenkins later claimed ignorance, denying that she had used the phrase in a racial manner.[9]

This was an embarrassing faux pas, especially since McCain and King had managed to rally Johnson's descendants in support of the pardon campaign, even though they had long hidden their relationship to him. Linda Haywood, a fifty-three-year-old seamstress in Chicago, remembered her parents' efforts to keep from her the truth about her notorious granduncle. As a sixth-grade student in 1966 she had seen Johnson's photo on her classroom wall. "It was up there next to pictures of Sojourner Truth and George Washington Carver as part of a black history week my teacher put together," Haywood recollected, yet she "didn't have the first clue who the man was."[10] When Haywood was twelve her mother finally told her the story of her Granduncle Jack, and she could see that "it pained her" to do so. "But it wasn't just her," Haywood recalled. "The shame was there for all members of my family." Even though Haywood's parents claimed that they had wanted to protect her from a "legacy of racial injustice," their silence most certainly stemmed from Johnson's ongoing demonization at the hands of the white establishment and some members of the black middle class.

In October 2009 McCain and King sent a letter to President Obama urging him to use his power to pardon the late boxer, but the White House offered no immediate comment. Some skeptics argued that Obama was not likely to bite since posthumous pardons are time-consuming and therefore rare.[11] Obama also had sound political reasons to avoid opening this racial can of worms. The black president had won the recent election based on a largely nonracial platform. He had also openly assailed the very black men—those living on the margins of respectable society—whom Johnson likely would have hung around if he were alive today.[12] Obama never personally responded to the request. Instead, in December 2009 the Justice Department announced that it would not grant Johnson a posthumous pardon. In a letter to Representative King, the department's pardon lawyer Ronald L. Rodgers stated that their general policy was not to process posthumous requests because they preferred to use their resources for people who were still alive and could "truly benefit" from their help.[13]

Since then, there have been murmurs about McCain and King's plan to reintroduce a congressional resolution for a posthumous pardon. Given their questionable attitudes of late toward undocumented workers and Muslims in the United States, it is curious that they remain steadfast in their desire to (in King's words) "correct an historic wrong,

FIGURE 19. U.S. senator John McCain (R-AZ) speaks as Dorothy Cross (in wheelchair), the grandniece of Jack Johnson; Cross's daughter, Constance Hines (center); Cross's family friend Betsy Victoria (right); and Representative Peter King (R-NY) (left) listen during a news conference on Capitol Hill, 1 April 2009. McCain and King introduced a resolution calling on President Barack Obama to posthumously pardon Johnson. © Getty Images.

and also, in a small way but significant way, help to bring the country together."[14] Linda Haywood has also expressed her continuing commitment to Johnson's fight for justice and plans to send a personal letter to President Obama on her granduncle's behalf. "I think having a letter from a family member will help put a face on our plea," she said.

However Johnson's prospects do not look good, for recent efforts to procure a posthumous pardon for the black leader Marcus Garvey—

who was convicted on trumped-up mail fraud charges in 1923—
have also fallen on deaf ears. In a letter to Obama about Garvey's
case, the Florida-based Jamaican-born attorney Donovan Parker
wrote, "It would be fitting if both you, Mr. President, and the first
lady visit Jamaica for the purposes of signing the executive order pardoning Marcus Mosiah Garvey."[15] Yet Parker received the same terse
rebuff from Rodgers as Johnson's supporters. In the midst of an economic downturn and with another presidential campaign underway, it
is hardly surprising that Obama and his administration have no real
interest in forging black Atlantic connections—except, perhaps, for
those that promote the expansion of U.S. capital and political influence. For now, it seems as if Johnson's pardon (as well as Garvey's)
might just be a dead issue.

Nevertheless, Johnson's insurgent legacy lives on at the fringes of
mainstream culture. In 2004 the socially conscious rap artist Mos Def
celebrated the black champion's special brand of defiance in his blues-
inflected songs "Zimzallabim" and "Blue Black Jack."[16] This Bike Is a
Pipe Bomb, a southern punk band known for their explicitly antiwar
and antiracist politics, also paid tribute to the black heavyweight's courageous stand against white supremacy in their raucous rendition of
"Jack Johnson."[17] More recently, the Guyanese-American comic book
writer and artist Trevor Von Eeden published a two-volume graphic
novel titled *The Original Johnson,* which George Gene Gustines of the
New York Times described as "unflinching in its depiction of racism in
America . . . and the tragedies and triumphs of Johnson's life, including
his sexual conquests."[18]

Perhaps it is best that President Obama has left the issue of Johnson's
pardon unresolved. Without the neat ending of the first black U.S. president publicly absolving the first black world heavyweight champion,
it is more difficult to put the icing on the cake of postracialism in the
United States. It also makes it much more difficult to reduce Johnson
and his global anticolonial legacy to a simplistic symbol of the triumph of U.S. neoliberal democracy. Over the past few decades we have
already seen this happen to the likes of Joe Louis and Muhammad Ali.
In the early 2000s, there was renewed interest in Louis's emergence as
an American hero during World War II, especially after his morale-
boosting victory over the Nazi-supported fighter Max Schmeling in
1938. Books and documentaries focused on this dimension of Louis's
career largely at the expense of exploring his more complex legacy
as a *black* hero who symbolized a variety of causes, from Ethiopian

autonomy in the face of Italian imperialism to the collective strength of the Brotherhood of Sleeping Car Porters in the face of the exploitative Pullman Company.[19]

Despite the fierce white backlash against Ali in the late 1960s, mainstream America has even managed to co-opt his irreverent slick talking, his membership in the Nation of Islam, his involvement with Malcolm X, and his resistance to the Vietnam War as proof of the United States' commitment to freedom of speech. Over the years, as his aging body has succumbed to the ravages of Parkinson's disease, it has become much easier to shape the slurring, shaking Ali into a nonthreatening symbol of American courage and righteousness in the face of adversity. This sanitizing process reached its apogee in the summer of 1996, when Ali lifted his palsied hand to light the Olympic flame in Atlanta, Georgia. By November 2009 President Obama saw no contradiction between publishing a letter of tribute to Ali as "a force for reconciliation and peace around the world" and then, a few days later, calling for an additional thirty thousand U.S. troops in Afghanistan during a speech at West Point.[20] As Ali's biographer and *Nation* sports editor David Zirin warned, "Today, Ali has been described as 'America's only living saint.' . . . But in a time when billions go to war and prisons while 50% of children will be on food stamps for the coming year, we can't afford Ali, the harmless icon." This domestication of Louis, Ali, and Johnson obscures the fact that despite the achievements of the black freedom struggle to date, there is still much unfinished business at both the local and global levels.

Using the success and visibility of black athletes as incontrovertible proof of black advancement has always been a dubious proposition. The growing demand for black performers in the late nineteenth century was intimately connected to the expanding trade in white supremacist entertainments that accompanied the intensification of Western imperialism. While Johnson and other black sojourners often found prosperity in the cultural arena, the color line kept them out of formal politics and barred them from more "legitimate" forms of employment. Their notoriety may have given them a unique platform from which to critique the racial world order, but it also made them vulnerable to white scrutiny and to being used in the service of white supremacy.

Their public visibility also influenced the tenor of black politics in subsequent decades. Although they laid the cultural groundwork for black global visions of the twentieth century, they also circumscribed black protest in other ways. Thanks to the stylized personas of Johnson and other black American athletes, masculine ideals of audacious bravado, physical strength, hyperheterosexuality, and conspicuous, over-the-top consumption have become an integral part of the aesthetics of black self-assertion and resistance, often to the detriment of black women and queer communities. At the same time, the global preponderance of African American images of blackness has served to marginalize the concerns and ideas of black people in different places throughout the diaspora, making it difficult to build racial solidarities across national borders. This form of African American cultural hegemony has only accelerated with the United States' rise to world dominance in the second half of the twentieth century.

Even today, the hypervisibility of black American athletes has not translated into increased black political power or racial equality more generally. Instead, this hypervisibility has become a frequent point of critique for white conservatives and certain members of the black middle class. There has been a tendency to blame black youth, particularly those from poor and working-class backgrounds, for their over-investment in the cultural arena and, in particular, for their supposed "sports fixation."[21] Yet this perspective ignores not only the problematic history of black spectacles but also the current conditions driving black hypervisibility in the sporting and entertainment industries. Black youths' focus on achieving success in the cultural realm is not just a simple matter of individual "choice." It is also symptomatic of their lack of access to formal political channels and their continued social and economic marginalization.[22] For professional sports teams, sporting manufacturers, and media companies—still predominantly white-owned enterprises—exploiting the vulnerability of black people and the disposability of young black bodies for the sake of profits has become business as usual.

Much as they did in Johnson's day, cultural representations of blackness now command the world's attention, even as nonwhite peoples continue to face repression of all kinds. The political and economic agendas of the global North have worked to install highly sophisticated and exploitative forms of neocolonialism in the global South. At the same time, people of color living in the global North still experience income and wealth disparities, unequal access to education, healthcare, and affordable housing, disproportionate arrests and prison time, and overexposure to environmental hazards. While politicians are rushing to declare the end of racism, increasingly strident calls for the closing of national borders to nonwhite peoples and for the preservation and reinvigoration of (white) nationalist cultures are reverberating across North America and Europe. How can we declare the end of "race" when these profound contradictions and inequalities remain? What transnational solidarities can be revived and reconfigured to combat this enduring problem?

In revealing the global stakes of the race question, Johnson's remarkable journeys at the turn of the twentieth century point to the need for reconceptualizing what race means to us at the beginning of the twenty-first. While he was certainly flawed, Johnson was also an incredible man of the world who defied white supremacy in its various manifestations. Although elements of his biography are certainly triumphant, his story is much more complicated than just a question of granting civil rights and ending de jure segregation; it is, in fact, much bigger than just the United States. Examining stories such as Johnson's in all their complexity will not only help us to understand why the color line continues to resonate with such breadth and intensity, but it will also help us to challenge the facile conceptions of "color blindness" and the "postracial" that often foreclose meaningful reflection and social change. After all, his global legacy speaks to the alternative, often buried ways of understanding the intrinsic relationship between racial ideas and practices and the rise of the modern world. It also points to a buried tradition of transnational alliances that must be renewed and reenvisioned. How we choose to remember Johnson will ultimately reveal the depth of our own racial conversations, and the scope of our own imagination for a more equitable future.

Notes

PREFACE

1. After an internal police review confirmed that two officers had chased the youths, the policemen were set to go on trial in October 2010. However, a Paris appeals court dropped the case in April 2011. See "French Police Criticised over Deaths of Youths That Led to Riots" (8 December 2006), www.guardian.co .uk/world/2006/dec/08/france.angeliquechrisafis?INTCMP=SRCH (accessed 1 September 2011); "2 French Police to Stand Trial in Deaths of Teens" (22 October 2010), http://abcnews.go.com/International/wireStory?id=11945881 (accessed 1 September 2011); "Paris Court Drops 2005 Riots Case against Police" (27 April 2011), www.guardian.co.uk/world/2011/apr/27/court-drops -france-riots-case-police (accessed 1 September 2011).

2. Quotations are taken from "France PM: Curfews to Stem Riots" (7 November 2005), www.cnn.com/2005/WORLD/europe/11/07/france.riots/index .html (accessed 10 November 2005). Also see Johanna McGeary, "Outside Looking In," *Time*, 13 November 2005; James Geary and James Graff, "Restless Youth," *Time*, 13 November 2005; Craig Smith, "Riots and Violence Spread from Paris to Other French Cities," *New York Times*, 6 November 2005; Mark Landler and Craig Smith, "French Officials Try to Ease Fear as Crisis Swells," *New York Times*, 8 November 2005; Olivier Roy, "Get French or Die Trying," *New York Times*, 9 November 2005.

3. Souhelia Al-Jadda, "In French Riots, a Lesson for Europe," *USA Today*, 8 November 2005.

4. "Letter to the Editor," *USA Today*, 13 November 2005.

5. David Crary, "Riots in France and Hurricane Katrina Have Forced Sparring Nations to Confront Race" (14 November 2005), http://blackvoices.aol

.com/black_news/canvas_directory_headlines_features/_a/riots-in-france-and
-hurricane-katrina/2005111409400999000I (accessed 17 November 2005).

6. Ibid.

7. Many articles dubbed Obama the "great black hope." See, for example, "Great Black Hope? The Reality of President-Elect Obama" (6 November 2008), www.nationalreview.com/articles/226264/great-black-hope/nro -symposium (accessed 12 August 2010); Benjamin Wallace-Wells, "The Great Black Hope: What's Riding on Barack Obama" (November 2004), www .washingtonmonthly.com/features/2004/0411.wallace-wells.html (accessed 12 August 2010); "The Great Black Hope," *New York Times,* 5 July 2009.

8. "Europe Obama Mania," *Sunday Times* (Perth), 20 July 2008, *Newspaper Source Plus,* EBSCO*host* (accessed 5 January 2011). Also see Shelley Emling, "Europe Looks to Obama as New Ray of Hope," *The Record* (Kitchener/Cambridge/Waterloo, ON), 23 July 2008, *Newspaper Source Plus,* EBSCO*host* (accessed 5 January 2011).

9. CNN *Situation Room,* "Europe's Racist Fringe: Reaction to Obama's Victory" (12 November 2008), www.cgi.cnn.com/TRANSCRIPTS/0811/12/ sitroom.01.html (accessed 4 January 2011).

10. CNN *Election Center,* "Election Night '08 Coverage Continues" (4 November 2008), http://transcripts.cnn.com/TRANSCRIPTS/0811/04/ec.03 .html (accessed 4 January 2011).

11. Nicholas Kristof, "Rebranding the U.S. with Obama," *New York Times,* 22 October 2008.

12. "Rioters Need Tough Love, Says David Cameron" (2 September 2011), www.bbc.co.uk/news/uk-politics-14760686 (accessed 2 September 2011); "Ex-NYC Top Cop Says He Is in Talks about Role in Riot-Hit UK" (12 August 2011), www.msnbc.msn.com/id/44116798/ns/world_news-europe/t/ex-nyc-top -cop-says-he-talks-about-role-riot-hit-uk/ (accessed 1 September 2011).

INTRODUCTION

1. Jack Johnson, *In the Ring—And Out* (1927; New York: Citadel Press, 1992), 21.

2. For cultural analyses of Johnson's fight against Jim Crow, see David Krasner, *A Beautiful Pageant: African American Theatre, Drama, and Performance in the Harlem Renaissance, 1910–1927* (New York: Palgrave Macmillan, 2002), 17–54; Kevin Mumford, *Interzones: Black/White Sex Districts in Chicago and New York in the Early Twentieth Century* (New York: Columbia University Press, 1997), 3–18; Gail Bederman, *Manliness and Civilization: A Cultural History of Gender and Race in the United States, 1880–1917* (Chicago: University of Chicago Press, 1995), 1–44; Davarian Baldwin, *Chicago's New Negroes: Modernity, the Great Migration, and Black Urban Life* (Chapel Hill: University of North Carolina Press, 2007), 194–204. There are some exceptions, including Patrick McDevitt, *May the Best Man Win: Sport, Masculinity, and Nationalism in Great Britain and the Empire, 1880–1935* (New York: Palgrave Macmillan, 2004), 76–78; Jeffrey Green, *Black Edwardians: Black People in Britain, 1901–1914* (London: Frank Cass Publishers, 1998),

172–80; Richard Broome, "The Australian Reaction to Jack Johnson, Black Pugilist, 1907–9," in *Sport in History,* ed. Richard Cashman and Michael McKernan (St. Lucia: University of Queensland Press, 1979); Claude Meunier, *Ring noir: Quand Apollinaire, Cendrars et Picabia découvraient les boxeurs nègres* (Paris: PLON, 1992); Jeff Wells, *Boxing Day: The Fight That Changed the World* (Sydney: HarperSports, 1998). McDevitt and Green discuss Johnson's difficulties in Britain, Broome and Wells explore Australia's reaction to Johnson, and Meunier examines his reception by the French avant-garde. For well-researched biographies of Johnson, see Al-Tony Gilmore, *Bad Nigger! The National Impact of Jack Johnson* (Port Washington, NY: Kennikat Press, 1975); Geoffrey Ward, *Unforgivable Blackness: The Rise and Fall of Jack Johnson* (New York: Knopf, 2004); Randy Roberts, *Papa Jack: Jack Johnson and the Era of White Hopes* (New York: Free Press, 1983). Although all of these biographers trace Johnson's journeys abroad, they are less interested in what these journeys reveal about the global dimensions of racial ideas, practices, and modes of resistance.

3. On the white American embrace of Joe Louis as a national hero, see Lauren Rebecca Sklaroff, "Constructing G.I. Joe Louis: Cultural Solutions to the 'Negro Problem' during World War II," *Journal of American History* 89, no. 3 (December 2002): 958–83.

4. Muhammad Ali quoted in David Remnick, "Struggle for His Soul," *Observer,* 2 November 2003. Also see Harvey Young, *Embodying Black Experience: Stillness, Critical Memory, and the Black Body* (Ann Arbor: University of Michigan Press, 2010), 108–9.

5. Martin Ritt, director, *The Great White Hope* (1970; Twentieth Century Fox, 2004); Howard Sackler, *The Great White Hope* (New York: Dial Press, 1968).

6. Miles Davis, *A Tribute to Jack Johnson* (1971; Columbia/Legacy, 2005).

7. Although Jack Johnson remained an obscure figure in the 1990s, the alternative country musician Tom Russell did produce a song named after him on the album *Hurricane Season* (Philo, 1991). Johnson also appeared in Joe R. Lansdale's fictional short story "The Big Blow" (1997), which the author later expanded into a novel of the same name. Joe R. Lansdale, *The Big Blow* (Burton, MI: Subterranean Press, 2000).

8. "Jazz Legend Miles Davis Pays Tribute to Boxing Great Jack Johnson," *Call and Post,* 5 May 2005.

9. Senator McCain quoted in Ken Burns, "Mr. President, Pardon Jack Johnson," *Los Angeles Times,* 13 July 2004.

10. Ken Burns, director, *Unforgivable Blackness: The Rise and Fall of Jack Johnson* (PBS Paramount, 2005). The documentary's screenwriter Geoffrey Ward also published a detailed biography of Johnson by the same name. Ward, *Unforgivable Blackness.*

11. Stanley Crouch quoted in Steve Kroner, "A Uniquely American Story," *San Francisco Chronicle,* 14 January 2005.

12. John Patterson, "On Film: Black Boxers Took on the World and Knocked It Flying," *Manchester Guardian,* 21 January 2005. See Clint Eastwood, director, *Million Dollar Baby* (Warner Brothers, 2004); Ron Howard,

director, *Cinderella Man* (Universal Pictures, 2005). This trend has continued. David O. Russell, director, *The Fighter* (Paramount Pictures, 2010); Gavin O'Connor, director, *Warrior* (Lionsgate, 2011).

13. I borrow the phrase "rebel sojourner" from Wayne Cooper's far-reaching biography of another itinerant black icon of the early twentieth century, Claude McKay. Wayne Cooper, *Claude McKay: Rebel Sojourner in the Harlem Renaissance* (Baton Rouge: Louisiana State University Press, 1996).

14. Black feminist scholars have examined the travels of black working-class women. Hazel Carby, *Cultures in Babylon: Black Britain and African America* (New York: Verso, 1999), 7–66; Jayna Brown, *Babylon Girls: Black Women Performers and the Shaping of the Modern* (Durham, NC: Duke University Press, 2008); Angela Davis, *Blues Legacies and Black Feminism: Gertrude "Ma" Rainey, Bessie Smith, and Billie Holiday* (New York: Vintage, 1999).

15. There is a growing literature on the global dimensions of the color line and the relationship between racial formations and globalization. Thomas Holt, *The Problem of Race in the 21st Century* (Cambridge, MA: Harvard University Press, 2000); Marilyn Lake and Henry Reynolds, *Drawing the Global Colour Line: White Men's Countries and the International Challenge of Racial Equality* (Cambridge: Cambridge University Press, 2008); Walter Gobel and Saskia Schabio, eds., *Beyond the Black Atlantic: Relocating Modernization and Technology* (New York: Taylor and Francis, 2006); Kamari Clarke and Deborah A. Thomas, eds., *Globalization and Race: Transformations in the Cultural Production of Blackness* (Durham, NC: Duke University Press, 2006).

16. W. E. B. Du Bois, "To the Nations of the World," in *W. E. B. Du Bois: A Reader,* ed. David Levering Lewis (New York: Henry Holt, 1995), 639.

17. W. E. B. Du Bois, "The Souls of White Folk," *Independent,* 18 August 1910. Also see Lake and Reynolds, *Drawing the Global Colour Line,* 9.

18. Du Bois, "The Souls of White Folk."

19. Bederman, *Manliness and Civilization,* 16–20.

20. Holt, *Problem of Race in the 21st Century,* 35. For more on the concept of biopolitics, see Michel Foucault, *History of Sexuality: Volume I, Introduction* (1978; New York: Vintage Books, 1990), 139–44.

21. Holt, *Problem of Race in the 21st Century,* 60. Historian Davarian Baldwin makes similar assertions about the importance of commercial culture as a site of racial formation in urban black communities. Baldwin, *Chicago's New Negroes,* 13.

22. On the late nineteenth-century shift to regulated, gloved fights under the Queensberry rules, see Elliot Gorn, *The Manly Art: Bare-Knuckle Prize Fighting in America* (Ithaca, NY: Cornell University Press, 1986), 207–47; Jeffrey Sammons, *Beyond the Ring: The Role of Boxing in American Society* (Urbana: University Illinois Press, 1988), 3–29.

23. Paul Gilroy's seminal book on the black Atlantic sparked an explosion of scholarly work on black internationalism and transnationalism. Paul Gilroy, *The Black Atlantic: Modernity and Double Consciousness* (Cambridge, MA: Harvard University Press, 1993). Much of this work has remained focused on

the interventions of black intellectuals, missionaries, activists, and artists. For example, James T. Campbell, *Songs of Zion: The African Methodist Episcopal Church in the United States and South Africa* (Chapel Hill: University of North Carolina Press, 1998); Penny Von Eschen, *Race Against Empire: Black Americans and Anticolonialism, 1937–1957* (Ithaca, NY: Cornell University Press, 1997); Brenda Gayle Plummer, *Rising Wind: Black Americans and U.S. Foreign Affairs, 1935–1960* (Chapel Hill: University of North Carolina Press, 1996); Robin Kelley, "But a Local Phase of a World Problem: Black History's Global Vision, 1883–1950," *Journal of American History* 86, no. 3 (December 1999): 1045–77; Nikhil Pal Singh, *Black Is a Country: Race and the Unfinished Struggle for Democracy* (Cambridge, MA: Harvard University Press, 2004); Michelle Rief, "Thinking Locally, Acting Globally: The International Agenda of African American Clubwomen, 1880–1940," *Journal of African American History* 89, no. 3 (Summer 2004): 203–22; Ifeoma Kiddoe Nwankwo, *Black Cosmopolitanism: Racial Consciousness and Transnational Identity in the Nineteenth-Century Americas* (Philadelphia: University of Pennsylvania Press, 2005); Brent Edwards, *The Practice of Diaspora: Literature, Translation, and the Rise of Black Internationalism* (Cambridge, MA: Harvard University Press, 2003); Michelle Stephens, *Black Empire: The Masculine Global Imaginary of Caribbean Intellectuals in the United States, 1914–1962* (Durham, NC: Duke University Press, 2005); Kevin Gaines, *American Africans in Ghana: Black Expatriates and the Civil Rights Era* (Chapel Hill: University of North Carolina Press, 2007); Carol Boyce Davies, *Left of Karl Marx: The Political Life of Black Communist Claudia Jones* (Durham, NC: Duke University Press, 2007); Kate A. Baldwin, *Beyond the Color Line and the Iron Curtain: Reading Encounters between Black and Red, 1922–1963* (Durham, NC: Duke University Press, 2002); Magdalena J. Zaborowska, *James Baldwin's Turkish Decade: Erotics of Exile* (Durham, NC: Duke University Press, 2008); Robert Carr, *Black Nationalism in the New World: Reading the African-American and West Indian Experience* (Durham, NC: Duke University Press, 2002); Frank Guridy, *Forging Diaspora: Afro-Cubans and African Americans in a World of Empire and Jim Crow* (Chapel Hill: University of North Carolina Press, 2010).

24. On the life and career of Thomas Molineaux, see Kevin Smith, *Black Genesis: The History of the Black Prizefighter 1760–1870* (Lincoln: iUniverse, 2003), 27–60.

25. Ibid., 95-105, 121–22.

26. Nat Fleischer, *Black Dynamite*, 5 vols., vol. 1, *Story of the Negro in Boxing* (New York: C.J. O'Brien, 1938), 87–88.

27. On Jackson's international career as a prizefighter and performer, see Susan F. Clark, "Up Against the Ropes: Peter Jackson as 'Uncle Tom' in America," *Drama Review* 44, no. 1 (2000): 157–82; David K. Wiggins, "Peter Jackson and the Elusive Heavyweight Championship: A Black Athlete's Struggle Against the Late Nineteenth Century Color-Line," *Journal of Sport History* 12, no. 2 (1985): 143–68.

28. Edwards, *The Practice of Diaspora*, 187.

29. Scholars have begun to explore the importance of proletarian travel

and resistance in the making of the Atlantic world, particularly through the lens of black maritime workers. Julius Scott, "The Common Wind: Currents of Afro-American Communication in the Era of the Haitian Revolution" (Ph.D. diss., Duke University, 1986); Peter Linebaugh and Marcus Rediker, *Many-Headed Hydra: Sailors, Slaves, Commoners, and the Hidden History of the Revolutionary Atlantic* (Boston: Beacon Press, 2000); Jeffrey Bolster, *Black Jacks: African American Seamen in the Age of Sail* (Cambridge, MA: Harvard University Press, 1997).

30. On the historical and experiential groundings of black radicalism, see Cedric Robinson, *Black Marxism: The Making of the Black Radical Tradition* (Chapel Hill: University of North Carolina Press, 2000); Robin Kelley, *Freedom Dreams: The Black Radical Imagination* (Boston: Beacon Press, 2002).

31. Stephens, *Black Empire*, 167–203; Edwards, *The Practice of Diaspora*, 187–240.

32. McKay's novel follows the exploits of the African American southerner Lincoln Agrippa Daily, otherwise known as "Banjo," as he lives among a motley group of drifters in the port city of Marseilles, France, in the 1920s. Claude McKay, *Banjo: A Story without a Plot* (1929; New York: Harvest Books, 1970).

33. Claude McKay, "Negroes in Sports," in *The Negroes in America* (1923; Port Washington, NY: Kennikat Press, 1979), 54.

34. McKay, *Banjo*, 331.

35. Alain Locke, ed., *The New Negro: Voices of the Harlem Renaissance* (1925; New York: Macmillan, 1992), 5.

36. A number of scholars have pointed to the "queer" (nonnormative) and anarchistic dimensions of black transnationalism. Omise'eke Natasha Tinsley, "Black Atlantic, Queer Atlantic: Queer Imaginings of the Middle Passage," *GLQ: A Journal of Lesbian and Gay Studies* 14, nos. 2–3 (2008): 191–215; Gary Edward Holcomb, *Claude McKay, Code Name Sasha: Queer Black Marxism and the Harlem Renaissance* (Gainesville: University Press of Florida, 2007).

37. Ward, *Unforgivable Blackness*, 5–6.

38. Ibid.

39. Ibid., 7–8.

40. Johnson quoted in ibid., 8.

41. Ibid., 10.

42. Johnson, *In the Ring—And Out*, 27–28.

43. Ibid., 27.

44. Ibid., 29; Ward, *Unforgivable Blackness*, 11.

45. Johnson, *In the Ring—And Out*, 31.

46. Ibid., 31–32; Ward, *Unforgivable Blackness*, 12.

47. Johnson, *In the Ring—And Out*, 34.

48. Ibid., 33–34; Ward, *Unforgivable Blackness*, 10.

49. Johnson, *In the Ring—And Out*, 36.

50. Johnson's unpublished prison memoir quoted in Ward, *Unforgivable Blackness*, 22.

51. Quotations in this paragraph are taken from Johnson, *In the Ring—And Out*, 37–38.

52. Ibid., 38–39; Ward, *Unforgivable Blackness*, 24.

53. On the competing ideals of black manhood, see Baldwin, *Chicago's New Negroes*, 195–96; Martin Summers, *Manliness and Its Discontents: The Black Middle Class and the Transformation of Masculinity, 1900–1930* (Chapel Hill: University of North Carolina Press, 2004), 151–53.

54. Quoted in Ward, *Unforgivable Blackness*, 56–57.

55. "The Black 'King' of the Pugilists," *Daily Chronicle*, 21 September 1911; Trevor Wignall, *Story of Boxing* (New York: Brentano's, 1924), 257; Baldwin, *Chicago's New Negroes*, 199.

56. J. B. Lewis quoted in Johnson, *In the Ring—And Out*, 7.

57. Paul Gilroy examines black Americans' historical association of cars with freedom within the context of their broader relationship to patterns of consumerism, suburbanization, and privatization. Paul Gilroy, *Darker Than Blue: On the Moral Economies of Black Atlantic Culture* (Cambridge: Belknap Press, 2010), 4–54.

58. Antonio Gramsci's concept of the "organic intellectual" provides a helpful framework for understanding the importance of traveling African American athletes and performers in the rise of a popular black global vision. Organic intellectuals maintain strong links with the working people and their everyday lives and struggles. They often come out of the working class, developing their critical awareness and radical imagination through experience rather than dispassionate study at traditional, elitist institutions. Antonio Gramsci, *Selections from the Prison Notebooks* (New York: International Publishers, 1971).

59. Rudyard Kipling, "The White Man's Burden," *McClure's Magazine* 12 (February 1899).

60. Alice L. Conklin, *A Mission to Civilize: The Republican Idea of Empire in France and West Africa, 1895–1930* (Stanford, CA: Stanford University Press, 1997); Paul Kramer, *Blood of Government: Race, Empire, the United States, and the Philippines* (Chapel Hill: University of North Carolina Press, 2006).

61. Historian Ann Laura Stoler argues that a shared interest in biopolitics linked together seemingly disparate examples of imperial rule. Ann Laura Stoler, *Race and the Education of Desire: Foucault's History of Sexuality and the Colonial Order* (Durham, NC: Duke University Press, 2002); "Tense and Tender Ties: The Politics of Comparison in North American History and (Post) Colonial Studies," *Journal of American History* 88, no. 3 (December 2001): 829–65; *Carnal Knowledge and Imperial Power: Race and the Intimate in Colonial Rule* (Berkeley: University of California Press, 2002). Stoler's work has inspired a growing field that examines the role of discourses of gender, sexuality, and the body in the theory and practice of Western imperialism. Ann Laura Stoler, ed., *Haunted by Empire: Geographies of Intimacy in North American History* (Durham, NC: Duke University Press, 2006); Tony Ballantyne and Antoinette Burton, eds., *Moving Subjects: Gender, Mobility, and Intimacy in an Age of Global Empire* (Urbana: University of Illinois Press, 2009); Tony Ballantyne and Antoinette Burton, eds., *Bodies in Contact: Rethinking Colonial Encounters in World History* (Durham, NC: Duke Uni-

versity Press, 2009); Eileen Suarez Findlay, *Imposing Decency: The Politics of Sexuality and Race in Puerto Rico, 1870–1920* (Durham, NC: Duke University Press, 1999).

62. Challenging conventional ideas of American exceptionalism, U.S. scholars have taken on the project of writing empire back into mainstream U.S. history. Richard Drinnon, *Facing West: The Metaphysics of Indian-Hating and Empire Building* (Minneapolis: University of Minnesota Press, 1980); Shelley Streeby, *American Sensations: Class, Empire, and the Production of Popular Culture* (Berkeley: University of California Press, 2002); Amy Kaplan and Donald Pease, eds., *Cultures of United States Imperialism* (Durham, NC: Duke University Press, 1993); Mary Renda, *Taking Haiti: Military Occupation and the Culture of U.S. Imperialism, 1915–1940* (Chapel Hill: University of North Carolina Press, 2001); Laura Wexler, *Tender Violence: Domestic Visions in an Age of U.S. Imperialism* (Chapel Hill: University of North Carolina Press, 2002); Amy Kaplan, *The Anarchy of Empire in the Making of U.S. Culture* (Cambridge, MA: Harvard University Press, 2002); Matthew Pratt Guterl, James T. Campbell, and Robert G. Lee, eds., *Race, Nation, and Empire in American History* (Durham, NC: Duke University Press, 2007); Gilbert Joseph, Catherine LeGrand, and Ricardo Salvatore, eds., *Close Encounters of Empire: Writing the Cultural History of U.S.-Latin American Relations* (Durham, NC: Duke University Press, 1998); Kramer, *Blood of Government;* Matthew Jacobson, *Barbarian Virtues: The United States Encounters of Foreign Peoples at Home and Abroad, 1876–1917* (New York: Hill and Wang, 2000).

63. Bernard Porter, *The Lion's Share: A Short History of British Imperialism, 1850–1995,* 3rd ed. (New York: Longman, 1996), 84–101.

64. Conklin, *Mission to Civilize,* 1–10.

65. This general interpretation of the late imperial moment can be found in Jacobson, *Barbarian Virtues;* Thomas G. August, *The Selling of Empire: British and French Imperialist Propaganda, 1890–1940* (Westport, CT: Greenwood Press, 1985).

66. President Cleveland quoted in Jacobson, *Barbarian Virtues,* 22. For more on empires and markets, see ibid., 15–58.

67. Porter, *Lion's Share,* 77–81; August, *Selling of Empire,* xii, 7. Much like their U.S. counterparts, European scholars have also taken on the task of restoring the importance of imperialism in the mainstream histories of their nations. Antoinette Burton, ed., *After the Imperial Turn: Thinking with and Through the Nation* (Durham, NC: Duke University Press, 2003); Gary Wilder, *The French Imperial Nation-State: Negritude and Colonial Humanism Between the Two World Wars* (Chicago: University of Chicago Press, 2005); Paul Gilroy, *Postcolonial Melancholia* (New York: Columbia University Press, 2006).

68. Lake and Reynolds, *Drawing the Global Colour Line,* 137, 178–80, 210. Also see John Cell, *The Highest Stage of White Supremacy: The Origins of Segregation in South Africa and the American South* (Cambridge: Cambridge University Press, 1982).

69. Charles Pearson quoted in Lake and Reynolds, *Drawing the Global Colour Line,* 3.

70. On the gendered anxieties of the late imperial moment, see Kristin Hoganson, *Fighting for American Manhood: How Gender Politics Provoked the Spanish-American and Philippine-American Wars* (New Haven, CT: Yale University Press, 1998); Bederman, *Manliness and Civilization.* On the concurrent rise of sport and body culture, see John F. Kasson, *Houdini, Tarzan, and the Perfect Man: The White Male Body and the Challenge of Modernity in America* (New York: Hill & Wang, 2001); Bederman, *Manliness and Civilization;* Joanna Bourke, *Dismembering the Male: Men's Bodies, Britain, and the Great War* (Chicago: University of Chicago Press, 1999); Michael A. Budd, *The Sculpture Machine: Physical Culture and Body Politics in the Age of Empire* (New York: New York University Press, 1997); Gerald R. Gems, *The Athletic Crusade: Sport and American Cultural Imperialism* (Lincoln: University of Nebraska Press, 2006); Lisa Grunberger, "Bernarr MacFadden's Physical Culture: Muscles, Morals and the Millennium" (Ph.D. diss., University of Chicago, 1997); McDevitt, *May the Best Man Win;* Clifford Putney, *Muscular Christianity: Manhood and Sports in Protestant America, 1880–1920* (Cambridge, MA: Harvard University Press, 2001).

71. Robert Rydell, *All the World's a Fair: Visions of Empire at American International Exhibitions, 1876–1916* (Chicago: University of Chicago Press, 1984), 6. Also see August, *Selling of Empire,* 127–41; Bernth Lindfors, ed., *Africans on Stage: Studies in Ethnological Show Business* (Bloomington: Indiana University Press, 1999); Jan Nederveen Pieterse, *White on Black: Images of Africa and Blacks in Western Popular Culture* (New Haven, CT: Yale University Press, 1992), 132–51.

72. John. A. Hobson, *The Psychology of Jingoism* (London: Grant Richards, 1901), 3.

73. Ibid., 12. For more on the importance of spectacle in the global imagination of imperialism, see Veit Erlmann, "'Spectatorial Lust': The Africa Choir in England, 1891–1893," in *Africans on Stage: Studies in Ethnological Show Business,* ed. Bernth Lindfors (Bloomington: Indiana University Press, 1999), 107–37.

74. For a discussion of race as fetish and commodity, see "The Fact of Blackness" in Frantz Fanon, *Black Skin, White Masks* (New York: Grove Press, 1967), 109–40; Anne McClintock, *Imperial Leather: Race, Gender and Sexuality in the Colonial Contest* (New York: Routledge, 1995), 207–31; Young, *Embodying Black Experience,* 87.

75. On the dissemination and impact of U.S. popular culture abroad in this period, see Robert Rydell and Rob Kroes, *Buffalo Bill in Bologna: The Americanization of the World, 1869–1922* (Chicago: University of Chicago Press, 2005); Rob Kroes, Robert Rydell, and D. F. J. Bosscher, eds., *Cultural Transmissions and Receptions: American Mass Culture in Europe* (Amsterdam: VU University Press, 1993).

76. Arjun Appadurai, *Modernity at Large: Cultural Dimensions of Globalization* (Minneapolis: University of Minnesota Press, 1996), 64.

77. *Life,* 24 November 1887.

78. See, for example, *Famous Irish Fighters in the Ring: John L. Sullivan* (London: Felix McGlennon, [1892]); John L. Sullivan, *Life and Reminis-*

cences of a 19th Century Gladiator (Boston: Jas. A. Hearn & Co.; London: Geo. Routledge & Sons, 1892); William Edgar Harding, *John L. Sullivan, the Champion Pugilist* (New York: 1883); Richard Kyle Fox, *Life and Battles of John L. Sullivan* (New York: Police Gazette, 1883); *Modern Gladiator: Being an Account of the Exploits and Experiences of the World's Greatest Fighter, John Lawrence Sullivan* (St. Louis, MO: Athletic Publishing Company, 1889); John Boyle O'Reilly, *Ethics of Boxing and Manly Sport* (Boston: Ticknor and Company, 1888); *Wehman's Book on the Art and Science of Boxing* (New York: Henry J. Wehman, 1892).

79. "J.L. Sullivan in Birmingham," *The Sportsman,* 14 November 1887. Also see Michael T. Isenberg, *John L. Sullivan and His America* (Urbana: University of Illinois Press, 1988), 241–42.

80. "The Triumph of the West," *Life,* 15 December 1887.

81. Edward Said, *Orientalism* (New York: Vintage Books, 1978); Louis Chude-Sokei, *The Last 'Darky': Bert Williams, Black-on-Black Minstrelsy, and the African Diaspora* (Durham, NC: Duke University Press, 2005), 58, 141; Veit Erlmann, "'A Feeling of Prejudice': Orpheus M. McAdoo and the Virginia Jubilee Singers in South Africa, 1890–1898," *Journal of South African Studies* 14, no. 3 (1988): 331–50; Richard Waterhouse, "The Minstrel Show and Australian Culture," *Journal of Popular Culture* 24, no. 3 (1990): 147–66. This analysis of the local and the global is informed by the theoretical insights of Walter Mignolo, *Local Histories/Global Designs* (Princeton, NJ: Princeton University Press, 2000).

82. Quoted in Douglas Lorimer, *Colour, Class and the Victorians* (New York: Holmes & Meier, 1978), 89.

83. Sarah Meer, *Uncle Tom Mania: Slavery, Minstrelsy and Transatlantic Culture in the 1850s* (Athens: University of Georgia Press, 2005).

84. Athos, "The World's Metropolis," *Indianapolis Freeman,* 16 July 1892.

85. Scholars have begun to explore the importance of popular culture as a conduit for black transnationalism and internationalism. Brown, *Babylon Girls;* Chude-Sokei, *The Last 'Darky';* Daphne Brooks, *Bodies in Dissent: Spectacular Performances of Race and Freedom, 1850–1910* (Durham, NC: Duke University Press, 2006); Harry Elam and Kennell Jackson, eds., *Black Cultural Traffic: Crossroads in Global Performance and Popular Culture* (Ann Arbor: University of Michigan Press, 2005).

86. Athos, "World's Metropolis."

CHAPTER 1. EMBODYING EMPIRE

1. Jack Johnson, "Ma Vie et mes combats," *La Vie au grand air,* 4 March 1911, 46.

2. Ibid., 11 March 1911, 161.

3. Quoted in Geoffrey Ward, *Unforgivable Blackness: The Rise and Fall of Jack Johnson* (New York: Knopf, 2004), 85.

4. Richard Waterhouse, "The Minstrel Show and Australian Culture," *Journal of Popular Culture* 24, no. 3 (1990): 147–49.

5. James J. Jeffries, "Mental and Moral Training through Boxing," *Physical Culture*, August 1909.

6. See, for example, "National Physique: Some Differences Explained," *Sandow's Magazine*, 2 August 1906; "The Editor's Ideas: Italians in the Ring," *Boxing*, 11 December 1909; "The Jew as a Physical Culturist," *Health & Strength*, 16 May 1908; "The Rise of the Black: A Short History of the Stages by Which the Negro Race Has Risen to a Commanding Position in the Ring," *Boxing*, 4 December 1909.

7. Jeffries, "Mental and Moral Training through Boxing."

8. Theodore Roosevelt to Mike Donovan, 10 February 1899, quoted in Dakin Burdick, "The American Way of Fighting: Unarmed Defense in the United States, 1845–1945" (Ph.D. diss., Indiana University, 1999), 101.

9. Gail Bederman, *Manliness and Civilization: A Cultural History of Gender and Race in the United States, 1880–1917* (Chicago: University of Chicago Press, 1995), 170, 190–92; Theodore Roosevelt, *Theodore Roosevelt: An Autobiography* (1913; Charleston: BiblioBazaar, 2007), 48.

10. Mike Donovan, *The Roosevelt That I Know: Ten Years of Boxing with the President, and Other Memories of Famous Fighting Men* (New York: B. W. Dodge & Co., 1909), 5.

11. Clifford Putney, *Muscular Christianity: Manhood and Sports in Protestant America, 1880–1920* (Cambridge, MA: Harvard University Press, 2001), 1–2.

12. Tom Pendergast, *Creating the Modern Man: American Magazines and Consumer Culture, 1900–1950* (Columbia: University of Missouri Press, 2000); Howard P. Chudacoff, *The Age of the Bachelor: Creating an American Subculture* (Princeton, NJ: Princeton University Press, 1999); John A. Dinan, *Sports in the Pulp Magazines* (London: McFarland & Company, 1998).

13. Michael A. Budd, *The Sculpture Machine: Physical Culture and Body Politics in the Age of Empire* (New York: New York University Press, 1997), xii, 33, 35–39.

14. The English philosopher Thomas Hobbes used many metaphors of the body to describe the character and function of governments in *Leviathan* (1651). On the recurring trope of the body politic, see A. D. Harvey, "The Body Politic: Anatomy of a Metaphor," *Contemporary Review* 275, no. 1603 (August 1999): 85-93.

15. Theodore Roosevelt, *The Strenuous Life: Essays and Addresses* (New York: Century, 1902), 3.

16. Budd, *Sculpture Machine*, 21, 37. Also see Max Nordau, *Degeneration* (1892; Lincoln: University of Nebraska Press, 2006).

17. See, for example, "Physical Culture in the City," *Health & Strength*, 11 April 1908; "Editorial Grips: A Physically Degenerated Army," *Health & Strength*, 5 September 1908; H. Mirville, "La Science de santé," *La Vie au grand air*, 29 March 1913, 245–46; Gordon Reeves, "Does Civilization Weaken the Physique?" *Physical Culture*, May 1914.

18. Bernarr MacFadden, "Are Americans Degenerating?" *Physical Culture*, [January] 1907. Also see Sydney Cummings, "America's Decreasing

Birth-Rate," *Physical Culture*, July 1909; Addison Berkeley, "The Decreasing Birth Rate," *Physical Culture*, November 1909.

19. Rene DuBois, "The French Nation Dying Out," *Physical Culture*, December 1908. French physical culturists also discussed degeneration in their own publications. "A propos des géants," *L'Education physique*, 31 January 1907; "Préservation contre la tuberculose," *L'Education physique*, 31 May 1907.

20. See, for example, "Are English Athletes Deteriorating?" *Sandow's Magazine*, 11 April 1907; "Editorial Grips: Why Are We Degenerating?" *Health & Strength*, 30 May 1908; "Editorial Grips: Is the Race Deteriorating?" *Health & Strength*, 12 September 1908; Viscount Hill, "Britain's Decline and How to Check It," *Health & Strength*, 9 October 1909; Samuel Cook, "Race Degeneration Threatening the British Empire," *Physical Culture*, April 1907; "Editorial Grips: The Decline of Our Physical Prestige," *Health & Strength*, 8 February 1908; Rachda Felley, "Foreign v. British Athletes," *Health & Strength*, 4 January 1908.

21. "Disease and Crime," *Sandow's Magazine*, 20 December 1906. Also see Daniel Pick, *Faces of Degeneration: A European Disorder, c. 1848–c. 1918* (Cambridge: Cambridge University Press, 1989), 176–221.

22. Budd, *Sculpture Machine*, 12, 95; Pick, *Faces of Degeneration*, 238.

23. Quotations in this paragraph are from John Terence McGovern, *How to Box to Win, How to Build Muscle* (New York: Rohde & Haskins, 1900), 7, 9.

24. Milwaukee *Free Press* quoted in Ward, *Unforgivable Blackness*, 84.

25. On the White Australia Policy and its legacy, see James Jupp, *From White Australia to. Woomera: The Story of Australian Immigration* (New York: Cambridge University Press, 2002); Keith Windschuttle, *White Australia Policy* (Sydney: Macleay Press, 2004); Jane Carey and Claire McLisky, eds., *Creating White Australia: New Perspectives on Race, Whiteness and History* (Sydney: Sydney University Press, 2009).

26. "Immigration Restriction Act 1901" (10 December 2004), www.peo .gov.au/resources/immigration_bill.htm (accessed 23 May 2006).

27. Katherine Ellinghaus, "Intimate Assimilation: Comparing White-Indigenous Intermarriage in the United States and Australia, 1880s–1930s," in *Moving Subjects: Gender, Mobility, and Intimacy in an Age of Global Empire*, ed. Tony Ballantyne and Antoinette Burton (Urbana: University of Illinois Press, 2009), 212.

28. "A Black Blot," *Sydney Truth*, 22 March 1908. The details regarding Toy's relationship with Johnson emerged during her libel suit against the *Sydney Referee* in 1908. For more on the Toy controversy, see Ward, *Unforgivable Blackness*, 88–89, 103–7; Jeff Wells, *Boxing Day: The Fight That Changed the World* (Sydney: HarperSports, 1998), 66–69.

29. "Lady and Pugilist: An Announced Engagement," *Argus*, 17 March 1908.

30. Ward, *Unforgivable Blackness*, 89; "Lady and Pugilist: The Sydney Libel Case," *Argus*, 18 March 1908.

31. "Boxing," *Punch*, 7 March 1907.

32. Ward, *Unforgivable Blackness,* 90–91; John Maynard, "Vision, Voice and Influence," *Australian Historical Studies* 34, no. 121 (2003): 94, 96.

33. "A Black Beano," *Sydney Truth,* 17 March 1907; Maynard, "Vision, Voice and Influence," 95.

34. Quotations in this paragraph and the next are from "A Black Beano."

35. Ibid.

36. John Maynard, "For Liberty and Freedom: Fred Maynard and the Australian Aboriginal Progressive Association," Lecture for New South Wales State Library, Sydney, 2004, 19–20.

37. Maynard, "Vision, Voice and Influence," 96. The photo is from the personal collection of Professor John Maynard, the grandson of Fred Maynard.

38. "Johnson-McLean Trouble," *Sunday Sun,* 24 March 1907.

39. Quoted in Ward, *Unforgivable Blackness,* 103.

40. Quoted in ibid., 104.

41. Quoted in ibid.

42. "A Black Blot."

43. Quotations in this paragraph and the next are from ibid.

44. Ibid.

45. Yorick Gradeley, "The Battle to the Strong: The Empire Builders," *Health & Strength,* 2 May 1908, 440.

46. Yorick Gradeley, "The Battle to the Strong: A Powerful and Exciting Physical Regeneration Story," *Health & Strength,* 4 January 1908, 14.

47. Gradeley, "The Battle to the Strong: The Empire Builders," 439–40.

48. Yorick Gradeley, "The Battle to the Strong: When Black Meets White," *Health & Strength,* 9 May 1908, 463.

49. Ibid., 464.

50. Dan McCaffery, *Tommy Burns: Canada's Unknown World Heavyweight Champion* (Toronto: James Lorimer & Company, 2000), 21–29.

51. Quoted in Daniel Streible, *Fight Pictures: A History of Boxing and Early Cinema* (Berkeley: University of California Press, 2008), 202.

52. Corinthian, "Boxing," *Punch,* 13 August 1908. Also see Richard Broome, "The Australian Reaction to Jack Johnson, Black Pugilist, 1907–9," in *Sport in History,* ed. Richard Cashman and Michael McKernan (St. Lucia: University of Queensland Press, 1979), 345.

53. Quoted in Wells, *Boxing Day,* 108.

54. Corinthian, "Boxing."

55. Wells, *Boxing Day,* 90. The *Bulletin* characterized O'Sullivan as "a combination of Samuel Plimsoll, Cicero, John L. Sullivan, and Caius Gracchus." See Bruce E. Mansfield, "O'Sullivan, Edward William (1846—1910)," *Australian Dictionary of Biography—Online Edition,* Australian National University, 2006, www.adb.online.anu.edu.au/biogs/A110117b.htm (accessed 4 February 2007).

56. Quoted in Broome, "Australian Reaction to Jack Johnson," 345. See also A.J. Hill, "Ryrie, Sir Granville de Laune (1865—1937)," in *Australian Dictionary of Biography—Online Edition,* Australian National University, 2006, www.adb.online.anu.edu.au/biogs/A110512b.htm (accessed 4 February 2007).

57. See photos of the *USS Brooklyn* (1898) and the *USS Oregon* (1898), Detroit Publishing Company Collection, Prints and Photographs Division, Library of Congress, Washington, D.C.

58. For an overview of Philippine boxing history, see J.R. Svinth, "The Origins of Philippines Boxing, 1899–1929," *Journal of Combative Sport,* July 2001, http://ejmas.com/jcs/jcsart_svinth_0701.htm (accessed 20 January 2005).

59. E. Hayward Conisby, "Our Fleet and Its Cruise in the Pacific," *Physical Culture,* February 1908. Conisby estimated that the total number of vessels was actually thirty to forty, since six torpedo boats and other noncombatant crafts followed the U.S. fleet. There were nearly fourteen thousand men onboard the battleships alone.

60. "Battle Fleet Sails West," *Boston Daily Globe,* 7 July 1908. Also see James R. Reckner, *Teddy Roosevelt's Great White Fleet* (Annapolis: Naval Institute Press, 1988); Kenneth Wimmel, *Theodore Roosevelt and the Great White Fleet: American Seapower Comes of Age* (Washington, DC: Brassey's, 1998).

61. "President to the Fleet," *Boston Daily Globe,* 7 July 1908.

62. Conisby, "Our Fleet and Its Cruise in the Pacific."

63. "16 Battleships Reach Auckland," *Atlanta Constitution,* 9 August 1908; "Sailors at the Races," *Washington Post,* 12 August 1908; Margaret Werry, "The Greatest Show on Earth: Political Spectacle, Spectacular Politics, and the American Pacific," *Theatre Journal* 57, no. 3 (October 2005): 366.

64. "Supremacy in the Pacific," *New York Times,* 22 July 1908.

65. "Our Fleet in Australia," *Washington Post,* 1 June 1908.

66. *Melbourne Age* quoted in Graeme Kent, *The Great White Hopes: The Quest to Defeat Jack Johnson* (Gloucestershire: Sutton Publishing, 2005), 3.

67. "America's Armada," *Argus,* 21 March 1908.

68. "Australia's Greeting Warm," *Chicago Daily Tribune,* 4 October 1908.

69. "Punch's Fleet Number," *Punch,* 10 September 1908. The *Bulletin* also printed a special edition in honor of the fleet and provided readers with the sheet music for "Yankee Doodle." "The White Supplement," *Bulletin,* 20 August 1908; "Yankee Doodle," *Bulletin,* 20 August 1908.

70. "Australia Plans Big Fleet Welcome," *New York Times,* 16 August 1908.

71. Wells, *Boxing Day,* 97–98; "Australia's Greeting Warm."

72. "A New Talk of Alliance," *Washington Post,* 16 August 1908.

73. "The Glad Hand," *Punch,* 10 September 1908. For similar cartoons, see "Tug of Peace," *Punch,* 10 September 1908; "The Enduring Bond," *Punch,* 13 August 1908. The first depicted the fleet as a rope used to pull the two nations together, while the second featured Lady Australia holding out her hand as Lady America walked across the Pacific on the tops of the U.S. battleships.

74. "New Relations," *Punch,* 10 September 1908.

75. "Our Fleet in Australia."

76. Werry, "The Greatest Show on Earth," 367.

77. "Big Fleet a Friend Maker," *Chicago Daily Tribune,* 16 August 1908.

78. "Australia and the Asiatic," *Bulletin,* 27 February 1908; "The Nigger Asserts Himself," *Bulletin,* 27 February 1908. The Anglo-Japanese Alliance (established in 1902 and renewed in 1905) had been a strategic move

for both nations. It had given Britain an ally in East Asia that would help not only to restrain Russia but also to preserve British commerce in China. For Japan, it offered official recognition as an important world power along with the chance to challenge Russian prerogatives in Manchuria and Korea. Yet the alliance clashed with Australia's own desire not only to control the Pacific region but also to remain a white nation. See Phillips Payson O'Brien, ed., *The Anglo-Japanese Alliance, 1902–1922* (New York: RoutledgeCurzon, 2004).

79. Wells, *Boxing Day*, 96; "Immigration to Australia," *Observer*, 19 December 1908; "Firm Policy in Far East," *New York Times*, 16 August 1908; "Description of an Imaginary War between the United States and Japan," *Washington Post*, 12 July 1908.

80. *Lone Hand* quoted in Wells, *Boxing Day*, 94–95.

81. "Last Shovelful of Coal: President Roosevelt's Warning," *Bulletin*, 20 August 1908.

82. "The Stowed Away Chinese," *Punch*, 10 December 1908; "A Medium in All Things," *Punch*, 10 December 1908.

83. "Threatening Mass," *Bulletin*, 20 August 1908.

84. "Immigration to Australia."

85. "Praise for our Sailors," *New York Times*, 7 September 1908. Also see "Notes and Queries," *Observer*, 9 January 1909; "Australian Immigration," *Punch*, 7 January 1909.

86. Maynard, "For Liberty and Freedom," 26.

87. "Melbourne Notes," *Tasmanian Mail*, 2 January 1909.

88. Broome, "Australian Reaction to Jack Johnson," 345; Wells, *Boxing Day*, 79–81. Also see Chris Cunneen, "McIntosh, Hugh Donald (1876–1942)," in *Australian Dictionary of Biography—Online Edition*, Australian National University, 2006, www.adb.online.anu.edu.au/biogs/A100280b.htm (accessed 4 February 2007).

89. Wells, *Boxing Day*, 82; Ward, *Unforgivable Blackness*, 113–14.

90. "White Australia Policy," *Tasmanian Mail*, 26 December 1908.

91. "More Perils of the Sea," *Bulletin*, 24 December 1908.

92. "The Nigger Asserts Himself."

93. "A Man and a Brother," *Bulletin*, 24 December 1908.

94. "Versatile Mr. Johnson," *Sydney Morning Herald*, 31 December 1908.

95. "The Great Fight in Plain Black and White," *Punch*, 31 December 1908.

96. Right-Cross, "Boxing," *Arrow*, 2 January 1909.

97. "Black versus White," *Health & Strength*, 7 March 1908; Romney, "'Tommy' Burns: An Appreciation of the Man and the Fighter," *Health & Strength*, 28 March 1908; "Sporting Notions," *Bulletin*, 31 December 1908.

98. "Mostly in New South Wales," *Bulletin*, 7 January 1909.

99. "Sporting Notions," *Bulletin*, 14 January 1909; "Gunner" James Moir, "Why Tommy Burns Will Win," *Health & Strength*, 21 November 1908.

100. "A Lady's Letter from Sydney," *Tasmanian Mail*, 9 January 1909.

101. Both quotations are from Right-Cross, "The Eve of a Great Battle," *Arrow*, 26 December 1908.

102. "Arrangements for Huge Crowd at Stadium," *Arrow*, 26 December 1908.

103. From 1907 to 1909 London and his wife toured the Pacific Islands, a voyage that later inspired his *South Sea Tales* (1911) and *Cruise of the Snark* (1913). London welcomed the opportunity to cover the Burns-Johnson match, since his Pacific voyage had left him ridden with debt and tropical disease. For more on London's coverage of Johnson, see Jeanne Campbell Reesman, *Jack London's Racial Lives: A Critical Biography* (Athens: University of Georgia Press, 2009), 179–205.

104. "Boxing Championship," *Australasian*, 2 January 1909.

105. "The Prize Fight," *Sydney Morning Herald*, 28 December 1908; "Boxing Day," *Sydney Morning Herald*, 28 December 1908; "Great Boxintg Mach [sic]," *Tasmanian Mail*, 2 January 1909.

106. "The Prize Fight."

107. "The Fight across the Wires," *Sydney Morning Herald*, 31 December 1908.

108. "Melbourne Notes."

109. "Sporting Notions," 31 December 1908.

110. "Boxing Championship"; Ward, *Unforgivable Blackness*, 122.

111. "Sporting Notions," 31 December 1908.

112. "Boxing Championship."

113. "Johnson Wins," *Sydney Morning Herald*, 28 December 1908.

114. "Boxing Championship."

115. "Sporting Notions," 31 December 1908.

116. "Boxing Championship."

117. Ibid; "Jack London on the Fight," *Australasian*, 2 January 1909. Numerous newspapers throughout the United States, the British Empire, and France reprinted London's postfight report.

118. "Melbourne Notes."

119. Ibid.

120. "Johnson Wins"; "Boxing Championship."

121. "The Great Fight in Plain Black and White."

122. "Back Johnson Heavily," *Indianapolis Freeman*, 23 January 1909.

123. All the quotations in this paragraph are from "Boxing Championship."

124. Ibid.

125. Ibid.

126. "The Great Fight in Plain Black and White."

127. "Sporting Notions," 31 December 1908.

128. "Johnson Wins."

129. "A Lady's Letter from Sydney."

130. "Melbourne Notes." Also see "Talk on Change," *Australasian*, 9 January 1909.

131. Lester A. Walton, "The Johnson-Burns Fight," *New York Age*, 31 December 1908.

132. "Back Johnson Heavily."

133. Walton, "The Johnson-Burns Fight."

134. "The Superiority of the Black," *New York Age*, 31 December 1908.

135. "The Black Gladiator. Veni, Vidi, Vici—Jack Johnson," *Indianapolis Freeman*, 23 January 1909.

136. *Cleveland Gazette,* 23 January 1909.

137. Lester A. Walton, "In the Sporting World," *New York Age,* 28 January 1909.

138. "Burns and Johnson," *Sydney Morning Herald,* 4 January 1909. A smoodge is someone who attempts to curry favor through flattery.

139. "Crowd Hoots Johnson," *Sydney Morning Herald,* 31 December 1908.

140. "Sporting Notions," 14 January 1909.

141. "The Great Fight," *Observer,* 2 January 1909.

142. "Boxing Championship."

143. Right-Cross, "Boxing," *Arrow,* 9 January 1909; "Boxing," *Punch,* 21 January 1909; "Sporting Notions," *Bulletin,* 7 January 1909.

144. "Topics of the Week," *Australasian,* 2 January 1909.

145. "Ladies' Letter," *Punch,* 31 December 1908.

146. All quotations in this paragraph are from "The Whit [sic] Australia," *Indianapolis Freeman,* 16 January 1909.

147. "The Boxing Contest," *Sydney Morning Herald,* 30 December 1908.

148. "Will Fight Johnson Again," *Health & Strength,* 9 January 1909.

149. "The Great Fight."

150. Quoted in "Johnson's Prophetic Vision," *Baltimore Afro-American,* 1 May 1909.

151. Tom Beasley, "Our Colored Brethren," *Bulletin,* 31 December 1908.

152. Ibid.

153. "The Great Fight," Henry Lawson, 1908, quoted in Humphrey McQueen, *A New Britannia: An Argument Concerning the Social Origins of Australian Radicalism and Nationalism,* 2nd ed. (1970; New York: Penguin Books, 1986), 107–8.

154. "Topics of the Week."

155. "Current Cartoons," *Punch,* 7 January 1909.

156. "Topics of the Week."

157. "Boxing," *Punch,* 21 January 1909.

158. "Current Cartoons."

159. "The Great Fight in Plain Black and White."

160. "Melbourne Notes."

161. Randolph Bedford, "White v. Black," *Melbourne Herald,* 26 December 1908. Also see Rodney G. Boland, "Bedford, George Randolph (1868–1941)," in *Australian Dictionary of Biography—Online Edition,* Australian National University, 2006, www.adb.online.anu.edu.au/biogs/A110512b.htm (accessed 4 February 2007).

162. "Theatres &c.," *Australasian,* 9 January 1909.

163. Bedford, "White v. Black."

164. Stanhope, "The Colour Question," *Times,* 23 September 1911.

165. All quotations in this paragraph are from Jack McLaren, *My Odyssey: South Seas Adventure* (1925; Melbourne: Oxford University Press, 1946), 175.

166. "The Boxing Contest," *Sydney Morning Herald,* 1 January 1909.

167. "The Editor's Ideas," *Boxing,* 23 October 1909.

168. James J. Jeffries, "The Need of an Athletic Awakening," *Physical Culture,* May 1909, 397.

CHAPTER 2. WHITE CENSORS, DARK SCREENS

1. Hugh D. McIntosh, "The Pride of the Blacks," *Boxing*, 24 September 1910. Also see Yorick Gradeley, "Jim Jeffries—The Outdoor Man," *Health & Strength*, 7 May 1910; "The Big Fight," *Star*, 11 July 1910.

2. McIntosh, "Pride of the Blacks."

3. Daniel Streible, *Fight Pictures: A History of Boxing and Early Cinema* (Berkeley: University of California Press, 2008), 9, 195. Streible provides an in-depth history of early interracial fight films within a U.S. context.

4. See Michael Rogin, "The Sword Became a Flashing Vision: D. W. Griffith's *The Birth of a Nation*," *Representations* no. 9 (Winter 1985): 150-95; Michele Wallace, "The Good Lynching and The Birth of a Nation: Discourses and Aesthetics of Jim Crow," *Cinema Journal* 43, no. 1 (Fall 2003): 85–104.

5. Streible, *Fight Pictures*, 24–25.

6. "Pictures and Pugilism," *Moving Picture World*, 18 December 1909.

7. On urban industrialism and the rise of early film, see Charles Musser, *The Emergence of Cinema: The American Screen to 1907* (New York: Scribner, 1990); Eileen Bowser, *The Transformation of Cinema, 1907–1915* (New York: Scribner, 1990).

8. Streible, *Fight Pictures*, 9.

9. "The Great Fight," *Observer*, 2 January 1909.

10. Streible, *Fight Pictures*, 204.

11. "Le Match Tommy Burns—Jack Jackson à Paris," *La Vie au grand air*, 6 March 1909, 155. There was no mention of any racial conflict caused by the film in the French colonies.

12. Streible, *Fight Pictures*, 207.

13. Ibid., 205–6.

14. "Some Comments on the Championship Contest," *Boxing World and Athletic Chronicle*, 14 July 1910.

15. Georges Dupuy, "Le Grand match Johnson-Jeffries," *La Vie au grand air*, 23 July 1910.

16. Geoffrey Ward, *Unforgivable Blackness: The Rise and Fall of Jack Johnson* (New York: Knopf, 2004), 170.

17. Ibid., 189, 191; "Ministerial Opposition to the Jeffries-Johnson Fight," *Indianapolis Freeman*, 4 June 1910.

18. Streible, *Fight Pictures*, 218; "Pictures and Pugilism."

19. "World's Championship at Frisco—July 4," *Mirror of Life and Sport*, 18 June 1910.

20. Streible, *Fight Pictures*, 219.

21. "How They Brought the News from Reno," *Indianapolis Freeman*, 30 July 1910. Also see Ward, *Unforgivable Blackness*, 192–93. *La Vie au grand air* had even contracted the African American heavyweight Joe Jeannette to report on the fight from a black perspective. Dupuy, "Le Grand match Johnson-Jeffries."

22. "To Cover Big Fight," *Moving Picture World*, 9 July 1910. Also see Streible, *Fight Pictures*, 219.

23. Ward, *Unforgivable Blackness*, 198–199, 202.

24. Ibid., 203; "Procession to the Fight," *Dublin Evening Mail,* 5 July 1910.

25. "Gate Receipts $270,775," *Boston Daily Globe,* 6 July 1910.

26. Ward, *Unforgivable Blackness,* 208–11.

27. "Fight Pictures Now Being Printed," *Moving Picture World,* 16 July 1910.

28. Streible, *Fight Pictures,* 13; "The Fight Films," *Englishman,* 8 July 1910; "Heavy Telegraph Tolls," *Boston Daily Globe,* 6 July 1910.

29. "To You, Mr. Jack Johnson," *Savannah Tribune,* 9 July 1910.

30. All quotations in this paragraph are from "City Wild over Result," *Indianapolis Freeman,* 9 July 1910.

31. R. Desmarets, "Après le championnat du monde," *L'Auto,* 6 July 1910.

32. "Excitement in London," *Dublin Evening Mail,* 5 July 1910.

33. "Sequel to the Jeffries-Johnson Fight," *Times,* 6 July 1910.

34. John Maynard, "For Liberty and Freedom: Fred Maynard and the Australian Aboriginal Progressive Association," Lecture for New South Wales State Library, Sydney, 2004, 27.

35. "Fight Pictures Now Being Printed."

36. "Government Prohibits Prize-fight Pictures," *Globe,* 8 July 1910; "Film Men Will Wait," *Washington Post,* 9 July 1910; Streible, *Fight Pictures,* 235.

37. "Fake Fight Pictures Stopped in Theatre," *New York Times,* 10 July 1910.

38. See *Greatest Fights of the Century: Jack Johnson vs. Jim Jeffries* (1965). Held in the Motion Picture, Broadcasting & Recorded Sound Division, Library of Congress, this film is an abridged version of the 1910 Jeffries-Johnson fight film. Also see Ward, *Unforgivable Blackness,* 199–200.

39. "Show Jeffries Tried," *Washington Post,* 10 July 1910.

40. "Mr. Johnson Talks," *Moving Picture World,* 20 August 1910.

41. Tim Brooks, *Lost Sounds: Blacks and the Birth of the Recording Industry* (Urbana: University of Illinois Press, 2004), 244.

42. "A vous . . . touché!" *La Boxe et les boxeurs,* 1 February 1911.

43. *Moving Picture World,* 2 July 1910; "One Roosevelt Hunt Fails," *Moving Picture World,* 1 May 1909; "Pictures of the Roosevelt Hunt," *Moving Picture World,* 18 December 1909.

44. Gerald R. Gems, *The Athletic Crusade: Sport and American Cultural Imperialism* (Lincoln: University of Nebraska Press, 2006), 48; Streible, *Fight Pictures,* 129; Amy Kaplan, *The Anarchy of Empire in the Making of U.S. Culture* (Cambridge, MA: Harvard University Press, 2002), 146–64. Kaplan maintains that the films of the Spanish-American War laid the groundwork for the production style and great popularity of *Birth of a Nation.*

45. "Sheriff Ignores Fight Films," *Chicago Daily Tribune,* 21 August 1910.

46. Rev. H.F. Jackson, "The Moving Picture in Relation to the World," *Moving Picture World,* 16 July 1910. Emphasis in the original.

47. "Paying the Fiddler," *Moving Picture World,* 30 July 1910.

48. Quoted in "Governors Urged to Aid Crusade," *Boston Daily Globe,* 6 July 1910. Also see "Pictures of the Prize Fight," *Christian Endeavour Times,* 14 July 1910.

49. Theodore Roosevelt, "The Recent Prizefight," *Outlook,* 16 July 1910.

50. Streible, *Fight Pictures*, 222.

51. "Cities Prohibit Fight Pictures," *Chicago Daily Tribune*, 6 July 1910; "Censors Pass on Reno Fight Views," *Chicago Daily Tribune*, 9 July 1910; "Chicagoans May See Fight Films," *Chicago Daily Tribune*, 10 July 1910; "Governors Oppose Pictures," *New York Times*, 8 July 1910.

52. Maine and Iowa had already passed fight film bans in 1897 and 1908, respectively. "Pictures from Reno Must Not Be Shown," *Globe*, 7 July 1910; Streible, *Fight Pictures*, 205. Also see "More Cities to Bar Fight Pictures," *Chicago Daily Tribune*, 7 July 1910; "Hornet's Nest Stirred up by Fight Picture Men," *Los Angeles Times*, 7 July 1910; "Syndicate Will Invoke Law," *Washington Post*, 7 July 1910; "The Prize Fight Moving Pictures," *Outlook*, 16 July 1910.

53. "Frisco Bars Fight Pictures of Jeffries-Johnson Scrap," *Chicago Daily Tribune*, 12 July 1910; "Censors Pass on Reno Fight Views."

54. "Picture Men to Fight Ban," *New York Times*, 7 July 1910; "May Withdraw Fight Pictures," *Los Angeles Times*, 9 July 1910. The Patent Company had paid $200,000 for the film rights in the hopes that Jeffries would win the fight. Lee Grieveson, *Policing Cinema: Movies and Censorship in Early-Twentieth-Century America* (Berkeley: University of California Press, 2004), 125.

55. "Pictures from Reno Must Not Be Shown."

56. "Governors Urged to Aid Crusade"; W. Knight Chaplin, *People's Society of Christian Endeavour Year Book* (London: Andrew Melrose, 1898), 8; W. Knight Chaplin, *People's Society of Christian Endeavour Year Book* (London: Andrew Melrose, 1899), 5, 7.

57. "Francis Edward Clark," in *Dictionary of American Religious Biography*, ed. Henry Warner Bowden (Westport, CT: Greenwood Press, 1993), 114. Also see "The Open-Air Cure," *Christian Endeavour Times*, 7 July 1910; "Fatness a Vital Matter," *Christian Endeavour Times*, 7 July 1910; "Shapely and Beautiful," *Christian Endeavour Times*, 7 July 1910; "The Religious Outlook in America," *Christian Endeavour Times*, 14 July 1910.

58. "Pictures of the Prize Fight."

59. "The Johnson-Jeffries Pictures," *Boxing World and Athletic Chronicle*, 14 July 1910.

60. "Fistic Gossip," *Boxing World and Athletic Chronicle*, 21 July 1910; "Telegrams," *Barbados Globe and Colonial Advertiser*, 11 July 1910; "Fight Pictures in Dublin," *New York Times*, 21 August 1910.

61. "Blacks & Whites," *Cape Times*, 7 July 1910.

62. Truman Harte, "American News and Notes," *Boxing*, 16 July 1910. Also see "The Big Fight," *Daily Gleaner*, 7 July 1910; "After the Fight," *Cape Argus*, 6 July 1910.

63. For the most part, this interpretation of the racial violence could be found only in the African American press. See, for example, N. Barnett Dodson, "Johnson the Real Victor," *Baltimore Afro-American*, 16 July 1910; "Negro Press on the Fight," *Washington Bee*, 16 July 1910; "Views of the Afro-American Press on the Johnson-Jeffries Fight," *Baltimore Afro-American*, 16 July 1910.

64. "Jack Johnson in his Pride," *Boxing*, 16 July 1910.

65. "Prohibition of Pictures," *Times of Natal,* 8 July 1910.

66. "And Not a Friendly Port in Sight," *San Francisco Examiner,* 9 July 1910.

67. "Glorifying the Coon," *Sunday Times,* 10 July 1910; "Johannesburg Action," *Star,* 9 July 1910; "Pictures of the Fight," *Star,* 14 July 1910; "Union Government Instructions," *Cape Times,* 9 July 1910; "Reno Pictures Prohibited in the Union," *Star,* 14 July 1910. The Wesleyan Methodist Church in Johannesburg and Pretoria also publicly opposed the fight film. "A Wesleyan Protest," *Star,* 9 July 1910; "A Wesleyan Protest," *Rand Daily Mail,* 7 July 1910.

68. "The Fight Films."

69. George S.C. Swinton, "The Colour Problem," *Times,* 19 September 1911.

70. "Case of Jamaica: An Agitation to Be Started," *Daily Gleaner,* 9 July 1910.

71. "Race Riots in America," *Mirror of Life and Sport,* 9 July 1910.

72. "The Moving Pictures," *Cape Times,* 9 July 1910.

73. "Fight Rouses Race Feeling," *Globe,* 6 July 1910.

74. "New Brunswick Picture Protest," *Boston Daily Globe,* 16 July 1910; "Telegrams"; "Government Prohibits Prize-fight Pictures." The Ontario government used a 1909 act regarding patron safety in movie houses to institute its ban.

75. "Jack Johnson Is 'In Bad' in Berlin," *Boston Daily Globe,* 16 July 1910. This article is a reprint from the *New York World.*

76. "Bar Johnson from Berlin," *Los Angeles Times,* 17 July 1910. On black entertainers in Berlin, see Jan Nederveen Pieterse, *White on Black: Images of Africa and Blacks in Western Popular Culture* (New Haven, CT: Yale University Press, 1992), 137–38.

77. "Jack Johnson Has Won the Double Crown," *Indianapolis Freeman,* 30 July 1910.

78. "Knocked Out! Two Ways of Looking at It," *Punch,* 7 July 1910.

79. Quotations in this paragraph and the next are from "Demoralisation," *Times of Natal,* 6 July 1910.

80. *Savannah Tribune,* 9 July 1910.

81. William Pickens, "Talladega College Professor Speaks on Reno Fight," *Chicago Defender,* 30 July 1910.

82. "Rev. G.E. Bevens' Opinion of Johnson's Victory," *Baltimore Afro-American,* 16 July 1910.

83. "Lessons of the Prize Fight," *Cleveland Gazette,* 23 July 1910.

84. *Pittsburgh Solidarity* quoted in "The Fight at Reno," *Cleveland Gazette,* 23 July 1910.

85. "What a Folly," *Washington Bee,* 9 July 1910; Dodson, "Johnson the Real Victor."

86. "Strong Arm of the American Law," *Chicago Defender,* 30 July 1910. Also see W.H. Bates, "The People's Forum," *Baltimore Afro-American,* 23 July 1910; "Those Moving Pictures, Prize Fights and Lynching," *Cleveland Gazette,* 16 July 1910; "Captain John T. Campbell Writes on the Moving Pictures of the Jeffries and Johnson Fight," *Broad Ax,* 23 July 1910.

87. "The Aftermath of the Great Johnson and Jeffries Fight at Reno, Nevada," *Broad Ax,* 16 July 1910.

88. All quotations in this paragraph and the next are from "How Scotland Received the Results of the Fight," *Indianapolis Freeman,* 6 August 1910. Throughout the 1910s Leo Daniels was a frequent correspondent for the *Freeman,* providing readers with updates on the state of European race relations. He later became the secretary of a local black political organization called the African Races Association of Glasgow. Jacqueline Jenkinson, "Black Sailors on Red Clydeside: Rioting, Reactionary Trade Unionism and Conflicting Notions of 'Britishness' Following the First World War," *Twentieth Century British History* 19, no. 1 (2008): 53.

89. John D. Clair, "Praise for Champion Johnson from Far-Off Cuba," *Indianapolis Freeman,* 21 May 1910.

90. John D. Clair, "How Cuba Rejoiced Over Jack Johnson's Victory," *Indianapolis Freeman,* 6 August 1910.

91. Aline Helg, *Our Rightful Share: The Afro-Cuban Struggle for Equality, 1886–1912* (Chapel Hill: University of North Carolina Press, 1995), 3, 162.

92. "From the Far Off Philippines," *Chicago Defender,* 20 August 1912; "$101,000 Purse for the Fight Is Now Up," *Manila Times,* 4 July 1910; Gems, *Athletic Crusade,* 56; Paul Kramer, *Blood of Government: Race, Empire, the United States, and the Philippines* (Chapel Hill: University of North Carolina Press, 2006), 298.

93. Gems, *Athletic Crusade,* 50, 53–54.

94. "A través de siete días," *Renacimiento Filipino,* 11 July 1910.

95. Quotations in this paragraph and the next are from Pedro Quinto, "El bofeton de Reno," *Renacimiento Filipino,* 11 July 1910.

96. "The Physical Strength of Indians," *Abhyudaya,* 2 October 1910. Also see Satadru Sen, "Schools, Athletes and Confrontation: The Student Body in Colonial India," in *Confronting the Body: The Politics of Physicality in Colonial and Post-Colonial India,* ed. Satadru Sen and James H. Mills (London: Anthem, 2004), 70–72. Unless otherwise noted, all Indian quotations are taken from articles compiled in the microfilm collection of *Indian Newspaper Reports, c1868–1942 from the British Library, London* (Adam Matthew Publications).

97. *Arya Prakásh,* 10 July 1910; *Kesari,* 12 July 1910.

98. "The White's Antipathy to the Black and the Colour Line," *Gujaráti Punch,* 31 July 1910; *Arya Prakásh,* 10 July 1910.

99. *Arya Prakásh,* 10 July 1910; *Bhála,* 18 July 1910.

100. *Indian Spectator,* 16 July 1910.

101. "Blacks and Whites," *Hitvarta,* 14 July 1910. Also see "Whites v. Blacks," *Daily Hitavadi,* 8 July 1910.

102. *Bhála,* 18 July 1910.

103. *Gujaráti,* 10 July 1910.

104. "Fistiana: The Great Battle," *Sunday Times,* 10 July 1910.

105. "Jeffries-Johnson," *Cape Times,* 4 July 1910.

106. "A Letter for Home: Sports, Sales, and Society," *Sunday Times,* 10 July 1910.

107. Marilyn Lake and Henry Reynolds, *Drawing the Global Colour Line:*

White Men's Countries and the International Challenge of Racial Equality (Cambridge: Cambridge University Press, 2008), 210.

108. Quoted in Leonard Thompson, *A History of South Africa*, 3rd ed. (New Haven, CT: Yale University Press, 2000), 144. Thanks to Andrew Offenburger for sharing this reference with me.

109. "Transition Stage," *Times of Natal*, 9 July 1910. In 1906 the Zulus revolted against British rule in Natal. Unfair practices of colonial taxation had sparked the armed uprising. Sean Redding, "A Blood-Stained Tax: Poll Tax and the Bambatha Rebellion in South Africa," *African Studies Review* 43, no. 2 (2000): 29–54.

110. "Native Affairs Department," *Times of Natal*, 9 July 1910.

111. James T. Campbell, *Songs of Zion: The African Methodist Episcopal Church in the United States and South Africa* (New York: Oxford University Press, 1995), 112–13; Zine Magubane, "Mines, Minstrels, and Masculinity: Race, Class, Gender, and the Formation of the South African Working Class, 1870–1900," *Journal of Men's Studies* 10, no. 3 (2002): 283–84.

112. Campbell, *Songs of Zion*, 126–27, 139–40.

113. Ibid., 127–28, 131. Also see Louis Chude-Sokei, *The Last 'Darky': Bert Williams, Black-on-Black Minstrelsy, and the African Diaspora* (Durham, NC: Duke University Press, 2005), 146–47.

114. Quoted in Veit Erlmann, "'A Feeling of Prejudice': Orpheus M. McAdoo and the Virginia Jubilee Singers in South Africa, 1890–1898," *Journal of South African Studies* 14, no. 3 (1988): 344.

115. "Demoralisation."

116. "Bioscope Pictures of the Fight," *Rand Daily Mail*, 6 July 1910.

117. "Effects of Reno Fight: A Natal Indian's Views," *Times of Natal*, 8 July 1910.

118. "White, Black and Coloured," *Times of Natal*, 8 July 1910.

119. "The Kaffir House Boy," *Sunday Times*, 10 July 1910. Also see "Nothing to Joke About," *Transvaal Critic*, 20 October 1911; "White Servants for Black," *Transvaal Critic*, 24 December 1908.

120. Martin H. Wilmot, "The Prize Fight," *Rand Daily Mail*, 14 July 1910.

121. "The Kaffir House Boy."

122. Magubane, "Of Mines, Minstrels, and Masculinity," 279–80; Zine Magubane, "The Boundaries of Blackness: African American Culture and the Making of a Black Public Sphere in Colonial South Africa," in *Empires and Boundaries: Rethinking Race, Class, and Gender in Colonial Settings*, ed. Harald Fischer-Tiné and Susanne Gehrmann (New York: Routledge, 2009), 227.

123. Gradeley, "Jim Jeffries—The Outdoor Man." White colonials in India also defended white Americans' repressive response to the fight and its moving picture. See "The Fight Films."

124. Yorick Gradeley, "The Great Fight—And After," *Health & Strength*, 16 July 1910.

125. Ibid.

126. Lake and Reynolds, *Drawing the Global Colour Line*, 124–25, 129–33, 214–16, 226.

127. Quotations in this paragraph are taken from "Is the Black Man Our Brother?" *Health & Strength*, 30 July 1910.

128. Samuel Coleridge-Taylor (1875–1911) was a famed black British composer, while Charles Peace (1832–79) was a notorious English murderer and thief.

129. "'Health & Strength' Debating Club: The Black Man in Natal," *Health & Strength*, 29 October 1910.

130. "'Health & Strength' Debating Club: What South Africans Think of the Blacks," *Health & Strength*, 3 December 1910.

131. Streible, *Fight Pictures*, 235–37; "Observations by Our Man about Town," *Moving Picture World*, 6 August 1910; "Show Fight Films in Chicago," *Chicago Daily Tribune*, 5 August 1910; "Will Show Fight Films on River," *Washington Post*, 10 September 1910.

132. "Les Films interdits," *La Boxe et les boxeurs*, 13 July 1910. Although the French press had paid close attention to the violent aftermath of the interracial fight, no editorials or protests emerged in opposition to the moving picture.

133. "Le Film du match Jeffries-Johnson," *La Boxe et les boxeurs*, 16 November 1910; "Le Film Jeffries-Johnson," *La Boxe et les boxeurs*, 11 January 1911.

134. Streible, *Fight Pictures*, 237; F. H. Lucas, "Parisian News and Notes," *Boxing*, 20 August 1910; R. Rufenacht, "La Boxe à l'étranger—en Allemagne, à Berlin: Le film Jeffries-Johnson," *La Boxe et les boxeurs*, 8 February 1911; "Berlin Sees Fight Films," *New York Times*, 17 September 1911; "Berlin to See Fight Films," *New York Times*, 16 December 1911.

135. George M. Johnson, "The Recent Big Fight as London Papers See It," *Indianapolis Freeman*, 6 August 1910.

136. *Times* quoted in ibid.

CHAPTER 3. JACK JOHNSON VERSUS JOHN BULL

The second epigraph on p. 101 is from "Johnson-Wells Match: Action by Earl's Court Freeholders," *Times*, 25 September 1911.

1. Sylvester Russell, "Jack Johnson in London," *Chicago Defender*, 17 June 1911.

2. Johnson's insistence on traveling first class had caused much consternation in the white American dailies. See "Johnson Departs with Glad Rags," *Chicago Daily Tribune*, 5 June 1911; "Johnson in Liner Knockout," *Chicago Daily Tribune*, 6 June 1911; "Champion Sails First-Class," *Washington Post*, 6 June 1911; "Gems Light His Cabin," *Washington Post*, 8 June 1911. His defiance on the high seas also became legendary among black Americans, inspiring "The Titanic," a popular song by the blues artist Lead Belly (Huddie Ledbetter) that gave a fictional account of Johnson being turned away from the infamous ship of the same name.

3. Russell, "Jack Johnson in London."

4. "The 'Fight,'" *Daily Chronicle*, 28 September 1911. In a reversal of the usual trend in compensation, £6,000 (approximately $30,000) would go to the

African American Johnson and only £2,000 (around $10,000) to the Englishman Wells—win, lose, or draw.

5. Bernard Porter, *The Lion's Share: A Short History of British Imperialism, 1850–1995*, 3rd ed. (New York: Longman, 1996), 84–101, 234-35.

6. "Stop the Fight," *Daily Chronicle*, 20 September 1911.

7. *Times* quoted in George M. Johnson, "The Recent Big Fight as London Papers See It," *Indianapolis Freeman*, 6 August 1910.

8. On the importance of the U.S. "negro problem" in shaping British discussions of race and democracy, see Marilyn Lake and Henry Reynolds, *Drawing the Global Colour Line: White Men's Countries and the International Challenge of Racial Equality* (Cambridge: Cambridge University Press, 2008), 49–74.

9. "Johnson-Wells Fight: Heated Controversy, Strong Pulpit Denunciations," *Daily Telegraph*, 18 September 1911.

10. Jeffrey Green, "Boxing and the 'Colour Question' in Edwardian Britain: The 'White Problem' of 1911," *International Journal of the History of Sport* 5, no. 1 (1988): 119.

11. "Johnson-Wells Fight: Heated Controversy, Strong Pulpit Denunciations."

12. "Jack Johnson's Ruse," *New York Times*, 27 August 1911.

13. "Afro-American Cullings," *Savannah Tribune*, 17 June 1911; "Afro-American Cullings," *Cleveland Gazette*, 17 June 1911. Both newspapers reprinted this article from the *New York Amsterdam News*.

14. Booker T. Washington, "Atlanta Compromise Speech," 1895.

15. Later published as a book, this series of articles was ghostwritten by white sociologist Robert E. Park, who had accompanied Washington on his European tour. Booker T. Washington, *The Man Farthest Down: A Record of Observation and Study in Europe* (New York: Doubleday, Page & Co., 1912).

16. Ibid., 34–35.

17. "Afro-American Cullings," *Savannah Tribune*. Washington's remarks fell in line with contemporary discourses about the supposedly superior living conditions of colonial subjects versus those of Europe's working-class population. European politicians often used this rhetoric to convince their national governments to develop more programs for their own poverty-stricken citizens. For example, John Burns, the first working-class man to rise to the British Cabinet, made similar comparisons between the slums of London and the west coast of Africa. Washington, *Man Farthest Down*, 361–62.

18. Washington, *Man Farthest Down*, 81.

19. "Doings of the Race," *Cleveland Gazette*, 1 July 1911.

20. Russell, "Jack Johnson in London." Also see "A Splendid Testimonial," *Cleveland Gazette*, 7 October 1911; "Doings of the Race." Reportedly, nine African American soldiers had also participated in the coronation parade.

21. On Johnson's vaudeville success see "Jack Has Music Hall Engagements Galore," *Indianapolis Freeman*, 2 September 1911; "Johnson Is a Big Hit," *Washington Post*, 9 July 1911. On the Universal Races Congress see "For a Better Understanding between Races," *Baltimore Afro-American*, 24 June 1911; "The First Universal Races Congress," *Indianapolis Freeman*, 2 Decem-

ber 1911; "Race Prejudice Being Fought by Educators," *Cleveland Gazette,* 26 August 1911; "Universal Races Congress," *Cleveland Gazette,* 9 September 1911.

22. "Johnson Jabs Uncle Sam," *Washington Post,* 19 July 1911. For the original article see "Johnson Interviewed: His Views about America," *Dublin Evening Herald,* 5 July 1911.

23. "La Caricature à l'étranger: 'Johnson Will Be Some Noise at Coronation with Those Loud Clothes,'" *La Boxe et les boxeurs,* 31 May 1911.

24. "Mr. Johnson, Anglomaniac," *Washington Post,* 20 July 1911.

25. "Jim Jeffries Is Home Again," *Washington Post,* 12 July 1911. Jeffries had visited England, Scotland, Ireland, Germany, Italy, France, Denmark, Norway, and Sweden.

26. "Mr. Johnson, Anglomaniac."

27. "From Germany," *Cleveland Gazette,* 9 September 1911.

28. "American and Foreign Negroes Honored in Europe," *Chicago Defender,* 29 July 1911.

29. *Savannah Tribune,* 10 June 1911.

30. Quoted in Lester A. Walton, "In the World of Sport: Search for a 'White Hope,'" *New York Age,* 21 September 1911.

31. "White Hopes," *Baltimore Afro-American,* 30 September 1911; "Search for White Hope Abandoned," *Indianapolis Freeman,* 1 July 1911.

32. Edgar Wallace, "From Fogopolis," *Sunday Times,* 18 October 1911.

33. "Will the Championship Change Colour?" *Boxing,* 9 September 1911.

34. "What the Two Men Think," *Health & Strength,* 7 October 1911.

35. "The Bombardier's Future," *Boxing,* 26 November 1910; "The Editor's Ideas," *Boxing,* 29 July 1911; "Is Wells Reckless?" *Boxing,* 22 July 1911; "Johnson to Fight Bombadier *[sic]* Wells in September," *Indianapolis Freeman,* 12 August 1911.

36. Oswald Frederick Snelling, *White Hope: The Story of the Jack Johnson Era* (London: Pendulum Publications, 1947), 16–17.

37. See "The Search for a White Champion," Official Tournament Program, 19 October 1910, Box 2, Sports, John Johnson Collection of Printed Ephemera, Bodleian Library, Oxford University, Oxford, England.

38. Most scholars have tracked Anglo-American rapprochement through foreign policy. Paul Kramer, "Empires, Exceptions, and Anglo-Saxons: Race and Rule between the British and United States Empires, 1880–1910," *Journal of American History* 88, no. 4 (2002): 1315–53; Stuart Anderson, *Race and Rapprochement: Anglo-Saxonism and Anglo-American Relations, 1895–1904* (East Brunswick, NJ: Associated University Presses, 1981).

39. Yorick Gradeley, "The Great Fight—And After," *Health & Strength,* 16 July 1910.

40. Frank Morely, "The Search for a White Champion," *Boxing,* 13 August 1910.

41. "Big London Pavilion for Important Fights," *Los Angeles Times,* 21 July 1911; "Papke to Fight Sullivan," *New York Times,* 5 June 1911.

42. The first match of the series occurred at King's Hall on 15 September 1910. "The Search for a White Champion," *Boxing,* 17 September 1910.

43. "Boxers and Wrestlers," *New York Times*, 24 January 1911.

44. Snelling, *White Hope*, 76.

45. "Un Espoir blanc," *La Boxe et les boxeurs*, 6 September 1911; "E. Henry, l'espoir blanc du Professeur Cuny," *La Boxe et les boxeurs*, 11 October 1911.

46. "Race Riot at Pittsburgh," *Globe*, 5 July 1910. Although the article claims that blacks "invaded" the Russian Quarter, this seems unlikely since most of the riots stemmed from white attacks on black Americans.

47. Other white American hopes included the German-Americans Al Kaufmann, Al Palzer, and Gunboat Smith (Edward Eckblad), the Italian-American journeyman Tony Ross (Antonio Rossilano), and the Irish-Americans Jim Barry, Sandy Ferguson, and Frank Moran. Snelling, *White Hope*, 32, 38, 46.

48. Frank Morely, "Where Is the Man to Beat Johnson?" *Boxing*, 30 July 1910.

49. "Boxing Clubs Plan for a Busy Week," *New York Times*, 22 May 1911; "Few White Hopes Show Up," *New York Times*, 11 August 1911; "Fireman Jim Flynn Whips Carl Morris," *New York Times*, 16 September 1911; "White Hopes Fizzle at Century Club," *New York Times*, 5 August 1911.

50. Randy Roberts, *Papa Jack: Jack Johnson and the Era of White Hopes* (New York: Free Press, 1983), 81–84, 131–37; Geoffrey Ward, *Unforgivable Blackness: The Rise and Fall of Jack Johnson* (New York: Knopf, 2004), 160–65, 281–83.

51. Trevor Wignall, *Story of Boxing* (New York: Brentano's, 1924), 257.

52. "Johnson to Do Barn Storming," *Los Angeles Times*, 16 July 1911; "Johnson-Bombadier [sic] Wells Fight Sure to Take Place," *Indianapolis Freeman*, 19 August 1911.

53. "In a Pugilistic Trust," *Washington Post*, 24 July 1911.

54. "Johnson to Do Barn Storming."

55. "Johnson-Wells Fight Picture Rights Important," *Indianapolis Freeman*, 16 September 1911.

56. "Home Rush from Paris," *New York Times*, 3 September 1911.

57. "The Black 'King' of the Pugilists," *Daily Chronicle*, 21 September 1911.

58. "Mons. Jaques [sic] D'Arthur Johnson," *Boxing World and Athletic Chronicle*, 28 September 1911.

59. On Johnson's resistance to training, obsession with clothes, and decadent eating habits, see "Jack Johnson, in Splendid Condition, Commences His Preparation for Bombardier Wells," *Boxing*, 2 September 1911; "Jack Johnson's Sudden Alarm," *Boxing*, 16 September 1911; "A Few Incidents of Johnson's Serious Preparation in Paris," *Boxing*, 16 September 1911.

60. "La Caricature à l'étranger: 'Boxing One of Most Popular Sports in France Just Now,'" *La Boxe et les boxeurs*, 7 June 1911.

61. Chester Mann, *F. B. Meyer: Preacher, Teacher, Man of God* (London: George Allen & Unwin, 1929), 20, 149–58.

62. Rev. F. B. Meyer, "The Dishonour of Manhood," *Health & Strength*, 4 April 1908.

63. "Johnson-Wells Match: An Appeal from the Pulpit," *Times*, 16 September 1911. The National Free Church Council was a breakaway association of

English churches that did not conform to Anglican doctrines. They used the Wells-Johnson protest to help raise their profile on the national scene.

64. "Johnson-Wells Match: Negotiations Broken Off," *Times*, 22 September 1911.

65. "Johnson-Wells Match: An Appeal from the Pulpit."

66. "Johnson-Wells Fight: Bishop of London's Protest," *Daily Telegraph*, 21 September 1911.

67. "Johnson-Wells Match: Mr. Churchill's Decision," *Times*, 26 September 1911.

68. Archbishop of Canterbury to Home Secretary Winston Churchill, 16 September 1911, "ENTERTAINMENTS: Boxing. Conditions under which contests are illegal. Law Officers' Opinion. 1911," Home Office Records 45/10487/110912, National Archives, London, England. HO (Home Office Records) and BNA (British National Archives) will be used in subsequent notes.

69. Ward, *Unforgivable Blackness*, 269. Also see "Will the Fight Be Stopped?" *Daily Chronicle*, 20 September 1911; "Protests Against the Match," *Daily Chronicle*, 21 September 1911; "To Stop the Fight," *Daily Chronicle*, 22 September 1911. For a more detailed discussion of the reaction in Britain, see Patrick McDevitt, *May the Best Man Win: Sport, Masculinity, and Nationalism in Great Britain and the Empire, 1880–1935* (New York: Palgrave Macmillan, 2004), 75–78.

70. "'Colour Feeling,' 'Times' Wants It Stopped in Interests of the Empire," *Daily Chronicle*, 20 September 1911.

71. "The Johnson-Wells Match," *Times*, 29 September 1911.

72. "The Primate and the Johnson-Wells Match," *Daily Telegraph*, 20 September 1911; "Our Note Book: Black Peril in the Prize-ring," *South African News*, 26 September 1911.

73. "Black v. White: South Africa against the Fight," *Daily Chronicle*, 22 September 1911; "Wells-Johnson Fight: Great Organized Protest," *South African News*, 21 September 1911.

74. "The Colour Question and the Fight," *Times*, 26 September 1911.

75. "Johnson Fight Stirs Clergy in England," *New York Times*, 24 September 1911.

76. Quoted in Ward, *Unforgivable Blackness*, 268.

77. "Will the Fight Be Stopped?"

78. Quoted in "Black v. White: South Africa against the Fight."

79. "Johnson-Wells Match: Attitude of the Owners of Earl's Court," *Times*, 23 September 1911.

80. "White Servants for Black," *Transvaal Critic*, 24 December 1908. Some believed that they should abandon this custom by replacing black male servants with white female servants.

81. Gareth Cornwell, "George Webb Hardy's *The Black Peril* and the Social Meaning of 'Black Peril' in Early Twentieth-Century South Africa," *Journal of Southern African Studies* 22, no. 3 (1996): 441–53; Timothy Keegan, "Gender, Degeneration and Sexual Danger: Imagining Race and Class in South Africa, ca. 1912," *Journal of Southern African Studies* 27, no. 3 (2001): 459–

77. For contemporary critiques see "The 'Black Peril' In South Africa," *African Times and Orient Review,* July 1912; "Black Peril: The Native View," *African Times and Orient Review,* October 1912; "The Black Peril: Mrs. MacFadyen's Appeal at the Races Congress," *South African News,* 19 September 1911. On the white American persecution of Johnson against the backdrop of antimiscegenation hysteria see Kevin Mumford, *Interzones: Black/White Sex Districts in Chicago and New York in the Early Twentieth Century* (New York: Columbia University Press, 1997), 3–18.

82. "What Readers Say: The So-called 'Black Peril,'" *South African News,* 26 September 1911.

83. "Our Note Book: Black Peril in the Prize-ring."

84. Jock McCulloch, *Black Peril, White Virtue: Sexual Crime in Southern Rhodesia, 1902–1935* (Bloomington: University of Indiana Press, 2000), 20–21. On 20 December 1910 Gladstone commuted the death sentence of Alukuleta, an African houseboy who was convicted of raping Bessie Comer in Southern Rhodesia (Zimbabwe). Alukuleta still had to serve a life sentence.

85. "Our Note Book: Black Peril in the Prize-ring."

86. "Legal Action to Stop the Fight," *Daily Chronicle,* 25 September 1911.

87. "The Rev. F. B. Meyer Interviewed," *Boxing,* 30 September 1911.

88. "The Editor Talks: Shall Boxing Be Abolished?" *Health & Strength,* 23 September 1911. Also see "What the Parsons Think of the Wells-Johnson Match," *Health & Strength,* 30 September 1911.

89. "The Editor's Ideas," *Boxing,* 30 September 1911.

90. "Johnson-Wells Fight Is Denounced in London," *Indianapolis Freeman,* 7 October 1911.

91. "No Fight in London," *Indianapolis Freeman,* 14 October 1911.

92. *Cleveland Gazette,* 7 October 1911.

93. "Johnson Is 'In Bad' in 'Dear Old England,'" *Indianapolis Freeman,* 18 November 1911. Also see "Jack Johnson in Bad," *Indianapolis Freeman,* 9 December 1911.

94. Sir John Simon, "Wells-Johnson Fight," 1911, HO 45/10487/110912, BNA.

95. Ward, *Unforgivable Blackness,* 267.

96. "Johnson-Wells Fight Picture Rights Important"; "Prize Fight Films," *Transvaal Critic,* 13 October 1911.

97. "Summonses for Fighters," *New York Times,* 27 September 1911.

98. "Johnson-Wells Match: Action by Earl's Court Freeholders."

99. "Johnson-Wells Match: Mr. Churchill's Decision."

100. "The 'Fight.'"

101. "Johnson-Wells Match: Summonses Against the Principals," *Times,* 28 September 1911.

102. "The 'Fight.'"

103. "Johnson-Wells Match: Injunction Against Earl's Court Company," *Times,* 28 September 1911.

104. "The Boxing Match," *Times,* 29 September 1911.

105. F. H. Lucas, "Parisian News and Notes," *Boxing,* 30 September 1911.

106. Leon Sée, "A propos d'une interdiction," *La Boxe et les boxeurs,* 4 October 1911.

107. Jacques Mortane, "Se Rencontreront-ils?" *La Vie au grand air,* 7 October 1911, 675.

108. "What the Two Men Think."

109. *Cleveland Gazette* quoted in "Some Higher Criticism; Or, Philosophy of the Fight That Failed," *Indianapolis Freeman,* 25 November 1911.

110. "Fight Didn't Go," *Indianapolis Freeman,* 7 October 1911.

111. "English Race Prejudice and Jack Johnson," *New York Age,* 5 October 1911.

112. "Some Higher Criticism."

113. Quotations in this paragraph and the next are from "English Race Prejudice and Jack Johnson."

114. "Some Higher Criticism."

115. Jeffrey Green, *Black Edwardians: Black People in Britain, 1901–1914* (London: Frank Cass Publishers, 1998), 178.

116. Wignall, *Story of Boxing,* 258.

117. "Lift the Colour Bar," [1947], British boxing: Colour Bar 1947, Colonial Office Records 876/89, BNA.

118. J.M. Batchman, "Prize Fighting and Prize Fighters," *Indianapolis Freeman,* 23 December 1911.

119. Lord Lonsdale to Frank McKenna, 16 March 1913, "ENTERTAINMENTS : Boxing. Contests between coloured men and white men," 1912–25, HO 45/11880, BNA.

120. Lord Lonsdale to Frank McKenna, 29 April 1914, HO 45/11880, BNA.

121. Frank McKenna to Lord Lonsdale, 1 May 1914, HO 45/11880, BNA.

122. "Black-and-White Boxing: Necessity of a 'Colour Line,'" *Morning Post,* 4 May 1914.

123. F.H. Lucas, "Should Coloured Boxers Be Ostracised?" *Boxing,* 30 May 1914.

124. "Snowy Baker's Search for an Aboriginal Hope," *Boxing,* 21 March 1914.

125. "Black and White in the Boxing Ring," *African Times and Orient Review,* 12 May 1914.

126. "Should Coloured Boxers Be Ostracised?" Known primarily as a wrestler in Europe, Crozier had taken up boxing in Paris in the 1910s with moderate success.

CHAPTER 4. THE BLACK ATLANTIC FROM BELOW

1. *Jack Johnson, In the Ring—and Out* (1927; New York: Citadel Press, 1992), 23.

2. Ibid., 25, 71, 101.

3. Ibid., 71.

4. Ibid., 126–27.

5. Geoffrey Ward, *Unforgivable Blackness: The Rise and Fall of Jack Johnson* (New York: Knopf, 2004), 298; Kevin Mumford, *Interzones: Black/White*

Sex Districts in Chicago and New York in the Early Twentieth Century (New York: Columbia University Press, 1997), 11.

6. Mumford, *Interzones*, 7, 10–12, 17. For a comprehensive treatment of the Mann Act, see David J. Langum, *Crossing over the Line: Legislating Morality and the Mann Act* (Chicago: University of Chicago Press, 1994).

7. "Jack Johnson's Case," *Indianapolis Freeman*, 17 May 1913.

8. Billy Lewis, "Jack Johnson Brought Down to Date," *Indianapolis Freeman*, 18 January 1913.

9. "Champ Jack up against the Wall," *Indianapolis Freeman*, 14 June 1913.

10. Johnson, *In the Ring—And Out*, 85.

11. Dr. M. A. Majors, "Jack Johnson Is Crucified for His Race," *Chicago Defender*, 5 August 1913.

12. Gary Edward Holcomb, *Claude McKay, Code Name Sasha: Queer Black Marxism and the Harlem Renaissance* (Gainesville: University Press of Florida, 2007), 25.

13. *Mirror of Life and Boxing World*, 19 July 1913. Also see Ward, *Unforgivable Blackness*, 348.

14. On the various efforts to prevent African American and Afro-Caribbean immigration into Canada in the early 1900s, see Sarah-Jane Mathieu, *North of the Color Line: Migration and Black Resistance in Canada, 1870-1955* (Chapel Hill: University of North Carolina Press, 2010), 22-60.

15. Billy Lewis, "Jack Johnson Cannot Enter Canada," *Indianapolis Freeman*, 22 March 1913.

16. "Jack Johnson Outwits His Uncle Sam," *New York Age*, 10 July 1913.

17. Ward, *Unforgivable Blackness*, 348-49.

18. "Jack Johnson Outwits His Uncle Sam"; Billy Lewis, "Jack Johnson Making History," *Indianapolis Freeman*, 5 July 1913.

19. Paul Gilroy, *The Black Atlantic: Modernity and Double Consciousness* (Cambridge, MA: Harvard University Press, 1993), 58.

20. A. F. Bettinson and W. Outram Tristram, eds., *The National Sporting Club: Past and Present* (London: Sands & Co., 1902), 53, 228.

21. Nat Fleischer, *Black Dynamite*, 5 vols., vol. 4, *"Fighting Furies": Story of the Golden Era of Jack Johnson, Sam Langford and their Negro Contemporaries* (New York: C. J. O'Brien, 1938), 228.

22. "Famous Coloured Quartette who Rule the Roast," *Boxing*, 12 August 1911. Also see Leon Sée, "Quadrille nègre," *La Boxe et les boxeurs*, 24 December 1913.

23. "A Bit of Langford's Early Days," *Boxing*, 4 December 1909. Also see Fleischer, *Black Dynamite*, 125–26.

24. Craig Lloyd, *Eugene Bullard: Black Expatriate in Jazz-Age Paris* (Athens: University of Georgia Press, 2000), 14–15.

25. Bullard's autobiography quoted in ibid., 16.

26. Fleischer, *Black Dynamite*, 126–27.

27. "A Bit of Langford's Early Days."

28. Joe Jeannette, "That World's Title," in *Boxing New Year's Annual 1914* (London, 1914).

29. Bob Scanlon, "The Record of a Negro Boxer," in *Negro: An Anthology,* ed. Nancy Cunard (1935; New York: Frederick Unger Publishing, 1970), 208.

30. Lloyd, *Eugene Bullard,* 33.

31. Ibid., 22–28.

32. Fleischer, *Black Dynamite,* 122, 126–27, 170–71.

33. Ibid., 173–74, 195. There are conflicting reports of McVea's hometown and year of birth. See Tracy Callis, International Boxing Research Organization, "Sam McVea" (3 September 2006), www.cyberboxingzone.com/boxing/mcvea-s.htm (accessed 20 September 2006).

34. See, for example, E. Desbonnet, "Mais Mac Vea troubla la fête," *La Boxe et les boxeurs,* 5 April 1911; "Joe Jeannette, automobiliste," *La Vie au grand air,* 21 March 1914, 267; Georges Dupuy, "Le Tigre et le bison," *L'Auto,* 21 February 1909; "Joe Jeannette et sa petite famille," *La Boxe et les boxeurs,* 7 January 1914.

35. "Billy McClain on Automobiling," *Indianapolis Freeman,* 18 November 1911; "Negro Fighters in the Old World," *Indianapolis Freeman,* 9 September 1911.

36. Lester A. Walton, "In the World of Sport: MacVea Showers Praise on MacClain," *New York Age,* 14 September 1911; "Billy MacClain Returns Home," *Chicago Defender,* 6 August 1912. On McClain's stage career, see Errol G. Hill and James V. Hatch, *A History of African American Theatre* (Cambridge: Cambridge University Press, 2005), 132–34.

37. "Billy MacClain Returns Home."

38. Claude McKay, *A Long Way from Home: An Autobiography* (London: Pluto Press, 1985), 231.

39. Quotations in this paragraph are from Jack Johnson, "Mes malheurs," *La Boxe et les boxeurs,* 16 July 1913. For the translation, see "French Board of Trade Honors Jack Johnson and Wife," *Chicago Defender,* 9 August 1913. The version in the *Defender* contains some errors but still maintains the basic meaning of Johnson's speech.

40. "Jack Johnson to Return October 1st," *Chicago Defender,* 12 August 1913. Also see Ward, *Unforgivable Blackness,* 352.

41. Cary B. Lewis, "Editor, R.S. Abbott to Go Abroad," *Indianapolis Freeman,* 18 April 1914.

42. "London Rejoices Over Colored Mayor and Mayoress," *Chicago Defender,* 29 November 1913.

43. See "Beauty of Paris," *Chicago Defender,* 19 July 1913; "Ghent Historic Old Town," *Chicago Defender,* 19 July 1913. For other examples of travel and lifestyle articles on Europe, see "Great Avenue Safe," *Washington Bee,* 9 July 1910; "Europe's Highest Village," *Washington Bee,* 16 July 1910; "This Queen Works," *Washington Bee,* 16 July 1910; "A Lapland Wedding," *Savannah Tribune,* 16 August 1913; "Travel in the Cotswolds," *Chicago Defender,* 6 September 1913; "In London," *Savannah Tribune,* 23 August 1913; "Bolden's Trip Abroad," *New York Age,* 17 July 1913.

44. "Chicago Defender Covers the World," *Chicago Defender,* 20 August 1912.

45. "Chicago Defender Sold in Europe," *Chicago Defender,* 15 November 1913.

46. Leo W. Daniels, "The Negro Is a World Question," *Indianapolis Freeman,* 17 January 1914.

47. Leo W. Daniels, "What They Think of Us Abroad," *Indianapolis Freeman,* 17 January 1914.

48. Ibid.

49. Jan Nederveen Pieterse, *White on Black: Images of Africa and Blacks in Western Popular Culture* (New Haven, CT: Yale University Press, 1992), 176.

50. "Une Publication sensationelle," *La Vie au grand air,* 14 January 1911, 21. Because of his somewhat limited French language skills, Johnson likely dictated or wrote out his memoirs for a French ghostwriter/translator.

51. Jack Johnson, *Mes Combats* (Paris: Pierre Lafitte & Co., 1914). There is now an English translation of this book, Jack Johnson, *My Life and Battles,* trans. Chris Rivers (Westport, CT: Praeger Publishers, 2007). Johnson's first English autobiography, *In the Ring—And Out,* did not appear until 1927.

52. Billy Lewis, "Preparing for the Big Scrap," *Indianapolis Freeman,* 13 June 1914.

53. McKay's works, *Banjo* and *A Long Way from Home,* have emerged as two of the most examined texts of early twentieth-century black American, particularly working-class, travel. Michelle Stephens, *Black Empire: The Masculine Global Imaginary of Caribbean Intellectuals in the United States, 1914–1962* (Durham, NC: Duke University Press, 2005), 129–203; Brent Edwards, *The Practice of Diaspora: Literature, Translation, and the Rise of Black Internationalism* (Cambridge, MA: Harvard University Press, 2003), 187–240. *Banjo* describes the multiracial working-class environment of the French port city of Marseilles, while McKay's autobiography traces his own international wanderings. Claude McKay, *Banjo: A Story without a Plot* (1929; New York: Harvest Books, 1970); McKay, *A Long Way from Home.*

54. Jack Johnson, "Ma Vie et mes combats," *La Vie au grand air,* 21 January 1911, 47.

55. Johnson also expressed his diasporic pride by hanging a wall-size picture of a black Cleopatra in his Chicago nightclub, the Café du Champion. Davarian Baldwin, *Chicago's New Negroes: Modernity, the Great Migration, and Black Urban Life* (Chapel Hill: University of North Carolina Press, 2007), 81, 199.

56. Johnson, "Ma Vie et mes combats," 21 January 1911, 47. On Theodore Roosevelt's ideas of the "strenuous life," see Gail Bederman, *Manliness and Civilization: A Cultural History of Gender and Race in the United States, 1880–1917* (Chicago: University of Chicago Press, 1995), 170–215.

57. Johnson, "Ma Vie et mes combats," 21 January 1911, 48.

58. Ibid; Johnson, "Ma Vie et mes combats," 4 February 1911, 79.

59. Johnson, "Ma Vie et mes combats," 28 January 1911, 64.

60. Johnson, "Ma Vie et mes combats," 18 February 1911, 114.

61. Johnson, "Ma Vie et mes combats," 4 March 1911, 146.

62. Elisa F. Glick, "The Dialectics of Dandyism," *Cultural Critique* 48 (Spring 2001): 131; Elisa F. Glick, "Harlem's Queer Dandy: African-American

Modernism and the Artifice of Blackness," *Modern Fiction Studies* 49, no. 3 (2003): 414.

63. Martin Summers, *Manliness and Its Discontents: The Black Middle Class and the Transformation of Masculinity, 1900–1930* (Chapel Hill: University of North Carolina Press, 2004), 151–53.

64. Johnson, "Ma Vie et mes combats," 18 February 1911, 114.

65. Johnson, "Ma Vie et mes combats," 29 April 1911, 275. *La Vie au grand air* printed the English verse and then translated it for readers.

66. Ironically, Kipling was one of Johnson's favorite poets. Ward, *Unforgivable Blackness*, 329.

67. "French Board of Trade." For photos of Johnson in the French press, see "M. et Mme Jack Johnson se plaisent fort chez Maitrot," *La Boxe et les boxeurs*, 6 August 1913; "Le Napoléon de la boxe," *La Boxe et les boxeurs*, 13 August 1913; "Jack Johnson, à son passage à Lyon," *La Boxe et les boxeurs*, 3 September 1913; "Jack Johnson et sa femme," *Excelsior*, 28 August 1913.

68. Billy Lewis, "England after Heavyweight Title," *Indianapolis Freeman*, 10 January 1914.

69. Johnson, *In the Ring—And Out*, 89.

70. Billy Lewis, "Jack Johnson in Paris," *Indianapolis Freeman*, 9 August 1913.

71. "French Board of Trade."

72. Ibid.

73. Lewis, "Preparing for the Big Scrap."

74. Lewis, "Jack Johnson in Paris."

75. "Jack Johnson to Appear in London," *Times*, 20 August 1913. Other reports claimed that he would earn $2,500 a week. See Lester A. Walton, "Theatrical Comment," *New York Age*, 4 September 1913.

76. "Johnson Ignores Protests," *New York Times*, 25 August 1913.

77. "The Americanisation of England," *African Times and Orient Review*, May 1913.

78. "Barred by Colour," *African Times and Orient Review*, May 1913. Also see "Color Line Drawn in Great Britain," 23 September 1913, Reel 2, 334, Tuskegee Clippings File, Division of Behavioral Science Research, Carver Research Foundation, Tuskegee Institute, Alabama (Sanford NC: Microfilming Corporation of America, 1981).

79. "African Students in London," *African Times and Orient Review*, May 1913.

80. "Strange Doings in London Town," *New York Age*, 10 July 1913. Also see "Prejudice Grows in London," *New York Age*, 3 July 1913.

81. Billy Lewis, "Jack Johnson in Paris, Says He Will Stick," *Indianapolis Freeman*, 19 July 1913.

82. *Dawson News* (Georgia), 16 September 1908, quoted in Lloyd, *Eugene Bullard*, 29. The population figures also come from this article.

83. "Got the 'Black Scare,'" *Indianapolis Freeman*, 15 March 1913.

84. Jeffrey Green, *Black Edwardians: Black People in Britain, 1901–1914* (London: Frank Cass Publishers, 1998), 1–14, 80–137.

85. Harry Reynolds, *Minstrel Memories: The Story of Burnt Cork Min-*

strelsy in Great Britain from 1836 to 1927 (London: Alston Rivers, 1928), 17, 70; Peter Fryer, *Staying Power: The History of Black People in Britain* (London: Pluto Press, 1984), 443.

86. Lloyd, *Eugene Bullard*, 30. Also see Reynolds, *Minstrel Memories*, 9.

87. Lester A. Walton, "Hooray for the British," *New York Age,* 10 July 1913.

88. Billy Lewis, "England Disappointing," *Indianapolis Freeman,* 6 September 1913.

89. "The Arena: Welsh Criticism," *African Times and Orient Review,* August 1912.

90. Fryer, *Staying Power,* 294–95. Unemployed black seamen could also be found in Newport, Barry, Liverpool, Hull, Tyneside, and Glasgow.

91. "The Arena: Welsh Criticism."

92. *Evening Standard* quoted in "Contesting the Negro's Right to Exist," *Indianapolis Freeman,* 22 March 1913.

93. "Negro Invasion Feared," *Atlantic Advocate,* 11 January 1913.

94. "The Dark Side of the White Hope Problem," in *Boxing New Year's Annual 1914* (London, 1914).

95. "Penny Plain and Twopence Coloured," in *Boxing New Year's Annual 1913* (London, 1913).

96. See "Miscegenation Abroad Excites No Comment," *Baltimore Afro-American,* 9 July 1910. This report used the marriage of Prince Dhuleep Singh, the eldest son of the maharaja of Lahore, to Lady Anne Coventry, the daughter of the Earl of Coventry, as an example of British racial tolerance.

97. "Contesting the Negro's Right to Exist."

98. Walton, "Theatrical Comment."

99. *Times,* 27 August 1913, quoted in Ward, *Unforgivable Blackness,* 350.

100. "Object to Jack Johnson," *New York Times,* 20 August 1913. The ban did not affect Johnson's engagements in Ireland and Scotland.

101. "Likely to Bar Johnson," *New York Times,* 22 August 1913.

102. "Jack Johnson's Engagement," *Times,* 23 August 1913.

103. "A Queensberry Revises an Indictment," *New York Times,* 27 August 1913.

104. "Johnson Upsets London Music Hall," *New York Times,* 26 August 1913. Also see "Cheer Jack Johnson in London Theaters," *Indianapolis Freeman,* 6 September 1913.

105. "Champion Jack Johnson Lionized in London," *Chicago Defender,* 30 August 1913.

106. *Era,* a London-based theatrical weekly, quoted in "Johnson at Euston," *New York Age,* 18 September 1913.

107. "Champion Jack Johnson Lionized in London."

108. "Johnson Upsets London Music Hall."

109. "Champion Jack Johnson Lionized in London."

110. Lewis, "England Disappointing."

111. Ward, *Unforgivable Blackness,* 352–53; Randy Roberts, *Papa Jack: Jack Johnson and the Era of White Hopes* (New York: Free Press, 1983), 190–91.

112. Pieterse, *White on Black,* 137–38.

113. "Johnson to Fight Moran and Pelkey," *Chicago Defender*, 4 October 1913.

114. "University of Budapest Entertains Jack Johnson," *Chicago Defender*, 15 November 1913.

115. "Ernest Stevens Visits Jack Johnson in Paris," *Chicago Defender*, 25 April 1914.

CHAPTER 5. TRADING RACE

1. "Ernest Stevens Visits Jack Johnson in Paris," *Chicago Defender*, 25 April 1914.

2. Ibid; Geoffrey Ward, *Unforgivable Blackness: The Rise and Fall of Jack Johnson* (New York: Knopf, 2004), 358.

3. Jacques Mortane, "Tous les nègres en Europe," *La Vie au grand air*, 9 May 1908, 292. Several scholars have noted the difficulty of translating the French word *nègre* into its English equivalent. Despite its visual similarity to "negro," *nègre* in the early 1900s was still a derogatory term whose meaning was likely closer to that of the word *nigger*. Since the word *nègre* appears most frequently in boxing publications that used colloquial language, I have chosen to translate it as "nigger." See Brent Edwards, *The Practice of Diaspora: Literature, Translation, and the Rise of Black Internationalism* (Cambridge, MA: Harvard University Press, 2003), 25–38; Jack Johnson, *My Life and Battles*, trans. Chris Rivers (Westport, CT: Praeger Publishers, 2007), xv–xvi.

4. "French Call Fight a Fake Unless a Knock-out Ends It," *Washington Post*, 19 February 1911.

5. French newspaper reports corroborate this story of African American independence. McVea took his white manager to court and then took over the management of his own affairs. "Sam Mac Vea devant le tribunal," *L'Auto*, 28 March 1909; "Sam Mac Vea manager," *L'Auto*, 15 October 1909.

6. "A vous . . . touché!" *La Boxe et les boxeurs*, 29 March 1911. Also see Claude Meunier, *Ring noir: Quand Apollinaire, Cendrars et Picabia découvraient les boxeurs nègres* (Paris: PLON, 1992), 39.

7. Michel Fabre, "The Ring and the Stage: African Americans in Parisian Public and Imaginary Space before World War I," in *Space in America: Theory, History, Culture*, ed. Klaus Benesch and Kerstin Schmidt (Amsterdam: Rodopi, 2005), 524.

8. "Why Black Men Favor France," *New York News*, [12] August 1914.

9. On the French civilizing mission in this period, see Alice L. Conklin, *A Mission to Civilize: The Republican Idea of Empire in France and West Africa, 1895–1930* (Stanford, CA: Stanford University Press, 1997).

10. Shawn Michelle Smith's critical analysis of the French praise for W. E. B. Du Bois's photographic exhibition of the American Negro at the Paris Exposition in 1900 exposes the same interimperial dynamic. Shawn Michelle Smith, *Photography on the Color Line: W. E. B. Du Bois, Race, and Visual Culture* (Durham, NC: Duke University Press, 2004).

11. See "La Caricature à l'étranger: 'Boxing One of Most Popular Sports in France Just Now,'" *La Boxe et les boxeurs*, 7 June 1911. A reprint from a

Notes to Pages 167–171 | 299

New York newspaper, this cartoon lampooned French sports fans for their fascination with black boxers.

12. I borrow the term "contact zone" from Mary Louise Pratt, *Imperial Eyes: Travel Writing and Transculturation* (New York: Routledge, 1992), 6–7.

13. Boxing manuals acquainted French fans with the basics of boxing technique and training, the Queensberry rules, the history of the ring, and the current championship scene. See Jacques Mortane and André Linville, *La Boxe* (Paris: Pierre Lafitte, 1908); Fernand Cuny, *La Boxe* (Paris: Éditions Nilsson, [1910]).

14. J. Delcroix, "Le 'Wonderland' français," *L'Education physique,* 31 December 1907.

15. See Jacques Mortane, "Les Critériums de boxe anglaise," *La Vie au grand air,* 19 January 1907, 48–49; Jacques Mortane, "Le Critérium international de boxe," *La Vie au grand air,* 26 January 1907, 53; Jacques Mortane, "Le Critérium de boxe," *La Vie au grand air,* 26 January 1907, 63; "Le Critérium de boxe," *La Vie au grand air,* 2 February 1907, 82; Jacques Mortane, "Tournois de boxe à Paris," *La Vie au grand air,* 19 October 1907, 275.

16. Much of the literature on African American performers and artists in France still focuses on the interwar years. Brett Berliner, *Ambivalent Desire: The Exotic Black Other in Jazz-Age France* (Amherst: University of Massachusetts Press, 2002); William Shack, *Harlem in Montmartre: A Paris Jazz Story between the Great Wars* (Berkeley: University of California Press, 2001); Tyler Stovall, *Paris Noir: African Americans in the City of Light* (New York: Houghton Mifflin, 1996).

17. Sieglinde Lemke, *Primitivist Modernism: Black Culture and the Origins of Transatlantic Modernism* (New York: Oxford University Press, 1998). Lemke describes primitivist modernism as a hybrid, multiracial, and transatlantic cultural formation.

18. On the American method, see Marc Gaucher, "Les Méthodes anglais et américaines," *La Vie au grand air,* 29 February 1908, 122–23; Mortane and Linville, *La Boxe,* 61–66. On the popularity of chewing gum, see "La Boxe gaie," *La Boxe et les boxeurs,* 29 December 1909. On American fashion, see "Mac Nab, American Tailor, 131, rue Montmartre," *La Boxe et les boxeurs,* 26 November 1913.

19. Jody Blake, *Le Tumulte noir: Modernist Art and Popular Entertainment in Jazz-Age Paris, 1900–1930* (University Park: Pennsylvania State University Press, 1999), 15, 37–38; Fabre, "The Ring and the Stage," 526, 528.

20. Jacques Mortane, "Athlétisme: un beau combat de boxe," *La Vie au grand air,* 11 January 1908, 26.

21. "Race Suicide in France," *Savannah Tribune,* 16 January 1909; C. C. Pagés, "Dégénérons-nous?" *La Culture physique,* 15 March 1910; E. Desbonnet, "Un grand défaut nationale," *La Santé par les sports,* 8 January 1913; Rene DuBois, "The French Nation Dying Out," *Physical Culture,* December 1908.

22. Sylvie Chalaye, *Nègres en images* (Paris: L'Harmattan, 2002), 110–11; Berliner, *Ambivalent Desire,* 9–10.

23. Charles Mangin, *La Force noire* (Paris: Hachette, 1910), 355.

24. Ibid., 343.

25. Chalaye, *Nègres en images*, 99–101; Blake, *Le Tumulte noir*, 23–25. Also see Jean-Michel Bergougniou, '*Villages noirs' et autres visiteurs africains et malgaches en France et en Europe, 1870–1940* (Paris: Karthala, 2001); Dana S. Hale, *Races on Display: French Representations of Colonized Peoples, 1886–1940* (Bloomington: Indiana University Press, 2008).

26. Henri Dispan, "Au fil des rounds: au Cirque de Paris," *La Boxe et les boxeurs*, 5 April 1911.

27. Louis Chude-Sokei, *The Last 'Darky': Bert Williams, Black-on-Black Minstrelsy, and the African Diaspora* (Durham, NC: Duke University Press, 2005), 124–25.

28. Chalaye, *Nègres en images*, 103; Hale, *Races on Display*, 91–96; Berliner, *Ambivalent Desire*, 9–36.

29. "Après le match—Sen-Sen chewing gum," *L'Auto*, 28 March 1909.

30. Blake, *Le Tumulte noir*, 11–36.

31. Segonzac quoted in Meunier, *Ring noir*, 35–36.

32. L. Manaud, "Un véritable championnat du monde," *L'Auto*, 6 January 1909.

33. "Comment s'entraînent Jeannette et Mac Vea," *L'Auto*, 12 February 1909.

34. See, for example, "Les deux terribles nègres s'entraînent avec ardeur," *L'Auto*, 15 January 1909.

35. L. Manaud, "Joe Jeannette au travail," *L'Auto*, 9 January 1909. Also see Jacques Mortane, "Joe Jeannette à l'entraînement," *La Vie au grand air*, 13 February 1909, 106–7.

36. "Les deux terribles nègres s'entraînent avec ardeur."

37. G. Dubois, "Leurs mensurations," *L'Auto*, 18 February 1909; "Silhouettes des combattants," *L'Auto*, 20 February 1909.

38. "Les grands combats de boxe," *L'Auto*, 14 January 1909; "Joe Jeannette contre Sam Mac Vea: Joe Jeannette à Paris," *L'Auto*, 8 January 1909; Mich, "Joe Jeannette ne trouve plus d'adversaires!" *L'Auto*, 29 January 1909; Mich, "Les grands champions," *L'Auto*, 1 February 1909. Mich's caricature of Jeannette shows the black fighter squaring off against a bucking horse.

39. Regarding his race, Jeannette wrote in a British sporting magazine, "Although I have been called a Canadian, I was born in Hoboken, N.J., of a white mother. I am the happy father of two children, also begot of white blood, so that we are none of us of the race known as 'niggers.'" "That World's Title," in *Boxing New Year's Annual 1914* (London, 1914), 43. While one could argue that Jeannette expressed an alarming level of racial self-hatred, his marketing of himself as a "mulatto" fighter certainly played into the prevailing narratives of whiteness and civilization in Europe, where the one-drop rule was less applicable than in the United States.

40. "Les deux terribles nègres s'entraînent avec ardeur." (Another newspaper claimed that there were more than five thousand people in attendance. "L'Opinion de la presse," *L'Auto*, 22 February 1909.) "Une grande soirée pugilistique," *L'Auto*, 21 February 1909; "Le grand match de samedi prochain," *L'Auto*, 17 February 1909; "Le Chiffre de la recette," *L'Auto*, 22 February 1909; *L'Auto*, 16 January 1909.

41. *La Patrie* quoted in "L'Opinion de la presse"; Georges Dupuy, "Le

Tigre et le bison," *L'Auto*, 21 February 1909; "A Coups de confetti," *L'Auto*, 24 February 1909.

42. *La Vie illustrée* quoted in "Après le grand match: que dit-on de la rencontre?" *L'Auto*, 23 February 1909.

43. J. Joseph-Renaud, "Un cinématographe? . . . !" *L'Auto*, 24 February 1909; Tristan Bernard, "Après le grand match: Sam et Joe," *L'Auto*, 22 February 1909.

44. "Les Jaloux," *L'Auto*, 3 March 1909.

45. Marcel Prévost of *Figaro* quoted in "L'Opinion de la presse."

46. "La Revanche aura lieu!" *L'Auto*, 30 March 1909.

47. Georges Dupuy, "Sam Mac Vea contre Joe Jeannette: après le grand match," *L'Auto*, 19 April 1909; Meunier, *Ring noir*, 33–34.

48. Segonzac quoted in Meunier, *Ring noir*, 35–36.

49. "Après le grand match: Impressions d'un monsieur chauve," *L'Auto*, 20 April 1909.

50. Tristan Bernard, "Le plus beau combat," *L'Auto*, 19 April 1909.

51. "Joe Jeannette—Sam Mac Vea," *L'Auto*, 8 December 1909.

52. "Lettres du kangourou boxeur," *L'Auto*, 14 December 1909.

53. "Au Cirque de Paris—match nul," *La Boxe et les boxeurs*, 15 December 1909.

54. *Le plein air*, 7 April 1911.

55. For descriptions of Grognet's school, see L. Manaud, "Le Rendez-vous des combattants," *L'Auto*, 30 September 1909; L. Manaud, "Maitres et champions: un grand établissement sportif à Paris," *L'Auto*, 16 September 1909.

56. *La Boxe et les boxeurs*, 22 December 1909; "A vous . . . touché !" *La Boxe et les boxeurs*, 15 December 1909.

57. Leon Sée, "Casse = Cou! Il ne faut pas que les nègres continuent," *La Boxe et les Boxeurs*, 1 June 1910.

58. "Les Sports et la politique," *L'Auto*, 1 March 1909.

59. Billy Lewis, "The War Has Broken up the Fight Game in Europe," *Indianapolis Freeman*, 12 September 1914.

60. Billy Lewis, "Jack Johnson in Paris, Says He Will Stick," *Indianapolis Freeman*, 19 July 1913.

61. Fabre, "The Ring and the Stage," 525.

62. Chalaye, *Nègres en images*, 106.

63. Henri Dispan, "Au fil des rounds," *La Boxe et les boxeurs*, 17 December 1913.

64. Gaston Mauvières, "La Gala de l'hippodrome," *Les Sports*, 15 March 1909.

65. Gaston Mauvières, "La Soirée de l'hippodrome," *Les Sports*, 22 March 1909.

66. Fabre, "The Ring and the Stage," 522.

67. Gus Muller, "Anecdote: souvenirs d'Amérique," *La Boxe et les boxeurs*, 15 April 1914. Also see Charles Ledoux, "Impressions d'Amérique," *La Boxe et les boxeurs*, 8 January 1913. This serial story recounted the French boxer's travels across the United States.

68. Muller, "Anecdote: souvenirs d'Amérique."

69. Ibid.

70. *Les Nègres contre Peaux-Rouges* (Paris: A. Eichler, 1913). This book was part of a French-language series of U.S. frontier stories.

71. "Le Retour de Major Taylor," *La Vie au grand air,* 27 April 1907, 279.

72. F.H. Lucas, "A Few Quaint Anecdotes and Curious Remarks of Well Known Boxers," *Boxing,* 13 June 1914.

73. L. Manaud, "Le dernier grand match de boxe de la saison," *L'Auto,* 26 June 1909.

74. L. Manaud, "Jim Barry disqualifié," *L'Auto,* 27 June 1909.

75. "Au Wagram boxing club: Bob Scanlon contre Charlie Hitte," *Les Sports,* 7 April 1910.

76. Henri Dispan, "Au fil des rounds," *La Boxe et les boxeurs,* 20 April 1910.

77. F.H. Lucas, "Parisian News and Notes," *Boxing,* 17 February 1912.

78. Bob Scanlon, "The Record of a Negro Boxer," in *Negro: An Anthology,* ed. Nancy Cunard (1934; New York: Frederick Ungar Publishing, 1970), 209.

79. "From Pit Boy to Champion Boxer," *Boxing,* 30 May 1914.

80. F.H. Lucas, "The French Boxer of To-day," in *Boxing New Year's Annual 1913* (London, 1913).

81. Daniel Rivoire, "Georges Carpentier contre Joe Jeannette," *Le Journal,* 21 March 1914. Also see L. Cams, "Un grand combat de boxe: Georges Carpentier contre Joe Jeannette," *L'Eclair,* 21 March 1914.

82. Joseph Galtier, "Propos de Paris," *Excelsior,* 22 March 1914.

83. "Le Match Carpentier—Joe Jeannette," *Excelsior,* 20 March 1914.

84. "Carpentier et Joe Jeannette seront sur le ring," *L'Auto,* 16 March 1914.

85. F.H. Lucas, "Carpentier Wins His Fight against Jeannette, but Loses the Verdict," *Boxing,* 28 March 1914.

86. "La Combat de l'année," *L'Auto,* 8 March 1914; Fighter, "Le grand combat de Carpentier," *L'Auto,* 17 March 1914; "Georges Carpentier contre Joe Jeannette," *L'Auto,* 5 March 1914; "Attention aux faux billets," *L'Auto,* 18 March 1914.

87. "A Few Mems on the Carpentier-Jeannette Contest," *Boxing,* 28 March 1914; "A vous . . . touché!" *La Boxe et les boxeurs,* 25 March 1914.

88. "Lettres d'un habitué du ring," *L'Auto,* 25 March 1914.

89. "A Few Mems on the Carpentier-Jeannette Contest."

90. Lucas, "Carpentier Wins His Fight against Jeannette, but Loses the Verdict." Also see Ch. A. Bernard, "Après le match: impressions d'un spectateur," *L'Intransigéant,* 23 March 1914.

91. Georges Dubujadoux, "Un grand soir," *La Boxe et les boxeurs,* 25 March 1914.

92. Daniel Rivoire, "Carpentier a battu aux points par Joe Jeannette," *Le Journal,* 22 March 1914; "A Few Mems on the Carpentier-Jeannette Contest."

93. "A vous . . . touché!" 25 March 1914; Leon Sée, "Le Match Carpentier = Jeannette," *La Boxe et les boxeurs,* 25 March 1914.

94. Daniel Cousin, "Joe Jeannette bat Carpentier," *La Presse,* 23 March 1914; "Apres le match Carpentier–Joe Jeanette," *L'Auto,* 23 March 1914; "A Few Mems on the Carpentier-Jeannette Contest."

95. F.H. Lucas, "Parisian News and Notes," *Boxing,* 25 April 1914

96. Jacques Mortane, "Joe Jeannette a battu Carpentier," *La Vie au grand air*, 28 March 1914.

97. Billy Lewis, "Interest in Sport Increasing in France," *Indianapolis Freeman*, 21 February 1914.

98. "The Editor's Ideas," *Boxing*, 4 July 1914.

99. "The Editor's Ideas," *Boxing*, 23 May 1914.

100. "The Editor's Ideas," *Boxing*, 27 June 1914; Georges Lefèvre, "L'Histoire d'un étudiant de Pittsburg," *L'Auto*, 16 June 1914.

101. "Toute l'Amérique espère en Frank Moran," *L'Auto*, 11 June 1914.

102. Ibid.

103. "Pour le championnat du monde toutes catégories," *L'Auto*, 24 June 1914.

104. Jacques Mortane, "Jack Johnson est-il toujours Jack Johnson?" *Excelsior*, 22 June 1914.

105. "Pour le championnat du monde toutes catégories"; "Dans neuf jours, le championnat du monde sera peut-être un blanc," *L'Auto*, 19 June 1914; "Le combat Jack Johnson–Frank Moran," *Excelsior*, 21 June 1914.

106. "L'Amérique espère, mais Jack Johnson 'a le sourire,'" *L'Auto*, 12 June 1914.

107. "Pour le championnat du monde toutes catégories"; "Jack Johnson contre Frank Moran," *L'Auto*, 18 June 1914.

108. *Indianapolis Freeman*, 4 July 1914.

109. "Jack Johnson demeure champion," *L'Auto*, 28 June 1914; F.H. Lucas, "Jack Johnson Retains His Title, but Moran Covers Himself with Glory," *Boxing*, 4 July 1914

110. Billy Lewis, "Jack Johnson Still in Evidence," *Indianapolis Freeman*, 29 August 1914.

111. "Bout Seemed Amateurish," *New York Times*, 28 June 1914. Also see J. Murray, "Johnson-Moran Impressions and an Answer to the Great Ladies Question," *Boxing*, 4 July 1914.

112. Colette, "Le Journal de Colette: Le 'chiqué,'" *Le Matin*, 2 July 1914.

113. "Bout Seemed Amateurish."; Lucas, "Jack Johnson Retains His Title, but Moran Covers Himself with Glory."

114. "Jack Johnson Still in Evidence," *Indianapolis Freeman*, 8 August 1914.

115. "Bout Seemed Amateurish."

116. Lewis, "Jack Johnson Still in Evidence."

117. *Chicago Defender*, 4 July 1914.

118. "Jack Johnson Still Master of 'White Hopes'," *New York Age*, 9 July 1914.

119. "Jack Johnson a Marvel," *New York Amsterdam News*, 3 July 1914.

120. Lewis, "Jack Johnson Still in Evidence."

121. Lewis, "The War Has Broken up the Fight Game in Europe."

122. "Johnson in the Eye's [sic] of Paris & General Public," *Indianapolis Freeman*, 16 May 1914.

123. Lewis, "The War Has Broken up the Fight Game in Europe."

124. "Jack Johnson Retains Championship without Extending Himself," *Philadelphia Tribune*, 4 July 1914.

125. Ward, *Unforgivable Blackness*, 362.

126. Quoted in *Indianapolis Freeman*, 3 October 1914.

127. "Jack Johnson Made Colonel of French Regiment," *Chicago Defender*, 8 August 1914.

128. Quoted in Ward, *Unforgivable Blackness*, 364.

129. On Scanlon's military service, see "Colored Boxer, French Lieutenant," *New York Amsterdam News*, 8 January 1915; "With the French Legion," *Chicago Defender*, 29 September 1917. On Bullard's war record, see Craig Lloyd, *Eugene Bullard: Black Expatriate in Jazz-Age Paris* (Athens: University of Georgia Press, 2000), 38–71.

130. Henri Dispan, "Au fil des rounds," *La Boxe et les boxeurs*, 28 January 1914.

131. "Johnson Eludes U.S. Offices," *Guardian*, 26 September 1914. Agents from the Department of Justice had reportedly followed Johnson to London hoping to apprehend him. Johnson always maintained that he had bribed U.S. officials during his escape in 1913, and a conspiracy to bribe was an extraditable offense in Britain.

132. Billy Lewis, "Jack Johnson Not a Citizen of France," *Indianapolis Freeman*, 3 October 1914.

133. Allison Blakely, "The Negro in Imperial Russia: A Preliminary Sketch," *Journal of Negro History* 61, no. 4 (1976): 355–56. For positive assessments of Russian race relations, see J. Bruce Grit, "Negro Poet of Royal Lineage," *Baltimore Afro-American*, 5 June 1909; "Negro Soldiers for French Army," *Baltimore Afro-American*, 21 August 1909.

134. "The Russian Mote and the Southern Beam," *Baltimore Afro-American*, 1 November 1913; "They Appeal to the Csar of Russia," *Baltimore Afro-American*, 27 January 1912. The *Baltimore Afro-American* had even noted that the conservative Russian newspaper *Novoe vremya* had used the antiblack riots in the wake of the Johnson's 1910 victory over Jeffries to argue for the inevitability of race prejudice, thereby justifying their own bloody campaigns against the Jews. "Foreign View of Race Prejudice," *Baltimore Afro-American*, 24 September 1910.

135. Jack Johnson, *In the Ring—And Out* (1927; New York: Citadel Press, 1992), 92–93. An African American jockey named Jimmy "Wink" Winkfield recalled that Johnson had arrived in the midst of the wartime festivities at Russia's racetracks. Ed Hotaling, *Wink: The Incredible Life and Epic Journey of Jimmy Winkfield* (New York: McGraw-Hill, 2005), 146.

136. Ward, *Unforgivable Blackness*, 363.

137. *Washington Post*, 26 August 1914.

138. "Jack Johnson Made Colonel of French Regiment."

CHAPTER 6. VIVA JOHNSON!

The English translation of the chapter epigraph is taken from Richard V. McGehee, "The Dandy and the Mauler in Mexico: Johnson, Dempsey, *et al.*, and the Mexico City Press, 1919–1927," *Journal of Sport History* 23, no. 1 (1996): 25.

1. By examining both formal and informal interventions in countries throughout the Caribbean, Latin America, Asia, and Africa, scholars have uncovered the many facets of U.S. influence abroad in this period. See, for example, Emily Rosenburg, *Financial Missionaries to the World: The Politics and Culture of Dollar Diplomacy* (Cambridge, MA: Harvard University Press, 1999); Louis Pérez Jr., *On Becoming Cuban: Identity, Nationality, and Culture* (New York: HarperCollins, 1999); Gilbert Joseph, Catherine LeGrand, and Ricardo Salvatore, eds., *Close Encounters of Empire: Writing the Cultural History of U.S.–Latin American Relations* (Durham, NC: Duke University, 1998); Gerald R. Gems, *The Athletic Crusade: Sport and American Cultural Imperialism* (Lincoln: University of Nebraska Press, 2006).

2. Daniel Fridman and David Sheinin, "Wild Bulls, Discarded Foreigners, and Brash Champions: US Empire and the Cultural Constructions of Argentine Boxers," *Left History* 12, no. 1 (2007): 54.

3. "Spanish a Popular Language," *Chicago Defender*, 13 February 1913.

4. "Chicago Woman Leads Fashion," *Chicago Defender*, 8 November 1913. Also see "Around and About Chicago," *Chicago Defender*, 10 October 1914.

5. "Brazil Welcomes Afro-Americans," *Chicago Defender*, 14 March 1914.

6. "Col. Marshall Accepts South American Military Post," *Chicago Defender*, 4 April 1914.

7. George Reid Andrews, "Race versus Class Association: The Afro-Argentines of Buenos Aires, 1850–1900," *Journal of Latin American Studies* 11, no. 1 (1979): 19–39; George Reid Andrews, "The Afro-Argentine Officers of Buenos Aires Province, 1800–1860," *Journal of Negro History* 64, no. 2 (1979): 85–100.

8. Robert G. Rodriguez, *The Regulation of Boxing: A History and Comparative Analysis of Policies among American States* (Jefferson, NC: McFarland & Company, 2009), 166–67. Also see "Buenos Aires," *Chicago Defender*, 12 December 1914; "Jack Johnson in South America," *Chicago Defender*, 12 December 1914.

9. Jack Johnson, *In the Ring—And Out* (1927; New York: Citadel Press, 1992), 97.

10. "Young Grand Pre Enjoys Buenos Aires," *Chicago Defender*, 8 May 1915. Grand Pre then left Buenos Aires, traveling to San Francisco by way of Ceylon, China, and Japan.

11. Willard's measurements are taken from "Johnson in Fine Form," *Chicago Defender*, 3 April 1915. For more on Jess Willard, see Graeme Kent, *The Great White Hopes: The Quest to Defeat Jack Johnson* (Gloucestershire: Sutton Publishing, 2005), 205–10; Geoffrey Ward, *Unforgivable Blackness: The Rise and Fall of Jack Johnson* (New York: Knopf, 2004), 365–66.

12. "Gibson to Bid for Jack Johnson Bout," *New York Times*, 5 January 1915. The negotiators included John McKee of Cincinnati, representing Curley Brown of the Havana racing interests; James Coffroth, representing interests in Tijuana; a representative of a Juárez syndicate; and Billy Gibson, who held the official Cuban government license for organizing fights in Havana.

13. "Johnson to Fight Willard in Mexico," *New York Times*, 9 January

1915. Born Doroteo Arango, Francisco "Pancho" Villa was a key leader in the Mexican Revolution against Porfirio Díaz's dictatorial regime. Villa's work on behalf of Mexico's peasants made him a popular hero in his homeland and an infamous figure around the world. See Friedrich Katz, *The Life and Times of Pancho Villa* (Stanford, CA: Stanford University Press, 1998).

14. Reverends Perry J. Rice, Wesley Webdell, and J.F. Williams to Secretary William Jennings Bryan, 13 January 1915, RG 59, 812.4066, National Archives, College Park, MD. In subsequent notes NARA will refer to the National Archives in College Park.

15. Ibid.

16. JRB and JBB (Office of the Solicitor) to Mr. Hitch, 21 January 1915, RG 59, 812.4066, NARA. Also see Robert Lansing, Counselor for the Secretary of State to Reverends Perry J. Rice, Wesley Webdell, and J.F. Williams, 27 January 1915, RG 59, 812.4066, NARA.

17. "Jack Johnson's Pleasant Visit to Barbados," *Chicago Defender,* 13 March 1915.

18. "Madam Walker Sails for Cuba," *Chicago Defender,* 29 November 1913; "Mound City Happenings," *Chicago Defender,* 25 April 1914.

19. Louis Martin Sears, "Frederick Douglass and the Mission to Haiti, 1889–1891," *Hispanic American Historical Review* 21, no. 2 (1941): 222–38; Daniel Brantley, "Black Diplomacy and Frederick Douglass' Caribbean Experiences, 1871 and 1889–1891: The Untold History," *Phylon* 45, no. 3 (1984): 197–209.

20. "American Influence Abroad," *Chicago Defender,* 26 March 1910.

21. On 28 July 1915 the United States invaded Haiti and began its nineteen-year occupation of the black nation. The U.S. military worked to install a puppet leader and pushed through a new constitution to make Haiti more amenable to foreign investment. African American journalists and intellectuals commented on this imperial conquest at length. See Mary Renda, *Taking Haiti: Military Occupation and the Culture of U.S. Imperialism, 1915–1940* (Chapel Hill: University of North Carolina Press, 2001); Brenda Gayle Plummer, *Haiti and the United States: The Psychological Moment* (Athens: University of Georgia Press, 1992); Henry Lewis Suggs, "The Response of the African American Press to the United States Occupation of Haiti, 1915–1934," *Journal of African American History* 87, no. 1 (2002): 70–82; Brenda Gayle Plummer, "The Afro-American Response to the Occupation of Haiti, 1915–1934," *Phylon* 43, no. 2 (1982): 125–43; Rayford Logan, "James Weldon Johnson and Haiti," *Phylon* 32, no. 4 (1971): 396–402.

22. "Jack Johnson Visits Barbados," *Barbados Globe and Colonial Advertiser,* 8 February 1915. Also see "Jack Johnson Is on His Way to Mexico," *Chicago Defender,* 27 February 1915.

23. "Jack Johnson's Pleasant Visit to Barbados."

24. The *Barbados Globe* described the man as a Demeraran named Stanley. "Jack Johnson's Exhibition," *Barbados Globe and Colonial Advertiser,* 10 February 1915.

25. "Jack Johnson Scores Victory in Barbados," *Chicago Defender,* 20 March 1915.

26. "Jack Johnson Visits Barbados"; Johnson, *In the Ring—And Out*, 199.

27. "Would Bar Jack Johnson," *New York Times*, 14 January 1915. Venustiano Carranza, one of the leaders of the Mexican Revolution, later became the president of Mexico in the post–Porfirio Díaz Mexican Republic. However, several factions, from reactionary landowners to the revolutionary forces of Emiliano Zapata and Francisco "Pancho" Villa, continued to dispute Carranza's leadership.

28. "Jack Johnson Sailing to Cuba," *New York Times*, 12 February 1915; "Slim Chance for Johnson to Fight," *New York Times*, 23 February 1915.

29. Pérez, *On Becoming Cuban*, 175; Gems, *Athletic Crusade*, 92.

30. "Havana Center of Boxing," *New York Times*, 1 January 1915.

31. "Gibson to Bid for Jack Johnson Bout." Also see "Interest in Boxing Grows," *Havana Daily Post*, 8 February 1915.

32. On white American interest in Cuba as a space of play, see Rosalie Schwartz, *Pleasure Island: Tourism and Temptation in Cuba* (Lincoln: University of Nebraska Press, 1997).

33. "The Fight in Cuba," *New York Times*, 3 February 1915.

34. Gems, *Athletic Crusade*, 93.

35. "The Fight in Cuba."

36. "Both Gladiators Are Confident of Victory," *Havana Daily Post*, 20 February 1915; "M'Vea Wins over Jim Johnson in 20 Rounds," *Havana Daily Post*, 21 February 1915.

37. On battle royals, see "Wednesday Night March 24 at the Stadium," *Havana Daily Post*, 23 March 1915; "Sweeney-M'Coy Saturday Night," *Havana Daily Post*, 2 April 1915; "'Knockout' Sweeney to Battle Al Mc Coy," *Havana Daily Post*, 3 April 1915.

38. Willard B. Gatewood, *Black Americans and the White Man's Burden, 1898–1903* (Urbana: University of Illinois Press, 1975), 17–19, 24–25, 30.

39. Ibid., 27, 62, 162, 164, 167.

40. See "Returns from Cuba," *Chicago Defender*, 4 May 1912; "Personal Mention," *Chicago Defender*, 2 November 1912; "Dr. Booker T. Washington and Dr. George C. Hall to Make Long Trip," *Chicago Defender*, 27 January 1912; "Sail for Africa and Cuba," *Chicago Defender*, 16 December 1911; "Mother Frances of Oblate Sisters Visits Chicago," *Chicago Defender*, 4 July 1914. Also see Lisa Brock and Digna Castañeda Fuertes, eds., *Between Race and Empire: African Americans and Cubans before the Cuban Revolution* (Philadelphia: Temple University Press, 1998); Frank Guridy, *Forging Diaspora: Afro-Cubans and African Americans in a World of Empire and Jim Crow* (Chapel Hill: University of North Carolina Press, 2010).

41. "A Queen of Song Elated over Cuba," *Chicago Defender*, 23 March 1912. Also see "Through Cuba with Madame Hackley," *Chicago Defender*, 13 April 1912. On Hackley's life, see Lisa Brevard, *A Biography of E. Azalia Smith Hackley: African-American Singer and Social Activist* (Lewiston, NY: Edwin Mellen Press, 2001).

42. "Cuba at Letts," *Chicago Defender*, 23 March 1912. Also see "Prominent Men Going to Cuba," *Chicago Defender*, 10 February 1912. African

American businesswomen were also traveling to Cuba in this period. See "Only Lady Manufacturer," *Chicago Defender*, 31 August 1912.

43. "Cuba in Throes of Revolt," *Chicago Defender*, 25 May 1912; "Cuban Revolt Seems Over," *New York Times*, 2 July 1912; "Revolt Bloodless to Cuban Troops," *New York Times*, 28 June 1912.

44. *Philadelphia Tribune* quoted in David J. Hellwig, "The African-American Press and United States Involvement in Cuba, 1902–1912," in *Between Race and Empire: African Americans and Cubans before the Cuban Revolution*, ed. Lisa and Digna Castañeda Fuertes Brock (Philadelphia: Temple University Press, 1998), 79. The *Washington Bee* reported on the potential barring of nonwhite immigrants.

45. Aline Helg, *Our Rightful Share: The Afro-Cuban Struggle for Equality, 1886–1912* (Chapel Hill: University of North Carolina Press, 1995), 3–6, 92.

46. Ibid., 146–47.

47. Ibid., 17–18, 194–226. Also see Aline Helg, "Black Men, Racial Stereotyping, and Violence in the U.S. South and Cuba at the Turn of the Century," *Comparative Studies in Society and History* 42, no. 3 (2000): 576–604.

48. "Annexing Cuba," *Chicago Defender*, 21 February 1914.

49. "Johnson at Havana," *New York Times*, 22 February 1915.

50. Jack Johnson, "Creo que vencere a Willard," *Diario de la Marina*, 21 March 1915.

51. "Johnson Agrees on Welch as Referee," *New York Times*, 26 March 1915.

52. "Johnson vs. Willard," *Havana Daily Post*, 24 March 1915.

53. Thanks to Brian Herrera for sharing his analysis of the racial implications of Johnson's fight in New Mexico.

54. Helg, *Our Rightful Share*, 16. Also see Alejandra Bronfman, *Measures of Equality: Social Science, Citizenship, and Race in Cuba, 1902–1940* (Chapel Hill: University of North Carolina Press, 2005).

55. "President of Cuba to See Big Fight," *New York Times*, 2 April 1915.

56. G. W. Krick, "Stadium Stabs," *Havana Daily Post*, 3 April 1915; "A las 12:30 p.m.," *La Lucha*, 5 April 1915.

57. "President of Cuba to See Big Fight."

58. "El Match Willard-Jhonson [sic]," *Diario de la Marina*, 31 March 1915.

59. Runyon quoted in Ward, *Unforgivable Blackness*, 376.

60. "Big Heavyweights in Cuba Sized Up," *New York Times*, 4 April 1915. Also see "La Guardia Rural," *Diario de la Marina*, 4 April 1915. The Rural Guard planned to have eight hundred horsemen in place to preserve the peace.

61. Quoted in Ward, *Unforgivable Blackness*, 375.

62. "Jack Johnson's Wife in Fight," *Los Angeles Times*, 26 March 1915.

63. See the correspondence between W. N. King and William Gonzales, 17 April to 7 May 1915, RG 84, 840.6, NARA. Although Gonzales admitted that reports of the incident had been "somewhat exaggerated," he agreed to pass along the group's money to Valdez.

64. *New York Sun*, 27 February 1915, quoted in Lester A. Walton, "The Cuban Negro," *New York Age*, 4 March 1915. Cushman Albert Rice was born in 1872 in Willmar, Minnesota. An officer in the Spanish-American War, he

later became one of the foremost Americans in Cuba, where he owned several cattle ranches. See Dan Hardy, "Cushman Rice: The Man who was Gatsby," *Writing in the Margins* (Spring 2008), www.stthomas.edu/english/margins/archives/Spring08%20WITM.pdf (accessed 24 August 2010).

65. Ibid.

66. "Big Heavyweights in Cuba Sized Up."

67. "Jack Johnson Is Favorite in Coming Fight," *Chicago Defender,* 27 March 1915.

68. "Menocal Rebukes Fight Gamblers," *New York Times,* 3 April 1915; Signor Pareada, "Vanderbilt Backs Champion to Win," *Chicago Defender,* 3 April 1915. Gonzales had warned President Menocal about the reports of his bet on Johnson in U.S. newspapers. Menocal then dispatched a statement denying the rumors to the Associated Press. See the statement dated 3 April in RG 84, 840.6, NARA.

69. "32,000 at Fight," *New York Times,* 7 April 1915; Herbert Swope, "Johnson Knockout Dramatic Climax to Battle," *Chicago Daily Tribune,* 6 April 1915; "Little Betting on Fight," *New York Times,* 6 April 1915.

70. Damon Runyon quoted in Ward, *Unforgivable Blackness,* 377.

71. "32,000 Saw the Fight," *La Lucha,* 6 April 1915; "W.A. Gaines Returns from Georgia Trip," *Chicago Defender,* 17 April 1915; Johnson, "Creo que vencere a Willard."

72. Swope, "Johnson Knockout Dramatic Climax to Battle."

73. Ibid. In this context the term "yellow" meant coward.

74. "Cowboy Wins Battle When Jack Weakens," *Chicago Daily Tribune,* 6 April 1915. For a summary of the fight, see Ward, *Unforgivable Blackness,* 377–79.

75. "The Downfall of Johnson," *Richmond Planet,* 10 April 1915.

76. Runyon quoted in Ward, *Unforgivable Blackness,* 379; Swope, "Johnson Knockout Dramatic Climax to Battle."

77. "Cowboy Wins Battle When Jack Weakens"; "32,000 at Fight"; "Story of the Battle," *New York Times,* 6 April 1915; Ward, *Unforgivable Blackness,* 380.

78. Swope, "Johnson Knockout Dramatic Climax to Battle"; "Story of the Battle."

79. Quoted in Ward, *Unforgivable Blackness,* 380.

80. Billy Lewis, "The Fight That Failed," *Indianapolis Freeman,* 17 April 1915.

81. "Willard's Punch Knocks Joy out of 'Black Belt,'" *Chicago Daily Tribune,* 6 April 1915; Lester A. Walton, "Fight Talk," *New York Age,* 15 April 1915.

82. James Weldon Johnson, "The Passing of Jack Johnson," *New York Age,* 8 April 1915. On James Weldon Johnson's international experiences, see James Weldon Johnson, *Along This Way: The Autobiography of James Weldon Johnson* (New York: Viking, 1933, reprint 1968).

83. Johnson, "The Passing of Jack Johnson." Also see "The Fall of Our Champion," *Chicago Defender,* 10 April 1915.

84. Johnson, "The Passing of Jack Johnson." The Battle of Hastings (1066)

was the decisive Norman victory in the Norman conquest of England, and the Battle of Agincourt (1415) was an important English triumph over the French in the Hundred Years' War.

85. "Laying Down His Crown," *New York Amsterdam News*, 9 April 1915.

86. "Willard Victor," *New York Times*, 6 April 1915.

87. M. Alvarez Marrón, "Sigue el boxeo," *Diario de la Marina*, 13 April 1915. Also see "Se acordó prohibir el boxeo," *Diario de la Marina*, 10 April 1915; "Miss Cecilia Wright y el Boxeo," *Diario de la Marina*, 28 March 1915.

88. Ricardo Perez Valdes, "Algo acerca de 'toros y boxeo,'" *Diario de la Marina*, 20 March 1915.

89. Jack Curley, "Forgive Their Enemies," *La Lucha*, 4 April 1915; "El Match Willard-Johnson," *Diario de la Marina*, 29 March 1915; "Had Curley Arrested," *La Lucha*, 7 April 1915; "Se Habla John Robinson," *La Lucha*, 8 April 1915.

90. Alvarez Marrón, "Sigue el boxeo."

91. "Boxing in Cuba Legal," *New York Times*, 13 May 1915; "Boxing Legal Says Supreme," *Havana Daily Post*, 13 May 1915. The court had rendered the decision in dismissing a case against Governor Bustillo of Havana province, which charged that he was guilty of breaking the law by personally attending the Willard-Johnson fight.

92. Havana also had the Arena Colon and the Stadium de Marina. Fernando Gil, "Cuba and Its Athletes," *The Ring*, December 1923; Pérez, *On Becoming Cuban*, 176.

93. Gil, "Cuba and Its Athletes."

94. Elio Menéndez and Victor Joaquin Ortega, *Kid Chocolate: 'El boxeo soy yo . . .'* (Havana: Editorial ORBE, 1980), 12; Gems, *Athletic Crusade*, 95. Sardiñias-Montalbo was born on 6 January 1910 in Cerro, Cuba. He turned professional in 1927 and was the world junior lightweight champion from 1931 to 1933.

95. "Jess Willard Is Not Considered Real Champion," *Chicago Defender*, 24 April 1915.

96. "No Passport for Johnson," *New York Times*, 10 April 1915; "American News and Notes," *Boxing*, 28 April 1915; "No Passagert [sic] for Johnson the Order," *La Lucha*, 9 April 1915; "Jack Johnson corre peligro de que lo extraditen," *La Lucha*, 9 April 1915; "Johnson Leaves Tonight," *La Lucha*, 8 April 1915; "Jack Johnson to Sail for Europe Today," *Havana Daily Post*, 20 April 1915.

97. Gus Rhodes wrote glowing reports of his uncle's activities in Europe. See "Ocean Trip Has No Terrors for Gus Rhodes," *Chicago Defender*, 17 July 1915; "Color No Barrier Here," *Chicago Defender*, 11 December 1915. In addition to Johnson's recruiting efforts, he also visited local hospitals to perform for wounded soldiers. The name "Jack Johnson" even became part of British wartime vernacular, used to describe Germany's destructive artillery shells as well as a popular dance (the Jack Johnson Glide) enjoyed by servicemen and their lady friends. See "Jack Johnson Still Helping," *Chicago Defender*, 11 December 1915; "Cupid Aids Recruiting," *New York Times*, 25 December 1914; "Dash of the Indian Troops: Dodging 'Jack Johnson's,'"

Times, 12 April 1915; "A Stoic of the Scots Guards," *Times,* 12 April 1915; "Advice to the O.T.C.'s," *Times,* 12 April 1915.

98. "Take Away Passport of American Writer," *New York Times,* 17 November 1916; "King's Bench Division: An Action against Jack Johnson," *Times,* 1 March 1916; Ward, *Unforgivable Blackness,* 388.

99. "Jack Johnson Boxing in Spain," *New York Times,* 1 June 1916; "King Alfonso Patron of Champ, Jack Johnson," *New York News,* 1 June 1916; "'Jack' Johnson in Charity Bull Fight," *Chicago Defender,* 12 August 1916; "J. Johnson, Bullfighter," *New York Times,* 20 June 1916. On 2 March 1916 Johnson fought against his friend and well-known dadaist poet Arthur Cravan. The match was a pitiful sight. As Johnson toyed with Cravan the Spanish public flooded the ring in protest. See Randy Roberts, *Papa Jack: Jack Johnson and the Era of White Hopes* (New York: Free Press, 1983), 206–7; Ward, *Unforgivable Blackness,* 388–89.

100. Johnson was not the only African American whose loyalty and patriotism were questioned during the Great War. Black newspapers and organizations came under a great degree of government surveillance. Theodore Kornweibel Jr., *Investigate Everything: Federal Efforts to Compel Black Loyalty during World War I* (Bloomington: Indiana University Press, 2001).

101. John W. Lang, Military Attaché, American Embassy, Madrid, to Director of Military Intelligence, Washington, DC, "Jack Johnson," 18 January 1919, RG 65, M1085, Reel 874, 5040, NARA.

102. *The Favorite Magazine* (Chicago), circa 1919, quoted in Gerald Horne, *Black and Brown: African Americans and the Mexican Revolution, 1910–1920* (New York: New York University Press, 2005), 28. For a detailed discussion of Johnson's exploits in Mexico, see Horne, *Black and Brown,* 25–38.

103. John W. Lang, Military Attaché, American Embassy, Madrid, to Director of Military Intelligence, Washington, DC, "Jack Johnson."

104. Horne, *Black and Brown,* 21–24. Also see Arnold Shankman, "The Image of Mexico and the Mexican-American in the Black Press, 1890–1935," *Journal of Ethnic Studies* 3, no. 2 (1975): 43–56; J. Fred Rippy, "A Negro Colonization Project in Mexico, 1894–1896," *Journal of Negro History* 6, no. 1 (1921): 66–73. Veracruz already had its own Afro-Mexican population dating back to the colonial period. Patrick J. Carroll, *Blacks in Colonial Veracruz: Race, Ethnicity, and Regional Development,* 2nd ed. (Austin: University of Texas Press, 2001).

105. Bob Scanlon, "The Record of a Negro Boxer," in *Negro: An Anthology,* ed. Nancy Cunard (1934; New York: Frederick Ungar Publishing, 1970), 208; G. W. Slaughter, "Mexico Offers Negroes of United States Great Opportunities," *Chicago Defender,* 26 March 1910.

106. "Mexico Gives Land to American Negroes," *Chicago Defender,* 21 January 1911.

107. *El Imparcial* quoted in "20,000 Negroes Coming to Mexico," *Chicago Defender,* 11 February 1911.

108. Horne, *Black and Brown,* 22–23. On the invisibility of blackness in the Mexican national imagination, see Marco Polo Hernandez Cuevas, *Afri-*

can Mexicans and the Discourse on Modern Nation (Lanham, MD: University Press of America, 2004).

109. See part III, "The Years of Revolution, 1910–1940," in John M. Hart, *Empire and Revolution: The Americans in Mexico since the Civil War* (Berkeley: University of California Press, 2002); Horne, *Black and Brown*, 128–32.

110. "Sergt. John Hunt Defends 9th Cavalry," *Chicago Defender*, 12 October 1912.

111. See Horne, *Black and Brown*, 69–87.

112. "General Villa of Mexico G. Goldsby Who Deserted United States Cavalry," *Chicago Defender*, 7 March 1914. Also see "'Villa a Negro' Says Explorer," *New York Age*, 26 March 1914; "Who is Gen. Villa?" *Indianapolis Freeman*, 4 April 1914; "General Villa, Head of Rebel Army Said to Be an American Negro," *New York Age*, 26 February 1914; "Says He Talked with Gen. Villa," *New York Age*, 12 March 1914; "General Villa Is George Goldsby, Lived in Vinita," *Chicago Defender*, 14 March 1914.

113. Although another report claimed that Pancho Villa was the 10th Cavalry veteran Spencer Young, it still espoused the same cautionary tale. After serving fifteen thankless years in the 10th Cavalry, Young found his fortune in Mexico. See "Baltimore Minister Brother of General Villa, Mexican Leader," *Chicago Defender*, 2 May 1914. Pancho Villa worked to cultivate a good image in the African American press. He sent an envoy to the *Chicago Defender* offices. One of Villa's top aides, General Felix Angeles, also told the *Defender*, "Our leading men in the army and in civil life are black men." He criticized white Americans' "persistent efforts to force their 'color prejudice' notions" on their Mexican counterparts. See "Rupert Jonas Here Is Envoy of Villa," *Chicago Defender*, 29 August 1914; "Color Line Mexico; Race Made Welcome," *Chicago Defender*, 26 June 1915.

114. "Defend the Flag," *Chicago Defender*, 2 May 1914. The invasion was in response to increasing assaults on U.S. citizens and their property. Horne, *Black and Brown*, 144–45.

115. See "Tenth Cavalry Are at Rest on the Border," *Chicago Defender*, 23 May 1914; "Peace and Quiet Reign along the Border," *Chicago Defender*, 4 July 1914; "Black Troops Ready for Mexico," *Chicago Defender*, 25 April 1914; "Wearing the Uniform of Blue," *Chicago Defender*, 9 May 1914; "Distinguishing Himself on Mexican Border," *New York Age*, 30 April 1914.

116. Ralph W. Tyler, "Why Fight for a Flag Whose Folds Do Not Protect," *Chicago Defender*, 14 March 1914; "Border Service for Our 'Boys,'" *New York Age*, 7 May 1914. On whether the war was just, see "Is the War with Mexico a Just One?" *New York Age*, 30 April 1914; "President Wilson with the Dead from Mexico," *New York Age*, 21 May 1914.

117. "South Carolina to Re-enslave Colored People," *Chicago Defender*, 31 January 1914.

118. Horne, *Black and Brown*, 157. On the Plan de San Diego, see Charles H. Harris III and Louis R. Sadler, "The Plan of San Diego and the Mexican–United States War Crisis of 1916: A Reexamination," *Hispanic American Historical Review* 58, no. 3 (1978): 381–408; Benjamin Johnson, *Revolution in Texas: How a Forgotten Rebellion and Its Bloody Suppression Turned Mexicans into*

Americans (New Haven, CT: Yale University Press, 2003). For a contemporary black press report, see "Doing Things in Texas," *Chicago Defender,* 24 June 1916.

119. Bolton Smith, "Notes on the Negro Problem," June 1918, Box I, RG 107, Emmett Scott Papers, NARA, quoted in Horne, *Black and Brown,* 165.

120. "George" to Lanier Winslow, U.S. State Department, no date, Reel 17, 832, "Federal Surveillance of Afro-Americans (1917–1925): The First World War, the Red Scare and the Garvey Movement," quoted in Horne, *Black and Brown,* 29.

121. McGehee, "The Dandy and the Mauler," 20–21.

122. On the Fifi, see Luis Alvarez, *The Power of the Zoot: Youth Culture and Resistance during World War II* (Berkeley: University of California Press, 2008), 82–83.

123. Hipolito Seijas, "Mas de dos mil personas," *El Universal,* 27 March 1919.

124. "Jack en Casa," *El Universal,* 31 March 1919.

125. McGehee, "The Dandy and the Mauler," 23; "Capt. Roper Goes to Train with J. Johnson," *Chicago Defender,* 31 May 1919.

126. "Plaza de Toros 'El Toreo,'" *El Universal,* 22 June 1919; "Johnson y Roper contenderán esta tarde en la Plaza 'El Toreo,'" *El Demócrata,* 22 June 1919; "Sensacional torneo de box," *El Demócrata,* 22 June 1919.

127. "Jack Johnson Hangs One on Ropes in Ten Round Bout in Mexico," *New York News,* [26 June?] 1919, Tuskegee Clippings File, Division of Behavioral Science Research, Carver Research Foundation, Reel 11, 107, Tuskegee Institute, Alabama (Sanford NC: Microfilming Corporation of America, 1981).

128. "Mexico to Bar Jack Johnson from Fighting," *Atlanta Constitution,* 11 March 1919; "Jack Johnson Riles Mexican Officials," *Washington Post,* 9 July 1919; "Jack Johnson in Bad in Mexico City," *Atlanta Constitution,* 9 July 1919; "Mexico to Deport Jack Johnson," *New York Times,* 29 July 1919.

129. "Jack Johnson Now Thrives as Medicine Man," *[Louisville News?],* 17 April 1919, Reel 11, 101, Tuskegee Clippings File. Also see Glenn Griswold, "Make J. Johnson Hero in Mexico," *Chicago Daily Tribune,* 16 April 1919; "Jack Johnson Rolling High," *Los Angeles Times,* 2 July 1919.

130. Johnson, *In the Ring—And Out,* 112.

131. "La Nota social de ayer," *El Universal,* 11 April 1919. Subsequent quotations are taken from this article unless otherwise noted.

132. Division Superintendent, Department of Justice to Frank Burke, Assistant Director and Chief, Bureau of Investigation, Washington, DC, "Negro Riot Propaganda and Activities of Jack Johnson at Mexico City," 15 October 1919, RG 65, M1085, Reel 874, 5040, NARA.

133. "Refused Johnson, License Revoked," *Chicago Defender,* 12 July 1919.

134. "Jack Johnson Gave Aid to Spain during War," *Chicago Defender,* 19 April 1919. Also see "Jack Idolized in Mexico," *Chicago Defender,* 10 May 1919.

135. As the *Defender* noted, a correspondent for the *New York Evening Sun* provided a completely different version of the events. He claimed a scuffle had ensued after Moore called Johnson a "nigger." Rather than siding with the black heavyweight, Mexico City officials had instructed local policemen

not to charge Moore and members of the chamber since they were the city's guests of honor. Regardless of which version is accurate, the *Defender* effectively used Johnson's experiences in Mexico to critique the hypocrisy of Jim Crow segregation.

136. A. A. Adee of the State Department to the U.S. Embassy in Mexico, quoted in Finis Farr, *Black Champion: The Life and Times of Jack Johnson* (London: MacMillan & Company, 1964), 220.

137. "Why Negroes Should Be Interested in Mexico," *Messenger,* July 1919. Also see "Mexico," *Messenger,* October 1919. This article discusses U.S. control over Mexican resources, particularly oil and copper.

138. "Refused Johnson, License Revoked."

139. "Jack Johnson Forms Land Co," *Chicago Defender,* 7 June 1919.

140. *Messenger,* July 1919. For other Mexican colonization schemes, see "600 Miles by Wagon Is Negro's Answer to Crackers," *Negro World,* [28?] February 1920, Reel 12, 280, Tuskegee Clippings File; "Mexico Open to Colored Emigrants," *Baltimore Afro-American,* 24 September 1920.

141. Captain W. Hanson, Texas Rangers to the Director of Military Intelligence, 15 October 1919, Reel 21, 284, *Surveillance Papers,* quoted in Horne, *Black and Brown,* 36.

142. Division Superintendent, Department of Justice to Frank Burke, Assistant Director and Chief, Bureau of Investigation, Washington, DC, "Negro Riot Propaganda and Activities of Jack Johnson at Mexico City," 15 October 1919, RG 65, M1085, Reel 874, 5040, NARA.

143. The San Antonio offices of the Bureau of Investigation advised that a study be conducted to "ascertain to what extent he [Johnson] is exciting the negroes of this country." Frank Burke, Assistant Director and Chief, Bureau of Investigation, to A. Lanier Winslow, Department of State, Washington, DC, 24 October 1919, RG 65 M1085, Reel 874, 5040, NARA. To make matters worse, Johnson had also become a hero among white American leftists who had fled to Mexico to escape the draft. Michael Gold ran into Johnson in the streets of Mexico City, where Johnson had given him a $10 donation toward his cause. Johnson also knew Charles Shipman. See Horne, *Black and Brown,* 32.

144. Langston Hughes, *The Big Sea* (1940; New York: Hill and Wang, 1993), 15, 39–40, 61–62.

145. This reference is from RG 165, Name Index to Correspondence of the Military Intelligence Division of the War Department General Staff, 1917–1941, M1194, Reel 109, NARA. Also see Division Superintendent, Department of Justice to Frank Burke, Assistant Director and Chief, Bureau of Investigation, Washington, DC, "Negro Riot Propaganda and Activities of Jack Johnson at Mexico City," 15 October 1919.

146. Military intelligence reports on Johnson, 1919, RG 165, NARA, quoted in Roberts, *Papa Jack,* 212.

147. Charles H. Boynton, Executive Director, National Association for the Protection of American Rights in Mexico to Mr. John Suter, Department of Justice, 7 November 1919, RG 65, M1085, Reel 874, NARA.

148. Mr. John Suter, Department of Justice, to Charles H. Boynton, Exec-

utive Director, National Association for the Protection of American Rights in Mexico, 8 November 1919, RG 65, M1085, Reel 874, NARA.

149. Horne, *Black and Brown*, 36.

150. Johnson, *In the Ring—And Out*, 115–16.

151. "Jack Johnson to Sail for America," *Chicago Defender*, 14 February 1920; "Eastern Sporting World," *Chicago Defender*, 6 March 1920; "Jack Johnson on Way to America," *Chicago Defender*, 27 March 1920.

152. Johnson, *In the Ring—And Out*, 121.

153. "Jack Johnson to Be Citizen of Mexico," *Chicago Defender*, 6 March 1920; "The Mexican Revolution," *Messenger*, August 1920.

CHAPTER 7. THE EMPIRE STRIKES BACK

1. "Seize Jack Johnson at Mexican Border," *New York Times*, 21 July 1920.

2. "Jack Johnson Is Jailed Here Despite Protest," *Los Angeles Times*, 21 July 1920.

3. Jack Johnson, *In the Ring—And Out* (1927; New York: Citadel Press, 1992), 256, 140.

4. Noah D. Thompson, "Jack Johnson Returns from Exile," *Chicago Defender*, 24 July 1920.

5. Johnson, *In the Ring—And Out*, 122–23.

6. Geoffrey Ward, *Unforgivable Blackness: The Rise and Fall of Jack Johnson* (New York: Knopf, 2004), 403–4.

7. Quotations in this paragraph are from Frederic J. Frommer, "90 Years Ago Today, Boxer Johnson Sought His Own Pardon" (28 June 2011), http://abcnews.go.com/Sports/wireStory?id=13945592 (accessed 1 September 2011). The records of Johnson's pardon request are held at the National Archives. Eventually released for good behavior, Johnson served only ten months of his original sentence.

8. Frank O'Neill, "The Brown Man in the Field of Sports," *The Ring*, November 1925.

9. "Interesting Letters from Our Readers," *The Ring*, December 1925.

10. Lothrop Stoddard, *The Rising Tide of Color Against White World-Supremacy* (1920; New York: Charles Scribner's Sons, 1922), vi, 9. On the growing popularity of eugenics in this period, see Marilyn Lake and Henry Reynolds, *Drawing the Global Colour Line: White Men's Countries and the International Challenge of Racial Equality* (Cambridge: Cambridge University Press, 2008), 310–31; Matthew Pratt Guterl, *The Color of Race in America, 1900–1940* (Cambridge, MA: Harvard University Press, 2001), 14–67.

11. Hubert Harrison, "The White War and the Colored Races," *Negro World*, 14 February 1920.

12. Lake and Reynolds, *Drawing the Global Colour Line*, 284–309.

13. Alain Locke, ed., *The New Negro: Voices of the Harlem Renaissance* (1925; New York: Macmillan, 1992), 5, 8.

14. Recent scholarship has emphasized the transnational, anticolonial, and Marxian character of black politics during the interwar years. See, for example, Glenda Gilmore, *Defying Dixie: The Radical Roots of Civil Rights, 1919–*

1950 (New York: W. W. Norton & Company, 2008); Michelle Stephens, *Black Empire: The Masculine Global Imaginary of Caribbean Intellectuals in the United States, 1914–1962* (Durham, NC: Duke University Press, 2005); Brent Edwards, *The Practice of Diaspora: Literature, Translation, and the Rise of Black Internationalism* (Cambridge, MA: Harvard University Press, 2003); Mamadou Badiane, *The Changing Face of Afro-Caribbean Cultural Identity: Negrismo and Negritude* (Lanham, MD: Lexington Books, 2010); Robert Philipson, "The Harlem Renaissance as Postcolonial Phenomenon," *African American Review* 40, no. 1 (2006): 145–60.

15. Quotations are taken from "Report of Brooklyn UNIA Meetings [23–24 January, 1922]," in *The Marcus Garvey and Universal Negro Improvement Association Papers, Volume 4*, ed. Robert A. Hill (Berkeley: University of California Press, 1991), 455–56, 458. For similar analyses see "Lord Chelmsford Admits Darker Races Are Revolting against White Rule," *Negro World*, 10 December 1921; "Black Peril Joins Hands with the Yellow Peril," *Chicago Whip*, 21 August 1920.

16. Claude McKay, *A Long Way from Home: An Autobiography* (London: Pluto Press, 1985), 61.

17. Ibid., 69–70.

18. On racial immigration restrictions in the early 1920s, see Lake and Reynolds, *Drawing the Global Colour Line*, 312–22. On assimilation programs, see James R. Barrett, "Americanization from the Bottom, Up: Immigration and the Remaking of the American Working Class, 1880–1930," *Journal of American History* 79, no. 4 (1992): 996–1020.

19. On boxing in the U.S. military during World War I, see Jeffrey Sammons, *Beyond the Ring: The Role of Boxing in American Society* (Urbana: University Illinois Press, 1988), 50–51; H. M. Spike Webb, "Boxing Helps Put Fighting Spirit in Jolly Tars," *The Ring*, July 1922. Boxing also found its way into Europe's wartime culture. See "Boxing a Man into the Army," *Health & Strength*, 19 June 1915; F. H. Lucas, "Boxing as the Best Training for a Soldier," *Boxing*, 9 June 1915. After the war boxing became an established part of U.S. military and police curriculum. See "Boxing at U.S. Naval Academy," *The Ring*, July 1922; "Boxing and the Criminal," *The Ring*, August 1922.

20. Dempsey, also known as the "Manassa Mauler," drew the color line, refusing to fight African American heavyweight Harry Wills. On Dempsey's life and career, see Randy Roberts, *Jack Dempsey, the Manassa Mauler* (Baton Rouge: Louisiana State University Press, 1979).

21. "The Ring Has Readers in All Parts of the World," *The Ring*, December 1924.

22. Peter Benson, *Battling Siki: A Tale of Ring Fixes, Race, and Murder in the 1920s* (Fayetteville: University of Arkansas Press, 2006), 12–14, 25–26, 37–39.

23. Bob Scanlon, "The Record of a Negro Boxer," in *Negro: An Anthology*, ed. Nancy Cunard (1934; New York: Frederick Ungar Publishing, 1970), 210. Scanlon escorted Siki away from the scene, helping him to avoid arrest.

24. Harry Reeve, "My Impressions of Battling Siki: A Good Man but a Wild One," *Boxing*, 15 November 1922.

25. Harry Reeve, "My Impressions of Battling Siki: Unjustified and Illogical Penalty," *Boxing,* 22 November 1922.

26. On Siki's childhood and wartime service, see Benson, *Battling Siki,* 89–112. Benson notes that there are many conflicting accounts of Battling Siki's origins. What follows are some of the key points from Benson's more detailed explanation of Siki's early life.

27. Dan Schocket, "Battling Siki—The Man They Turned into a Joke," *World Boxing,* September 1974, quoted in ibid., 89. Also see Ed Cunningham, "Siki Denies Coming from Jungle," *The Ring,* August 1925.

28. Benson, *Battling Siki,* 27–28.

29. "Americanism in France," *Messenger,* September 1922. In the same issue another journalist argued that economic imperatives had led to another form of "Americanism" in France. A new law was to limit the number of foreigners allowed in French orchestras, thereby protecting French artists from the arrival of black American jazz musicians. "As a result of this economic competition," the correspondent asserted, "the French who have never yielded to race prejudice, who have no qualms about social equality, who are by no means disturbed about amalgamation or miscegenation with colored races— have passed a law which for sheer economic discrimination takes rank with anything to be found in the South's Black Code and vagrancy laws during the reconstruction following our Civil War." See "The Nickle [sic] under Frenchman's Foot," *Messenger,* September 1922. Comments on the spread of Jim Crow racism in France were not limited to the *Messenger.* See "Prejudice in France," *Cleveland Gazette,* 3 May 1919; "Spreading Anti-Negro Propaganda," *Savannah Tribune,* 7 September 1922; "Americans Draw Color Line in Paris," *Negro World,* 2 July 1921; "Voice of Americans in Europe," *Chicago Tribune European Edition,* 5 January 1923; "Color Line Raises Furore in France," *Negro World,* 15 September 1923; "What the French Say," *Negro World,* 15 September 1923. For French reports of this phenomenon, see "Informations diverses, les étrangers en France," *Le Temps,* 2 August 1923; Gratien Candace, "Préjuge de couleur: il est temps que cela cesse," *L'Homme libre,* 11 August 1923; Robert Boucard, "Français de couleur molestes, l'attitude de certains étrangers est intolérable," *La Presse,* 7 August 1923; Jacques Barty, "Le Noir et le blanc," *L'Homme libre,* 8 August 1923. Black French colonials wrote some of these articles in response to bad treatment at the hands of white Americans.

30. "The Rising Tide of Color," *Chicago Defender,* 22 May 1920.

31. R. T. Brown, "The Spirit of the Age," *Negro World,* 28 October 1922. Also see J. Jackson Tilford, "The New Psychology of the Negro," *Negro World,* 28 October 1922.

32. "Le Gentleman," *La Boxe et les boxeurs,* 2 August 1922; "Le Match Carpentier-Siki: un match de propagande," *L'Auto,* 24 September 1922.

33. Paul Olivier, "Le Match Carpentier-Siki," *L'Auto,* 24 September 1922.

34. "A vous . . . touché!" *La Boxe et les boxeurs,* 6 September 1922.

35. "Siki Is a Gorilla Says His Manager," *New York Times,* 26 September 1922.

36. Trevor Wignall, *Story of Boxing* (New York: Brentano's, 1924), 261.

37. "Résultat du match Carpentier-Siki," *La Presse,* 24 September 1922. Although this report claims there were sixty thousand fans in attendance, other articles set the number closer to thirty thousand.

38. Max Abbat, "Carpentier's Film Fiasco," *Boxing,* 27 September 1922.

39. "Siki Has Heart of Gold, but Is a Baby," *Chicago Whip,* 25 November 1922.

40. Frank Withers, "Siki Conquers Idol of France," *Chicago Defender,* 30 September 1922.

41. "Negro Knocks Out French Idol," *Savannah Tribune,* 28 September 1922.

42. Scanlon, "The Record of a Negro Boxer," 210.

43. "Carpentier Conquered," *Boxing World, Mirror of Life, & Sporting Observer,* 30 September 1922; "Carpentier s'effondre devant Battling Siki," *L'Auto,* 25 September 1922; "Battling Siki, A Senegalese Negro, Knocks Out Carpentier, the French Idol, in Six Rounds," *Negro World,* 30 September 1922.

44. Scanlon, "The Record of a Negro Boxer," 210.

45. "Negro Knocks Out French Idol."

46. "Carpentier Conquered"; "La Résultat de la semaine," *La Boxe et les Boxeurs,* 27 September 1922. The fight film later confirmed that Siki had not fouled Carpentier. J. Bissell, "Doubt That Siki 'Doubled Crossed,'" *Boxing World, Mirror of Life, & Sporting Observer,* 14 October 1922.

47. "The Editor's Ideas: Spoils and Spoof," *Boxing,* 4 October 1922; "Battling Siki vient à 'L'Auto,'" *L'Auto,* 26 September 1922; Basil D. Woon, "Siki, a Former Dishwasher, Now Is Idol of Boulevards," *Negro World,* 7 October 1922.

48. "Boxe," *La Dépêche coloniale et maritime,* 1 October 1922; "Les Noirs veulent fêter la victoire de Siki," *L'Auto,* 30 September 1922. Contributions for the commemorative piece were to be addressed to a M. Senghor.

49. "Siki," *Messenger,* October 1922.

50. "Vive la France," *Chicago Whip,* 30 September 1922.

51. "Paris Beauties Kink Their Hair in Siki Glory," *Chicago Defender,* 14 October 1922; "That Siki Silhouette," *Chicago Defender,* 28 October 1922; "Dark Skins Again All the Rage in Cafes of Paris," *Chicago Whip,* 14 October 1922.

52. "Battling Siki résume aux lecteurs de 'l'Auto,'" *L'Auto,* 29 September 1922.

53. "Battling Siki Fears Dempsey's Old Color Line," *Chicago Defender,* 23 September 1922. Picking up on Siki's public declarations, a reporter for the *Chicago Defender* claimed the Senegalese boxer was better off than his African American counterparts Jack Johnson and Harry Wills. Though Johnson and Wills were born U.S. citizens, they still went about "with fear and trembling," while Siki had become a full "CITIZEN of a country in which yesterday he was but a colonial." Roscoe Simmons, "The Week," *Chicago Defender,* 30 September 1922. This article ran next to Simmons's comments about the failure of the Dyer Anti-Lynching Bill.

54. Boulland de L'Escale, "La Propagande coloniale par le tourisme les beaux-arts et les sports," *L'Autre France,* 14 October 1922; "The Race Ques-

tion in Pugilism," *Brooklyn Citizen*, 26 September 1922; "Siki Victory Precipitates Negro Officer Proposition," *California Eagle*, 11 November 1922.

55. "The Last Scene of the Tragedy," *Boxing*, 27 September 1922; "L'impression en Angleterre," *L'Auto*, 28 September 1922. German and Italian sportsmen reportedly were also stupefied by Carpentier's quick defeat. See "Après le défaite de Carpentier," *L'Auto*, 27 September 1922.

56. "'Le péril du champion c'est le cinéma,'" *L'Auto*, 30 September 1922.

57. The Crusader News Service provided black American publications with descriptions of these disturbances. See "Siki's Victory Stirs Americans in France to Protest Equality," *Chicago Defender*, 7 October 1922; "Siki's Victory Causing Racial Disturbances," *Savannah Tribune*, 5 October 1922; "Siki Victory Stirs Paris Race Fights," *Chicago Whip*, 7 October 1922. Run by Cyril Briggs of the African Blood Brotherhood, an organization that advocated black self-determination and Marxist revolution, the Crusader Service supplied many of the reports on Siki that appeared in the black American press.

58. "Battling Siki as a Dark Cloud on the Horizon," *Literary Digest*, 14 October 1922. Also see "The Rise of Siki," *New York Times*, 27 September 1922.

59. On the principles of British indirect rule, see Mahmood Mamdani, *Citizen and Subject: Contemporary Africa and the Legacy of Late Colonialism* (Princeton, NJ: Princeton University Press, 1996). On the early twentieth-century French civilizing mission, see Alice L. Conklin, *A Mission to Civilize: The Republican Idea of Empire in France and West Africa, 1895–1930* (Stanford, CA: Stanford University Press, 1997).

60. *Republican* quoted in "Battling Siki as a Dark Cloud."

61. Quotations in this paragraph are taken from ibid. Also see "Byproducts," *New York Times*, 1 October 1922.

62. "England's White Hope to Take a Swing at Siki," *Chicago Whip*, 28 October 1922. The Crusader News Service supplied this report.

63. Lord Lonsdale to R. McKenna, 1 November 1922, Home Office Records 45/11880, British National Archives, London, England. In subsequent notes, HO denotes Home Office and BNA denotes British National Archives.

64. Major Arnold Wilson to Lord Lonsdale, 1 November 1922, HO 45/11880, BNA.

65. "Siki Has Heart of Gold, but Is a Baby."

66. *L'Echo des sports* quoted in Benson, *Battling Siki*, 255.

67. "Sports Writers Trying to Prejudice U.S. against Siki," *New York Age*, 28 October 1922.

68. "Siki and the American Press," *New York Age*, 4 November 1922.

69. J. Bissell, "The Bar Up to Siki," *Boxing World, Mirror of Life, & Sporting Observer*, 18 November 1922; "Battling Siki Suspended," *Times*, 11 November 1922; "Major Arnold Wilson's Attitude," *Times*, 11 November 1922; "Siki Is Deprived of French Title," *New York Times*, 10 November 1922; "Siki Now Barred from Boxing Here," *New York Times*, 11 November 1922; "Italian Boxing Clubs Close Their Doors to Battling Siki," *New York Times*, 15 November 1922; "Siki's License Is Canceled by French Boxing Federation," *New York Times*, 22 November 1922; "Opens Competition for Siki's Title," *New York Times*, 23 November 1922.

70. "Battling Siki Deprived of Title, Call the 'Jack Johnson' of Europe," *New York Age,* 18 November 1922.

71. Letter to Home Office, 10 November 1922, HO 45/11880, BNA. Also see E. B. Osborn, "English Writer Admits Negro's Physical Advantages over Other Men," *Negro World,* 20 January 1923; "Let the Gorilla Fight the Winner," *Saturday Blade,* 28 October 1922.

72. *African World* quoted in "Our Readers' Own Opinions," *Health & Strength,* 11 November 1922. Also see "Our Readers' Own Opinions: Sir Arthur Conan Doyle and the Home Office," *Health & Strength,* 25 November 1922.

73. "Siki Case to Be Aired in French Chamber," *New York Times,* 30 November 1922.

74. "Dark-Hued Deputy Loses Plea for Siki," *New York Times,* 1 December 1922. Also see "L'Affaire Siki à la chambre," *La Dépêche coloniale et maritime,* 3 December 1922. Diagne claimed that Carpentier's handlers had tried unsuccessfully to get Siki to throw the match against their charge. A civil tribunal made a full investigation of the fight. Despite much damning evidence, the tribunal found nothing illegal in the fight's promotion, exonerating Carpentier and his management from any wrongdoing. "French Courts to Unravel Siki Fight," *New York Times,* 4 December 1922; "Siki Relates How Bout Was Framed," *New York Times,* 5 December 1922; "Clears Carpentier of Siki's Charges," *New York Times,* 16 January 1923.

75. Ho Chi Minh, "About Siki," *Le Paria,* 1 December 1922.

76. Reportedly, film producers had considered hiring Siki to star in a moving picture version of *Batuoula.* See "Siki's Victory Stirs Americans in France to Protest Equality."

77. "De Siki à la révolution mondiale," *Le Paria,* November 1922.

78. "Siki's Knockout," *Chicago Whip,* 18 November 1922. Also see "Prime Sport News," *Cleveland Gazette,* 18 November 1922; "The 'Color' Folly," *Chicago Defender,* 30 December 1922.

79. Claude McKay, "Negroes in Sports," in *The Negroes in America* (1923; Port Washington, NY: Kennikat Press, 1979), 50–52.

80. Ibid., 53.

81. Home Office to the Earl of Lonsdale, 26 January 1923, HO 45/11880, BNA. On 31 January the Home Office instructed immigration officers to keep Battling Siki from entering Britain. "Battling Siki est déchu de tous ses titres de Champion de France, d'Europe et du Monde," *L'Auto,* 13 January 1923.

82. "Boxing: Death of Battling Siki," *Times,* 16 December 1925. Also see "Battling Siki Shot Dead in the Street," *New York Times,* 16 December 1925.

83. "Thug Murders Battling Siki," *Chicago Defender,* 19 December 1925.

84. *New York Amsterdam News,* 23 December 1925, quoted in Gerald Early, "Battling Siki: The Boxer as Natural Man," in *The Culture of Bruising: Essays on Prizefighting, Literature, and Modern American Culture* (Hopewell, NJ: Ecco Press, 1994), 78.

85. Gary Edward Holcomb, *Claude McKay, Code Name Sasha: Queer Black Marxism and the Harlem Renaissance* (Gainesville: University Press of Florida, 2007), 25. Also see Theodore Kornweibel Jr., *Investigate Everything:*

Federal Efforts to Compel Black Loyalty during World War I (Bloomington: Indiana University Press, 2001).

86. John Henrik Clarke, "Marcus Garvey: The Harlem Years," *Transition*, no. 46 (1974): 18.

EPILOGUE

1. James Thurber quoted in Geoffrey Ward, *Unforgivable Blackness: The Rise and Fall of Jack Johnson* (New York: Knopf, 2004), 431.

2. Thurber quoted in ibid., 432–33.

3. Ada "Bricktop" Smith quoted in ibid., 436.

4. Randy Roberts, *Papa Jack: Jack Johnson and the Era of White Hopes* (New York: Free Press, 1983), 220–21.

5. Quoted in Ward, *Unforgivable Blackness*, 438.

6. Ibid., 439; Theresa Runstedtler, "In Sports the Best Man Wins: How Joe Louis Whupped Jim Crow," in *In the Game: Race, Identity, and Sports in the Twentieth Century*, ed. Amy Bass (New York: Palgrave Macmillan, 2005), 65.

7. Roberts, *Papa Jack*, 225; Ward, *Unforgivable Blackness*, 442–43.

8. Joe Markman, "Pardon for Boxer Jack Johnson May Be Elusive" (26 October 2009), http://articles.latimes.com/2009/oct/26/nation/na-boxer-pardon 26 (accessed 5 November 2010); "Congress Approves Jack Johnson Pardon" (30 July 2009), www.cbsnews.com/stories/2009/07/30/sportsline/main5197355 .shtml (accessed 12 August 2010).

9. Michael Saul, "Kansas Pol Lynn Jenkins Tells Crowd: GOP Needs 'Great White Hope' to Battle Obama, Dems," *New York Daily News* (27 August 2009), www.nydailynews.com/news/politics/2009/08/27/2009-08-27 _kansas_pol_lynn_jenkins_tells_crowd_gop_needs_great_white_hope_to_ battle_obama_d.html (accessed 6 January 2011); "Jenkins Says She Supported Resolution, Didn't Read It," *Ottawa Herald* (Kansas), 1 September 2009, *Newspaper Source Plus*, EBSCO*host* (accessed 6 January 2011).

10. Alan Silverleib, "Family of Boxer Fights for Pardon of 1913 Racist Conviction" (22 April 2009), http://articles.cnn.com/2009-04-22/us/jack.johnson .pardon_1_first-african-american-world-heavyweight-jack-johnson-all-white -jury?_s=PM:US (accessed 12 August 2010).

11. "Posthumous Pardon Sought for Johnson" (21 October 2009), http:// sports.espn.go.com/sports/boxing/news/story?id=4565549 (accessed 12 August 2010); Markman, "Pardon for Boxer Jack Johnson May Be Elusive."

12. See, for example, Julie Bosman, "Obama Sharply Assails Absent Black Fathers," *New York Times*, 16 June 2008; Geoff Earle, "Kick in Pants from O: 'Brother's, Stop Sagging,'" *New York Post*, 4 November 2008.

13. "No Posthumous Pardon," *New York Times*, 11 December 2009.

14. Quotations in this paragraph are from Frederic J. Frommer, "Backers Making Another Run at Pardon for Boxer" (21 February 2011), www.scpr .org/news/2011/02/21/24278/backers-making-another-run-pardon-boxer/ (accessed 1 September 2011). Also see "McCain and King Seek Pardon for Boxing Great Jack Johnson (25 May 2011), www.reuters.com/article/2011/05/25/ us-boxing-johnson-idUSTRE74O06420110525 (accessed 1 September 2011).

15. Quoted in Karyl Walker, "No Pardon for Garvey" (21 August 2011), www.jamaicaobserver.com/news/No-pardon-for-Garvey_9489036#ixzz1 XISZyfzk (accessed 1 September 2011).

16. Mos Def, "Zimzallabim" and "Blue Black Jack," *The New Danger* (Geffen Records, 2004).

17. This Bike Is a Pipe Bomb, "Jack Johnson," *Three Way Tie for a Fifth* (Plan-It-X South, 2004).

18. Trevor Von Eeden, *The Original Johnson,* vol. I (San Diego: IDW Publishing, 2009); Trevor Von Eeden, *The Original Johnson,* vol. II (San Diego: IDW Publishing, 2011); George Gene Gustines, "Comic Book Takes Unflinching Look at a Boxing Champion," *New York Times,* 24 December 2008.

19. See, for example, David Margolick, *Beyond Glory: Joe Louis vs. Max Schmeling, and a World on the Brink* (New York: Random House, 2006); Patrick Myler, *Ring of Hate: Joe Louis vs. Max Schmeling, the Fight of the Century* (New York: Arcade Publishing, 2005); Barak Goodman, director, *The Fight* (Social Media Productions, 2004). On Louis as a black icon, see Runstedtler, "In Sports the Best Man Wins."

20. David Zirin, "Message to Obama: You Can't Have Muhammad Ali" (3 December 2009), www.huffingtonpost.com/dave-zirin/message-to-obama -you-cant_3_b_378429.html (accessed 10 January 2011). Obama's tribute appeared in *USA Today* as part of a special edition titled "Ali: Celebrating 50 Years on the World Stage."

21. John Hoberman, *Darwin's Athletes: How Sport Has Damaged Black America and Preserved the Myth of Race* (New York: Houghton Mifflin, 1997). Bill Cosby has made similar comments about black youth and their fascination with rap music. Bill Cosby and Alvin Poussaint, *Come on, People: On the Path from Victims to Victors* (Nashville: Thomas Nelson, 2007).

22. Richard Iton, *In Search of the Black Fantastic: Politics & Popular Culture in the Post–Civil Rights Era* (New York: Oxford University Press, 2008), 16–17. Also see David J. Leonard and C. Richard King, eds., *Commodified and Criminalized: New Racism and African Americans in Contemporary Sports* (Plymouth, UK: Rowman & Littlefield, 2011).

Bibliography

NEWSPAPERS AND PERIODICALS

African American

Baltimore Afro-American, Broad Ax, California Eagle, Call and Post, Chicago Defender, Chicago Whip, Cleveland Gazette, Crisis, Indianapolis Freeman, Messenger, Negro World, New York Age, New York Amsterdam News, Philadelphia Tribune, Richmond Planet, Savannah Tribune, Washington Bee

Australia

Age, Argus, Arrow, Australasian, Bulletin, Melbourne Herald, Observer, Punch, Sunday Sun, Sydney Morning Herald, Sydney Truth, Tasmanian Mail

Barbados

Barbados Globe and Colonial Advertiser

Britain

African Times and Orient Review, Daily Chronicle, Daily Telegraph, Dublin Evening Herald, Dublin Evening Mail, Guardian, Morning Post, Times

Canada

Toronto Globe

Cuba

Havana Daily Post, Diario de la Marina, La Lucha

France

L'Autre France, Chicago Tribune European Edition, La Dépêche coloniale et maritime, L'Eclair, L'Excelsior, Le Figaro, L'Homme libre, L'Humanité, L'Intransigéant, Le Journal, Le Matin, Le Paria, La Presse, Le Temps

India

The Englishman; Abhyudaya, Arya Prakásh, Bhála, Daily Hitavadi, Gujaráti, Gujaráti Punch, Hitvarta, Indian Spectator, and Kesari (translated and excerpted in Indian Newspaper Reports, c1868–1942 from the British Library, London, Adam Matthew Publications)

Jamaica

Daily Gleaner

Mexico

Excélsior, El Demócrata, El Universal

Philippines

Manila Times, Renacimiento Filipino

South Africa

Cape Argus, Cape Times, Rand Daily Mail, South African News, Star, Sunday Times, Times of Natal, Transvaal Critic

United States

Atlanta Constitution, Boston Daily Globe, Chicago Daily Tribune, Life, Literary Digest, Los Angeles Times, McClure's Magazine, National Police Gazette, New York Post, New York Times, Outlook, San Francisco Chronicle, Time, USA Today, Washington Post

SPORT AND SPECIALTY PUBLICATIONS
Australia
Sydney Referee

Britain

Boxing, Boxing New Year's Annual, Boxing World and Athletic Chronicle, Boxing World, Mirror of Life, & Sporting Observer, Christian Endeavour Times, Health & Strength, Mirror of Life and Boxing World, Mirror of Life and Sport, Sandow's Magazine, Sportsman

France

L'Auto, La Boxe et les boxeurs, La Culture physique, L'Education physique, La Santé par les sports, Les Sports, La Vie au grand air

United States

Moving Picture World, Physical Culture, The Ring

ARCHIVAL COLLECTIONS

Detroit Publishing Company Collection, Prints and Photographs Division, Library of Congress, Washington, D.C.

Herbert Lazarus Collection, Beinecke Library, Yale University, New Haven, Connecticut.

Jack Johnson Photograph Collection, Schomburg Center for Research in Black Culture, New York Public Library.

John Johnson Collection of Printed Ephemera, Bodleian Library, Oxford University, Oxford, England.

Tuskegee Clippings File, Division of Behavioral Science Research, Carver Research Foundation, Tuskegee Institute, Alabama. Sanford, NC: Microfilming Corporation of America, 1981.

National Archives, London, England

"British boxing: Colour Bar 1947," Colonial Office Records, 876/89.

"ENTERTAINMENTS: Boxing. Conditions under which contests are illegal. Law Officers' Opinion. 1911; LAW OFFICERS OPINIONS: Boxing—conditions under which contests are illegal. 1911," Home Office Records, 45/10487/110912.

"ENTERTAINMENTS: Boxing. Contests between coloured men and white men," Home Office Records 45/11880.

"Prize Fight—Earls Court between Bombardier Wells and Jack Johnson on Oct 2—objections 1911," Metropolitan Police Records, 2/1474.

National Archives II, College Park, Maryland

Record Group 59, State Department Decimal Files, "Boxing," 812.4066.

Record Group 65, Investigative Case Files of the Bureau of Investigation, 1908–1922, "Jack Johnson," M1085.

Record Group 84, American Embassy Files, "Amusements & Sports," 840.6.

FILMS AND RECORDINGS

Burns, Ken, director. *Unforgivable Blackness: The Rise and Fall of Jack Johnson.* PBS Paramount, 2005.

Davis, Miles. *A Tribute to Jack Johnson.* 1971; Columbia/Legacy, 2005.

Eastwood, Clint, director. *Million Dollar Baby.* Warner Brothers, 2004.

Goodman, Barak, director. "The Fight." *American Experience.* Social Media Productions, 2004.

Greatest Fights of the Century: Jack Johnson vs. Jim Jeffries. 1965. Available at the Library of Congress's Motion Picture, Broadcasting & Recorded Sound Division.

Howard, Ron, director. *Cinderella Man*. Universal Pictures, 2005.

O'Connor, Gavin, director. *Warrior*. Lionsgate, 2011.

Ritt, Martin, director. *The Great White Hope*. 1970; Twentieth Century Fox, 2004.

Russell, David O., director. *The Fighter*. Paramount Pictures, 2010.

PUBLISHED PRIMARY AND SECONDARY SOURCES

Alvarez, Luis. *The Power of the Zoot: Youth Culture and Resistance During World War II*. Berkeley: University of California Press, 2008.

Anderson, Stuart. *Race and Rapprochement: Anglo-Saxonism and Anglo-American Relations, 1895–1904*. East Brunswick, NJ: Associated University Presses, 1981.

Andrews, George Reid. "The Afro-Argentine Officers of Buenos Aires Province, 1800–1860." *Journal of Negro History* 64, no. 2 (1979): 85–100.

———. "Race versus Class Association: The Afro-Argentines of Buenos Aires, 1850–1900." *Journal of Latin American Studies* 11, no. 1 (1979): 19–39.

Appadurai, Arjun. *Modernity at Large: Cultural Dimensions of Globalization*. Minneapolis: University of Minnesota Press, 1996.

August, Thomas G. *The Selling of Empire: British and French Imperialist Propaganda, 1890–1940*. Westport, CT: Greenwood Press, 1985.

Badiane, Mamadou. *The Changing Face of Afro-Caribbean Cultural Identity: Negrismo and Negritude*. Lanham, MD: Lexington Books, 2010.

Baldwin, Davarian. *Chicago's New Negroes: Modernity, the Great Migration, and Black Urban Life*. Chapel Hill: University of North Carolina Press, 2007.

Baldwin, Kate A. *Beyond the Color Line and the Iron Curtain: Reading Encounters between Black and Red, 1922–1963*. Durham, NC: Duke University Press, 2002.

Ballantyne, Tony, and Antoinette Burton, eds. *Bodies in Contact: Rethinking Colonial Encounters in World History*. Durham, NC: Duke University Press, 2009.

———, eds. *Moving Subjects: Gender, Mobility, and Intimacy in an Age of Global Empire*. Urbana: University of Illinois Press, 2009.

Barrett, James R. "Americanization from the Bottom, Up: Immigration and the Remaking of the American Working Class, 1880–1930." *Journal of American History* 79, no. 4 (1992): 996–1020.

Bederman, Gail. *Manliness and Civilization: A Cultural History of Gender and Race in the United States, 1880–1917*. Chicago: University of Chicago Press, 1995.

Benson, Peter. *Battling Siki: A Tale of Ring Fixes, Race, and Murder in the 1920s*. Fayetteville: University of Arkansas Press, 2006.

Bergougniou, Jean-Michel. *'Villages noirs' et autres visiteurs africains et malgaches en France et en Europe, 1870–1940*. Paris: Karthala, 2001.

Berliner, Brett. *Ambivalent Desire: The Exotic Black Other in Jazz-Age France*. Amherst: University of Massachusetts Press, 2002.

Bettinson, A. F., and W. Outram Tristram, eds. *The National Sporting Club: Past and Present.* London: Sands & Co., 1902.

Blake, Jody. *Le Tumulte noir: Modernist Art and Popular Entertainment in Jazz-Age Paris, 1900–1930.* University Park: Pennsylvania State University Press, 1999.

Blakely, Allison. "The Negro in Imperial Russia: A Preliminary Sketch." *Journal of Negro History* 61, no. 4 (1976): 351–61.

Bolster, Jeffrey. *Black Jacks: African American Seamen in the Age of Sail.* Cambridge, MA: Harvard University Press, 1997.

Bourke, Joanna. *Dismembering the Male: Men's Bodies, Britain, and the Great War.* Chicago: University of Chicago Press, 1999.

Bowser, Eileen. *The Transformation of Cinema, 1907–1915.* New York: Scribner, 1990.

Boyce Davies, Carol. *Left of Karl Marx: The Political Life of Black Communist Claudia Jones.* Durham, NC: Duke University Press, 2007.

Brantley, Daniel. "Black Diplomacy and Frederick Douglass' Caribbean Experiences, 1871 and 1889–1891: The Untold History." *Phylon* 45, no. 3 (1984): 197–209.

Brevard, Lisa. *A Biography of E. Azalia Smith Hackley: African-American Singer and Social Activist.* Lewiston, NY: Edwin Mellen Press, 2001.

Brock, Lisa, and Digna Castañeda Fuertes, eds. *Between Race and Empire: African Americans and Cubans before the Cuban Revolution.* Philadelphia: Temple University Press, 1998.

Bronfman, Alejandra. *Measures of Equality: Social Science, Citizenship, and Race in Cuba, 1902–1940.* Chapel Hill: University of North Carolina Press, 2005.

Brooks, Daphne. *Bodies in Dissent: Spectacular Performances of Race and Freedom, 1850–1910.* Durham, NC: Duke University Press, 2006.

Brooks, Tim. *Lost Sounds: Blacks and the Birth of the Recording Industry.* Urbana: University of Illinois Press, 2004.

Broome, Richard. "The Australian Reaction to Jack Johnson, Black Pugilist, 1907–9." In *Sport in History,* edited by Richard Cashman and Michael McKernan, 343–64. St. Lucia: University of Queensland Press, 1979.

Brown, Jayna. *Babylon Girls: Black Women Performers and the Shaping of the Modern.* Durham, NC: Duke University Press, 2008.

Budd, Michael A. *The Sculpture Machine: Physical Culture and Body Politics in the Age of Empire.* New York: New York University Press, 1997.

Burdick, Dakin. "The American Way of Fighting: Unarmed Defense in the United States, 1845–1945." Ph.D. diss., Indiana University, 1999.

Burton, Antoinette, ed. *After the Imperial Turn: Thinking with and Through the Nation.* Durham, NC: Duke University Press, 2003.

Campbell, James T. *Songs of Zion: The African Methodist Episcopal Church in the United States and South Africa.* Chapel Hill: University of North Carolina Press, 1998.

Carby, Hazel. *Cultures in Babylon: Black Britain and African America.* New York: Verso, 1999.

Carey, Jane, and Claire McLisky, eds. *Creating White Australia: New Perspec-*

tives on Race, Whiteness and History. Sydney: Sydney University Press, 2009.

Carr, Robert. *Black Nationalism in the New World: Reading the African-American and West Indian Experience*. Durham, NC: Duke University Press, 2002.

Carroll, Patrick J. *Blacks in Colonial Veracruz: Race, Ethnicity, and Regional Development*. 2nd ed. Austin: University of Texas Press, 2001.

Cell, John. *The Highest Stage of White Supremacy: The Origins of Segregation in South Africa and the American South*. Cambridge: Cambridge University Press, 1982.

Chalaye, Sylvie. *Nègres en images*. Paris: L'Harmattan, 2002.

Chaplin, W. Knight. *People's Society of Christian Endeavour Year Book*. London: Andrew Melrose, 1898.

———. *People's Society of Christian Endeavour Year Book*. London: Andrew Melrose, 1899.

Chudacoff, Howard P. *The Age of the Bachelor: Creating an American Subculture*. Princeton, NJ: Princeton University Press, 1999.

Chude-Sokei, Louis. *The Last 'Darky': Bert Williams, Black-on-Black Minstrelsy, and the African Diaspora*. Durham, NC: Duke University Press, 2005.

Clark, Susan F. "Up Against the Ropes: Peter Jackson as 'Uncle Tom' in America." *Drama Review* 44, no. 1 (2000): 157–82.

Clarke, John Henrik. "Marcus Garvey: The Harlem Years." *Transition*, no. 46 (1974): 14–19.

Clarke, Kamari, and Deborah A. Thomas, eds. *Globalization and Race: Transformations in the Cultural Production of Blackness*. Durham, NC: Duke University Press, 2006.

Conklin, Alice L. *A Mission to Civilize: The Republican Idea of Empire in France and West Africa, 1895–1930*. Stanford, CA: Stanford University Press, 1997.

Cooper, Wayne. *Claude McKay: Rebel Sojourner in the Harlem Renaissance*. Baton Rouge: Louisiana State University Press, 1996.

Cornwell, Gareth. "George Webb Hardy's *The Black Peril* and the Social Meaning of 'Black Peril' in Early Twentieth-Century South Africa." *Journal of Southern African Studies* 22, no. 3 (1996): 441–53.

Cosby, Bill, and Alvin Poussaint. *Come on, People: On the Path from Victims to Victors*. Nashville: Thomas Nelson, 2007.

Cuevas, Marco Polo Hernandez. *African Mexicans and the Discourse on Modern Nation*. Lanham, MD: University Press of America, 2004.

Cuny, Fernand. *La Boxe*. Paris: Éditions Nilsson, [1910].

Davis, Angela. *Blues Legacies and Black Feminism: Gertrude "Ma" Rainey, Bessie Smith, and Billie Holiday*. New York: Vintage, 1999.

Dinan, John A. *Sports in the Pulp Magazines*. London: McFarland & Company, 1998.

Donovan, Mike. *The Roosevelt That I Know: Ten Years of Boxing with the President, and Other Memories of Famous Fighting Men*. New York: B. W. Dodge & Co., 1909.

Drinnon, Richard. *Facing West: The Metaphysics of Indian-Hating and Empire Building.* Minneapolis: University of Minnesota Press, 1980.

Du Bois, W.E.B. "To the Nations of the World." In *W.E.B. Du Bois: A Reader,* edited by David Levering Lewis, 639–41. New York: Henry Holt, 1995.

Early, Gerald. "Battling Siki: The Boxer as Natural Man." In *The Culture of Bruising: Essays on Prizefighting, Literature, and Modern American Culture,* 66–85. Hopewell, NJ: Ecco Press, 1994.

Edwards, Brent. *The Practice of Diaspora: Literature, Translation, and the Rise of Black Internationalism.* Cambridge, MA: Harvard University Press, 2003.

Elam, Harry, and Kennell Jackson, eds. *Black Cultural Traffic: Crossroads in Global Performance and Popular Culture.* Ann Arbor: University of Michigan Press, 2005.

Erlmann, Veit. "'A Feeling of Prejudice': Orpheus M. McAdoo and the Virginia Jubilee Singers in South Africa, 1890–1898." *Journal of Southern African Studies* 14, no. 3 (1988): 331–50.

———. "'Spectatorial Lust': The African Choir in England, 1891–1893." In *Africans on Stage: Studies in Ethnological Show Business,* edited by Bernth Lindfors, 107–37. Bloomington: Indiana University Press, 1999.

Fabre, Michel. "The Ring and the Stage: African Americans in Parisian Public and Imaginary Space before World War I." In *Space in America: Theory, History, Culture,* edited by Klaus Benesch and Kerstin Schmidt, 521–28. Amsterdam: Rodopi, 2005.

Famous Irish Fighters in the Ring: John L. Sullivan. London: Felix McGlennon, [1892].

Fanon, Frantz. *Black Skin, White Masks.* New York: Grove Press, 1967.

Farr, Finis. *Black Champion: The Life and Times of Jack Johnson.* London: Macmillan & Company, 1964.

Findlay, Eileen Suarez. *Imposing Decency: The Politics of Sexuality and Race in Puerto Rico, 1870–1920.* Durham, NC: Duke University Press, 1999.

Fleischer, Nat. *Black Dynamite.* 5 vols. Vol. 1, *Story of the Negro in Boxing.* New York: C.J. O'Brien, 1938.

———. *Black Dynamite,* 5 vols. Vol. 4, *"Fighting Furies": Story of the Golden Era of Jack Johnson, Sam Langford and their Negro Contemporaries.* New York: C.J. O'Brien, 1938.

Foucault, Michel. *History of Sexuality: Volume I, Introduction.* 1978; New York: Vintage Books, 1990.

Fox, Richard Kyle. *Life and Battles of John L. Sullivan.* New York: Police Gazette, 1883.

"Francis Edward Clark." In *Dictionary of American Religious Biography,* edited by Henry Warner Bowden, 113–14. Westport, CT: Greenwood Press, 1993.

Fridman, Daniel, and David Sheinin. "Wild Bulls, Discarded Foreigners, and Brash Champions: US Empire and the Cultural Constructions of Argentine Boxers." *Left History* 12, no. 1 (2007): 52–77.

Fryer, Peter. *Staying Power: The History of Black People in Britain.* London: Pluto Press, 1984.

Gaines, Kevin. *American Africans in Ghana: Black Expatriates and the Civil Rights Era.* Chapel Hill: University of North Carolina Press, 2007.

Gatewood, Willard B. *Black Americans and the White Man's Burden, 1898–1903.* Urbana: University of Illinois Press, 1975.

Gems, Gerald R. *The Athletic Crusade: Sport and American Cultural Imperialism.* Lincoln: University of Nebraska Press, 2006.

Gilmore, Al-Tony. *Bad Nigger! The National Impact of Jack Johnson.* Port Washington, NY: Kennikat Press, 1975.

Gilmore, Glenda. *Defying Dixie: The Radical Roots of Civil Rights, 1919–1950.* New York: W. W. Norton & Company, 2008.

Gilroy, Paul. *The Black Atlantic: Modernity and Double Consciousness.* Cambridge, MA: Harvard University Press, 1993.

———. *Darker Than Blue: On the Moral Economies of Black Atlantic Culture.* Cambridge: Belknap Press, 2010.

———. *Postcolonial Melancholia.* New York: Columbia University Press, 2006.

Glick, Elisa F. "The Dialectics of Dandyism." *Cultural Critique* 48 (Spring 2001): 129–63.

———. "Harlem's Queer Dandy: African-American Modernism and the Artifice of Blackness." *Modern Fiction Studies* 49, no. 3 (2003): 414–42.

Gobel, Walter, and Saskia Schabio, eds. *Beyond the Black Atlantic: Relocating Modernization and Technology.* New York: Taylor and Francis, 2006.

Gorn, Elliot. *The Manly Art: Bare-Knuckle Prize Fighting in America.* Ithaca, NY: Cornell University Press, 1986.

Gramsci, Antonio. *Selections from the Prison Notebooks.* New York: International Publishers, 1971.

Green, Jeffrey. *Black Edwardians: Black People in Britain, 1901–1914.* London: Frank Cass Publishers, 1998.

———. "Boxing and the 'Colour Question' in Edwardian Britain: The 'White Problem' of 1911." *International Journal of the History of Sport* 5, no. 1 (1988): 115–19.

Grieveson, Lee. *Policing Cinema: Movies and Censorship in Early-Twentieth-Century America.* Berkeley: University of California Press, 2004.

Grunberger, Lisa. "Bernarr MacFadden's Physical Culture: Muscles, Morals and the Millennium." Ph.D. diss., University of Chicago, 1997.

Guridy, Frank. *Forging Diaspora: Afro-Cubans and African Americans in a World of Empire and Jim Crow.* Chapel Hill: University of North Carolina Press, 2010.

Guterl, Matthew Pratt. *The Color of Race in America, 1900–1940.* Cambridge, MA: Harvard University Press, 2001.

Guterl, Matthew Pratt, James T. Campbell, and Robert G. Lee, eds. *Race, Nation, and Empire in American History.* Durham, NC: Duke University Press, 2007.

Hale, Dana S. *Races on Display: French Representations of Colonized Peoples, 1886–1940.* Bloomington: Indiana University Press, 2008.

Harding, William Edgar. *John L. Sullivan, the Champion Pugilist.* New York, 1883.

Harris, Charles H., III, and Louis R. Sadler. "The Plan of San Diego and the Mexican–United States War Crisis of 1916: A Reexamination." *Hispanic American Historical Review* 58, no. 3 (1978): 381–408.

Hart, John M. *Empire and Revolution: The Americans in Mexico since the Civil War.* Berkeley: University of California Press, 2002.

Harvey, A.D. "The Body Politic: Anatomy of a Metaphor." *Contemporary Review* 275, no. 1603 (August 1999): 85-93.

Helg, Aline. "Black Men, Racial Stereotyping, and Violence in the U.S. South and Cuba at the Turn of the Century." *Comparative Studies in Society and History* 42, no. 3 (2000): 576–604.

———. *Our Rightful Share: The Afro-Cuban Struggle for Equality, 1886–1912.* Chapel Hill: University of North Carolina Press, 1995.

Hill, Errol G., and James V. Hatch. *A History of African American Theatre.* Cambridge: Cambridge University Press, 2005.

Hoberman, John. *Darwin's Athletes: How Sport Has Damaged Black America and Preserved the Myth of Race.* New York: Houghton Mifflin, 1997.

Hobson, John. A. *The Psychology of Jingoism.* London: Grant Richards, 1901.

Horne, Gerald. *Black and Brown: African Americans and the Mexican Revolution, 1910–1920.* New York: New York University Press, 2005.

Hoganson, Kristin. *Fighting for American Manhood: How Gender Politics Provoked the Spanish-American and Philippine-American Wars.* New Haven, CT: Yale University Press, 1998.

Holcomb, Gary Edward. *Claude McKay, Code Name Sasha: Queer Black Marxism and the Harlem Renaissance.* Gainesville: University Press of Florida, 2007.

Holt, Thomas. *The Problem of Race in the 21st Century.* Cambridge, MA: Harvard University Press, 2000.

Hotaling, Ed. *Wink: The Incredible Life and Epic Journey of Jimmy Winkfield.* New York: McGraw-Hill, 2005.

Hughes, Langston. *The Big Sea.* 1940; New York: Hill and Wang, 1993.

Isenberg, Michael T. *John L. Sullivan and His America.* Urbana: University of Illinois Press, 1988.

Iton, Richard. *In Search of the Black Fantastic: Politics & Popular Culture in the Post–Civil Rights Era.* New York: Oxford University Press, 2008.

Jacobson, Matthew. *Barbarian Virtues: The United States Encounters of Foreign Peoples at Home and Abroad, 1876–1917.* New York: Hill and Wang, 2000.

Jenkinson, Jacqueline. "Black Sailors on Red Clydeside: Rioting, Reactionary Trade Unionism and Conflicting Notions of 'Britishness' Following the First World War." *Twentieth Century British History* 19, no. 1 (2008): 29–60.

Johnson, Benjamin. *Revolution in Texas: How a Forgotten Rebellion and Its Bloody Suppression Turned Mexicans into Americans.* New Haven, CT: Yale University Press, 2003.

Johnson, Jack. *In the Ring—And Out.* 1927; New York: Citadel Press, 1992.

———. *Mes Combats.* Paris: Pierre Lafitte & Co., 1914.

———. *My Life and Battles.* Translated by Chris Rivers. Westport, CT: Praeger Publishers, 2007.

Johnson, James Weldon. *Along This Way: The Autobiography of James Weldon Johnson.* 1933; New York: Viking, reprint 1968.

Joseph, Gilbert, Catherine LeGrand, and Ricardo Salvatore, eds. *Close Encounters of Empire: Writing the Cultural History of U.S.–Latin American Relations.* Durham, NC: Duke University Press, 1998.

Jupp, James. *From White Australia to Woomera: The Story of Australian Immigration.* New York: Cambridge University Press, 2002.

Kaplan, Amy. *The Anarchy of Empire in the Making of U.S. Culture.* Cambridge, MA: Harvard University Press, 2002.

Kaplan, Amy, and Donald Pease, eds. *Cultures of United States Imperialism.* Durham, NC: Duke University Press, 1993.

Kasson, John F. *Houdini, Tarzan, and the Perfect Man: The White Male Body and the Challenge of Modernity in America.* New York: Hill & Wang, 2001.

Katz, Friedrich. *The Life and Times of Pancho Villa.* Stanford, CA: Stanford University Press, 1998.

Keegan, Timothy. "Gender, Degeneration and Sexual Danger: Imagining Race and Class in South Africa, ca. 1912." *Journal of Southern African Studies* 27, no. 3 (2001): 459–77.

Kelley, Robin. "But a Local Phase of a World Problem: Black History's Global Vision, 1883–1950." *Journal of American History* 86, no. 3 (December 1999): 1045–77.

———. *Freedom Dreams: The Black Radical Imagination.* Boston: Beacon Press, 2002.

Kent, Graeme. *The Great White Hopes: The Quest to Defeat Jack Johnson.* Gloucestershire: Sutton Publishing, 2005.

Kornweibel, Theodore, Jr. *Investigate Everything: Federal Efforts to Compel Black Loyalty during World War I.* Bloomington: Indiana University Press, 2001.

Kramer, Paul. *Blood of Government: Race, Empire, the United States, and the Philippines.* Chapel Hill: University of North Carolina Press, 2006.

———. "Empires, Exceptions, and Anglo-Saxons: Race and Rule between the British and United States Empires, 1880–1910." *Journal of American History* 88, no. 4 (2002): 1315–53.

Krasner, David. *A Beautiful Pageant: African American Theatre, Drama, and Performance in the Harlem Renaissance, 1910–1927.* New York: Palgrave Macmillan, 2002.

Kroes, Rob, Robert Rydell, and D. F. J. Bosscher, eds. *Cultural Transmissions and Receptions: American Mass Culture in Europe.* Amsterdam: VU University Press, 1993.

Langum, David J. *Crossing over the Line: Legislating Morality and the Mann Act.* Chicago: University of Chicago Press, 1994.

Lake, Marilyn, and Henry Reynolds. *Drawing the Global Colour Line: White Men's Countries and the International Challenge of Racial Equality.* Cambridge: Cambridge University Press, 2008.

Lansdale, Joe R. *The Big Blow.* Burton, MI: Subterranean Press, 2000.

Lemke, Sieglinde. *Primitivist Modernism: Black Culture and the Origins of Transatlantic Modernism.* New York: Oxford University Press, 1998.

Leonard, David J., and C. Richard King, eds. *Commodified and Criminalized: New Racism and African Americans in Contemporary Sports.* Plymouth, UK: Rowman & Littlefield, 2011.

Les Nègres contre Peaux-Rouges. Paris: A. Eichler, 1913.

Lindfors, Bernth, ed. *Africans on Stage: Studies in Ethnological Show Business.* Bloomington: Indiana University Press, 1999.

Linebaugh, Peter, and Marcus Rediker. *Many-Headed Hydra: Sailors, Slaves, Commoners, and the Hidden History of the Revolutionary Atlantic.* Boston: Beacon Press, 2000.

Lloyd, Craig. *Eugene Bullard: Black Expatriate in Jazz-Age Paris.* Athens: University of Georgia Press, 2000.

Locke, Alain, ed. *The New Negro: Voices of the Harlem Renaissance.* 1925; New York: Macmillan, 1992.

Logan, Rayford. "James Weldon Johnson and Haiti." *Phylon* 32, no. 4 (1971): 396–402.

Lorimer, Douglas. *Colour, Class, and the Victorians.* New York: Holmes & Meier, 1978.

Lynch, Bohun. *Knuckles and Gloves.* London: W. Collins & Sons, 1922.

Magubane, Zine. "The Boundaries of Blackness: African American Culture and the Making of a Black Public Sphere in Colonial South Africa." In *Empires and Boundaries: Rethinking Race, Class, and Gender in Colonial Settings,* edited by Harald Fischer-Tiné and Susanne Gehrmann, 212–32. New York: Routledge, 2009.

———. "Mines, Minstrels, and Masculinity: Race, Class, Gender, and the Formation of the South African Working Class, 1870–1900." *Journal of Men's Studies* 10, no. 3 (2002): 271–89.

Mamdani, Mahmood. *Citizen and Subject: Contemporary Africa and the Legacy of Late Colonialism.* Princeton, NJ: Princeton University Press, 1996.

Mangin, Charles. *La Force noire.* Paris: Hachette, 1910.

Mann, Chester. *F. B. Meyer: Preacher, Teacher, Man of God.* London: George Allen & Unwin, 1929.

Margolick, David. *Beyond Glory: Joe Louis vs. Max Schmeling, and a World on the Brink.* New York: Random House, 2006.

Mathieu, Sarah-Jane. *North of the Color Line: Migration and Black Resistance in Canada, 1870–1955.* Chapel Hill: University of North Carolina Press, 2010.

Maynard, John. "For Liberty and Freedom: Fred Maynard and the Australian Aboriginal Progressive Association." Lecture for New South Wales State Library, Sydney, 2004.

———. "Vision, Voice and Influence." *Australian Historical Studies* 34, no. 121 (2003): 91–105.

McCaffery, Dan. *Tommy Burns: Canada's Unknown World Heavyweight Champion.* Toronto: James Lorimer & Company, 2000.

McClintock, Anne. *Imperial Leather: Race, Gender and Sexuality in the Colonial Contest.* New York: Routledge, 1995.

McCulloch, Jock. *Black Peril, White Virtue: Sexual Crime in Southern Rhodesia, 1902–1935.* Bloomington: University of Indiana Press, 2000.

McDevitt, Patrick. *May the Best Man Win: Sport, Masculinity, and Nationalism in Great Britain and the Empire, 1880–1935.* New York: Palgrave Macmillan, 2004.

McGehee, Richard V. "The Dandy and the Mauler in Mexico: Johnson, Dempsey, *et al.,* and the Mexico City Press, 1919–1927." *Journal of Sport History* 23, no. 1 (1996): 20–33.

McGovern, John Terence. *How to Box to Win, How to Build Muscle.* New York: Rohde & Haskins, 1900.

McKay, Claude. *Banjo: A Story without a Plot.* 1929; New York: Harvest Books, 1970.

———. "Negroes in Sports." In *The Negroes in America,* 49–55. 1923; Port Washington, NY: Kennikat Press, 1979.

———. *A Long Way from Home: An Autobiography.* London: Pluto Press, 1985.

McLaren, Jack. *My Odyssey: South Seas Adventure.* 1925; Melbourne: Oxford University Press, 1946.

McQueen, Humphrey. *A New Britannia: An Argument Concerning the Social Origins of Australian Radicalism and Nationalism.* 2nd ed. 1970; New York: Penguin Books, 1986.

Meer, Sarah. *Uncle Tom Mania: Slavery, Minstrelsy and Transatlantic Culture in the 1850s.* Athens: University of Georgia Press, 2005.

Meunier, Claude. *Ring noir: Quand Apollinaire, Cendrars et Picabia découvraient les boxeurs nègres.* Paris: PLON, 1992.

Mignolo, Walter. *Local Histories/Global Designs.* Princeton, NJ: Princeton University Press, 2000.

Modern Gladiator: Being an Account of the Exploits and Experiences of the World's Greatest Fighter, John Lawrence Sullivan. St. Louis, MO: Athletic Publishing Company, 1889.

Mortane, Jacques, and André Linville. *La Boxe.* Paris: Pierre Lafitte, 1908.

Mumford, Kevin. *Interzones: Black/White Sex Districts in Chicago and New York in the Early Twentieth Century.* New York: Columbia University Press, 1997.

Musser, Charles. *The Emergence of Cinema: The American Screen to 1907.* New York: Scribner, 1990.

Myler, Patrick. *Ring of Hate: Joe Louis vs. Max Schmeling, the Fight of the Century.* New York: Arcade Publishing, 2005.

Nordau, Max. *Degeneration.* 1892; Lincoln: University of Nebraska Press, 2006.

Nwankwo, Ifeoma Kiddoe. *Black Cosmopolitanism: Racial Consciousness and Transnational Identity in the Nineteenth-Century Americas.* Philadelphia: University of Pennsylvania Press, 2005.

O'Brien, Phillips Payson, ed. *The Anglo-Japanese Alliance, 1902–1922.* New York: RoutledgeCurzon, 2004.

O'Reilly, John Boyle. *Ethics of Boxing and Manly Sport.* Boston: Ticknor and Company, 1888.

Ortega, Elio Menéndez and Victor Joaquin. *Kid Chocolate: 'El boxeo soy yo . . .'* Havana: Editorial ORBE, 1980.

Pendergast, Tom. *Creating the Modern Man: American Magazines and Consumer Culture, 1900–1950.* Columbia: University of Missouri Press, 2000.

Pérez, Louis, Jr. *On Becoming Cuban: Identity, Nationality, and Culture.* New York: HarperCollins, 1999.

Philipson, Robert. "The Harlem Renaissance as Postcolonial Phenomenon." *African American Review* 40, no. 1 (2006): 145–60.

Pick, Daniel. *Faces of Degeneration: A European Disorder, c. 1848—c. 1918.* Cambridge: Cambridge University Press, 1989.

Pieterse, Jan Nederveen. *White on Black: Images of Africa and Blacks in Western Popular Culture.* New Haven, CT: Yale University Press, 1992.

Plummer, Brenda Gayle. "The Afro-American Response to the Occupation of Haiti, 1915–1934." *Phylon* 43, no. 2 (1982): 125–43.

———. *Haiti and the United States: The Psychological Moment.* Athens: University of Georgia Press, 1992.

———. *Rising Wind: Black Americans and U.S. Foreign Affairs, 1935–1960.* Chapel Hill: University of North Carolina Press, 1996.

Porter, Bernard. *The Lion's Share: A Short History of British Imperialism, 1850–1995.* 3rd ed. New York: Longman, 1996.

Pratt, Mary Louise. *Imperial Eyes: Travel Writing and Transculturation.* New York: Routledge, 1992.

Putney, Clifford. *Muscular Christianity: Manhood and Sports in Protestant America, 1880–1920.* Cambridge, MA: Harvard University Press, 2001.

Reckner, James R. *Teddy Roosevelt's Great White Fleet.* Annapolis: Naval Institute Press, 1988.

Redding, Sean. "A Blood-Stained Tax: Poll Tax and the Bambatha Rebellion in South Africa." *African Studies Review* 43, no. 2 (2000): 29–54.

Reesman, Jeanne Campbell. *Jack London's Racial Lives: A Critical Biography.* Athens: University of Georgia Press, 2009.

Renda, Mary. *Taking Haiti: Military Occupation and the Culture of U.S. Imperialism, 1915–1940.* Chapel Hill: University of North Carolina Press, 2001.

"Report of Brooklyn UNIA Meetings [23–24 January, 1922]." In *The Marcus Garvey and Universal Negro Improvement Association Papers, Volume 4,* edited by Robert A. Hill, 452–59. Berkeley: University of California Press, 1991.

Reynolds, Harry. *Minstrel Memories: The Story of Burnt Cork Minstrelsy in Great Britain from 1836 to 1927.* London: Alston Rivers, 1928.

Rief, Michelle. "Thinking Locally, Acting Globally: The International Agenda of African American Clubwomen, 1880–1940." *Journal of African American History* 89, no. 3 (Summer 2004): 203–22.

Rippy, J. Fred. "A Negro Colonization Project in Mexico, 1894–1896." *Journal of Negro History* 6, no. 1 (1921): 66–73.

Roberts, Randy. *Jack Dempsey, the Manassa Mauler.* Baton Rouge: Louisiana State University Press, 1979.

———. *Papa Jack: Jack Johnson and the Era of White Hopes.* New York: Free Press, 1983.

Robinson, Cedric. *Black Marxism: The Making of the Black Radical Tradition.* Chapel Hill: University of North Carolina Press, 2000.

Rodriguez, Robert G. *The Regulation of Boxing: A History and Comparative Analysis of Policies among American States.* Jefferson, NC: McFarland & Company, 2009.

Rogin, Michael. "The Sword Became a Flashing Vision: D. W. Griffith's *The Birth of a Nation.*" *Representations* 9 (Winter 1985): 150–95.

Roosevelt, Theodore. *The Strenuous Life: Essays and Addresses.* New York: Century, 1902.

———. *Theodore Roosevelt: An Autobiography.* 1913; Charleston: Biblio-Bazaar, 2007.

Rosenburg, Emily. *Financial Missionaries to the World: The Politics and Culture of Dollar Diplomacy.* Cambridge, MA: Harvard University Press, 1999.

Runstedtler, Theresa. "In Sports the Best Man Wins: How Joe Louis Whupped Jim Crow." In *In the Game: Race, Identity, and Sports in the Twentieth Century,* edited by Amy Bass, 47–92. New York: Palgrave Macmillan, 2005.

Rydell, Robert. *All the World's a Fair: Visions of Empire at American International Exhibitions, 1876–1916.* Chicago: University of Chicago Press, 1984.

Rydell, Robert, and Rob Kroes. *Buffalo Bill in Bologna: The Americanization of the World, 1869–1922.* Chicago: University of Chicago Press, 2005.

Sackler, Howard. *The Great White Hope.* New York: Dial Press, 1968.

Said, Edward. *Orientalism.* New York: Vintage Books, 1978.

Sammons, Jeffrey. *Beyond the Ring: The Role of Boxing in American Society.* Urbana: University Illinois Press, 1988.

Scanlon, Bob. "The Record of a Negro Boxer." In *Negro: An Anthology,* edited by Nancy Cunard, 208–11. 1934; New York: Frederick Ungar Publishing, 1970.

Schwartz, Rosalie. *Pleasure Island: Tourism and Temptation in Cuba.* Lincoln: University of Nebraska Press, 1997.

Scott, Julius. "The Common Wind: Currents of Afro-American Communication in the Era of the Haitian Revolution." Ph.D. diss., Duke University, 1986.

Sears, Louis Martin. "Frederick Douglass and the Mission to Haiti, 1889–1891." *Hispanic American Historical Review* 21, no. 2 (1941): 222–38.

Sen, Satadru. "Schools, Athletes and Confrontation: The Student Body in Colonial India." In *Confronting the Body: The Politics of Physicality in Colonial and Post-Colonial India,* edited by Satadru Sen and James H. Mills, 58–79. London: Anthem, 2004.

Shack, William. *Harlem in Montmartre: A Paris Jazz Story between the Great Wars.* Berkeley: University of California Press, 2001.

Shankman, Arnold. "The Image of Mexico and the Mexican-American in the Black Press, 1890–1935." *Journal of Ethnic Studies* 3, no. 2 (1975): 43–56.

Singh, Nikhil Pal. *Black Is a Country: Race and the Unfinished Struggle for Democracy.* Cambridge, MA: Harvard University Press, 2004.

Sklaroff, Lauren Rebecca. "Constructing G.I. Joe Louis: Cultural Solutions to the 'Negro Problem' during World War II." *Journal of American History* 89, no. 3 (December 2002): 958–83.

Smith, Kevin. *Black Genesis: The History of the Black Prizefighter 1760–1870*. Lincoln: iUniverse, 2003.

Smith, Shawn Michelle. *Photography on the Color Line: W.E.B. Du Bois, Race, and Visual Culture*. Durham, NC: Duke University Press, 2004.

Snelling, Oswald Frederick. *White Hope: The Story of the Jack Johnson Era*. London: Pendulum Publications, 1947.

Stephens, Michelle. *Black Empire: The Masculine Global Imaginary of Caribbean Intellectuals in the United States, 1914–1962*. Durham, NC: Duke University Press, 2005.

Stoddard, Lothrop. *The Rising Tide of Color Against White World-Supremacy*. 1920; New York: Charles Scribner's Sons, 1922.

Stoler, Ann Laura. *Carnal Knowledge and Imperial Power: Race and the Intimate in Colonial Rule*. Berkeley: University of California Press, 2002.

———. *Race and the Education of Desire: Foucault's History of Sexuality and the Colonial Order*. Durham, NC: Duke University Press, 2002.

———. "Tense and Tender Ties: The Politics of Comparison in North American History and (Post) Colonial Studies." *Journal of American History* 88, no. 3 (December 2001): 829–65.

———, ed. *Haunted by Empire: Geographies of Intimacy in North American History*. Durham, NC: Duke University Press, 2006.

Stovall, Tyler. *Paris Noir: African Americans in the City of Light*. New York: Houghton Mifflin, 1996.

Streeby, Shelley. *American Sensations: Class, Empire, and the Production of Popular Culture*. Berkeley: University of California Press, 2002.

Streible, Daniel. *Fight Pictures: A History of Boxing and Early Cinema*. Berkeley: University of California Press, 2008.

Suggs, Henry Lewis. "The Response of the African American Press to the United States Occupation of Haiti, 1915–1934." *Journal of African American History* 87, no. 1 (2002): 70–82.

Sullivan, John L. *Life and Reminiscences of a 19th Century Gladiator*. Boston: Jas. A. Hearn & Co.; London: Geo. Routledge & Sons, 1892.

Summers, Martin. *Manliness and Its Discontents: The Black Middle Class and the Transformation of Masculinity, 1900–1930*. Chapel Hill: University of North Carolina Press, 2004.

Thompson, Leonard. *A History of South Africa*. 3rd ed. New Haven, CT: Yale University Press, 2000.

Tinsley, Omise'eke Natasha. "Black Atlantic, Queer Atlantic: Queer Imaginings of the Middle Passage." *GLQ: A Journal of Lesbian and Gay Studies* 14, nos. 2–3 (2008): 191–215.

Von Eeden, Trevor. *The Original Johnson*. Vol. 1. San Diego: IDW Publishing, 2009.

———. *The Original Johnson*. Vol. 2. San Diego: IDW Publishing, 2011.

Von Eschen, Penny. *Race Against Empire: Black Americans and Anticolonialism, 1937–1957*. Ithaca, NY: Cornell University Press, 1997.

Wallace, Michele. "The Good Lynching and *The Birth of a Nation:* Discourses and Aesthetics of Jim Crow." *Cinema Journal* 43, no. 1 (Fall 2003): 85–104.

Ward, Geoffrey. *Unforgivable Blackness: The Rise and Fall of Jack Johnson.* New York: Knopf, 2004.

Washington, Booker T. *The Man Farthest Down: A Record of Observation and Study in Europe.* New York: Doubleday, Page & Co., 1912.

Waterhouse, Richard. "The Minstrel Show and Australian Culture." *Journal of Popular Culture* 24, no. 3 (1990): 147–66.

Wehman's Book on the Art and Science of Boxing. New York: Henry J. Wehman, 1892.

Wells, Jeff. *Boxing Day: The Fight That Changed the World.* Sydney: Harper-Sports, 1998.

Werry, Margaret. "The Greatest Show on Earth: Political Spectacle, Spectacular Politics, and the American Pacific." *Theatre Journal* 57, no. 3 (October 2005): 355–82.

Wexler, Laura. *Tender Violence: Domestic Visions in an Age of U.S. Imperialism.* Chapel Hill: University of North Carolina Press, 2002.

Wiggins, David K. "Peter Jackson and the Elusive Heavyweight Championship: A Black Athlete's Struggle Against the Late Nineteenth Century Color-Line." *Journal of Sport History* 12, no. 2 (1985): 143–68.

Wignall, Trevor. *Story of Boxing.* New York: Brentano's, 1924.

Wilder, Gary. *The French Imperial Nation-State: Negritude and Colonial Humanism Between the Two World Wars.* Chicago: University of Chicago Press, 2005.

Wimmel, Kenneth. *Theodore Roosevelt and the Great White Fleet: American Seapower Comes of Age.* Washington, DC: Brassey's, 1998.

Windschuttle, Keith. *White Australia Policy.* Sydney: Macleay Press, 2004.

Young, Harvey. *Embodying Black Experience: Stillness, Critical Memory, and the Black Body.* Ann Arbor: University of Michigan Press, 2010.

Zaborowska, Magdalena J. *James Baldwin's Turkish Decade: Erotics of Exile.* Durham, NC: Duke University Press, 2008.

Index

Note: Page numbers in italics indicate figures.

Al-Jadda, Souhelia, xviii
Jeannette, Joe, 138–39, 140, 165, 170–71,
 174–78, 185–87
Jeffries, Jim: agreement to fight Johnson,
 67; at coronation of George V, 108; as
 great white hope, xix; on Johnson, 108;
 physical condition of, 71; on physical
 fitness and fighting, 33; retirement of,
 46; white South African sportsmen and,
 91–92. *See also* Jeffries-Johnson fight
Jeffries-Johnson fight: action of, 74, *75;*
 aftermath of, 85–87; censorship of film
 of, 78–84, 87–90, 92, 99; controversy
 about, 69–70; deal for, 72; fan reaction
 to, 74–76, 85; film of, 73, 76–77, 99–
 100; as international event, 73; location
 of, 72–73; promotion of, 72; spectators,
 73–74; Union of South Africa and,
 91–100
Jenkins, Lynn, 255–56
Jim Crow racism and segregation: black
 working men and, 133; Britain and, 104,
 152–53; commercial mass culture and,
 26–27; France and, 180, 182; Mexico
 and, 226–27; rise of, 20–21; search for
 equality beyond reach of, 105–6; South
 Africa and, 96–97; in sporting realm,
 14; U.S. Army and, 150; on world stage,
 24
J. & J. Company, 73
Johannesburg, South Africa, calls for censorship of fight film in, 82
Johnson, Battling Jim, 206
Johnson, Eddie Bernice, 3
Johnson, Henry, 12
Johnson, John Arthur "Jack": on Aboriginal culture, 53; Ali on, 3; on Anglo-
 Saxon supremacy, 189; arrest of, 134;
 autobiography of, 162; birth and early
 life of, 12, 13; on British racism, 124,
 126–27; career of, 1, 4–5; cars and, 16,
 53, *54;* cultural and political significance of, 2–4, 253, 258, 259–60, 261;
 as dandy, 16, 38–39, 148–49, 169, 224;
 Davis on, 3; death of, 255; early travels
 of, 14–15, 16–18, 148; French memoir
 of, 145–50; French sportswriters on,
 180; on life and career, 132; lifestyle
 of, 1–2, 7–8, 15–16, 179–80; on match
 with Wells, 125; photos of, *17, 41, 112,
 142, 215, 254;* prison time of, 232–33;
 as "rebel sojourner," 5, 17–18; Segonzac
 on, 173–74; as showman, 189; style of,
 16, *17;* surrender to authorities, 230, 231;

Toy and, 37, 38, 42–44; on white Ameri-
 can racism, 107, 141, 161, 189, 218–19,
 227; on white degeneration, 63–64;
 world championship reign, xix. *See also*
 Burns-Johnson fight; Jeffries-Johnson
 fight; Wells-Johnson match; Willard-
 Johnson fight
Johnson, Lucille: in Paris, 150; photo of,
 142; travels of, 136, 141, 151, 202, 218;
 Valdez and, 211–12
Johnson, Lucy, 147
Johnson, Tina "Tiny," 12, 132, 135, 148
"Johnson Fifi!" cartoon, *197*
Johnson Land Company, 227–28
Johnson-Moran fight, 188–93
Johnson-Roper fight, 224–25
Juárez, Mexico, 201–2, 204–5

"The Kaffir House Boy" (cartoon), 97
Kelly, Walter, 108
Kennedy, Edward, 3
Ketchell, Stanley, 115
Kid Davis, 166
King, Peter T., 255, 256–57, *257*
King, W.N., 212
Kingsley, Tom, 181
Kingston, Jamaica, calls for censorship of
 fight film in, 82
Kipling, Rudyard, 18; "The Ballad of East
 and West," 149–50
Klaus, Frank, 129
Kristof, Nicholas, xxi

Lang, Bill, 38–39, 114, 118
Lang, John, 219
Langford, Sam: in Coloured Quartette,
 138; in Cuba, 206; earnings of, 140; in
 London, 118; Lonsdale and, 129; man-
 agement of, 165–66; McIntosh and, 115
Lascars, mutiny of, 52–53
Lawson, Henry, 64
Leonard, Sugar Ray, 3
Les Nègres contre les Peaux-Rouges, 182
Lewis, Billy: on black Americans in Britain,
 155; on Johnson, 136, 151, 161, 191–92;
 on Johnson-Moran fight, 191; on John-
 son's memoir, 145–46; on McVea in
 Paris, 179; on use of term "nigger" by
 white French boys, 190; on Willard, 215
Lewis, Calvin C., 203
Lewis, Harry, 182–83
Lewis, Walter, 15
Locke, Alain, 11, 235
London: Jackson in, 26; Johnson in, 104–5,

TEXT
10/13 Sabon

DISPLAY
Din

COMPOSITOR
BookMatters, Berkeley

PRINTER AND BINDER
Maple-Vail Book Manufacturing Group